Treating ADHD and Comorbid Disorders

Treating
ADHD
and Comorbid
Disorders

Psychosocial and
Psychopharmacological
Interventions

Steven R. Pliszka

THE GUILFORD PRESS
New York   London

The author has checked with sources believed to be reliable in his efforts to provide information that is complete and generally in accord with the standards of practice that are accepted at the time of publication. However, in view of the possibility of human error or changes in medical sciences, neither the author, nor the editor and Publisher, nor any other party who has been involved in the preparation or publication of this work warrants that the information contained herein is in every respect accurate or complete, and they are not responsible for any errors or omissions or the results obtained from the use of such information. Readers are encouraged to confirm the information contained in this book with other sources.

Library of Congress Cataloging-in-Publication Data

Pliszka, Steven R.
   Treating ADHD and comorbid disorders: psychosocial and psychopharmacological interventions / Steven R. Pliszka.
      p. ; cm.
   Includes bibliographical references and index.
   ISBN 978-1-60623-266-8 (hardcover: alk. paper)
   1. Attention-deficit hyperactivity disorder.   2. Comorbidity.   I. Title.
   [DNLM: 1. Attention Deficit Disorder with Hyperactivity—drug therapy.   2. Attention Deficit Disorder with Hyperactivity—complications.   WS 350.8.A8 P728t 2009]
   RJ506.H9P553   2009
   616.92′8589—dc22
                                                                2009006665

With thanks to my wife, Alice,
who carefully read the manuscript of this book
and provided invaluable advice and support

About the Author

Steven R. Pliszka, MD, is Professor of Psychiatry at the University of Texas Health Science Center at San Antonio, where he serves as Vice Chair of the Department of Psychiatry and Chief of the Division of Child and Adolescent Psychiatry. Dr. Pliszka has been involved in numerous clinical trials of psychopharmacological agents in the treatment of attention-deficit/hyperactivity disorder (ADHD) as well as bipolar disorder of childhood. Recent research activities include the neuroimaging of stimulant response in patients with ADHD and the study of mood-stabilizing medication in the treatment of aggression. Dr. Pliszka personally cares for over 500 children with ADHD, developmental disabilities, and other psychiatric disorders; he also teaches psychopharmacology and neurobiology to medical students and psychiatry residents. He was the principal author of the Practice Parameters of the American Academy of Child and Adolescent Psychiatry for the diagnosis and treatment of ADHD. He is currently the principal investigator for Services Uniting Pediatrics and Psychiatry Outreaching to Texas (SUPPORT), a state-funded initiative to increase the availability of mental health services to children in the Medicaid program by placing mental health professionals in pediatric primary care offices.

Preface

Children who have attention-deficit/hyperactivity disorder (ADHD) frequently present with other serious problems, such as aggression, mood lability, tics, anxiety, or depression. *Treating ADHD and Comorbid Disorders: Psychosocial and Psychopharmacological Interventions* is designed for mental health professionals looking for guidance in dealing with these challenging cases. The book draws heavily on my two decades of experience as a clinician in traditional outpatient services as well as in residential treatment centers for developmentally delayed and severely emotionally disturbed youth. I have utilized evidence-based guidelines for the use of pharmacological and psychosocial treatments, but there is less emphasis on compiling and integrating the research findings than in *ADHD with Comorbid Disorders: Clinical Assessment and Management,* written with Caryn Carlson and James M. Swanson (Guilford, 1999). The earlier book was an in-depth scientific review of the diagnostic and treatment issues surrounding comorbidity in ADHD; it also contained an extensive section on behavior therapy for problems in the home, at school, and at the playground. *Treating ADHD and Comorbid Disorders* is not a second edition of that book; rather, it takes an accessible, case-based approach to the issues surrounding treatment.

Each chapter focuses on one or more related comorbid disorders and reviews the relevant literature, but the emphasis is on clinical cases in which the approaches of clinicians are described in detail. I address the most vexing comorbidities confronting child mental health professionals who deal with ADHD, including oppositional defiant and conduct disorders, impulsive aggression, mania, and autism spectrum disorders. For many of these conditions there is no research database showing how to use multiple medications to treat the comorbid disorders. Each case presented carefully details the clinical reasoning that leads to the combination of various agents and interventions.

One of the most difficult and controversial issues in mental health discussed in the book is the evaluation and treatment of children with ADHD who exhibit severe mood lability and aggression. Such children often receive diagnoses of bipolar disorder. But when is this diagnosis appropriate and when is the clinician engaging in "over-diagnosis"? A child with ADHD and bipolar disorder may be treated with a stimulant, a second-generation antipsychotic, and two mood stabilizers. When is this treatment appropriate and when is it excessive? More important, what are the logical steps leading to the right pharmacological treatment?

There has been increasing criticism regarding the use of powerful antipsychotic medications in children, given the propensity of these medications to cause serious weight gain, which carries the long-term risks of diabetes and heart disease. Indeed, studies comparing the second-generation antipsychotics with the first generation in treating adult- and child-onset schizophrenia have not always shown the expected superiority of the newer drugs (Leucht et al., 2009; Sikich et al., 2008). Where does that leave the clinician who treats seriously ill children and teenagers with ADHD? Are we inappropriately exposing these youth to the risks of side effects without any added benefit? The answer, of course, is complex. We must be judicious in the use of powerful psychotropics, but we cannot afford to go the way of therapeutic nihilism, which would discourage the use of *any* psychiatric medication in children. By combining clinical judgment and research findings, we can address these treatment issues in a balanced way.

The book also illustrates how to modify psychosocial interventions for each comorbid disorder. What is the best way to coach families on implementing behavior therapy programs, especially with an explosive or mood-labile child with ADHD? How should cognitive-behavioral therapy be applied with an impulsive, inattentive, or depressed teenager? There is a strong focus on describing family interactions, as well as situations involving foster care or residential settings. I emphasize how to cope with the practical difficulties of bringing complex therapies into the office setting. Often, this is not as straightforward as suggested in practice guidelines or research studies.

The ultimate goal of *Treating ADHD and Comorbid Disorders* is to provide clinicians with a ready toolkit for dealing with the most difficult cases. Therefore, Appendix I provides structured interviews that help the clinician sort out symptoms and distinguish between different comorbid disorders. Appendix II contains a concise update on child and adolescent psychopharmacology, as well as an in-depth discussion of the side effects and long-term risks associated with each psychotropic medication commonly used to treat children.

This is a challenging time for clinicians who deal with children and teenagers suffering from ADHD and significant comorbid disorders. When I began working in the mental health field as a child-care worker in the 1970s, the average length of stay in a state hospital children's unit was several years. By the time I began my residency in the 1980s, an acute hospitalization still lasted 30 to 90 days. Today, an acute hospitalization rarely lasts longer than a week, residential programs are fewer in number, and managed care places limitations on outpatient sessions. Children who were out of sight in generations past are now in our neighborhoods and schools. While this change brings a welcome integration into the community, it places a heavy burden on clinicians and families to help seriously ill children cope with the demands of daily life. This book is dedicated to all mental health professionals—from those with advanced degrees to child-care workers on the front lines in our residential facilities. It is my sincere hope that *Treating ADHD and Comorbid Disorders* will enable clinicians to approach their work with these challenging patients with greater confidence.

Contents

Chapter 1

Overview of Comorbid Disorders in ADHD

There are thousands of scientific studies examining the comorbidity of psychiatric disorders with attention-deficit/hyperactivity disorder (ADHD), but for the clinician, it is the individual patient that is most important. My colleagues and I (Pliszka, Carlson, & Swanson, 1999) opened our previous work on this topic with the case of Justin:

Justin was a 13-year-old seventh grader. He was first diagnosed with ADHD when he was 5 years of age. His doctor prescribed methylphenidate, which led to increased agitation. He was managed without medication until the age of 7, when his severe hyperactivity and aggression led to a suspension from school. He was treated with dextroamphetamine with modest results. Psychological testing at age 8 showed marked reading delay; Justin had particular difficulty sounding out words. His handwriting was very poor. He began attending special education classes 2 hours a day. In the fifth grade, he exploded and threw a chair at a teacher, which led to a 5-day psychiatric hospitalization. An electroencephalogram (EEG) showed "right temporal slowing" but no actual seizure activity. He was started on carbamazepine in the hope this would reduce the aggressive outbursts. After 6 months of treatment, however, it was still unclear if the anticonvulsant was helpful and it was eventually discontinued. Justin barely passed the sixth grade. Repeat of psychological testing showed he was reading at the third-grade level. During the seventh grade, his aggressive outbursts increased, and he began making suicidal statements such as "How'd you feel if I wasn't around anymore?" He was caught with a small amount of marijuana in his school locker and was expelled. In the midst of an argument with his mother that night, he made a cut on his wrist and was hospitalized again. The managed care company approved a 3-day stay.

Justin was a patient of mine. By pure coincidence, I ran into Justin's father about seven years after this. The father reported that Justin had gone to residential treatment. There, he was diagnosed with bipolar disorder and tried on multiple medications, some of which clearly helped for at least a short time. When he turned 18, he left the residential center, began to use illegal drugs, and was arrested for burglary. He spent about a year in jail, then lived with various friends but kept in contact with his parents. While on probation, he found employment, stopped abusing drugs and drinking, and against all expectations he established a positive relationship with a woman whom he married. The marriage and his job remained stable, and he repaired his relations with his parents. He has returned to community college part time, is now a parent himself, and currently shows no signs of bipolar disorder or antisocial personality.

How do we explain Justin's developmental course? Was he "misdiagnosed" as bipolar? Was comorbid conduct disorder the most accurate diagnosis all along? If so, what accounts for the remission of these symptoms with age? Did the aggressive intervention with residential treatment and psychotropic medication alter his long-term course? Cases like Justin's give us hope that while current research does not have all the answers, careful integration of findings from the literature and clinical experience can map the way to effective intervention. The previous work of my colleagues and I (Pliszka et al., 1999) was an in-depth scientific review of the topic of ADHD with comorbid disorders. This book takes a more clinical approach. While it is informed by the significant advances in the study of comorbidity of mental disorders with ADHD over the last decade, the study of each condition in the subsequent chapters revolves around a series of case studies. The goal here is to inform the practicing clinician of the variety of both pharmacological and psychosocial interventions that can be brought to bear in these difficult situations. While I have been involved in clinical and neuroimaging research in the last 20 years, I have spent half my time involved in the care of patients in a variety of settings ranging from a "private practice" university clinic to residential treatment centers. Moreover, the data from literally thousands of these patients has been consistently entered into a computer database that allows accurate documentation of the patients' clinical course. As Yogi Berra allegedly said, "You can observe a lot by just looking." This database contains a rich source of cases of children and adolescents with ADHD who also have conduct problems, affective and anxiety disorders, autism spectrum disorders (ASD), and substance abuse issues, among other serious complications. We mine this database to explore the management of very complex cases.

Defining Comorbidity

Comorbidity can be simply defined as two or more diseases occurring in the same individual. Angold, Costello, and Erkanli (1999) discussed several factors that influence this definition, and their framework is useful for developing the questions that we address in this book.

Disorder versus Disease

In general medicine, the pathophysiologies of many diseases are at present much better understood than in mental health. When we speak of the comorbidity of lung cancer and emphysema, each individual disease is a clearly separate clinical entity with a specific clinical course and treatment. Our knowledge of their pathophysiology allows us to understand that smoking is a major etiological agent for both. In mental health, we define *disorders* as "behavioral and psychological syndromes that deviate from some standard of normality" (Angold et al., 1999, p. 58). We do not know for certain if separation anxiety and generalized anxiety disorder (GAD) are truly different diseases or whether they are one disease with varied presentations at different developmental levels. If they are one disease there is no "comorbidity"; rather the problem is with our classification system. Similar issues will complicate our discussion of ADHD and comorbid bipolar disorder (BP)—particularly in distinguishing severe mood lability/aggression from manic cycling. Of course, clinicians cannot wait for nomenclature debates to resolve themselves in the DSM-V (or VI or VII!) before making a diagnosis for the patient who is in the office today.

Primary versus Secondary Disorders

Patients with diabetes frequently have impaired eyesight as they age; so one might say that blindness is often comorbid with diabetes. Diabetes can also lead to atherosclerosis in small blood vessels (microaneurysms), which in turn leads to hemorrhages in the retina. Through our knowledge of the pathophysiology of the disease, it is clear that the impaired vision is secondary to the diabetes (diabetic retinopathy). Again, we have no such detailed knowledge in psychiatry to make such a determination when two mental disorders coexist in a patient. When treating a child with comorbid ADHD and oppositional defiant disorder (ODD), clinicians often observe that the defiance and argumentativeness frequently resolve after medication treatment of the ADHD (Newcorn, Spencer, Biederman, Milton, & Michelson, 2005; Spencer et al., 2006). Does this mean that the ODD is "secondary" to the ADHD? In contrast, in children with ADHD and bipolar disorder, the onset of ADHD usually precedes the onset of mood symptoms by several years, and clinical experience is that treatment of ADHD does not improve the mood symptoms per se. Few would argue that bipolar is "secondary" to ADHD simply because it occurred later in the child's clinical course. Despite our imprecision in these matters, a critical clinical decision point is whether or not to regard a comorbid disorder as secondary to ADHD. Declaring comorbid disorder truly secondary to ADHD suggests that treatment of the ADHD should occur first. We examine a variety of cases where this approach is either warranted or contraindicated.

Developmental Comorbidity

When we say that two disorders are present *at the same time* in a patient, what time frame are we referring to? Do we mean at the exact moment a patient is in the clinic? Or do we mean the last week, month, or 6 months? Or perhaps even the child's entire lifetime? Angold et al. (1999) use the terms "concurrent" and "successive" comorbidity to refer to two different clinical situations: in concurrent comorbidity the child clearly meets criteria for two or more disorders at the present time (i.e., at the visit, has 8/9 inattention symptoms of ADHD and 6/9 symptoms of ODD), while successive comorbidity refers to a child who meets criteria for ADHD at one point in his or her life and, while the ADHD symptoms resolve with age, develops a new disorder such as dysthymia. In this latter case, has the ADHD "morphed" into depression or has it gone "underground"? Will the ADHD reemerge once the depression is treated? Or has the ADHD truly resolved such that the clinician is seeing the emergence of an unrelated condition?

Familial Comorbidity

The substantial role of genetics in the etiology of ADHD is now well established. Family studies consistently have shown that if a child has ADHD, 10–35% of first-degree relatives are likely to have the disorder as well (Biederman et al., 1992). If a parent has

ADHD, the risk of the child developing ADHD is as high as 57% (Biederman et al., 1995b). In adoptive children who were hyperactive, higher rates of hyperactivity were found in their biological parents relative to their adoptive parents (Cantwell, 1972; Morrison, 1980; Morrison & Stewart, 1971). Sprich, Biederman, Crawford, Mundy, and Faraone (2000) examined the rates of ADHD in the relatives of both adopted (i.e., nonbiological) and nonadopted children with ADHD. The rate of ADHD in biological relatives of children with ADHD was 18% compared to only 6% in the adopted relatives, suggesting a strong genetic effect. Twin studies compare conductance rates for ADHD in monozygotic and dizygotic twins to determine the relative influence of genes and environment on the variance in the symptoms of ADHD. Reviews of these studies consistently show that about 75% of the variance in ADHD traits is attributable to genetics (Faraone et al., 2005).

Angold et al. (1999) point out that comorbidity also is influenced by genetics. Relatives of children with ADHD have not only elevated rates of ADHD but higher than expected rates of antisocial personality, alcoholism, and substance abuse. It is also noteworthy that sometimes comorbidity will "breed true." For instance, children with ADHD alone do not have elevated rates of comorbidity of conduct disorder (CD) in their relatives, while children with comorbid ADHD/CD do. Moreover, the ADHD and CD "cosegregate," that is, the relatives of the child with ADHD/CD also tend to have *both* ADHD and antisocial behavior, suggesting that ADHD/CD is a separate genetic subtype from ADHD alone (Biederman et al., 1992). Similarly, while parents with depression have higher than expected rates of depression among their children, children of depressed parents also have higher rates of a range of disruptive behavior disorders (Angold et al., 1999). Family history, therefore, plays a role in helping us untangle comorbidity in the child. Yet, we must not "jump the gun." A parent with bipolar disorder may bring his or her child for treatment of defiance and argumentativeness, but we would not conclude the child has bipolar disorder based only on the parent history. Nonetheless, how should the parent's history inform treatment?

When Does Comorbidity Matter?

If a child with ADHD presents to your office with a runny nose, the child can be said to have ADHD with a comorbid rhinitis. For the mental health professional, it is difficult to think of any long-term consequence of such "comorbidity." We must have a set of rules for determining when a comorbid disorder really has clinical significance in the management of the patient. Otherwise we run the risk of concluding that everything is comorbid with ADHD, as every disorder in the DSM and every known disease has occurred in people with ADHD at one time or another. Fortunately, Jensen, Martin, and Cantwell (1997) have developed such rules for determining if a comorbid disorder (CM) associated with ADHD is clinically relevant.

Distinctive Clinical Picture

Children with ADHD/CM should differ in substantial ways from children with ADHD on measures other than the diagnostic criteria themselves. For instance, children with ADHD and social phobia should be seen as withdrawing from social interactions on the playground by observers blind to the child's diagnostic status. If children with ADHD with and without a comorbid diagnosis differ only on the clinician's interview, without any "real-world" differences on behavior rating scales, peer interactions, educational achievement, and so forth, then the validity of the distinction is questionable.

Distinctive Demographic Factors

The ADHD/CM group may differ from the children with ADHD alone in terms of sex, ethnicity, or social class.

Differences in Psychosocial Factors

The ADHD/CM group may have a differential exposure to major societal stressors such as poverty, crime, urban decay, or exposure to violence.

Differences in Biological Factors

Are there differences between the ADHD/CM and ADHD groups in terms of genetic markers, brain anatomy, neuroimaging, or physiology? This approach is still in its infancy but holds great promise for the future.

Distinctive Family Genetic Factors

Does the ADHD/CM condition "breed true"? That is, if a child has ADHD/CM, is there an increased prevalence of both ADHD and CM in his or her relatives? Furthermore, do the ADHD and CM almost always occur in the same relative or does the child have some relatives with CM and others with ADHD? In the former situation, the case for ADHD/CM being a distinct genetic subtype is strengthened. In the latter case, the child most likely inherited two independent disorders from separate relatives and ADHD/CM is not distinct.

Distinctive Family Environmental Factors

Has the child with ADHD/CM been exposed to certain family experiences not shared by the child with ADHD alone? Have children with ADHD and anxiety disorders experienced more divorce or separation than those with ADHD alone? Are children with ADHD and CD more likely to have been exposed to domestic violence?

Distinctive Clinical Course and Outcome

Are children with ADHD with and without comorbid disorders different at follow-up? Do children with ADHD/CD have more criminal convictions? Do children with ADHD and depression have a higher rate of adult affective disorder than nondepressed children with ADHD? Are there differences in the life course of the ADHD itself for comorbid and noncomorbid children? Does the presence of the comorbid disorder make continuation of ADHD into adulthood more or less likely?

Unique Response to Specific Treatments

Do children with ADHD with and without comorbid disorders differ in their response to either psychopharmacological or psychosocial interventions?

　　In the subsequent chapters, we pay particularly close attention to each of these factors as we look at the different comorbidities.

Comorbidity in the Community and the Clinic

Epidemiologists and clinicians look at the world quite differently. The epidemiologist wishes to establish the true prevalence and incidence in a population. While clinicians tend to use these terms interchangeably, they are quite different (see Box 1.1), and it is prevalence that is most important to the study of comorbidity. Epidemiologists do not

---

BOX 1.1. Defining Prevalence and Incidence

　　Prevalence—defined as the total number of cases of the disease in the population at a given time, or the total number of cases in the population, divided by the number of individuals in the population. It is presented as a percentage. For instance, the prevalence of ADHD was found to be 8.7% by the U.S. National Health and Nutrition Survey for the period 2001–2004 (Froehlich et al., 2007). Prevalence is subtyped into:

- *Point prevalence*—a measure of the proportion of people in a population who have a disease or condition at a particular time, such as a particular date. It is like a snapshot of the disease in time.
- *Period prevalence*—a measure of the proportion of people in a population who have a disease or condition over a specific period of time (last month, last year).
- *Lifetime prevalence*—the number of individuals in a statistical population that at some point in their lives (up to the time of assessment) have experienced a "case" (e.g., a disorder), compared to the total number of individuals. (It is expressed as a ratio or percentage.)

　　Incidence—the number of new cases of a disease during a given time interval, usually 1 year. It can be expressed as a proportion or as a rate.

- *Incidence proportion* (also known as *risk*)—the number of new cases divided by the size of the population at risk. For example, if a stable population contains 1,000 persons and 43 develop a condition over 2 years of observation, the incidence proportion is 43 cases per 1,000 persons.
- *Incidence rate*—the number of new cases per unit of person-time at risk. In the same example as above, the incidence rate is 21.5 cases per 1,000 person-years, because the incidence proportion (43 per 1,000) is divided by the number of years of the study (2). *Incidence* is sometimes used alone as a shorthand for *incidence rate*, though this should be avoided.

look at clinical samples, but rather at samples of hundreds or thousands of children drawn from the community. If we take the prevalence of ADHD to ~7%, we then look at the prevalence of another disorder of interest (e.g., ODD/CD) in the general population and find that in a particular study, it is 8.0%. By chance alone, we would expect 8% of the children with ADHD to have comorbid ODD/CD. If this were the case, then the odds ratio of having ODD if the child has ADHD would be 1.0 (i.e., not different from chance). Suppose the prevalence of ODD/CD in the ADHD sample is 16%; then the odds ratio would be 2.0 (i.e., double the rate). Figure 1.1 resulted from a meta-analysis of 21 epidemiological studies of mental disorders in children. As can be seen, relative to the general population, patients with ADHD had greater than expected prevalence of ODD/CD (10 times), depression (5.5 times), and anxiety (3 times). These epidemiological studies are critical in showing us that comorbidity is not simply an artifact of children with more severe conditions being referred for treatment (i.e., referral bias).

These epidemiological studies can inform us about the comorbidity of common conditions such as depression, ODD, and ADHD. They are less well suited for the study of more rare conditions such as bipolar or tic disorders. For instance, only 6 of 1,420 (0.42%) children in the Great Smokey Mountain Study had a manic or hypomanic episode during the 3 months preceding the interview (Costello et al., 1996). For the study of these conditions, we must rely on clinical samples. Here, I would like to make

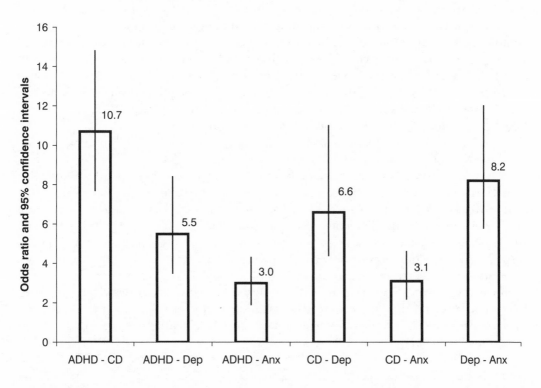

FIGURE 1.1. Risk of conduct, anxiety, and depressive disorders in children and adolescents with ADHD. From Angold, Costello, and Erkanli (1999). Copyright 1999 by Blackwell Publishing Ltd. Reprinted by permission.

an important point before presenting some prevalence data from my own practice—data from tertiary referral centers tell us what we are facing *in the clinic*. For instance, a child psychiatrist receiving referrals (as I do) of difficult-to-treat patients may see, in a given day, eight children with ADHD alone, six with ADHD and ODD/CD, and six with ADHD and bipolar disorder. This does not mean, however, that the prevalence of bipolar disorder in patients with ADHD in the community at large is 6/20, or 30%! So, I should not view the rates of bipolar disorder in my clinic as though they applied to the whole world. At the same time, I must deal with the reality that 30% of my patients with ADHD do have bipolar disorder, and I should not see the low rates of bipolar disorder in epidemiological samples as invalidating the reality I see in my clinic every day.

The Division of Child and Adolescent Psychiatry at the University of Texas Health Science Center at San Antonio is affiliated with several major clinical enterprises: (1) a "private practice University Clinic," (2) two private nonprofit child mental health clinics serving low-income children, and (3) two residential treatment centers for severely psychiatrically ill children (most of whom have suffered physical, sexual, or emotional abuse). One facility is for children of average IQ or above, the other treats children with mental retardation and/or ASD. For the last 5 years, data on these children's treatment have been systematically entered into our database. As one might imagine, the breadth and diversity of psychopathology in these children and adolescents is great, thus it is hoped that there is "something for everyone" in the data—regardless of discipline or practice setting.

These patients were not research subjects; all data were gathered as part of their routine clinical care (and deidentified for analysis here). Diagnoses were made according to the structured interview in Appendix Ib. This interview is not a fully validated structured research interview such as the Kiddie Schedule for Affective Disorders and Schizophrenia (K-SADS; Kaufman et al., 1997) or the Diagnostic Interview Schedule for Children (DISC; Fisher et al., 1997; Shaffer, Fisher, Lucas, Dulcan, & Schwab-Stone, 2000). It was developed to train medical students and psychiatric residents to conduct their standard clinical interviews with children and their parents in a systematic fashion, but it has proven useful for all our faculty clinicians.

For the first broad look at the data, I extracted the diagnoses from all patients with ADHD who were active patients of any of the sites (defined as having had at least one visit in the last year); this yielded 1,035 patients for a snapshot of what is happening "right now" in the clinic. The comorbidity of these patients is shown in Table 1.1. The simplest way to look at comorbidity is to pair each comorbid disorder with ADHD. An inspection of this table shows how the San Antonio practice is atypical in some ways, yet is atypical in a fashion useful for the study of comorbidity. There are a substantial number of children (27%) with no comorbidity ("ADHD simplex"), though this number of patients with uncomplicated ADHD is clearly smaller than might be found in a primary care practice. Not surprisingly, ODD and CD are quite common (32% of the children with ADHD).

Comorbidity data are frequently displayed in research studies as in Table 1.1, yet reality is more complex, as shown in Figure 1.2. This Venn diagram illustrates that many children with ADHD have more than one comorbid disorder; in particular, there is a common phenomenon of "triple comorbidity" with ODD/CD. Of these patients with ADHD, 167 have an additional diagnosis of ODD/CD and nothing else (these

TABLE 1.1. Overall Comorbidity of Diagnoses among Patients with ADHD in a Medical School Setting

Diagnoses	San Antonio (*n* = 1035)		MTA study (*n* = 579)	
	Count	%	Count	%
No comorbidity	282	27.2		
ODD/CD	327	31.6	314	54.2
Intermittent explosive disorder	74	7.1		
Mood disorder not otherwise specified	90	8.7		
Depressive disorders[a]	109	10.5	22	3.8
Bipolar disorder (all subtypes)	121	11.7	13[c]	2.2
Anxiety disorders	149	14.4	194	33.5
Autism spectrum disorders[b]	50	4.8		
Psychotic disorder not otherwise specified	29	2.8		
Learning disabilities	101	9.8		
Tic disorder	17	1.6	63	10.9

[a]Includes major depressive disorder, dysthymic disorder, and depressive disorder not otherwise specified.
[b]Includes Asperger's disorder.
[c]Mania/hypomania.

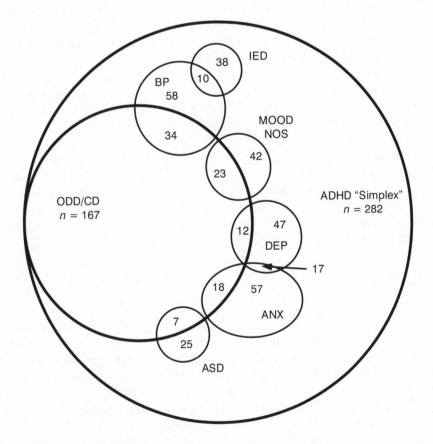

FIGURE 1.2. Overlap of diagnoses in children and adolescents with ADHD with more than one comorbid diagnosis.

patients are the focus of Chapter 2). Note, however, that when other major disorders are comorbid with ADHD, it is highly likely that ODD/CD is present as well. Note how ASD, anxiety, depression, nonspecific mood disorders, and BP tend to line up on the edge of the ODD/CD prevalence circle. This leads to one of the central arguments of this book—that argumentative, negativistic, and aggressive behaviors in children with ADHD are frequently (but not always) fueled by other comorbidities. The treatment of ADHD + ODD/CD and that of ADHD + ODD/CD combined with yet other comorbid disorders can be markedly different. This is a major focus of Chapter 2. In Chapters 5 and 6, we also examine two important but little researched phenomena. The diagnosis of mood disorder not otherwise specified was given to 8.7% of our ADHD population and these children are clearly separate from those with depression or bipolar disorder. What type of symptomatology leads to this diagnosis and how does it influence treatment? Note that 38 children were diagnosed with intermittent explosive disorder (IED) and no other disorder besides ADHD. Thus, clinicians separate out those with explosive aggression who do not have prominent mood symptoms. Is this a clinically relevant distinction? Chapter 3 will explore this issue. It is of interest to compare the rates of comorbidity in this database to that in the subjects of the National Institute of Mental Health Multimodal Treatment Study of ADHD (MTA; MTA Cooperative Group, 1999a, 1999b). The MTA study was designed to look at the treatment of ADHD per se, so major mental disorders such as bipolar disorder or ASD were excluded. Nonetheless, the comorbidity of ODD/CD was also highly prevalent in the MTA sample, as were depressive disorders. Despite the exclusion of children with BP, a small subgroup still met criteria for hypomania/mania. The difference in the rate of tic disorders between the two samples is harder to explain, but further illustrates the differences in comorbidity that can occur with different sampling strategies, even when focused on a clinical population.

There are also small groups of children with more than two comorbid diagnoses in addition to ADHD ("quadruple comorbidity"), as listed in Table 1.2. These children rarely find themselves in research projects (they meet exclusionary criteria), but they show up at the clinician's office and have stormy clinical courses. By looking in detail at these complex cases, we can have some approaches ready when these infrequent but serious situations arise.

Clinical Interview

Owing to its origins in psychoanalysis, the child mental health field has always emphasized the "open-ended" clinical interview, allowing both parent and child to state the reason for the visit and then to expand spontaneously, with the clinician following the interviewee's lead and in particular paying attention to his or her emotional state. Since the emergence of the successive versions of the *Diagnostic and Statistical Manual of Mental Disorders* (DSM) over the last several decades, mental health has moved to a more structured approach. Similarly, extensive interviews such as the DISC and K-SADS have been developed to make valid and reliable diagnoses in the research area. These research interviews can take several hours to administer and are rarely practical for use in the typical clinician's office. At the same time, when a child presents with multiple prob-

TABLE 1.2. "Quadruple Comorbidity" Children with ADHD Who Have More Than Two Comorbid Disorders

ODD/CD + mood disorder not otherwise specified + tic disorder	1
ODD/CD + mood disorder not otherwise specified + learning disabilities	4
ODD/CD + intermittent explosive disorder + mood disorder not otherwise specified	1
ODD/CD + intermittent explosive disorder + depression	1
ODD/CD + intermittent explosive disorder + BP + anxiety	1
ODD/CD + intermittent explosive disorder + anxiety	2
ODD/CD + depression + mood disorder not otherwise specified	1
ODD/CD + depression + BP	2
ODD/CD + depression + anxiety	7
ODD/CD + BP + anxiety	4
ODD/CD + BP + tic disorder	2
ODD/CD + BP + learning disabilities	2
ODD/CD + BP + anxiety + learning disabilities	1
ODD/CD + ASD + learning disabilities	1
ODD/CD + anxiety + tic disorder	1
ODD/CD + anxiety + learning disabilities	2
Intermittent explosive disorder + depression + BP	1
Depression + BP + anxiety	1
BP + ASD + tic disorder	1
BP + anxiety + ASD	4

lems, an open-ended approach can lead to confusion as the parent mixes the description of symptoms of ADHD, oppositional behavior, aggression, mood lability, anxiety and so on. The interview in Appendix Ib represents a compromise between the highly structured research interview and the very open-ended approach traditionally used by child mental health clinicians. This interview follows a number of basic principles:

The Interview Is Time Limited

It is designed such that information about even severely ill children can be obtained in 1 to 1½ hours, including interviews of both child and parent.

Preliminary Data Have Been Gathered

It is assumed that a demographic/developmental questionnaire and parent rating scales (see next section) have been obtained before the interaction with the parent. An example of the scale used in our clinic is in Appendix Ia. The questionnaire may either be mailed to the parent beforehand or the parent may arrive half an hour early to fill it out. The questionnaire should cover the child's medical history and developmental milestones. Ideally, a rating scale (particularly for ADHD symptoms) also has been obtained from the teacher. The interview format assumes that the clinician has had time to review these forms prior to meeting with the parent.

Both Parent and Child Will Be Interviewed

The degree to which the child provides key information for the diagnoses can be a contentious issue. With increasing demands on the time of mental health professionals, some clinicians have been interviewing only the parent, often with the child in the room. With the child present, however, the parent may not be frank in discussing many aspects of the history; furthermore the child may disrupt the interview. While interviewing *only* the parent alone may alleviate the problem with parental openness, not seeing the child might lead the clinician to miss internalizing symptoms (particularly suicidal ideation) as well as possible signs of abuse.

Interviewing both the parent and the child brings up the issue of integrating possibly incongruent data from both informants. What should the clinician do if the child states she is sad but the parent denied that the child was depressed? If the child denies any hyperactivity, should the clinician give this any weight? A long-standing clinical practice has emerged that adults (parents and teachers) are better reporters of children's disruptive behaviors whereas children themselves are more reliable when it comes to internalizing symptoms, such as depression or anxiety (Edelbrock, Costello, Dulcan, Conover, & Kalas, 1986; Loeber, Green, Lahey, & Stouthamer-Loeber, 1989; Reich & Earls, 1987; Welner, Reich, Herjanic, Jung, & Amado, 1987). Bird, Gould, and Staghezza (1992) performed DISC interviews on several hundred parent–child pairs. DISC diagnoses were generated, and then a clinician made a separate diagnosis of the child, which served as the external validating criterion (the "gold standard"). Statistical methods were used to determine if, for a given diagnosis, the parent or child data were most critical to make the diagnosis. For instance, if a child was given a diagnosis of ADHD by the clinician, did the parent or the child endorse the inattention and hyperactivity items on the DISC? Or did they both endorse symptoms of ADHD? For ADHD and ODD, *only* the parent DISC predicted the diagnoses, whereas for anxiety and depressive diagnoses, *both* the parent and child DISC contributed to the diagnosis.

The data of Bird et al. (1992) clearly showed that parents and children agree only about 20% of the time. Using the method of Loeber et al. (1989), they examined the percentage of time children endorsed a symptom if their parent had said the child had it. Of note, if the parent said the child fidgeted, about 45% of the children agreed that they fidgeted. If, however, the parent said the child failed to finish things, only 18% of the children agreed that they had this problem. A similar pattern was found for internalizing symptoms. If the parent stated the child worried a great deal, 58% of the children agreed. If the parent stated the child was depressed, only 20% of the children agreed. If a child says he or she has a symptom, what percent of parents agree? The pattern is not any more consistent. Bird et al. (1992) next looked at the prevalence of diagnoses in their sample if they based the diagnoses on the parent interview only, the child interview only, or a combination of the parent and child interview. In the latter method, if either the parent or the child DISC interview yielded a diagnosis, that diagnosis is regarded as present. Basically, the either–or method yields somewhat higher prevalence estimates of the disorders. Children will deny they have ADHD or ODD when adults clearly state it is present, but they will report more internalizing symptoms than adults have observed. As we explore each major comorbid disorder in subsequent chapters, we discuss in more detail how to handle specific situations.

The Format for the Parent Is Structured

The interview assumes only a brief time for assessing the chief complaint before the clinician moves in to gather systematic information from the parent about each major DSM-IV childhood diagnostic criterion—I refer to this as "therapeutic interrupting." If the parent begins to move into an extensive discussion of how his or her divorce may be affecting the child, I say, "That is very important information and we will need to come back to it, but let me be sure that I have all the information about your child's symptoms." This allows me to launch into asking specific questions. Naturally, since we are dealing with ADHD with comorbid disorders, documenting the presence of ADHD and the most common comorbidities (ODD and CD) takes the stage first. The first page of the interview contains blanks to enter the result of whichever DSM-IV-based rating scale for ADHD, ODD, and CD the clinician has chosen (see Table 1.3), as well as a section for the clinician to use clinical judgment in interpreting the rating scale.

The interview for affective disorders focuses first on the child's *current* mood state and places heavy emphasis on quantifying the frequency and magnitude of abnormal mood states. The boxes on the form are only an endpoint—a series of clinical probes needs to be used to gather the data needed for differential diagnosis of an explosively aggressive, mood-labile child with ADHD. Is it intermittent explosive disorder, a manic or mixed episode of bipolar disorder, or a severe major depressive episode with psychomotor agitation? In the affective disorder chapters, we go into detail about such critical issues as how to distinguish irritable mania from irritable depression (or the irritability of ODD) and mixed states versus ultra-rapid cycling, and how to determine the time of onset of an abnormal mood state. Once the current mood state is established, the presence or absence of both neurovegetative signs and first-rank symptoms of mania should be determined.

It is then most logical to proceed to asking about past history of mood disorder, in particularly distinguishing between the child who has clear-cut episodes of depression or mania versus those who seem to have had a chronic course of abnormal mood. Issues including age of onset of mood disorder, chronicity, and phenomenology have been much debated in the literature (Biederman, 1998; Carlson, 2007; Klein, Pine, & Klein, 1998). They have also been much debated in the lay media since the emergence of data showing that the prevalence rate of visits to clinicians for bipolar disorder in children has grown from 25/100,000 in 1994–1995 to 1,003/100,000 in 2002–2003 (Moreno et al., 2007). Chapters 3 and 4 focus on this issue in detail.

The interview proceeds with questions that screen for the anxiety disorders, psychotic symptoms, and substance abuse issues. There are also screening questions for ASD, but the presence of these on this interview would only trigger further evaluation, not serve as a definitive diagnosis. As always, data about the child's past psychiatric treatment would need to be documented. (It is assumed that medical history is covered in the developmental questionnaire.)

The Format for the Child Is Unstructured, Combined with Self-Report Rating Scales

Most children (and many adolescents) would be bored repeating such a full format of structured questions, and given that children often add limited information to the diagnosis of ADHD/ODD/CD (Biederman et al., 2007b), the interview focuses instead on internalizing symptoms, where the child can give the clinician the greatest insight. After a period of establishing rapport, it is useful to get the child's sense of externalizing symptoms by asking, "Your parents have mentioned that you seem to have a lot of trouble paying attention, sitting still, or staying organized. What do you think about that?" The same can be done for the symptoms of ADHD or ODD/CD. It is generally a good sign if the child has insight into the presence of these problems, but his or her awareness of them is not necessary to confirm the diagnosis of an externalizing disorder, nor would the child's denial of them negate reports from teacher and parents. Fairly quickly, the clinician should move to exploring internalizing symptoms by saying, "I would like to ask some questions about your feelings." We administer self-report depression and anxiety scales (see below) and then use these scales to explore the problems related to these feelings. Specific questions are asked regarding substance abuse, suicidal thoughts and actions, and possible abuse. Finally, the child's current mental status is documented.

Rating Scales

Table 1.3 describes a variety of rating scales useful in the assessment of the child with ADHD and comorbidity. Since assessment of ADHD is always the starting point, a scale that covers all 18 of the DSM-IV-defined symptoms of ADHD is key; all of the scales also include well-validated ratings of ODD and CD. The clinician dealing with comorbidity should also gather information from the parent dealing with a broad range of symptoms. The table contains scales that explore depressive, manic, and anxiety symptoms. The Child Mania Rating Scale (CMRS; Pavuluri, Henry, Devineni, Carbray, & Birmaher, 2006b) has proven particularly helpful in conjunction with the clinical interview in the differential diagnoses of mood lability. Parent and teacher measures of aggression, independent of diagnosis, are also helpful as aggression is often a target symptom regardless of the type of comorbidity.

The child should fill out any self-report scales during the visit, either in the presence of the clinician or with a trained administrative staff in the office. Children should not fill out such scales at home or in the waiting room with the parent looking over their shoulder. Having the child fill out the questionnaire in the presence of the clinician allows him or her to follow up immediately on any statements that cause concern (such as items related to suicidality) as well as assess the validity of the child's responses.

We have used the Mood and Feelings Questionnaire (MFQ; Angold et al., 1995; Messer et al., 1995) and the Screen for Child Anxiety Related Emotional Disorders (SCARED; Birmaher et al., 1997) as our child self-report forms. They are straightforward scales, make clinical sense, and are available without charge. This does not detract from the other scales in the table—scales that are commercially available often have better and more up-to-date normative data; they are more likely to be available in computerized form.

TABLE 1.3. Common Behavior Rating Scales Used in the Assessment of ADHD and the Most Common Comorbid Disorders

Domain	Name of scale	Description and reference
ADHD	Academic Performance Rating Scale (APRS)	The APRS is a 19-item scale for determining a child's academic productivity and accuracy in grades 1–6. It has six scale points. Construct, concurrent, and discriminant validity data, as well as norms ($n = 247$), are available (Barkley, 1990).
ADHD	ADHD Rating Scale–IV	The ADHD Rating Scale–IV is an 18-item scale using DSM-IV criteria (DuPaul, Power, Anastopoulos, & Reid, 1998).
ADHD	Brown ADD Rating Scales for Children, Adolescents and Adults (BADDS)	Brown ADD Rating Scales consists of four separate scales with norms for preschoolers, children, adolescents, and adults and assess a wide range of symptoms of executive function impairments associated with ADHD/ADD. They contain items beyond the DSM-IV ADHD criteria which assess organization skills, regulating alertness, and managing frustrations and emotions as well as working memory (Brown, 2001).
Broad	Child Behavior Checklist (CBCL)	The CBCL is available in preschool and school age (6–18 years) forms, and each has about 100 items assessing a wide variety of problems in the areas of Aggressive Behavior; Anxious/Depressed; Attention Problems; Rule-Breaking Behavior; Social Problems; Somatic Complaints; Thought Problems; and Withdrawn/Depressed. The school-age form contains six DSM-oriented scales: Affective Problems, Anxiety Problems, Somatic Problems, Attention Deficit/Hyperactivity Problems, Oppositional Defiant Problems, and Conduct Problems. Scoring yields T scores (> 65 borderline, >70 is the clinical cutoff) for each scale as well as broad Externalizing and Internalizing symptoms.
ADHD	Conners 3	The parent form includes 110 items, the teacher form 115 items, and the self-report form 99 items. The short form, consisting of 43 items on the parent form, 39 on the teacher form, and 39 on the self-report form, can be used for screening. ADHD and Global Indexes are included. (Conners, 2008).
Broad	Home Situations Questionnaire—Revised (HSQ-R), School Situations Questionnaire—Revised (SSQ-R)	The HSQ-R (14 items) and the SSQ-R (8 items) are filled out by the caretaker and teacher, respectively (Barkley & Murphy, 2005). Each has the same structure: The informant responds "Yes" or "No" as to whether the child has problems in common situations (playing with other children, being in the car, individual desk work in class, recess). If the informant responds "Yes," they rate the severity of the problems on a scale from 1 (mild) to 9 (severe).
Broad	Swanson, Nolan, and Pelham (SNAP-IV) and SWANP	The SNAP-IV is a 26-item scale that contains DSM-IV criteria for ADHD and screens for other DSM diagnoses. The SWANP is a 30-item scale that measures impairment of functioning at home and at school (Swanson, 1992).
ADHD and ODD/CD	Vanderbilt ADHD Diagnostic Parent and Teacher Scales	Teachers rate 35 symptoms and 8 performance items measuring ADHD symptoms and common comorbid conditions (Wolraich et al., 2003a). The parent version contains all 18 ADHD symptoms with items assessing comorbid conditions and performance (Wolraich et al., 2003b).
Depression	Children's Depression Inventory (CDI)	The CDI is a 27-item scale. On each item, the child selects the option that best fits him or her—"I am sad all the time," "I am sad some of the time," "I am never sad." Not diagnostic, but useful in screening and documenting response to treatment (Kovacs, 1992).

(cont.)

TABLE 1.3. *(cont.)*

Domain	Name of scale	Description and reference
Depression	Mood and Feelings Questionnaire (MFQ)	The MFQ comprises parent and child self-report versions of a 37-item scale covering a wide range of depressive symptoms (Angold et al., 1995; Messer et al., 1995). No charge for use, but permission of author required (see *devepi.mc.duke.edu/MFQ.html*).
Mania	Child Mania Rating Scale—Parent Version (CMRS-P)	The CMRS-P is a mania rating scale designed to be completed by parents. It includes 21 items reflecting the DSM-IV criteria for a manic episode. Each item is answered on a 4-point Likert-type scale anchored by 0 (Never/Rare), 1 (Sometimes), 2 (Often), and 3 (Very Often) (Pavuluri et al., 2006b).
Anxiety	Revised Manifest Anxiety Scale (RCMAS)	The RCMAS has 37 items written at third-grade level. The child answers "Yes" or "No" to each item. Well-established norms, not diagnostic, but useful in screening and documenting response to treatment (Reynolds & Richmond, 1997).
Anxiety	Screen for Child Anxiety Related Emotional Disorders (SCARED)	The SCARED is a 38-item scale with parent and child forms. The subject responds to each item with 0—not true, 1—sometimes true, or 2—often true. Yields five factors: somatic/panic, general anxiety, separation anxiety, social phobia, and school phobia. Discriminates depressed/anxious children from those with disruptive behavior disorders. No norms as yet (Birmaher et al., 1997).
Anxiety	Multidimensional Anxiety Scale for Children (MASC)	The MASC is a 39-item scale with four factors: physical symptoms, social anxiety, separation anxiety, and harm avoidance. Fourth-grade reading level (March et al., 1997).
Aggression	Modified Overt Aggression Scale	This is a clinician-rated scale covering verbal and physical aggression against others, self, property, and animals (Coccaro, Harvey, Kupsaw-Lawrence, Herbert, & Bernstein, 1991).
Aggression	Overt Aggression Scale	This is a 20-item scale filled out by parent or teacher regarding the child's aggressive behavior toward others, self, or property in last week (Kronenberger, Giauque, & Dunn, 2007).
Aggression	Children's Aggression Scale	This scale includes parent and teacher ratings of specific aggressive acts (Halperin, McKay, Grayson, & Newcorn, 2003; Halperin, McKay, & Newcorn, 2002).

Dual versus Differential Diagnosis

The clinician must have an algorithm in his or her head for classifying the many symptoms encountered in the psychiatric interview, as well as knowing how to sort them into diagnostic categories. A case example (Pliszka et al., 1999) is helpful in illustrating this process:

Nine-year-old James was brought to the clinic by his mother because of poor school performance. Currently a third grader, he had been described by his teachers throughout elementary school as careless, sloppy, and unable to finish his work. He fidgets and makes noises but does not get out of his seat or run around the classroom. On the playground, he is shy and does not play with the other children. The teacher reported that he has said, "I'm ugly and stupid," when asked why he does not get along with the other children.

The mother also has trouble getting James to complete tasks at home. He seems unable to concentrate on his homework. He throws temper tantrums when pushed to do things. He cries, stamps his feet, and throws things. He does not become physically aggressive. He often says, "I hate you" or "I hate my life" when very angry. He does not want to go to bed at night and calls out for water and says he can't sleep. Once asleep, he stays asleep through the night. He has always been a picky eater. He is very nervous in new situations. He has never tried to deliberately hurt himself. His mother states that James is in a "bad mood" much of the time, but does not say he is sad.

During the examination, James is cooperative and friendly. He doesn't seem restless during the interview, but it is difficult to get James to concentrate on the questions asked. He says he hates school because "it is boring and the kids are mean." He states he is sad because there is no one to play with in his neighborhood and his dad does not always visit him. He is scared of the dark and worries that something bad will happen to his mom. He once wished he was dead when his mom grounded him but denies any suicidal ideation currently.

This case presents with a mixture of anxiety, depressive, and inattentive/hyperactive symptoms. The clinician must determine whether this is a case of ADHD, depression, or a truly comorbid case of ADHD and depression. Figure 1.3 illustrates how a clinician can step through the data to arrive at the appropriate conclusion. After a structured interview, one of several patterns may be evident. James may meet full criteria for ADHD, with onset of the symptoms before age 7. The interviewer detects symptoms of depression, but the child does not meet the full criteria for major depressive disorder (MDD) or dysthymia. The depressive symptoms may stem from a variety of issues. They may be centered on the child's unhappiness over the consequences of his ADHD behavior. Children will not play with him because he acts silly or is irritating. He might miss activities because of frequent misbehavior. It does not constitute a true depressive disorder, though it certainly may be the focus of psychosocial intervention. The psychotropic management would focus on the ADHD, most likely beginning with stimulant treatment. Antidepressant medication would not be the first-line treatment in such a child. The primary diagnosis made would be ADHD, though a diagnosis of adjustment disorder with depressed mood might be entertained if the demoralization symptoms were significantly impairing. The child would not be regarded as truly comorbid.

In the middle box of the chart, a somewhat more complex outcome of the interview is illustrated. The child clearly meets full criteria for MDD, and the child reports pervasively depressed mood. ADHD symptoms are present, but the child does not meet the full criteria for ADHD. He has a number of inattentive symptoms, as well as three impulsive–hyperactive symptoms. Age of onset is a critical issue. If these symptoms were not present before age 7, by definition he does not have ADHD. Equally important is whether these ADHD symptoms had their onset only after the depressive symptoms emerged. If so, it is likely they may be secondary to the MDD. The depression would be the focus of the psychotropic management, as well as any psychological intervention. It would be expected that the inattentive and impulsive symptoms would resolve once the child's depression lifted. Again, this would not be a truly comorbid case.

The box to the far right of Figure 1.3 illustrates the most complex situation of all. After the interview, the child is found to fully meet criteria for both disorders. The child is inattentive, impulsive, and hyperactive; these symptoms are pervasive and have

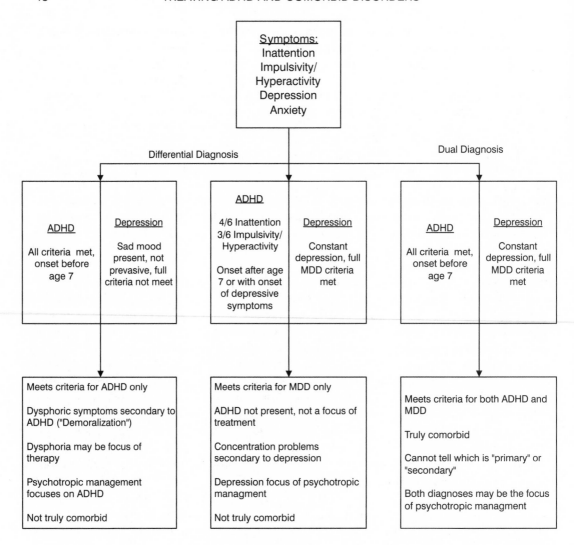

FIGURE 1.3. Differential versus dual diagnosis in the evaluation of comorbid disorders in ADHD.

been present since early childhood. The child is also pervasively depressed, and has multiple neurovegetative signs. This is a truly comorbid case. There is no way to tell for sure which diagnosis is "primary" or "secondary." Indeed, the child may be suffering from two independent disorders, each requiring its own treatment. Thus both diagnoses may be the focus of psychotropic or psychological treatment.

Treatment Issues in Comorbidity

Treatment of ADHD with comorbid disorders involves a multifaceted, multidisciplinary approach, with both pharmacological and psychosocial treatment (primarily behavior therapy) playing central roles. Appendix II provides a review of the major pharmacological agents used in the treatment of ADHD, affective and anxiety disorders, psychosis, tics, and aggression. This information is concentrated in one place so that it will not be necessary to repeat details about dosing, side effects, and monitoring in each chapter, particularly as some agents (such as atypical antipsychotics and antidepressants) can be used for a variety of conditions. In the chapters themselves, the focus will be on the combination of agents used to treat both ADHD and the comorbid condition. Here there is limited research data to guide us, but the database should provide a wealth of case examples.

It is not the intent of this book to provide a detailed instruction manual on behavior or other forms of psychotherapy. The original work of my colleagues and I (Pliszka et al., 1999) contains an excellent overview of the principles of behavior therapy; there are also many textbooks on this topic (Barkley, 1997b; Barkley, 2006a; McMahon, Wells, & Kotler, 2006; Smith, Barkley, & Shapiro, 2006). For the treatment of severe oppositional and aggressive behaviors, we examine a number of social, cognitive, and collaborative approaches that show promise in this population (Greene & Ablon, 2006; Larson & Lochman, 2002). As we move toward the internalizing disorders, the focus will shift to when cognitive therapy is appropriate. Again, there is rich literature on this topic regarding the treatment of both depressive and anxiety disorders with this technique (Reinecke, Dattillio, & Freeman, 2006). The case examples focus on the implementation of these therapies in unique or difficult situations. The MTA is a valuable source of information on how comorbid disorders affect the clinical course of ADHD. Because we refer to this study so often, an overview of its many findings is in order.

The MTA Study

The MTA is one of the few long-term studies of treatment outcomes for ADHD. Subjects underwent a year of active treatment (MTA Cooperative Group, 1999a, 1999b), then had follow-up assessments 2 years (MTA Cooperative Group, 2004a, 2004b), 3 years (Jensen et al., 2007a; Molina et al., 2007; Swanson et al., 2007a, 2007b), and most recently 6–8 years (Arnold & Molina, 2007; Elliott & Swanson, 2007; Molina, 2007) after the formal research treatment ended. Subjects will most likely be followed into adulthood. A large number of children with ADHD ages 7–10 years ($n = 579$) were randomized to one of four groups for 13 months of active intervention:

1. Medication management (Med-Mgt), wherein children first underwent a 28-day double-blind placebo-controlled methylphenidate trial to determine the best dose of stimulant for symptom reduction and then received 13 months of regular medication follow-up. Pharmacotherapists had regular access to parent and teacher behavior rating scales.
2. Intensive behavior therapy (Beh), consisting of 35 parent training sessions, biweekly consultation with the child's teacher, an 8-week summer camp program designed for children with ADHD, and 3 months of classroom aide support.
3. Combined treatment (Comb), consisting of Med-Mgt and Beh together.
4. Community comparison (CC).

It would not be ethical to deprive children with ADHD of all treatments for a year, so the control group was referred for standard treatment in the community. About two-thirds of these children received medication treatment, primarily with stimulants.

Among the many strengths of the MTA were the large sample, the high degree of comorbidity (see Table 1.1), the fact that girls made up 25% of the sample, and the significant number of Hispanics and African Americans included. The MTA findings address several major areas: (1) how comorbidity affects symptoms at entry to the study, (2) outcome of acute treatment at the end of the year, and (3) outcome at future time points *after active treatment had ended.* This latter point is particularly important in understanding the results of the MTA. After the first year of the study families chose whichever standard treatment they wished, or they could drop out of treatment. Children who were in the behavior group could go on medication, while children in the medication group could stop medication. For the purposes of the analyses in years 2, 3, and 6–8, children were still classified according to the group in which they were originally randomized.

Figure 1.4 is the now famous figure showing how the children undergoing different treatments in the first year of the MTA fared over time. All of the children met DSM-IV criteria at study entry; at 14 months all four groups showed improvement in symptoms such that many children no longer officially met criteria for ADHD (MTA Cooperative Group, 1999a). As shown, the two groups that were treated with rigorous medication management were significantly better than the CC and Beh groups, which were not different from each other. Beh appeared to do as well as the "standard" CC group in reducing symptoms, so it might be claimed that behavior therapy works as well as medication and is an alternative to medication. However, when children who had not received any medication were excluded from the CC group, the CC group in fact did better than the Beh group. Thus, behavior therapy is not as effective as medi-

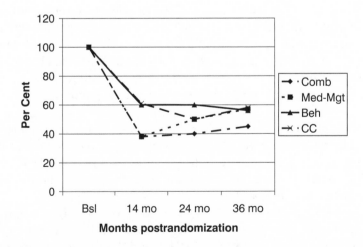

FIGURE 1.4. The long-term outcome of children with ADHD in the Med-Mgt, Beh, Comb, and CC groups of the MTA study. From Jensen et al. (2007a). Copyright 2007 by Wolters Kluwer. Reprinted by permission.

cation treatment. The American Academy of Child and Adolescent Psychiatry (2007) practice parameters regard pharmacological intervention as the first-line treatment for ADHD.

Before moving to the long-term outcome, it is critical to look at moderators that affected the response of subgroups in the sample. Not surprisingly, comorbidity was a key factor, as shown in Figure 1.5 (Jensen et al., 2001; MTA Cooperative Group, 1999b). The y-axis represents effect size (see Box 1.2 for a discussion of effect sizes) over CC, that is, how much greater the effect of the structured treatment was over CC. Note that for children with ADHD alone, Beh did not have any effect greater than CC (effect size = 0), whereas there was a significantly larger effect size for Med-Mgt and Comb over CC (though not different from each other). The comorbidity of ODD/CD did not moderate treatment—the lines for ADHD plus ODD/CD essentially overlap with the ADHD group. This means that the children with comorbid ODD/CD responded to treatment just like the ADHD group. The pattern was quite different for comorbid anxiety, however. Note that children with comorbid anxiety were much more responsive to all treatments, with a large effect size compared with the CC group. Comb was more effective than Med-Mgt. This was particularly true for the group with dual comorbidity, that is, children with ADHD, ODD/CD, *and* anxiety. Hinshaw (2007) described other moderators of outcome in the MTA. Children on public assistance and African American children responded better to Comb treatment. In contrast, children with depressed parents and those with more severe ADHD or low IQ showed worse response to both Med-Mgt and Comb. As Hinshaw (2007) points out, "these results are sobering, as they reveal a relative failure of the intensive MTA treatment algorithms to help those children in the study who were most in need of intervention" (p. 96).

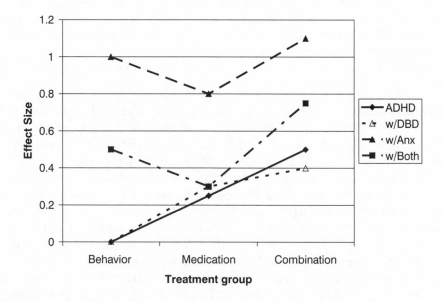

FIGURE 1.5. Effect of comorbidity on treatment outcome in the MTA study. From Jensen et al. (2001). Copyright 2001 by Wolters Kluwer. Reprinted by permission.

BOX 1.2. Effect Size for Clinicians

The concept of effect size is important because it has become a common way to present results from treatment studies. It gets beyond statistical significance and helps tell us when a treatment is clinically significant. The effect size of a treatment is calculated from the simple equation below:

$$\frac{\text{Mean } RX_1 - \text{Mean } RX_2}{\text{Standard Deviation}}$$

The two treatments may be an active treatment and a placebo, or two different active treatments. The effect size is unitless because the values of the outcome measures (laboratory value, rating scale scores, etc.) appear in both the numerator and denominator. Thus, effect sizes can be used to compare results from studies using different measures. To use a stimulant trial as an example, suppose two groups of children with ADHD are randomized to placebo or drug and a rating scale is obtained after 2 weeks of treatment. Assume the mean of the placebo group is 2.1 and the stimulant group is 1.0, with a standard deviation of 0.8. The effect size is calculated as 1.4. Contrast this with an antidepressant trial that uses a depression rating scale as an outcome variable. The active drug group has a mean of 52, while the placebo group has a mean of 64, with a standard deviation of 35. The effect size is 0.46. Thus, effect sizes range between 0 and 2.0, though in clinical practice they are rarely above 1.0. The stimulant effect size is "large," indicating that it is observable by the family and clinician, so a relatively small sample will be required to show statistical significance. In contrast, the effect size for the antidepressant is moderate, and a much larger sample is required for that difference in the means to be significant. It also means the effect will not be as strongly noticed at the level of the individual patient. Effect sizes of 0.2–0.3 are less likely to be clinically significant, as they would only become statistically significant with very large samples. Many public health practices (e.g., eating low-fat foods) have very small effect sizes, but they have great public health significance if millions of people can be induced to adopt them.

Once active treatment stopped, the four groups converged, and many children returned to active ADHD diagnostic status at 24 months (MTA Cooperative Group, 2004a) (again, see Figure 1.4). The Med-Mgt group continued to show significant superiority over the Beh and CC groups for ADHD and ODD symptoms at 24 months, although not as great as at 14 months. Additional benefits of Comb over Med-Mgt and of Beh over CC were not found. By 36 months, however, there were no differences at all between the groups in ADHD status. All four groups remained improved over their baseline status, and 40% of the children no longer met criteria for ADHD even though many were not on medication (Jensen et al., 2007a). At 36 months, 70% of the Med-Mgt and Comb groups were still taking medication, compared with 60% of the CC group and 45% of the Beh group. While there were differences in outcome between those taking and not taking medication at 24 months, there was no such difference at 36 months (Swanson et al., 2007b)! These findings were not any different at the 6- to 8-year follow-up. All four groups showed declines in impulsivity–hyperactivity (though still more impaired than controls), and they were not different from each other in clinically meaningful ways (Arnold et al., 2007). Is it possible that taking medication for ADHD really makes no difference in the long run?

Looking at data in a naturalistic outcome study is very complex. One possibility is that only the most severely ill children stayed on medication, thus masking the beneficial effect of the treatment. How could this happen? Imagine a group of 200 children with ADHD, half very severely impaired, the other half only mildly impaired. All are treated with medication. Over time, the mildly impaired group ends up with 20 on medication and 80 off medication (because the less severe children "grew out" of their ADHD). In contrast, 80 of the severely ill group are on medication, and only 20 are off medication. Assume we are using a scale like the SNAP (Swanson, Nolan, and Pelham Questionnaire) with a 0–3 range. The 80 severely ill children on medication have a SNAP of 2.0, while the 20 off medication have a SNAP of 2.5. The mildly ill children on medication have a SNAP of 1.0; the mildly ill children off medication have a SNAP of 1.5. Thus both groups show a beneficial effect of medication, but when you average the two groups together to compare all subjects on and off medication, both groups have a mean SNAP of about 1.8. Swanson and colleagues (2007b) performed a "propensity score" analysis to rule out this possibility. They *did not* find the above scenario. They divided the MTA sample into five quintiles based on severity of symptoms and did find that those with greater severity were more likely to take medication, but being on or off medication did not affect outcome within any given quintile. So what is going on?

First, none of the 36-month data take away from the fact that medication showed strong effects in the 14- and 24-month follow-up, superior to the only alternative to medication, that is, behavior therapy. Behavior therapy also showed no effect in the 36-month data. Most likely, there are biological changes in the subjects that are not related to initial severity. Thus, some children with ADHD do have improvement in their symptoms that is likely based on brain maturation (Shaw et al., 2007); these children no longer need medication. Others have deterioration (perhaps based on development of comorbidities) that leads to poor outcome in spite of being on medication. What is needed to really resolve the issue is a long-term (5–10 years) *controlled* trial of medication, as difficult as this might be. An analogy to the long-term treatment of asthma might be helpful. As asthmatic children mature, some outgrow their asthma while others go on to develop serious airway problems. Inhalers improve breathing during an asthma attack, but if we followed up these asthmatic children into adolescence we might also find that inhaler use was unrelated to outcome. Yet, no one would suggest not using inhalers during acute asthmatic attacks.

We will have much more to say about the MTA in subsequent chapters. Let us close our discussion of the MTA with a final, important graph (Figure 1.6) examining outcome for the children (Swanson et al., 2007b). Using a specialized statistical technique, it was shown that the children with ADHD fell into three classes: (1) those who showed gradual improvement over time (34% of the sample), (2) those who showed immediate strong improvement and maintained it (52%), and (3) those who showed initial gains but then deteriorated over time such that by year three they were as impaired as at baseline (14%). None of the classes were in remission; all remained more impaired than a normative control group. Class 2 was less impaired at baseline. But, classes 1 and 3 were similar in baseline impairments, despite their very different patterns of outcome, again showing that baseline severity is not the only factor influencing outcome.

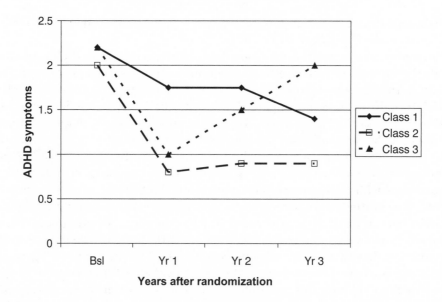

FIGURE 1.6. Three different types of outcome in the MTA study. From Swanson et al. (2007b). Copyright 2007 by Wolters Kluwer. Reprinted by permission.

Moving Forward

Given the wide variety of diagnoses that can be comorbid with ADHD, what is the most logical way to work through them? Many clinicians report what I have seen in my own practice: that severely dysregulated mood and aggression are the chief complaint in a growing number of cases. It therefore seems most prudent to begin with the study of the most common comorbidity in ADHD, that of ODD and CD. Dealing with oppositional and antisocial behavior invariably brings up the topic of aggression. Aggression, in turn, may be a symptom of other comorbid disorders, including sequelae of abuse, psychosis, and mania. Impulsive aggression may be a disorder separate from these, as in IED. Therefore, it would be best to step through these in an orderly manner: Chapter 2 deals with ODD and CD per se and emphasizes the differential diagnosis of irritability. It focuses also on behavioral approaches for ODD/CD to be used in combination with medication for the child's ADHD. Chapter 3 focuses on aggression more directly, particularly impulsive aggression in the absence of mood disorders. Since aggression of this sort is more common in children with a history of child abuse, this chapter is a good place to explore the treatment of children with ADHD who find themselves in foster care and not able to handle their placements due to their disruptive behavior.

Having explored the comorbidity of aggressive behavior, we are ready to move on to the diagnosis and management of patients with ADHD and bipolar disorder (Chapter 4). We then move on to the "internalizing disorders," such as depression (Chapter 5) and anxiety disorders (Chapter 6). The final two chapters concern tic and obsessive–compulsive disorders (Chapter 7) as well as developmental disorders such as intellectual disability (ID) and ASD (Chapter 8).

Case Material

Each chapter contains two to three cases from my clinical practice. To protect the privacy of patients, information not germane to the clinical situation has been removed or changed, including names, gender, and parent profession. Occasionally, composites were created from two or three very similar cases. I have not identified the ethnicity of patients to enhance protection of confidentiality, and I have used very common, nonethnic first names. In each chapter, the cases include some patients from more well-to-do families with plenty of resources, while others focus on families with very limited means and many psychosocial stressors. The point here is to show how comorbid disorders affect patients regardless of social standing, as well as how a clinician can respond in any of these settings. I have adopted another convention regarding generic or brand names of medication. In literature surveys about medications, I use generic names only. In the case reports, I use the brand name of the medication the child or adolescent was actually on. This allows a more realistic presentation of the case, and given the wide variety of the cases, the use of multiple brand names will be illustrated in a way that does not imply superiority of a particular brand when there is not scientific evidence to do so.

Chapter 2

Oppositional Defiant and Conduct Disorders

It is not uncommon for families to call our clinic and ask if there is a medication for oppositional defiant disorder (ODD). The question suggests that parents are thinking of ODD in the same way they think of ADHD—as a fairly discrete disorder with a specific pharmacological intervention. Yet, as heterogeneous as ADHD is in terms of possible etiologies and range of treatments, ODD and conduct disorder (CD) are even more so. ODD and CD are in some instances viewed as behaviors that the child chooses to engage in, while in others they may be viewed as secondary to ADHD or to other severe comorbidities. ODD and CD are discussed together in this chapter, but it must be borne in mind that they are separate entities that influence the course of ADHD in unique ways. Certain of the items in the ODD diagnostic criteria imply a degree of negative arousal/affectivity, such as losing one's temper, getting annoyed, and arguing. Mick, Spencer, Wozniak, and Biederman (2005) have carefully studied qualitative aspects of irritability in children with ADHD who have ODD alone or ODD with mood disorders; this information is helpful in sorting out when negative affect is just ODD as opposed to something more ominous. While CD symptoms can be affect neutral, as in a child who stealthily plans the theft of money from a classmate's desk, other children with CD can be explosively and impulsively aggressive and not plan their antisocial behavior at all. Bipolar disorder (BP) is frequently comorbid with CD (Biederman et al., 1997, 2003; Biederman, Mick, Faraone, & Burback, 2001; Kovacs & Pollock, 1995; Pliszka, Sherman, Barrow, & Irick, 2000). Perhaps most important, this chapter emphasizes that ODD and CD are not "grab bags" into which children behaving badly are simply dumped. We discuss the diagnostic interview and treatment protocol for those children with ADHD and ODD/CD who do not have a mood disorder. In Chapter 3, we explore the troublesome diagnosis of intermittent explosive disorder (IED; i.e., the presence of severe aggressive behavior in the absence of a mood or psychotic disorder). This will allow us to segue into Chapter 4, which covers mood disorders and children with severe mood dysregulation.

ODD and CD are the most common comorbidities associated with ADHD. In the MTA study, 40% of the children with ADHD met criteria for ODD, while 14.3% met criteria for CD (MTA Cooperative Group, 1999a). In a variety of studies done over the last two decades, the prevalence of ODD with or without CD in children with ADHD has been shown to range from 45 to 84%, averaging about 55% across studies (Barkley, 2006b). One study showed that 63% of preschoolers with ADHD also had ODD (Wilens et al., 2002). Long-term follow-up studies are beginning to show that ODD may be viewed as a "gateway diagnosis," predisposing children with ODD to develop not only the more serious diagnosis of CD, but other major psychiatric disorders. Burke, Loeber, Lahey, and Rathouz (2005) followed 177 boys with disruptive behavior disorders for 13 years from the time of their first assessment (when they were 7–12 years of age); the average retention rate in the study was 92%. The children were assessed for psychiatric diagnoses and other measures of psychopathology, psychosocial impairment, substance abuse, parental psychopathology, parenting skill, and a wide variety of psychosocial predictors and correlates. Not surprisingly, ADHD and ODD at earlier ages predicted persistence of these diagnoses, though it was only hyperactive–impulsive (vs. inattentive) symptoms of ADHD that predicted ODD at later ages. Only ODD (and not ADHD itself) predicted the development of CD. Interestingly, ODD, CD, and anxiety were predictive of later depression as well. Depression, in turn, predicted alcohol use. The authors then tested how psychosocial factors influenced the development of additional diagnoses. Figure 2.1 shows the author's hypotheses of how ADHD, ODD, and other psychiatric diagnoses are related. Once a child with ADHD has developed ODD, there are several routes to anxiety, depression, and CD. The route to depression can be directly from ODD, or through the route of CD as a reaction to psychosocial impairment. This raises the question as to what pushes a child with ADHD to ODD alone, or ODD plus CD or affective disorders. The sample of Burke et al. (2005) was not large enough to have any subjects with BP, but it is likely that the road to that diagnosis runs through ODD as well. The task for the clinician is how to differentiate between ADHD and ODD alone versus ADHD/ODD associated with additional comorbid disorders.

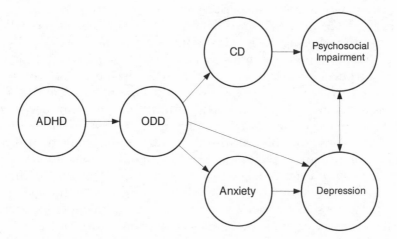

FIGURE 2.1. The model of Burke, Loeber, Lahey, and Rathouz (2005) hypothesizing about ODD is related to the development of other comorbid disorders. From Burke et al. (2005). Copyright 2005 by Blackwell Publishing Ltd. Reprinted by permission.

Assessing Irritability

There are two serious mistakes a child mental health professional can make in this area, and they are unfortunately the mirror images of each other. The first mistake is thinking that every child with temper outbursts has a mood disorder, the second that temper outbursts are nothing but "acting out," calling for the application of firm limits and not much else. The first mistake may lead to excessive prescriptions of powerful psychotropics, but the second is to be feared as well—it may lead to the withholding of life-saving treatments. DSM-IV is of limited help in this area. One of the most common questions of medical students is how the irritability of ODD, mania, and major depressive episode are to be differentiated. Few faculty members have a good answer. Eric Mick and his colleagues (2005) got down to basics on this issue by looking at the specific questions that assess irritability in structured interviews such as the Kiddie Schedule for Affective Disorders and Schizophrenia (K-SADS). For depression, the K-SADS asks, "Has there ever been a period of two weeks or longer in which you were feeling mad (or cranky) most of the day, nearly every day?" In contrast, in the mania section, the irritability question is phrased differently: "Have you ever had a period of one week or longer when you felt super angry, grouchy (or cranky) all of the time?" Mick et al. (2005) note that in DSM-IV, items about depression and mania follow a "two-tier" format. That is, the question about irritability is asked first, and only if the abnormal mood is present 50% of the time does the clinician query the parent or patient about other symptoms of either depression or mania. Manic-irritability is characterized as extreme ("super-angry") and pervasive ("all the time"), while depressive irritability is characterized by primarily negative mood and attitude that can be punctuated by some good days. Explosive outbursts are far less likely to be a part of the picture in depression, but they are present in mania. In contrast, ODD follows a one-tier format—all nine symptoms are queried. While there is no specific "irritability" item, three of the symptoms of ODD clearly tap into this construct: "Do you often lose your temper?" "Are you often angry or resentful?" and "Is it easy to make you mad or to annoy you?" In the case of ODD, the symptoms must be present "more often than not" for a period of 6 months or more.

Mick et al. (2005) next examined data from 274 children with ADHD ages 6–17 years who were studied using the KSADS. Many (*n* = 144) had no mood disorder diagnosis, while 100 had unipolar depression and 30 had BP. Figure 2.2 shows how the three different types of irritability were distributed across these groups of children with ADHD. ODD-only type irritability (easily annoyed, losing temper, angry or resentful) was highly prevalent in all three groups. In contrast, children with ADHD and comorbid depression were more likely to endorse the "mad/cranky" item than those without a mood disorder. Those with bipolar disorder endorsed the "super-angry" criterion in addition to the mad/cranky item in the depressive module. Even if the angry mood is extreme, this is not sufficient to diagnose a mood disorder. Only 46% of these children met criteria for bipolar disorder, because it is also necessary to show other symptoms including inflated self-esteem, decreased need for sleep, pressured speech, flight of ideas, or excessive involvement in pleasurable/dangerous activities.

Table 2.1 lays out a template to guide the clinician's thinking on this issue. The table assumes children in all four groups meet criteria for ADHD and have associated mood/oppositional symptoms. The key is how to place these diverse children into the appropriate category. For ODD alone, there is the "irritability triad" identified by Mick et al. (2005). The "mood" part of ODD alone is characterized by a rapid onset of anger

	Non Mood	Depression	Bipolar Disorder
ODD-type irritablity	67	85	90
Mad/Cranky	17	57	83
Super-angry/Grouchy	8	16	77

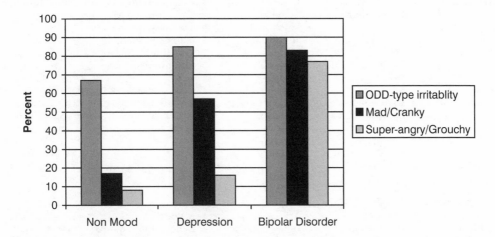

FIGURE 2.2. Distribution of types of irritability among children with ADHD with and without an affective disorder. Adapted from Mick, Spencer, Wozniak, and Biederman (2005). Copyright 2005 by Elsevier Limited. Adapted by permission.

(usually in response to limit setting or frustration) that rarely lasts more than an hour. Children with ODD/CD alone have long periods of euthymia in between their angry periods. Indeed, if they are in a setting where no limits are set (e.g., spending the summer with an indulgent grandparent), they may have no anger episodes for extended periods of time (days to weeks). For major depressive disorder (MDD), negative and pessimistic mood predominates and is present on a regular basis, even in the absence of frustrating events. The irritability is more restrained; such children look angry, won't talk about their feelings, and have a sullen facial expression. They do a "slow burn" and direct anger at themselves as well as others. Most important, they show an array of neurovegetative symptoms and suicidality. We take up ADHD with comorbid MDD in Chapter 5.

The great debate among child and mental health professionals is about the diagnoses in the middle two columns. The dividing line between these columns is dashed to indicate the fluidity of the situation; there is not great scientific or clinical consensus as to how to place a patient in either of these columns. For a diagnosis of mania, the clinician should elicit the history of extreme anger, but there is often a mixed picture of elation and abnormal silliness/giddiness. Unlike the irritability of ODD alone, the mood is pervasive with euthymia present only when everything in the child's life is going exactly to his or her liking (and sometimes not even then). The irritability of mania is much more overt than that of MDD and less associated with a negative self-image.

IED is a pattern of verbal and physical aggression in response to minor provocations not better explained by other DSM diagnoses such as mood disorder. While manic children and adolescents are angry but not necessarily aggressive, those with IED are always significantly aggressive by definition. Bursts of physical and verbal aggression are

TABLE 2.1. The Differential Diagnosis of Mood Instability

Diagnostic category	ODD/CD	IED	Mania/mixed	MDD
Nature of irritability	• Loss of temper • Angry/resentful • Easily annoyed	• Super-angry • Extreme outbursts • Physical aggression	• Super-angry • Extreme outbursts • Can be mixed with elation, silliness ("So happy you think something is wrong with him/her")	• Negative mood and attitude
Time course of irritability	• Rapid onset • Lasts minutes to no more than 1 hour • Euthymic mood between outbursts • Adequate self-esteem	• High level of arousal during outbursts • Euthymic between outbursts	• Lasts several hours a day at least • Present at least 50% of the time	• Present "more days than not" • "Slow-burn" anger • Low self-esteem ("Everybody hates me")
Associated symptoms	• Argues • Defies adult requests • Does mean things to others • Annoys others • For CD, aggression and antisocial behaviors must be present	• Argues • Defies adult requests • Does mean things to others • Annoys others • Physical damage to property • Injury to others • Serious verbal threats ("I'll kill you")	• Argues • Defies adult requests • Does mean things to others • Annoys others • Grandiosity • Decreased need for sleep • Increased sexual interest • Flight of ideas • Increased pleasure seeking; dangerous, daredevil acts	• Argues • Defies adult requests • Does mean things to others • Annoys others • Suicidal ideation • Low energy • Low self-esteem • Sleep/appetite problems

extreme (resulting in injury or damage to property); the outbursts also have a strong arousal component. Patients describe themselves as out of control, excited, red-faced, or having "smoke coming out of the ears." The outbursts are far more extreme than in ODD, but as with ODD, there is no mood disturbance between the episodes. In Chapter 4 we take up the issue of the differentiation between bipolar I, bipolar "not otherwise specified," and general severe mood dysregulation (Leibenluft, Charney, Towbin, Bhangoo, & Pine, 2003). In this chapter the focus is on the child with ADHD who has ODD/CD alone without impulsive aggression.

How Do ODD and CD Influence the Course of ADHD?

Before getting to specific cases, it is important to review how children and adolescents with ADHD and ODD/CD are different from those with ADHD alone in terms of family environment and history, cognition, long-term outcome, and treatment response.

Family Environment and History

One of the most consistent findings in the study of ADHD is that parents of children with ADHD and ODD/CD have far greater rates of psychopathology than parents of children with ADHD alone. This higher rate of mental illness in families includes not only antisocial problems but depressive and anxiety disorders (Biederman et al., 1992; Faraone, Biederman, Jetton, & Tsuang, 1997a; Faraone, Biederman, Keenan, & Tsuang, 1991; Goldstein et al., 2007a; Lahey et al., 1988; Pfiffner, McBurnett, Rathouz, & Judice, 2005). As noted in Chapter 1, Biederman et al. (1992) found that ADHD and CD co-segregated in families, indicating that ADHD + CD is a separate genetic subtype; a recent molecular genetic study (Jain et al., 2007) is consistent with this notion.

Pfiffner et al. (2005) showed that the family history of children with ADHD and CD was significantly more likely to include maternal depression and paternal antisocial behavior than that of children with ADHD alone or those with only ADHD and ODD. Parents of 3-year-olds with both hyperactivity and oppositional behavior had significantly more antisocial behavior (fathers only), depression, and anxiety than parents of preschoolers who were only hyperactive (Goldstein et al., 2007a). In contrast, they found that adult ADHD was equally elevated in the parents of both hyperactive and hyperactive/oppositional preschoolers. Parents of hyperactive/oppositional preschoolers were in conflict with each other significantly more than parents of control or hyperactive-only children.

These differences in parental psychopathology appear to have an impact on family functioning. Compared to children with ADHD alone, children with ADHD and ODD/CD are more likely to experience divorce (August & Stewart, 1983) or be placed in foster care (Reeves, Werry, Elkind, & Zametkin, 1987). Mothers of hyperactive/oppositional preschoolers experienced more parental distress, had more dysfunctional interactions with their child, and rated the child more difficult than did parents of hyperactive-only preschoolers (Goldstein, Harvey, & Friedman-Weieneth, 2007b). In a study of older children with ADHD, this pattern of negative parent–child interactions in those with ODD/CD was even more apparent. Pfiffner et al. (2005) obtained measures of parenting in three groups of children with ADHD: those with ADHD only (*n* = 66), ADHD/ODD (*n* = 48), and ADHD/CD (*n* = 35). Both ODD and CD were associated with negative/ineffective maternal discipline, while CD only was associated with lack of maternal warmth and ineffective parental discipline as well as parental antisocial personality. In the MTA study, a co-diagnosis of ODD/CD was associated with more deviant scores on the Wells Parenting Index and more negative parent–child interactions (Jensen et al., 2001).

Cognition

Children with ADHD and comorbid CD (or delinquency) are far more likely to show reading and learning disabilities relative to those with ADHD alone (McGee, Williams, & Silva, 1984; Moffitt & Silva, 1988). Children with ADHD and CD show lower reading scores when compared with children with CD alone (who were not different from controls) (Schachar & Tannock, 1995). Moffitt (1990) followed an epidemiological sample of children with ADHD and controls from ages 3 to 13. Children who showed lower verbal IQ, ADHD, *and* high family adversity at age 3 were more likely to become delinquent later in life. Compared with children with ADHD alone, those with comorbid ODD/CD show more severe hyperactive–impulsive symptoms on both parent and teacher ratings (Jensen et al., 2001; Newcorn et al., 2001); the comorbid group made more impulsive errors on a laboratory measure of impulsivity as well (Newcorn et al., 2001).

Long-Term Outcome

Without doubt, children with ADHD and comorbid disruptive behavior disorders (particularly CD) have a much higher likelihood of developing antisocial behaviors as adults relative to those with ADHD alone. Both hyperactivity and aggression independently contribute to the prediction of criminal behavior in childhood and adolescence. Loeber, Brinthaupt, and Green (1988) found that 3.4% of those with ADHD alone were later convicted of multiple criminal offenses, compared with 1.7% of controls. In contrast, 21% of adolescents with CD (without ADHD) and nearly a third (30.8%) of adolescents with comorbid ADHD/CD had committed multiple crimes by adulthood. More recent studies confirm this pattern. Satterfield et al. (2007) examined the criminal histories of 179 children with ADHD and 75 controls over a 30-year period. Almost 30% of the children with ADHD were convicted of an offense (17% for a felony); the comparable rates in controls were 8.0 and 2.7%. Felony convictions, in particular, were much higher among the subjects with ADHD who had higher CD ratings in childhood. Kindergarteners who are rated high in hyperactivity, antisocial behavior, and fearlessness are far more likely to be involved in deviant peer activities 12 years later than kindergarteners who are only hyperactive (Lacourse et al., 2006).

The path to substance abuse for children with ADHD is mediated by CD. Adolescent drug use outcomes were compared between ADHD-only ($n = 27$), ADHD externalizing (mostly ODD; $n = 82$), and normal control ($n = 91$) groups; only the externalizing group had a higher rate of substance and alcohol use disorders than the ADHD-only group or controls (August et al., 2006). Conduct, not attentional problems, predicted drug abuse in a 25-year follow-up of 1,265 adolescents in New Zealand. Any association between early attentional problems and later substance abuse was mediated via the association between conduct and attentional problems (Fergusson, Horwood, & Ridder, 2007).

Response to Pharmacological Treatment

Early studies showed that the core symptoms of ADHD in children with ADHD and ODD/CD respond as well to psychopharmacological treatment as symptoms in children with ADHD alone (Barkley, McMurray, Edelbrock, & Robbins, 1989; Pliszka, 1989). In addition, stimulants have been shown to reduce both oppositional as well as covert and overt antisocial behavior (Hinshaw, Heller, & McHale, 1992; Klein et al., 1997). In the MTA study, the stimulant response of children with ADHD and ODD/CD was just as good as that of the noncomorbid ADHD group (Jensen et al., 2001). Recent studies of both long-acting stimulants and atomoxetine have shown robust effects on symptoms of ODD (Newcorn et al., 2005; Spencer et al., 2006). Thus, it is a maxim of treatment of ADHD with comorbid ODD/CD that the ADHD should be aggressively treated with psychopharmacology in hopes of also having a positive effect on the oppositional/antisocial symptoms. One key point here is that the ADHD symptoms should never be attributed to the ODD symptoms ("He just doesn't want to pay attention; he could do it if he wanted to").

Table 2.2 shows the distributions of medications used in both the ADHD only and ADHD/ODD/CD groups in our clinical database. Not surprisingly, stimulants were the mainstay in over 95% of these children. Atomoxetine, bupropion, and alpha-agonists were used to some degree in both groups, as well as low doses of antidepressants such as mirtazapine and trazodone, usually for sleep difficulties. Note that 10% of children with ADHD and ODD/CD were on second-generation antipsychotics (SGAs) and only a very few patients were on alpha-agonists or mood stabilizers. Review of the 17 cases of ADHD and ODD/CD on SGAs showed that these children were already showing aggressive outbursts and severe temper tantrums, even though they did not yet carry the diagnoses of IED or mood disorder. The clinicians were clearly using the SGAs to treat aggression and anger, not ODD or CD per se. Given the side-effect profile of these classes of medication (see Appendix II), this is a prudent practice; Chapter 3 deals with the psychopharmacology of aggression in detail. For ODD/CD itself, medications for ADHD also treat the ODD/CD.

Short of using SGAs and mood stabilizers for aggression, are there medications that can be added to stimulants to "augment" their effect on symptoms of ODD or CD? Ever since alpha-agonists have been used for the treatment of ADHD (Hunt, Minderaa, & Cohen, 1986), clinical lore has held that clonidine in particular is effective for impulsive, oppositional, and aggressive symptoms. However, until recently, only very small uncontrolled trials have suggested this was an effective approach (Kemph, DeVane, Levin, Jarecke, & Miller, 1993; Schvehla, Mandoki, & Sumner, 1994). Only two controlled trials have examined the effect of combining clonidine with stimulants in the treatment of ODD/CD comorbid with ADHD. In a 2-month randomized comparison of clonidine, methylphenidate, and clonidine combined with methylphenidate for the treatment of 24 children and adolescents (ages 6–16 years) with ADHD and CD or ODD, it was found that all three treatment groups showed significant improvement in oppositional and conduct disordered symptoms (i.e., there was no beneficial effect of adding clonidine to the stimulant) (Connor, Barkley, & Davis, 2000). A sample of children with ADHD and ODD/CD were treated with methylphenidate, and a subgroup ($n = 67$) were identified who did not have full resolution of their hyperactive and/or aggressive behavior (Hazell & Stuart, 2003). These patients were randomized to placebo or clonidine in a double-blind fashion. At the end of 6 weeks, there were significantly more responders on clonidine than placebo, although the effect was modest and not present

TABLE 2.2. Medication Status as a Function of Comorbid ODD/CD

Medication class	ADHD only ($n = 282$)		ADHD and ODD/CD ($n = 167$)	
Alpha-agonist	7	(2.5%)	8	(4.8%)
Atypical neuroleptic	0		17	(10.1%)
Miscellaneous antidepressant	5	(1.8%)	14	(8.4%)
Mood stabilizer	0		1	(0.6%)
Atomoxetine	13	(4.6%)	8	(4.8%)
Bupropion	2	(0.7%)	0	
Selective serotonin reuptake inhibitor	0		2	(1.2%)
Stimulant	270	(96%)	156	(93.4%)

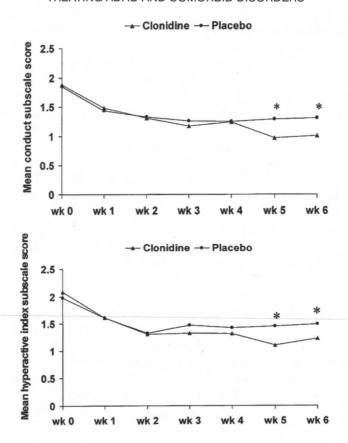

FIGURE 2.3. The effect on conduct disorder symptoms of adding clonidine to methylphenidate. Asterisks indicate significant difference of clondine from placebo. From Hazell and Stuart (2003). Copyright 2003 by Wolters Kluwer. Reprinted by permission.

until week 5 of the study (see Figure 2.3). While using alpha-agonists to treat ODD/CD is a viable option, clinicians should not be overly optimistic about their effects.

Response to Behavioral Treatment

It is an irony that while behavior therapy was designed for ODD-type behaviors, it has not yet been *proven* to alter the long-term clinical course of ADHD plus ODD/CD beyond medication alone. The sample of Satterfield et al. (2007) consisted of children with ADHD who had been treated with medication alone (*n* = 81) and those who also participated in a multimodality treatment (MMT) program (*n* = 51). An earlier study found that MMT subjects had a significantly lower number of felony arrests and prison time than medication-only comparison subjects (Satterfield, Satterfield, & Schell, 1987) . In the 30-year follow-up, however, the medication-only and MMT groups were not significantly different on any outcome measure of criminal behavior. In the MTA study (see Figure 1.5), the effect size for combined treatment was not greater than that of medication alone for those with ADHD and ODD/CD alone (but see effects for those with anxiety disorders with and without ODD/CD, Chapter 6). More encouragingly, however, children treated with a combination of medication and therapy in the treatment did have lower levels of substance abuse at the 36-month follow-up, although delinquency itself was not affected differentially by treatment (Molina, 2007). At present, behavior therapy in combination with medication treatment is the best (if not the only) option we have to treat the child with ADHD and ODD/CD. It clearly can provide short-term benefit, if only to avoid antisocial outcome in adolescence (Satterfield et al., 1987). Furthermore, while the MTA did not show ODD/CD itself to be a moderator of treatment outcome, severity of ADHD, being on public assistance, and ethnicity were related to better outcome with combination treatment (Hinshaw, 2007). These variables are often more present in children with comorbid ADHD/ODD.

The Case of Caitlin

Chief Complaint

"Medication is wearing off in the afternoon."

History of Presenting Illness

Caitlin is an 8-year-old girl who was first diagnosed with ADHD at the age of 6. In the first grade, she was treated by her pediatrician with Ritalin 5 mg in the morning and at noon; the parents reported that she showed marked improvements in both classroom behavior and academic achievement. In the second grade, the teacher noted that the medication was wearing off toward the end of the day and that Caitlin began to have difficulty even with the small amount of homework she was receiving at that time. The dosage of Ritalin was gradually increased over the course of the year to 10 mg three times a day (A.M., noon, and after school); she was then switched to Concerta 36 mg once in the morning. While the Concerta was more helpful than the immediate-release methylphenidate, she continued to struggle with homework.

Caitlin attended an after-school program until her parents returned from work. According to the policy of the after-school program, she was supposed to do her homework before joining activities. The staff at the day care reported that Caitlin would refuse to do her work, argue with them about it, or tell them that she did not have any homework. As a result, Caitlin would need to do all of her homework when she arrived at home around 6:00 P.M. in the evening. This seriously disrupted the family's evening routine as Caitlin's mother needed to care for Caitlin's 3-year-old brother as well as prepare dinner. Caitlin's mother described nightly scenes in which she would reprimand her daughter and Caitlin would throw a temper tantrum. These consisted of crying, throwing objects around the room, and yelling, "I hate you" at her mother. Caitlin also argued with both her mother and her father every time a request was made to pick up her toys, clean her room, or carry out any task. Caitlin would often throw tantrums in public places, such as stores. Her parents would often have to leave the store or buy her toys simply in order to terminate the embarrassing tantrum. Caitlin's behavior on the weekends was equally oppositional and occurred *throughout the day*. She often had to do makeup work on the weekend, and she was equally oppositional whether the parents worked with her in the morning or the afternoon. However, Caitlin was never physically aggressive at home.

Caitlin's parents were amazed that her disruptive behaviors were never displayed at school. The teacher described her as a "good student," though she noted that Caitlin could sometimes be bossy with her friends on the playground. Nonetheless, the other children did not seem to mind and often followed her lead in games. Caitlin's academic average was 87, and she received a satisfactory grade in conduct. Children in the second-grade class brought a conduct folder home every week. Caitlin usually earned a "Smiley Face" 4 days out of 5. When she did receive a conduct mark, it was usually for some minor infraction. She had never been to the principal's office for a serious offense at school.

A SNAP behavior rating scale was sent to the teacher. This confirmed that Caitlin's symptoms of ADHD were well controlled during the school day. The inattention score was 1.0, while the hyperactivity–impulsivity score was only 0.5. The ODD score was zero. Review of Caitlin's report card showed that she was making A's and B's in all subjects. Caitlin was in all regular classes.

The parents wondered if Caitlin was depressed, but they denied that Caitlin showed any overt symptoms of sadness. Her energy level was very good; she had never expressed any suicidal ideation. Her appetite was suboptimal when she took her stimulant medication, but rebounded immediately if she skipped a dose (as did the ADHD behaviors). Caitlin was oppositional about bedtime nearly every night but slept through the night. She was also oppositional about getting up on school days but often got up earlier than expected on the weekends. While Caitlin was very active and fidgety, there was no evidence of manic hyperactivity. Her speech always made sense, and there was no suggestion of any psychotic symptoms.

Past Psychiatric and Medical History

Caitlin had not been treated with any other medication besides those mentioned above. She had no history of psychiatric hospitalization. She had a history of ear infections as a toddler, but these had resolved. Recent hearing screening was entirely within normal limits. She took an antihistamine on an as-needed basis for symptoms of hay fever. The parents restricted sugar and foods they thought were high in additives after reading information about this on a website about ADHD. This also led to many arguments with their daughter. Her weight is 55 pounds/25 kg (~0.4 mg/kg dose in IR methylphenidate equivalent).

Family and Social History

Caitlin's mother is a supervisor for a regional office of an insurance company; her hours are generally from 8:00 A.M. to 5:00 P.M. Her father is a certified public accountant who has his own firm. He often works 10 to 12 hours a day, particularly during the tax season. Caitlin has a 3-year-old brother (Sam) who attends the day care where Caitlin attends her after-school program. Her brother is very active and intrusive and requires a lot of supervision by their mother. He frequently wants to play with Caitlin's toys, resulting in further temper tantrums by her. As noted, Caitlin's mother comes home at 6:00 P.M., fixes dinner, tries to get Caitlin to do her homework, puts Sam to bed, and cleans the kitchen. The father often gets home at 7:30 P.M., eats by himself, and then goes to the study to either watch television or surf the Internet.

Weekends are taken up by shopping at the grocery store, completing household chores, and trying to get Caitlin to assist with chores. The family watches three to seven movies each weekend. Caitlin has a television and DVD player in her room, where she watches movies by herself. She also enjoys Internet sites where she reads about actors from the Disney Channel and plays games. Parental controls are set on the computer to prevent her accessing inappropriate sites. While Caitlin is often "grounded" for poor behavior, restrictions on television or the Internet are not consistently enforced during these periods. The mother and father also often watch separate movies. While Caitlin's parents feel they do not spend enough time together, there are no overt marital problems. The parents have been married for 10 years.

Mental Status Examination

Caitlin is an 8-year-old girl who appears her stated age. She makes good eye contact and engages the examiner easily. Her rate of speech is appropriate, and her vocabulary is above average for a child of her age. Her mood is neither elevated nor depressed, and her affect is appropriate to thought content. She is alert and oriented, and her thought is logical, coherent, and goal directed. She denies suicidal ideation, as well as any auditory or visual hallucinations. When asked about her behavioral problems at home, Caitlin initially denies such problems but then agrees that she does lose her temper. She denies any chronic anger toward her parents and states that their rules are fair. She admits that she does not like to do her homework and does not like to stop playing on the computer.

Formulation

The diagnoses of ADHD and ODD seem well established, although the oppositional symptoms are present only at home. Caitlin shows a significant amount of irritability during her temper outbursts, but it is important to note that there is no evidence of mood disturbance in between her temper tantrums. There is also no evidence of any neurovegetative signs, thus the parents can be told that their child does not suffer from a depressive disorder. Is the Concerta wearing off early? This possibility should always be considered when parents complain of difficulties completing homework in the evening. What is significant in this case, however, is that Caitlin's parents describe oppositional behaviors throughout the day on the weekends. They do not describe a pattern of her doing well in the early morning and afternoon and then deteriorating late Saturday and Sunday. If such a pattern had emerged, a dose increase to 45 or 54 mg could be considered. In this case, it was decided to address her oppositional symptoms through the use of behavioral techniques.

Treatment Course

After the initial evaluation, the parents were advised that no change to the medication regimen should be made at the present time. They were scheduled to return for a single 1-hour session of family therapy with just the parents present. Even scheduling this session presented some difficulties as both parents were reluctant to miss work, but with persistence a time was found. The clinician first engaged in psychoeducation about the use of behavior management for children with ADHD.

Often behavior management programs are not well accepted by parents. They feel that the therapist is telling them they do not know how to raise their children or feel they are already using behavioral management techniques but these have not born any fruit. The best way to approach this problem with parents of children with ADHD is by emphasizing the need to use *specialized* behavior management techniques. Before proceeding with the treatment plan, it is important to elaborate on this point. As reviewed by Barkley (1997a), children with ADHD think only in the short term, lack self-awareness, cannot see long-term consequences, and often respond better to immediate and concrete reinforcement. They cannot tolerate delay. This makes their responses to the usual behavior management techniques different from those of children without ADHD. Box 2.1 reviews the definitions of reinforcement and punishment in behavior theory. How does the application of these concepts differ in children with ADHD/ODD relative to typically developing children?

Developmentally, parents begin discipline in the toddler and preschool years using positive punishment—they say "No!" when a child grasps the lamp cord (adding the aversive stimulus to the environment to decrease the unwanted behavior). Time out is a form of positive punishment when it is given to a child for an undesirable act, like biting a peer. Although parents often do begin using positive reinforcement (e.g., "If you stay in your stroller, Mommy will give you candy when we're done shopping"), there is in fact a strong bias in Western culture against rewarding children for what "they should do anyway." Nonetheless, as children enter school, parents will provide reinforcement, such as paying the child $2 for each good grade earned on a report card. Furthermore, as children age, it is social reward (parental approval/disapproval) that becomes the main agent of discipline. This includes positive reinforcement (e.g., "What great grades, good job!") but also positive punishment (e.g., "A 60 on your spelling test? What's wrong with you?"). Many parents make extensive use of negative reinforcement by means of nagging. The parent issues a long string of aversive stimuli (e.g., "Do you think I was put on this earth to be your slave! Every day I clean this house and you turn it into a pigsty. Don't look at me like that when I talk to you. ..."). The child can only terminate the tirade by performing the required act, such as going ahead and cleaning his room. Finally, there is negative punishment (response cost) as when the child is restricted from an activity (e.g., riding a bike) because her grades are low. As inefficient as nagging is, typically developing children respond to it because parental approval is

---

BOX 2.1. Defining Reinforcement and Punishment

Everyone uses the term *positive reinforcement* and most people think that the word *positive* refers to its rewarding aspect, when this is not in fact the case. *Reinforcement* is anything that results in an increased probability of the behavior occurring, while *punishment* is something that decreases the probability of the behavior. Positive and negative do not refer to reward or aversion, but to whether the reinforcing or punishing agent is being added to or subtracted from the environment, as illustrated below:

Positive reinforcement—Every time a rat presses a bar, a food pellet is *added* to the cage. The rat increases the number of times it presses the bar.

Negative reinforcement (often erroneously thought to be synonymous with punishment)— A noxious, continuous noise occurs in the rat's cage. The rat happens to press the bar and the noise stops. If the noise reoccurs, then the rat presses the bar again. The noise is a reinforcer even though it is aversive because the behavior (pressing the bar) is increasing. It is negative because the noise is subtracted from the environment when the rat acts.

Positive punishment—The rat presses the bar and receives a blast of air. The rat stops pressing the bar. Obviously, the air blast is not pleasurable, but adding it to the environment causes a decrease in the bar-pressing behavior.

Negative punishment—This is also referred to as response cost. The rat has free access to water. If it presses a particular bar in the cage, the water flow stops. The rat stops pressing that bar. *Negative* refers to the fact that the water is subtracted from the environment; it is punishment because, again, the bar presses are reduced.

such a rewarding stimulus, while parental disapproval is so noxious. So, why don't they work in children with ADHD/ODD?

While children with ADHD and ODD are as attached to their parents as other children, they are less sensitive to parental expressions of disapproval. Being highly distractible, they simply don't find a long parental tirade that aversive, so they have no motivation to escape it by performing the behavior the parent wants. Simple expressions of parental approval are also less motivating as positive reinforcements. Parents are then usually advised to use more concrete reinforcers, but here they run up against the other problem that children with ADHD have: reasoning within only a very short time frame and being unable to delay gratification (Solanto et al., 2001). Suppose a parent tells the child that he can have a dollar for each good grade he brings home at the end of the 6-week grading period. At the end of the class day, the child with ADHD can focus solely on his wish to play videogames when he gets home. If the teacher assigns homework, this prevents him from playing, so he does not bring the work home. He tells his parent there is no homework and proceeds to play; he cannot focus on the fact that he will get a zero on the assignment tomorrow and that this will adversely affect his 6-week grade. While all children with ADHD show these cognitive failings, those with ADHD/ODD have one additional trait that is unique to them—the tendency to use positive punishment (a tantrum) to decrease the probability of their parents issuing a command or following through on a limit. So, when the parent discovers that the child lied about the homework, the child is restricted from videogames—but the child promptly screams and yells to the point that the parent is reluctant to follow through. The key to circumventing this pattern is to use very concrete reinforcements and punishment.

Treatment Course, Continued

The clinician began by describing how children with ADHD, particularly those with ODD, have this very different way of looking at the world. For instance, it was noted that Caitlin's mother responded to her daughter's refusal to do homework by giving lengthy lectures about the need to do well in school, particularly in order to get into a good college. For a child with ADHD, however, even references to a report card that will arrive in 3 to 6 weeks is too long. The clinician described how their use of grounding was not an effective behavior management tool. By restricting her from television and the Internet, they hoped that Caitlin would be motivated to work to gain these privileges back.

Without knowing it, the mother was trying to couple negative punishment with negative reinforcement. By negative punishment (response cost) we mean that when Caitlin threw her tantrum, her Internet privileges were suspended; the mother hoped this would decrease the tantrum behavior. This then placed Caitlin in a deprived state—if she did the homework, the restriction would be lifted (negative reinforcement). The mother, however, was often grounding her for a week at a time. Once the grounding was in force, Caitlin had no motivation to change her behavior. Indeed by throwing continued tantrums, Caitlin was using positive punishment against her parents, decreasing the probability of them upholding the grounding.

The next major issue the clinician brought up was the parents' lifestyle. From a mental health perspective, this is a very healthy and loving family. There was no spousal abuse, and there were no substance use problems. The parents were, in general, happy with their marriage. Nonetheless, they had fallen into a pattern all too common today: long working hours, lack of family time, and excessive reliance on entertainment technology. The clinician pointed out to Caitlin's father that he was not participating sufficiently in Caitlin's discipline. He responded by saying that he needed to work long hours to keep his business afloat. The clinician suggested that he adjust his working hours: he should arrive home at 6:00 P.M., the family should eat dinner together, and then he could finish any remaining work after Caitlin had gone to bed. As an accountant, he could finish much of his work on his home computer. Similarly, the family was advised to change their weekend schedule so that they spend more time together. They should watch family movies together, and the parents should watch movies together after the children go to bed. Indeed, they should cut back the movie watching in general. The family should go on hikes or visit a children's museum. It was suggested that Caitlin join the Brownies or a soccer team.

The clinician then turned to the design of the behavior management program. He suggested a daily report card as shown in Figure 2.4. Three goals were selected for Caitlin: complete homework at after-school program, don't lose temper, and do things first time asked. The latter goal included not arguing with her parents. At the end of each day, the parents were to give her a rating of 0, 1, or 2 for each goal, with 2 being "excellent." Caitlin was to be given an "allowance" where each point was worth 10 cents. At first, the parents balked, stating that they did not believe in an allowance. They were asked to recall how much money they spent on Caitlin in any given week. They discovered to their surprise that when they added up the toys, requested soft drinks or candy, and extra clothing, the amount came to at least $15 a week. They were told that in the future, Caitlin could only spend the money that she earned from the behavior management program. If, on a given day, Caitlin received a zero on any of her goals, she was restricted from television and the

GOALS FOR THE WEEK

GOAL	SAT	SUN	MON	TUE	WED	THU	FRI
Do homework at after-school program	0 1 2	0 1 2	0 1 2	0 1 2	0 1 2	0 1 2	0 1 2
Don't lose temper	0 1 2	0 1 2	0 1 2	0 1 2	0 1 2	0 1 2	0 1 2
Do things first time asked	0 1 2	0 1 2	0 1 2	0 1 2	0 1 2	0 1 2	0 1 2
DAILY TOTALS							

0 TO 15: BAD WEEK   Each point is worth 10 cents.

16 TO 27: OK WEEK

28 TO 42: GREAT WEEK!

WEEKLY TOTAL	

My Name_____   Week of_____

FIGURE 2.4. A behavior management system for a child with ADHD and ODD.

Internet for that night. If she earned at least all 1's on the following day, she could regain her television and Internet privileges. If she earned 28 or more points in a given week, she could do an extra special activity. It turned out that Caitlin loved to go to the zoo, so it was agreed that this would be her special activity. Conversely, if the number of points fell below 16, then Caitlin would be restricted from playing videogames for the entire weekend.

One more session was held, this time including Caitlin. The behavior management system was described to her. To her parents' surprise, Caitlin enthusiastically embraced the system. An appointment was scheduled 1 month later to follow up on its implementation. The parents reported that her tantruming behavior had substantially decreased. The father had made the requested change to his work schedule, and this appeared to substantially increase Caitlin's compliance with both parents. The parents returned to their pediatrician for long-term medication management of the Concerta. The psychiatrist told them to return on an as-needed basis for booster sessions.

There were many advantages to dealing with Caitlin's family. The parents had a good marriage and were willing to reassess their lifestyle. They also had the resources to participate actively in the intervention, and there was a minimum of psychosocial stress. As noted earlier, many children with ADHD and ODD come from more disadvantaged backgrounds where implementing a treatment plan can run into any number of hurdles.

The Case of James

Chief Complaint

Auto theft.

History of Presenting Illness

James is a 14-year-old seventh grader who had had a history of truancy and curfew violations since he was 12 years old. He was well known to police officers in his community, and his mother reported that he frequently hung out with other teenagers who got into similar types of trouble. After he missed 15 days of school, he was brought to court for truancy and placed on probation. He then attended school, but did not do his work and was frequently oppositional with teachers. One day, he skipped school and was hanging out with his friends at a local convenience store. A man drove up and left his keys in his car while he ran in to buy a lottery ticket. One of James's peers dared him to steal the car and to his peer's surprise, James jumped into the car and drove off. When the man emerged from the convenience store, he immediately recognized James as he drove away. James drove the car around the neighborhood for about half an hour and then returned home to find the police waiting for him. He was placed in juvenile detention. Although this was his first serious criminal offense, it occurred while he was on probation, and as a result, he was sent to a local group home for nonviolent juvenile offenders.

James was told by his probation officer that he would stay at the group home for at least 3 months, but that his stay could be extended if his behavior was disruptive. He was required to do well at school as well as follow all the rules of the group home. James appeared to get along well with the group home staff and with the other residents, but he had considerable difficulty completing chores and his schoolwork continued to be extremely poor. The probation department performed a psychological evaluation that showed a Full Scale

IQ of 110. Despite the fact that James was failing every class in school, he was found to be on grade level according to the achievement testing. There was no evidence of any learning disability. According to the standard practice of the group home, James had to have a psychiatric screening within 30 days of his admission. The psychiatrist was notified by the group home staff that "this would be a simple evaluation" since James was "just a conduct disorder who would do well with just some firm limits." The evaluation proceeded with the group home staff. They filled out a SNAP checklist, which revealed an *absence* of inattention or impulsivity–hyperactivity symptoms. They reported that while James was a "nice kid," he could often be argumentative, he annoyed his peers and staff, deliberately broke rules, and was generally uncooperative. They denied that James showed any aggressive or angry outbursts. Indeed, one of the staff members stated that James had a "shit-eating grin" whenever he misbehaved—that is, they saw James as excessively mischievous rather than angry. While James had a history of fighting at school, he had not been aggressive since admission to the group home. Nonetheless, he warned the staff that if anyone "got in his face," he would react aggressively. The staff denied that James showed any depressive symptoms. Since he had arrived in the group home, his sleep and appetite were within normal limits, as was his energy level. He had no history of suicidal ideation and had not shown any self-injurious behavior since admission. The staff also had not observed any behavior suggesting delusions or hallucinations. The psychological evaluation did not suggest any evidence of a thought disorder.

A SNAP rating scale was sent to the school James was attending at the group home, as well as to his previous school. The teachers at his previous school did not fill out the rating scale as they felt James had not attended enough for them to get a good sense of his behavior. The group home teacher, however, rated James as very high on symptoms of inattention—his inattention score was 2.5 and his hyperactive–impulsive score was 1.8. She also noted that he was argumentative and frequently tried to be the class clown.

The group home social worker contacted the mother. Her history was consistent with that provided by the group home child care staff. His mother reported that teachers always told her that James was very bright but did not apply himself. He was retained in second grade because of immaturity. A fourth-grade teacher had suggested an evaluation for ADHD, but the mother was afraid to do this because of concerns about the side effects of medication. The mother denied that James had ever shown any significant depressive or manic symptoms. The mother did report that James had intermittently smoked marijuana, but she had no clear idea as to how frequently this occurred. At the group home, James denied that he had any craving for marijuana.

Past Psychiatric and Medical History

James had no history of prior psychological or psychiatric treatment of any kind. While on probation, he had met briefly with his probation officer, who counseled him on his behavior. His birth and development were unremarkable, and he had no history of any chronic medical illness.

Family and Social History

James lives with his mother and two younger siblings in a housing project. His father is in the state penitentiary serving a sentence for involuntary manslaughter as a result of a drunk-driving incident. Even prior to his incarceration, James's father was in and out of the household and James had had little contact with him. His father had been a poor student and dropped out of school in the ninth grade. James's mother was receiving disability for depression; she took antidepressants on and off when she could make her appointments at the Community Mental Health Center. While James's mother had difficulty supervising the activities of her children, there was no evidence of gross abuse or neglect.

Mental Status Examination

James is a 14-year-old boy who appeared his stated age. He was very pleasant in the interview; he smiled and made good eye contact with the examiner. His vocabulary was age appropriate. He became bored with the interview, looked around the room, and asked how soon he could get back to his activities. Psychomotor activity was slightly increased for his age. He was oriented to person, place, and time; recent and remote memory were clearly intact based on the clear history that he gave to the examiner. His mood was neither elevated nor depressed and affect was appropriate. Thought content was logical, coherent, and goal directed. There was no evidence of any delusions, and James denied any visual or auditory hallucinations. He could not explain why he had stolen the car. He did not have a plan for doing anything with the car; he could only state that his friend had dared him and he felt that he could not back down. He smiled and said that it was a dumb thing to do, but otherwise he showed no remorse over the action.

Treatment Course

The psychiatrist's suggestion that James had ADHD was met with a good deal of skepticism. Several of the child care staff remarked that James could pay attention if he wanted to and felt they wished to work with James behaviorally. The group had a well-established behavior management program. Residents earned green points for positive behaviors (completing schoolwork and chores) and red points for inappropriate behaviors (cursing, defiance, etc.). Green points were summed at the end of the day, then the sum of red points was subtracted from the total of green points. Privileges were based on James being able to remain in the "green zone" each day.

   A therapist from the group home met with James on a weekly basis. The therapist suspected that the absence of James's father had a negative impact on him and that he needed to work through this issue. However, the therapist found that James had little interest in discussing this topic. James would acknowledge missing his father at times, but in fact, he had very few clear memories of his father. The therapist found it increasingly difficult to maintain James's attention during the sessions. During the therapy session, the therapist would often play pool, checkers, or even videogames with James in an attempt to engage him. The therapist found, however, that James would refuse to stop playing to discuss any issues of consequence. The therapist interpreted this as James's denial of his feelings of abandonment by his father. James also attended group therapy as part of his treatment. During one of the sessions, James told the group that he felt it was actually the car owner's fault that the car had been stolen. James stated that he did not understand why the car owner had left the keys where someone could so easily get to them.

   One afternoon, a child care worker was taking James and two other boys from the group home on an outing to buy clothes. When the child care worker turned his back, James was gone; this runaway was reported to the police, but James was found by the caseworker about half an hour later simply wandering up and down the street. When asked why he had run off, James simply said he wanted to see what the town looked like. James's behavior was discussed at the team meeting. All of the team members now agreed that James was highly impulsive; the teacher, in particular, noted that James was capable of very good work but rarely concentrated in class. A discussion was held with James's mother. The benefits and risks of using stimulant medication were explained to her. Her principal fear was that the medicine would turn him into a "zombie" or that it might cause him to have a heart attack.

The mother was reassured that James's psychological status would be monitored closely and that since he had no history of heart disease, there was no reason to think that any serious cardiovascular event would occur. While James had no dramatic history of substance abuse, the fact that he had so many antisocial peers led to concerns that he might be tempted to divert his medication. As a result, he was started on Vyvanse 30 mg/day, and the dose was increased at weekly intervals until he reached a dose of 70 mg/day.

At a dose of 70 mg/day, the teacher reported marked improvement in his classroom behavior. Daytime staff also noted that James was more cooperative with chores and generally thought things through more clearly. James began to have more "green days" and began to earn privileges. Unfortunately, it was discovered that after earning a weekend pass James had smuggled some cigarettes into the group home on his return. At this point, the psychiatrist and therapist consulted about the case.

In the consultation, an overview of the therapist's use of an interpersonal model of psychotherapy was undertaken. The hypothesis that James was in some sort of emotional turmoil due to the absence of his father was discussed. It was noted that in fact James hardly knew his father, denied being upset or depressed about his father's absence, and was bored and irritated by discussions of his father. It appeared clear that James was not suffering from "denial"; rather, the issue of his father was not relevant to his current oppositional behavior. The therapist was somewhat skeptical and noted his own emotional turmoil when his own parents divorced when he was 10 years old and his father moved to another town. It was pointed out that unlike James, the therapist had a strong, established relationship with his own father. Thus, the therapist had something to lose emotionally. In addition, James's ADHD was influencing his emotional response to events. Like Caitlin, James focused only on his immediate situation—stealing the car in response to a peer's dare or responding to curiosity about the town by walking off. James's social impulsivity was made worse by a lifetime of living in an unstructured home environment. Moreover, like so many adolescents with ADHD and ODD, he did not reflect on the impact of his behavior on himself or others. He developed a view of the world not uncommon in patients with ADHD/ODD—that it was permissible and inevitable that he respond to temptation. Indeed, it was the world's fault if temptations appeared in front of him. This high degree of sensation seeking combined with impulsivity (and not suppressed emotional conflict) led to his bad decision making.

The group home behavior management system clearly was the most critical part of James's intervention, since it provides immediate reinforcement or punishment for desired or undesired behaviors. Was there a way to get James to internalize these rules faster? Clearly, treatment of the ADHD helped, as he now at least had time to think about his actions. It is also clear that the therapist should abandon the interpersonal approach. Children with ADHD have proven to be resistant to cognitive-behavioral therapy (Abikoff et al., 1988; Abikoff, 1991; Abikoff & Gittelman, 1985), so the therapist should not expect to cognitively restructure James. Nonetheless, some of the principles of both cognitive-behavioral and traditional behavior therapy were integrated into his approach.

Treatment Course, Continued

The therapist began to base James's access to the pool table or checkers in therapy on whether James was in the green zone at the time of the therapy session. If he was in the red zone, then therapy could consist only of talking. The focus of therapy was shifted from James's past to his future. Each session reviewed how close James was to earning discharge, and how poor judgment might delay it. His oppositional behavior was discussed with particular reference to how it made others feel. His auto theft was reviewed in detail. With the permission of the mother and the probation officer, the victim of the car theft joined a session by phone. He told James how the theft of the car had resulted in his missing an important meeting that led to a lower paycheck for him that month. This had an impact on James, who had viewed the theft as "no big deal" because the man got his car back. James was encouraged to apologize to the man, something he had never done to a victim before.

The therapist sought other ways to make James more future oriented. James was big for his age and a good athlete; he was encouraged to join the football team at the local school. He had to maintain his grades in order to remain eligible. This gave him an important short-term goal beyond the green zone of the group home behavior management system. James earned several passes and behaved well during them. There were no further incidents of James leaving the group home without permission. Before he was discharged, arrangements were made for him to join the football team at his neighborhood school.

Since James did not have a mood disorder, or evidence of impulsive aggression of a serious nature, he was not a candidate for mood stabilizers or SGA treatment. The therapist's hypothesis of depression would not justify treatment with antidepressants. As with most cases of ADHD with ODD/CD (which do not involve dangerous aggression), treatment of the underlying ADHD combined with a strong behavioral approach is the key. To the degree that psychotherapy is directed at the child or teen, the focus should be on developing a greater future orientation and developing empathy for others. Working with James and Caitlin was in many ways a pleasure—they related well to their caregivers, had pleasant personalities, and responded to treatment. When children with ADHD and ODD/CD present with aggression, the diagnostic and therapeutic tasks become more difficult.

Chapter 3

Impulsive Aggression

During a presentation regarding the psychopharmacological treatment of aggression, I was asked if I thought aggression was a "medical or a social problem." I responded that the same question could be applied to Type II diabetes, as the growth in that disorder in the Western world has a great deal to do with changes in diet and attitudes about obesity. Are these not social issues? Just as diabetes can result from an interplay of genetic and environmental factors, so can impulsive aggression. Connor (2002) defines maladaptive aggression as that which occurs outside a socially acceptable context. Furthermore, its intensity, frequency, and duration are excessive; and the aggression is not terminated in response to feedback (e.g., a schoolyard scuffle may be developmentally appropriate but should not end in injury and should stop when the teacher appears). Impulsive aggression is a subset of maladaptive aggression in that it is unplanned and overt, and often the aggressor feels negative emotions during the episode. Indeed, impulsive aggression is characterized by high levels of very negative arousal (Donovan et al., 2003; Jensen et al., 2007b). In their review of findings from a consensus conference, Jensen and colleagues (2007b) noted that impulsive aggression is a common symptom in children with a wide variety of psychiatric disorders, including ADHD, BP, and pervasive developmental disorders. Thus, the evaluation and treatment of aggression in children and adolescents with ADHD is important not only in its own right, but as a precursor to the treatment of comorbidities such as BP and ASD.

Aggression in ADHD

As noted in the previous chapter, 30–50% of children and adolescents with ADHD meet criteria for ODD and CD. The DSM-IV criteria for ODD/CD contain limited items referring to aggression—"Often loses temper" for ODD; "Starts fights," "Bullies or threatens," "Steals using force," and "Destroys property" for CD. Yet, these items do not often refer to aggression per se, particularly impulsive aggression. Thus while the comorbidity of ADHD and ODD/CD has been extensively studied, the same is not true for ADHD and aggression. Jensen et al. (2007b) reexamined data from the MTA study and found that 267 of the original sample of 579 children (46%) exhibited clinically significant aggression. Of even greater concern, 44% of the aggressive subgroup remained so even after treatment of ADHD with medication. Clearly, the issue needs closer attention.

Intermittent Explosive Disorder: Is It a Useful Construct?

On their face, the DSM-IV criteria for intermittent explosive disorder (IED) are very straightforward. First, the patient must exhibit "several" discrete episodes of *failure to resist* aggressive impulses that result in serious assaultive acts or destruction of property. This excludes deliberate aggression to obtain a specific goal. Secondly, the aggressive acts must be grossly out of proportion to any precipitating stressor. The difficulty arises in the third part of the criteria—that the aggression is not better accounted for by diagnosis of another mental disorder or the direct effect of a substance (e.g., drug abuse). The criteria give antisocial and borderline personality disorder, ADHD, CD, psychosis, and mania as specific examples of disorders that might be causing the aggression. For many clinicians, this makes the IED disorders pointless, as they feel that nearly every child or adolescent with aggressive behavior will meet criteria for one of these diagnoses. Indeed, particularly for inpatient psychiatrists, it is common to diagnose every aggressive child admitted as having either BP or "mood disorder not otherwise specified." So, why would anyone want to use the IED diagnosis? In reality, clinicians deal with children with ADHD who have aggressive outbursts and simply do not meet the criteria for mood disorder. They have no pressured speech, decreased need for sleep, or racing thoughts, and there is no disturbance in mood between their aggressive episodes. The diagnosis of "bipolar not otherwise specified" is often used in this circumstance, but is there not a point at which we are being dishonest with ourselves and our patients? More to the point, research has established both the validity and reliability of the IED diagnosis (Coccaro, Kavoussi, Berman, & Lish, 1998); and epidemiological studies show it to be a fairly common disorder (Coccaro, Posternak, & Zimmerman, 2005; Coccaro, Schmidt, Samuels, & Nestadt, 2004; Kessler et al., 2006).

The National Comorbidity Survey Replication (NCSR; Kessler & Merikangas, 2004) interviewed nearly 10,000 adults face to face regarding many major DSM-IV disorders. The interview included questions regarding IED, but the diagnosis of IED was not made if the patient already met criteria for BP. The lifetime prevalence of IED was found to be 7.3% when the disorder was broadly defined (three attacks in a lifetime) and 5.4% when narrowly defined (three attacks in a single year). Nearly all of those with IED had onset of the disorder before age 18, with 60% of the sample having onset before age 15. Childhood onset (30%) was common. Persons with the narrow IED reported committing a mean of 56 attacks over their lifetimes, causing an average of $1,600 of damage to property. More ominously, an average of 233 victims per 100 cases of IED required medical attention as a result of the attacks.

Comorbidity findings were intriguing. ADHD was present in about 20% of those with IED. Mood disorders other than bipolar (38%), anxiety disorders (60%), and alcohol/substance abuse disorders (35–40%) were also highly prevalent. With the exception of ADHD, nearly all of these disorders had onset *after* the IED. It is difficult to say if the IED is an early marker of the mood or anxiety disorder, but since IED has such early onset one cannot argue that it is simply an epiphenomenon of the other DSM-IV disorders. The data from Kessler et al. (2006) clearly tell us that if we diagnose a child or adolescent with IED, we must be on the lookout for the emergence of mood or anxiety disorders in the future. Some children with IED do not go on to develop other psychiatric disorders, and their aggression may resolve with time. When this occurs, it is reasonable to say that IED has resolved. In contrast, if an aggressive child is diagnosed with BP but is symptom free in 3 years, how is this to be explained? Thus IED is highly useful as an intermediate diagnosis if the child does not yet meet criteria for a manic episode.

Another key piece of information is that IED may have a neurobiological contribution, no less than in other neuropsychiatric disorders. When individuals undergoing functional magnetic resonance imaging (fMRI) look at angry faces, there is a strong activation of both the amygdala and the orbitofrontal cortex (OFC). While the amygdala directly assesses the degree of threat, the OFC activation is more related to inhibition, so we do not act immediately on the possible threat (Dougherty et al., 1999, 2004). Coccaro, McKloskey, Fitzgerald, and Phan (2007) obtained fMRI on 10 healthy men and 10 with IED while they looked at happy, surprised, disgusted, sad, angry, and neutral faces. Subjects with IED activated their amygdala more strongly in response to angry faces than controls, and this activation correlated strongly with the IED subject's lifetime history of aggression. In contrast, the IED subjects had less activation of their OFC than controls and less correlation between the activity levels of their OFC and amygdala, suggesting less adequate control of amygdala reaction by the OFC. These findings do not mean that IED is hardwired into the brain, as the brain can be shaped by experience, but it clearly goes against the idea that IED is just a "dumping ground" diagnosis. Of course, it is important to note that neuroimaging is not useful for the clinical diagnosis of IED. As has been previously noted (Pliszka, 1991; Pliszka et al., 1999), IED and impulsive aggression are not forms of epilepsy, and while anticonvulsant mood stabilizers have a role in the treatment of aggression, EEG is not useful in the workup of aggression unless there are specific signs and symptoms suggesting neurological disease (e.g., history of severe head injury, loss of consciousness, automatisms).

The diagnosis of IED should not be made when a child has only loss of temper without verbal or physical aggression, while CD alone should be diagnosed if the aggression (starting fights, bullying) has a specific goal and the impulse to fight is not in any way resisted by the child. As noted in Table 2.1 in the previous chapter, IED is associated with a euthymic mood between episodes of aggression. It is common for children and teens with IED to have poor insight into their aggression, to blame others for it, and even to have a poor memory or complete denial of the aggression. Here is a typical conversation that I had with one of my 10-year-old patients with ADHD and comorbid IED regarding his behavior in the last week. (I had already interviewed his mother.)

DR. P: So, how has your week gone?

JASON : Good.

DR. P: Did you have any particular problems this week?

JASON : No, not really.

DR. P: Your mom told me that you were suspended for a fight at school.

JASON : Well, not suspended exactly, I'm in ISS [in-school suspension].

DR. P: Can you tell me what happened?

JASON : This kid called me an asshole, so I pushed him—he started crying, so the teacher thought it was all my fault.

DR. P: Didn't he get hurt? Your mom said he got stitches.

JASON : Yeah, he fell against the locker and there was this metal thing sticking out—I didn't mean to hurt him.

DR. P: How are you feeling about all this now?

JASON : (*Shrugs.*) I shouldn't have done it, but he just made me mad.

DR. P: Did you try to control yourself?

JASON : I just couldn't.

The diagnosis of IED (when properly made) justifies the use of more aggressive psychopharmacology than that used to treat ADHD alone, but we need more than medication. To intervene psychotherapeutically, we need to look at how aggressive children misinterpret social cues and how they operate on a different set of social conventions than typically developing children.

How Do Aggressive Children Look at the World?

The example of Jason illustrates why parents and teachers find children with ADHD who are aggressive so frustrating. They seem clueless to the mayhem they produce. They just don't "get it" when it comes to their anger—they view the fact that someone "made them mad" as the most reasonable justification for "going off." Aggressive children with ADHD are perhaps the polar opposite of mental health professionals, who tend to be sensitive and introspective. Often we are convinced that if we can just get inside them and understand what conflict is causing them to be aggressive, the problem will be solved. However, when no conflict seems to emerge from many sessions of play or individual therapy, we conclude the child is a sociopath and feel nothing further can be done.

Social information processing theory (Dodge, 2006; Dodge & Schwartz, 1997) provides a mechanism to better understand how aggressive children think. Dodge and Schwartz (1997) reviewed the stages of Dodge's social information processing model: encoding, interpretation of social cues, goal selection, response access and construction, and response decision. When looking at social situations, aggressive children encode fewer relevant cues and do not seek out additional information when the situation is ambiguous. They are more likely to interpret ambiguous cues as hostile. Dodge (2006) points out (as shown in the imaging study discussed above) that recognizing hostile intent may be a hardwired function of the amygdala, while attributing benign intent to an ambiguous situation is a learned process. As for goal selection, aggressive children seek dominance and control and generate fewer potential responses to a problematic social situation. There is a negative correlation between the number of responses and the child's rate of aggression. In terms of response decision, aggressive children view aggression as producing more desirable outcomes—they are more likely to see aggression as leading to tangible rewards and peer group approval, and they do not see their victims as suffering any real harm. The encoding and the response-decision phases differ in children with different subtypes of aggression (Dodge, Harnish, Lochman, & Bates, 1997).

Dodge et al. (1997) classified both a large population of third graders and a group of adjudicated juvenile offenders as showing either proactive or reactive aggression. Subjects viewed videotapes of social interactions. The subject was asked to imagine being the protagonist. In the community sample, encoding errors were found in the reactive aggressive children, while the proactive aggressive children were more likely to anticipate positive outcomes for aggression. Similar findings were found for the offender sample. Reactively aggressive offenders made more encoding errors, while the proactively aggressive offenders expected aggression to reduce aversion, leaving them feeling more competent and effective. Reactively aggressive children were more likely to have been abused; both encoding errors and hostile attributions are associated with aggression even when studies control for the degree of impulsivity (Dodge, 2006). Box 3.1 summarizes Dodge's model.

It is important to note that Dodge's model is *not* a purely biological one. While our tendency to recognize hostile intent (through amygdala-mediated recognition of threatening faces) is inborn, we learn how to recognize benign intent through our experiences with parents and the larger culture we grow up in. Physical abuse, modeling of hostility by adults, and rearing in a culture that values self-defense, personal honor, and retaliation can lead to the child developing chronically hostile attributions. A secure attachment and modeling of prosocial behavior lead to the ability to accurately interpret social cues in conflictual situations. As we will see in the cases of Mark

---

BOX 3.1. Social Information Processing and Aggressive Behavior: How Aggressive Kids See the World

Aggressive and nonaggressive children are asked to view a videotape of two children playing with a toy in a sandbox. A third child comes into the sandbox, plays briefly with the other two boys, then suddenly grabs the toy and runs off. One of the boys looks very sad. Note that the situation is ambiguous. Was the toy stolen? Did it belong to the third boy? The videotape is inconclusive. The experimenter then asks the children questions about the scenario that assess the children's skills at processing social information.

- *Encoding*—Healthy controls provide a great deal of information. They pick up on facial expression, the fact that all the boys played together briefly. Perhaps, they notice that the third boy looked off as though a parent had called. In contrast, the aggressive children tend to miss these cues and focus nearly exclusively on the possible theft or say that the third boy was "mean."
- *Attribution*—This is where some of the most pronounced differences between aggressive and nonaggressive children are noted. The nonaggressive children construct many hypotheses about what happened: a theft, maybe it belonged to the third boy anyway, maybe the first two boys said he could have it, and so forth. The aggressive children almost universally make a hostile attribution—that the toy was stolen and the third boy was the enemy of the first two.
- *Response construction*—Nonaggressive children are also able to generate many different responses. They will mention aggression as a possibility ("I'll go grab it back") but also provide a number of other alternatives: ask for it back, tell a parent, find another toy to play with. Aggressive children have difficulty coming up with any response other than confronting and possibly being aggressive with the alleged thief.
- *Decision*—Healthy controls may think of aggression as a possible response, but they are less likely to view it as a potentially successful option. They are more aware that they might get in trouble or get hurt themselves, or that the toy might be broken. The aggressive children almost always have the expectation that aggression will have a desirable outcome (getting the toy back) and no real downside, even for the victim.

and John, this model allows the therapist to take a more active role in changing the child's view of the world, thus reducing his or her hostile attributions.

Aggression, ADHD, Abuse, and Posttraumatic Stress Disorder

Clinical experience tells us that verbal and physical abuse lead to aggression in children and adolescents and ultimately to violent criminal behavior; large-scale epidemiological surveys confirm this. Interviewing over 1,300 urban youth about their exposure to violence and mental health problems, Ruchkin, Henrich, Jones, Vermeiren, and Schwab-Stone (2007) found that the development of posttraumatic stress disorder (PTSD) fully mediated the relationship between victimization and depression and anxiety in girls, while in boys, PTSD partially mediated the relationship between violence exposure and later commission of violent acts. Lansford et al. (2007) followed 574 children from age 5 to age 21; those who had been abused before age 5 were at greater risk of being arrested for violent, nonviolent, and status offenses as teenagers. The relationship of ADHD, abuse, and aggression is complex, however. Wozniak et al. (1999) assessed exposure to trauma (physical and sexual abuse as well as violence and accidents) in 140 children with ADHD and 120 controls who had been participants in a family history study. There was no statistically significant difference in the rate of trauma exposure in the ADHD (12%) and control (7%) groups. While major depression was associated with exposure to trauma, ADHD was not. The authors concluded there was no meaningful relationship between ADHD and exposure to trauma or the development of PTSD. (Indeed, development of formal PTSD after trauma was rare in this group.)

Ford and colleagues (Ford et al., 1999, 2000) examined the problem from a different angle, looking at a large sample of children treated in an outpatient clinic for trauma exposure. This is a unique sample, unlikely to be representative of children with ADHD in general. Once they controlled the variety of family factors associated with trauma (parental psychopathology, social adversity, poor parenting), they found PTSD to be associated primarily with ODD rather than ADHD itself. Only 6% of the children with ADHD alone had PTSD versus 22% of the children with ADHD and ODD. From this, we can discern the pathway from ADHD to PTSD and aggression more clearly. ADHD is *not* caused by trauma; nor, by itself, does it predispose a child to be traumatized. In contrast, a child with ODD or CD (regardless of the presence of ADHD) is more likely to be exposed to the family pathology that leads to PTSD. In some cases, PTSD then leads to aggression; in others, the child may develop IED with no signs of PTSD.

I am often asked how I differentiate ADHD from PTSD or IED in a child who has been traumatized. The underlying premise of the question is that trauma can induce ADHD symptoms, leading PTSD to masquerade as ADHD. As we have seen from the Wozniak et al. (1999) study, this is an unlikely event. If it weren't, then the rate of trauma in the ADHD group would have been much higher than in the control group. The key is to utilize only the criteria of PTSD (see Box 3.2) to make the diagnosis; when it is present, it should be viewed as a comorbid diagnosis with ADHD. In contrast (as we shall see in the case of John), an aggressive child with a history of trauma may not report any intrusive memories, flashbacks, or hyperarousal related to memories. In this case, a diagnosis of PTSD would be inappropriate. The distinction becomes critical when choosing a pharmacological intervention, as IED and PTSD require very differ-

BOX 3.2. DSM-IV-TR Diagnostic Criteria
for Posttraumatic Stress Disorder (PTSD)

A. The person has been exposed to a traumatic event in which both of the following were present:

(1) the person experienced, witnessed, or was confronted with an event or events that involved actual or threatened death or serious injury, or a threat to the physical integrity of self or others
(2) the person's response involved intense fear, helplessness, or horror. **Note:** In children, this may be expressed instead by disorganized or agitated behavior

B. The traumatic event is persistently reexperienced in one (or more) of the following ways:

(1) recurrent and intrusive distressing recollections of the event, including images, thoughts, or perceptions. **Note:** In young children, repetitive play may occur in which themes or aspects of the trauma are expressed.
(2) recurrent distressing dreams of the event. **Note:** In children, there may be frightening dreams without recognizable content.
(3) acting or feeling as if the traumatic event were recurring (includes a sense of reliving the experience, illusions, hallucinations, and dissociative flashback episodes, including those that occur on awakening or when intoxicated). **Note:** In young children, trauma-specific reenactment may occur.
(4) intense psychological distress at exposure to internal or external cues that symbolize or resemble an aspect of the traumatic event
(5) physiological reactivity on exposure to internal or external cues that symbolize or resemble any aspect of the traumatic event

C. Persistent avoidance of stimuli associated with the trauma and numbing of general responsiveness (not present before the trauma), as indicated by three (or more) of the following:

(1) efforts to avoid thoughts, feelings, or conversations associated with the trauma
(2) efforts to avoid activities, places, or people that arouse recollections of the trauma
(3) inability to recall an important aspect of the trauma
(4) markedly diminished interest or participation in significant activities
(5) feeling of detachment or estrangement from others
(6) restricted range of affect (e.g., unable to have loving feelings)
(7) sense of a foreshortened future (e.g., does not expect to have a career, marriage, children, or a normal life span)

D. Persistent symptoms of increased arousal (not present before the trauma), as indicated by two (or more) of the following:

(1) difficulty falling or staying asleep
(2) irritability or outbursts of anger

(cont.)

BOX 3.2. *(cont.)*

   (3) difficulty concentrating
   (4) hypervigilance
   (5) exaggerated startle response

E. Duration of the disturbance (symptoms in Criteria B, C, and D) is more than 1 month.

F. The disturbance causes clinically significant distress or impairment in social, occupational, or other important areas of functioning.

From American Psychiatric Association (2000). Copyright 2000 by the American Psychiatric Association. Reprinted by permission.

ent approaches. In Chapter 6, we return to the topic of PTSD from the perspective of an anxiety disorder.

Psychopharmacological Treatment of Aggression

Two major clinical consensus conferences have been held regarding the pharmacological treatment of aggression. The Treatment Recommendations for the use of Antipsychotics for Aggressive Youth (TRAAY; Pappadopulos et al., 2003; Schur et al., 2003) focused on the use of second generation antipsychotics (SGAs) for aggression generally, while revision of the Children's Medication Algorithm Project (CMAP) focused on the treatment of aggression in children with ADHD (Pliszka et al., 2006). TRAAY emphasized the need for thorough psychiatric evaluation of the aggressive child and treatment of any primary underlying condition (ADHD, psychosis, depression); if aggression remained seriously problematic, then treatment with SGAs for the aggression per se was indicated. CMAP followed this logic for the aggressive child with ADHD, making the physician's first step a full pharmacological intervention for the ADHD (See Figure 3.1). Two large-scale reviews of the effects of stimulant medication on aggression have been undertaken. Connor, Glatt, Lopez, Jackson, and Melloni (2002) reviewed 28 studies published from 1970 to 2001 that measure stimulant effect on aggression; a mean effect size of 0.84 was found for overt aggression and 0.69 for covert aggression. Similarly, Pappadopulos et al. (2006) reviewed 19 stimulant studies involving over 1,000 subjects and found stimulants to have an effect size of 0.78 in the treatment of aggression. These effect sizes are equivalent to those of stimulants on the core symptoms of ADHD. There has been a long-standing belief that stimulants *cause* aggression, so much so that the Food and Drug Administration (FDA) convened a special panel to study this issue. The FDA meta-analysis of six placebo-controlled clinical trials (involving the long-acting stimulants) is shown in Table 3.1 (Mosholder, Gelperin, Hammad, Phelan, & Johann-Liang, 2009). No significant difference was found between placebo and stimulant in the prevalence of psychotic, manic, or suicidal events or aggression, but all the 11 psychotic events occurred during stimulant treatment.

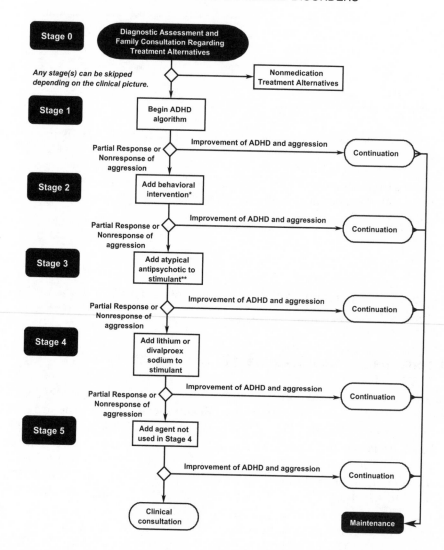

FIGURE 3.1. CMAP algorithm for treatment of comorbid ADHD and aggression. *Evaluate adequacy of behavior treatment after inadequate response at any stage. **If patient is an imminent threat to self or others, atypical antipsychotic may be started with behavior treatment.

After a stimulant trial, the physician must assess the response to both the ADHD and aggression. If there has been no response whatsoever of the ADHD symptoms to the stimulant, then progression down the CMAP algorithm for ADHD itself (See Appendix II) is recommended. The next step would be atomoxetine, whose package insert contains warnings regarding hostility and suicidal ideation. The meta-analyses of such events in controlled trials are reassuring, however (Polzer et al., 2007). In pooled studies of 2,114 children (atomoxetine = 1,308; placebo = 806), the rate of hostile/aggressive events was 21 in the active drug group and 9 in the placebo group (a non–statistically significant difference). If the ADHD did not respond to atomoxetine, then other medications in the algorithm could be considered. In many cases, however, the child does have a clinically significant response of his or her ADHD symptoms to the stimulant, but the aggression remains problematic. The physician and family wish to continue the stimulant, but clearly more needs to be done.

CMAP next recommends the implementation of a psychosocial intervention; these are covered in the next section. If the psychosocial intervention is not successful or there is an emergent situation (the child is physically attacking others), then psychopharmacology for the aggression per se should be initiated concurrent with a psychosocial intervention. (Psychopharmacological treatment alone for the aggression is appropriate if the parent cannot, for some reason, participate in a psychosocial intervention.) CMAP recommends the addition of an SGA to the stimulant as the initial step in treating the aggression, a position that is not without controversy (Sharp, 2007). Note also that the one controlled trial of this practice did not show risperidone to be superior to placebo in treating aggression when added to a stimulant (Armenteros, Lewis, & Davalos, 2007). Clinicians should recognize that starting an SGA is a major event in a

TABLE 3.1. Food and Drug Administration Meta-Analysis of Psychiatric Side Effects of Stimulants in the Treatment of ADHD

Drug	Type of trial	No. of trials	Duration of trials (range)	Category of exposure	n	Patient-years	Psychosis/mania events	Suicidal events	Aggression events
Concerta	DB	4	6–28 days	Placebo	317	10.20	0	0	0
				Drug DB	321	12.68	0	0	0
	OL	7	≤12 months	Drug OL	2,824	1,397.40	8	6	52
Metadate CD	DB	4	7–21 days	Placebo	572	19.44	0	0	3
				Drug DB	493	19.13	0	0	3
	OL	2	NS	Drug OL	322	19.55	0	0	6
MTS	DB	8	1–49 days	Placebo	464	23.84	0	0	1
				Drug DB	471	30.26	4	0	6
	OL	4	NS	Drug OL	617	341.97	6	1	7
Modafinil	DB	6	1–9 weeks	Placebo	366	39.87	0	0	5
				Drug DB	722	85.50	2	4	9
	OL	3	≤1 year	Drug OL	924	383.53	2	0	14
Adderall XR	DB	7	1–4 weeks	Placebo	678	28.00	0	0	6
				Drug DB	1,236	77.18	0	1	20
	OL	6	≤2 years	Drug OL	5,177	1,767.47	14	8	166
Atomoxetine	DB	20	≤78 weeks	Placebo	1,443	350.73	0	4	18
				Drug DB	2,459	654.87	4	9	49
	OL	10	≤96 weeks	Drug OL	5,270	5,095.27	12	44	198
Ritalin LA	DB	5	1–14 days	Placebo	259	11.31	0	1	0
				Drug DB	383	25.66	2	0	2
	OL	1	NS	Drug OL	125	25.95	0	1	0
d-MPH	DB	8	≤49 days	Placebo	468	53.24	0	0	0
				Drug DB	588	64.75	4	0	1
	OL	5	≤1 year	Drug OL	740	362.09	3	1	13

Note. DB, double blind; OL, open label.

child or adolescent's life, not to be taken lightly; all should be aware of the significant safety issues with SGAs discussed in Appendix II. The SGAs have the largest database showing efficacy in aggression, with risperidone being the most studied medication (see Table 3.2). The onset of their therapeutic action is rapid, and laboratory monitoring is less problematic than for mood stabilizers such as lithium or divalproex. Weight gain, extrapyramidal symptoms (EPS), and possible neuromalignant syndrome (NMS) always are present as threats.

CMAP placed "classic" mood stabilizers, such as lithium and divalproex, in the next stage if SGAs are not effective for the treatment of aggression. Over the last several decades, lithium was found to be superior to placebo in reducing the aggression of inpatient children with CD (Campbell et al., 1984, 1995; Malone, Delaney, Luebbert, Cater, & Campbell, 2000), but one study was negative (Rifkin et al., 1997). This latter study administered lithium for only 2 weeks versus 6 weeks in the studies showing efficacy. A placebo-controlled crossover study in 20 adolescents found divalproex superior to placebo (Donovan et al., 2000). Steiner, Petersen, Saxena, Ford, and Matthews (2003) randomized 71 adolescents with CD in a residential facility for juvenile offenders to either therapeutic or low doses of divalproex for 7 weeks; both subjects and outcome raters were blind to treatment status. Reduction in aggression severity ($p = .02$), improvement in impulse control ($p < .05$), and global improvement ($p = .0008$) were greater in the group with therapeutic divalproex levels than in the low-dose condition. Carbamazepine has never been show to be effective for aggression (Cueva et al., 1996). Newer anticonvulsant medications such as gabapentin, oxcarbamazepine, and topiramate have never been studied for their anti-aggressive effects in children; gabapentin has been reported to cause behavioral dyscontrol in children with epilepsy (Lee et al., 1996; Tallian, Nahata, Lo, & Tsao, 1996). Therefore, these medications do not appear in the algorithm in Figure 3.1. In severe cases, it may be necessary to combine a stimulant, an SGA, and lithium or divalproex to get full response; in extraordinary cases, lithium and divalproex may need to be combined with the stimulant and the SGA. The cases to follow illustrate this process.

Readers may be surprised to see that clonidine is not included as an anti-aggressive agent in the revised algorithm, as it was in the original (Pliszka et al., 2000). The data for the effectiveness of clonidine as an anti-aggressive agent are limited to a small series of case reports/open label studies (Kemph et al., 1993); the one small controlled trial of clonidine for aggression was negative (Connor et al., 2000), and modest improvement in oppositional conduct symptoms was noted when clonidine was added to methylphenidate in children with ADHD (Hazell & Stuart, 2003). In this latter study, aggression per se was not the focus of treatment. The CMAP panel felt the data did not exist to warrant clonidine's inclusion in the aggression treatment algorithm. One practice that has emerged is the combination of clonidine (whether for aggression or insomnia) in combination with SGAs. Physicians should be very cautious because of the additive effects of alpha-agonists and SGAs on sedation and hypotension. In December 2006, Rebecca Riley, a 4-year-old in Boston, Massachusetts, died after an alleged overdose of clonidine (Carey, 2007). The clonidine had been prescribed in combination with quetiapine and divalproex. Even when this combination is administered as prescribed, dangers abound. A number of years ago, an obese, aggressive patient with autism admitted to a San Antonio inpatient hospital died during a restraint; the patient entered the hospital on haloperidol and guanfacine. The day before his death, he had been switched

TABLE 3.2. Studies of the Efficacy of Second-Generation Antipsychotics in the Treatment of Aggression

Study	Age (years)	n	Medication	Dose	Duration	Results
Findling et al. (2000)	6–14	20	Risperidone	0.7–1.5 mg/day	6 weeks	Risperidone > placebo in reducing aggression.
Buitelaar, Van der Gaag, Cohen-Kettenis, & Melman (2001)	12–17	38	Risperidone	1.5–4 mg/day	6 weeks	Risperidone > placebo in reducing aggression, weight gain of 3.5% of body weight in risperidone group.
Aman et al. (2002)	5–12	118	Risperidone	0.02–0.06 mg/kg/day	6 weeks	Risperidone > placebo in reducing conduct, irritability, aggression. Mean weight gain of 2.2 kg in risperidone group.
Snyder et al. (2002)	5–12	110	Risperidone	0.02–0.06 mg/kg/day	6 weeks	47% reduction in conduct scores in risperidone group versus 21% reduction in placebo group. Extrapyramidal symptoms in 13% of risperidone group, 2.2 kg weight gain.
LeBlanc et al. (2005)	5–12	163	Risperidone	0.01–0.06 mg/kg/day	6 weeks	Pooled analysis of above two studies. 87% of risperidone subjects showed global improvement versus 40% in placebo group. Risperidone group has 2.7 kg weight gain, 72% rate of somnolence.
Turgay, Binder, Snyder, & Fisman (2002)	5–12		Risperidone	0.02–0.06 mg/kg/day	48 weeks	Open label. Improvement in aggression maintained, prolactin rose and then returned to normal levels, 8.5 kg weight gain, half attributed to normal growth.
Caldwell, Malterer, Umstead, & McCormick (2008)	13–18	129	Risperidone	Mean dose 2.5 mg/day		69 subjects at a juvenile correctional facility received a behavioral program alone, 69 had risperidone added to regimen after 21 days in behavioral program. Open label, no randomization. Risperidone groups showed significantly greater improvements in behavior, decreased aggression.
Armenteros et al. (2007)	7–12	25	Risperidone	Mean dose 1.08 mg/day	4 weeks	Aggression scores declined in both placebo and risperidone groups when study drug added to stimulant, no significant difference in rating scale of aggression, but significantly more responders in the risperidone group (100%) compared to the placebo group (70%).

(cont.)

TABLE 3.2. *(cont.)*

Study	Age (years)	n	Medication	Dose	Duration	Results
Findling et al. (2006b)	6–12	17	Quetiapine	4.4 ± 1.1 mg/kg/day	8 weeks	Open label, significant improvement in aggression ratings at endpoint over baseline. No extrapyramidal symptoms, no discontinuations due to adverse events.
Findling et al. (2007c)	6–12	9	Quetiapine	75–350 mg/day	26 weeks	Open label follow-up of above sample. Stimulants added to Quetiapine for treatment of ADHD. Improvement was maintained over course of study, 3 subjects dropped for noncompliance. Median weight gain was 0.5 kg, but one subject gained 8.2 kg.
Kronenberger et al. (2007)	12–16	30	Quetiapine and MPH	50–600 mg, mean 329 mg	3 weeks MPH, 9 weeks Quetiapine	24/30 subjects did not enter remission with MPH alone. Open label Quetiapine resulted in significant reduction in aggression over baseline, 79% response rate. Mean weight gain of 1.2 kg.
Stephens, Bassel, & Sander (2004)	7–13	10	Olanzapine	2.5–20 mg/day	8 weeks	2-week placebo run, 8 weeks active treatment, tics and aggression significantly decreased at endpoint versus placebo, mean 5.5 kg weight gain.
Handen & Hardan (2006)	13–17	16	Olanzapine	5–20 mg	8 weeks	Open label. Significant improvement in irritability and hyperactivity, weight gain 12.7 kg.
Masi et al. (2006b)	11–17	23	Olanzapine	5–20 mg	6–12 months	Open label. Subjects had failed a trial of valproate or lithium. Significant reduction in aggression over baseline. Weight gain 4.6 kg.
Findling et al. (2003)	6–17	23	Aripiprazole	1–15 mg	2 weeks	Open label. 64% response rate in children, 45% in adolescents.
Rugino & Janvier (2005)	5–17	17	Aripiprazole	5–20 mg	2–30 weeks	Open label. High comorbidity with autism and bipolar, 25% response rate. High degree of adverse events when combined with alpha-agonists.

from haloperidol to quetiapine. As shown in Appendix II, most SGAs have significant alpha-1 blocking capacity; these combined with the presynaptic alpha-2 stimulating effects of clonidine/guanfacine (both reducing the input of norepinephrine in both the central and peripheral nervous system) can be dangerous.

What about antidepressants for the treatment of aggression? In Appendix II, we review the issues of manic activation and suicidal ideation as they relate to antidepressant treatment in children and adolescents. While there is evidence for the efficacy of antidepressants for depression in the pediatric population (Bridge et al., 2007), there is no such evidence for the treatment of aggression (Connor et al., 2006). Fluoxetine has been shown to be helpful for irritability and explosiveness in a small sample of men with IED (Coccaro & Kavoussi, 1997). A psychopharmacological study of the treatment of borderline personality disorder (often associated with mood lability and explosiveness) sheds some light on this issue (Zanarini, Frankenburg, & Parachini, 2004). Female patients were randomized to receive fluoxetine alone ($n = 14$), olanzapine alone ($n = 16$), or a combination of the two ($n = 15$) for an 8-week trial. There was no placebo control and the study was not double blind. Over the course of the study, all three groups improved significantly relative to baseline levels of dysphoria and aggression. Olanzapine alone and the combination of the two medications were superior to fluoxetine alone for the treatment of aggression; the combination was not superior to olanzapine alone. In contrast, depressive symptoms responded better to the combination than to olanzapine alone, yet olanzapine alone was still superior to fluoxetine alone. Interestingly, over 90% of the subjects in this study had a unipolar mood disorder. This suggests that in mood-labile, explosive individuals, antidepressants alone are not as helpful as SGAs or a combination of SGA and antidepressants.

Table 3.3 shows the types of medications used in children and adolescents in our clinic with ADHD and IED who did not have BP or an ASD. None of these 67 patients

TABLE 3.3. Psychotropic Usage in Children with ADHD and IED

Medication type	n (67)	%
Alpha-agonist	4	6.0
SGA	51	76.1
Aripiprazole	13	19.4
Ziprasidone	1	1.5
Risperidone	20	29.9
Quetiapine	14	20.9
Olanzapine	3	4.5
SSRI	4	6.0
SNRI	1	1.5
Other antidepressant	7	8.5
Anticonvulsant mood stabilizer	18	26.9
Stimulant	53	79.1
Atomoxetine	4	6.0

Note. SGA, second-generation antipsychotic; SSRI, selective serotonin reuptake inhibitor; SNRI, serotonin–norepinephrine reuptake inhibitor.

carried a psychotic diagnosis; eight had a depressive diagnosis. Nearly all of these children were on a stimulant medication for ADHD; a small number were on atomoxetine. SGAs were clearly the most prevalent medication combined with stimulants in this group. Anticonvulsant mood stabilizers (primarily divalproex) were the second most prescribed medication in this group, with only a very small proportion on alpha-agonists. There was a small group of children with IED on antidepressants, but the seven who were on miscellaneous antidepressants were on trazodone or mirtazapine (at low doses) for sleep difficulties. Only seven were on a selective serotonin reuptake inhibitor (SSRI) or a mixed serotonin–norepinephrine reuptake inhibitor (SNRI). This again suggests that in the real-life clinic, physicians were not finding antidepressants helpful for aggression

Psychosocial Interventions for Aggression

There are many excellent reviews and textbooks on psychosocial interventions with aggressive children (Connor, 2002; Connor et al., 2006; McMahon et al., 2006). Most interventions for aggressive behavior are closely linked to the treatment of ODD and CD, but particular elements need to be added. As McMahon et al. (2006) point out, there are four broad categories of intervention: family based (with a strong behavior management focus), skill training, community programs, and school-based groups. I focus on the first two as they are the ones likely to be used in the clinician's office (though as we shall see, the clinician will often need the school as a partner). All of the programs discussed below have been validated by controlled, randomized trials. In the family-based methods, parents are taught behavior management techniques; this is the focus of programs such as Helping the Noncompliant Child (HNC; McMahon & Forehand, 2003). In the most elaborate forms, parents interact with their child in a room with a one-way mirror and the therapist gives advice via a "bug in the ear" device. While this is clearly not practical for the average therapist, the theme of HNC is very important—the therapist goes beyond lecturing to the parent about behavior management principles and "gets in there" with the parent and child. How is this practically applied in the office? One way is for the therapist to ask the parent and child to perform some task in the office that when attempted at home leads to an aggressive outburst. This might be doing homework, cleaning up, playing quietly with toys. The therapist directly models the behaviors that the parent needs to adopt. Even in my medication appointments, I find this technique useful. The child is playing on the floor with toys while I discuss how the medications are working.[1] As I announce the end of the session, I may ask if cleaning up is a problem at home and ask the child to pick up. If he begins to tantrum, I work on three issues: (1) helping the child develop empathy—"Other children need to play with toys"; (2) giving the child no choice about picking up—"I really need you to begin picking up"; and (3) discussing with the mother what an appropriate reward/consequence will be—getting a drink from the machine for a rapid response

---

[1]A running issue with psychiatrists is how to devote any time to psychotherapy in the course of a medication management visit, as these run 10–20 minutes. This has led to the joke "What's the problem with a 15-minute med check? What do you do with the other 10 minutes." As described above, there are things that can be done.

versus not listening to CDs in the car on the way home. Note that the rewards must be immediate—it will not do for the parent to "ground" the child for a week. This is dealt with in the office, with real behaviors, rather than abstractly.

Families who produce aggressive children are characterized by high levels of hostility (Dodge, 2006). Their needs go beyond learning behavior management skills— parent and child often have active hostility toward each other: "He just enjoys making me mad"; "He's just like his good-for-nothing father"; "I don't have time for this nonsense, he can just act the way he is supposed to. I'm not going to reward him for being good." Parent–Child Interaction Therapy (PCIT; Bell & Eyberg, 2002; Brinkmeyer & Eyberg, 2003) was heavily influenced by attachment theory and works not only to teach behavior management but to enhance a nurturing parent–child relationship. In this program, parent and child play together in the office in an initial child-directed interaction. Parents are taught the PRIDE skills—praising the child, reflecting child statements, imitating the play, describing child behavior, and using enthusiasm in play with the child. Behavior management skills are taught in a second, parent-directed interaction. Again, there are lessons in this approach even for the clinician not formally using the program. It is easy, in a busy office, to become exasperated yourself with these difficult children, and you can find yourself lapsing into the same habits as the parent— "Get down off that couch!," "Please don't touch my papers" (with irritated voice). Clinician, heal thyself. Go out of your way to praise some skill or accomplishment of the child, praise siblings who are very patient, or ask the child if he is aware of how hard his mother is working to help him.

The Incredible Years (Webster-Stratton, 2000; Webster-Stratton & Reid, 2003) program is an efficient way to disseminate behavior management principles by videotape. It uses a standard package of 250 video vignettes presented during a 12- to 14-week program. Parents learn a variety of techniques and are given homework to practice the skills with their children. A program for the children themselves (Dinosaur School) has also been developed.

Earlier, we noted the tendency of aggressive children to fail to read social cues, make hostile attributions, and expect that aggressive behavior will be successful for them (Dodge, 2006). The Anger Coping and Coping Power programs (Larson & Lochman, 2002; Lochman & Wells, 1996, 2002, 2003, 2004) are designed to cognitively modify the social information processing deficits that aggressive children often show. The Anger Coping program is formally a series of school-based groups. Teachers nominate students who have problems with anger or aggression; these students then attend 11 sessions of groups. Videotapes and pictures of conflictual social situations are presented, and the group is encouraged to develop solutions. This allows the therapist to reframe aggressive responses and encourage less hostile attributions. In one exercise, the group members listen individually to a tape of a socially problematic situation. Each member reports to the group his or her own view of the situation, helping children see how many different views of a situation there may be.

The Collaborative Problem Solving approach (Greene & Ablon, 2006) has become increasingly popular with clinicians and parents of "explosive kids." Parents appreciate the very matter-of-fact descriptions of the situations that trigger aggression. Greene and Ablon (2006) have used the analogy of the parent (or other responsible adult) becoming the child's "surrogate frontal lobe"—that is, the adult must teach skills. Greene points out that many parents react to an impending tantrum by simply repeating the command more forcefully and applying a punishment (Plan A). This invariably leads to a full-blown aggressive outburst. Other parents simply give in (Plan C). Greene teaches "Plan B," in which the parent first uses empathy, allowing the parent to connect with the child, then tries to shift into a problem-solving mode. Thus, if the child is refusing to brush his teeth, the parent should not simply say, "You need to brush them right now, young man, or you are grounded." Rather, the parent should say, "I know it is hard to stop playing and brush your teeth." Next, the parent shifts into a problem-solving mode ("We have a new toothpaste that tastes really good" or "Doing things the first time asked is one of your goals, and you have been doing really well so far.") The program advances from these basics to more advanced problem-solving skills. In each of the cases below, therapists using combinations of these principles collaborated with the psychiatrist to try to bring the aggression under control.

The Case of Mark

Chief Complaint

Anger and aggression.

History of Presenting Illness

Mark is 8 years old and had been diagnosed with ADHD and ODD when he was in kindergarten. He was referred to the psychiatrist because of the emergence of serious aggressive behavior both at home and at school. Mark's parents reported that he would become impulsive and strike out (either physically or verbally) whenever he was angry or frustrated. Despite treatment with both immediate-release Adderall and clonidine his parents reported that Mark would lose his temper, argue constantly with them, and defy their requests. He frequently threw objects around the house. He had kicked holes in several walls of the house. These episodes would erupt suddenly and generally last anywhere from 5 minutes to half an hour. The parents reported that they remained upset about the event far longer than Mark did. Indeed, a further outburst often occurred because the parents would insist upon an apology and Mark would refuse to give one. The headmaster of Mark's exclusive private school told the psychiatrist that Mark would become enraged in the classroom and on the playground over what he perceived as insults. Mark would even curse at teachers. The headmaster noted that Mark had particular difficulty during periods of transition. These aggressive outbursts occurred three to five times a week; Mark was in danger of being expelled.

   Both the headmaster and teachers denied that Mark showed any chronic disturbance of mood. When he was not having a temper tantrum, he was described as a happy child; indeed, his parents were concerned by his apparent lack of awareness about how serious his outbursts were. The parents denied Mark showed any symptoms of depression. He did not make negative comments about himself, and there was no history of suicidal ideation or self-injurious behavior. Mark had taken Adderall since he was in kindergarten—his sleep and appetite were not robust, but these symptoms did not appear to be neurovegetative in nature. Teachers described Mark as highly intelligent. He had an excellent vocabulary; indeed, he would debate with adults until the adults became quite irritated. Mark had a sharp wit and frequently offended friends and neighbors with rash comments. There were many houses in the neighborhood where Mark was not welcomed. The parents denied that Mark showed any periods of elated mood, and his periods of irritability were limited to the aggressive outbursts. The parents denied any history of auditory or visual hallucinations.

Past Psychiatric History

Mark's pediatrician had tried him on a variety of medications. The parents had heard "bad things" about Ritalin, and Mark's treatment began before the availability of long-acting stimulants. In kindergarten, the pediatrician started Mark on short-acting Adderall; the dose of this medication was gradually increased to 15 mg in the morning and at noon. When Mark was 8 years old, the pediatrician had thought that the aggressive outbursts might be caused by an underlying depression. Mark had been angry and nonverbal during one visit to the pediatrician. The pediatrician initiated a trial of Zoloft, but Mark became more aggressive. He hit three children, and the Zoloft was discontinued. A trial of Prozac was then initiated, but curiously Mark developed tics while on this SSRI. No change in the aggressive behavior was noted, and the Prozac was discontinued. The pediatrician initiated clonidine 0.05 mg at bedtime. This was gradually increased to 0.1 mg in the morning, 0.05 mg at noon, and 0.1 mg at bedtime. After the most recent increase in the dose of the clonidine, the pediatrician referred Mark for a second opinion by the psychiatrist.

The family had been in psychotherapy on and off for the last 2 years. The first therapist they saw engaged Mark in play therapy on a weekly basis. The parents discontinued this when they saw no improvement in the aggressive behavior. Mark did not like the second therapist he saw because "it was boring just to talk." The therapist told the parents he could not get Mark to open up about his underlying problems. At the time of their consultation with the psychiatrist, Mark had just enrolled in a social skills group, which he seemed to enjoy.

Past Medical History

The mother's pregnancy and Mark's birth history was unremarkable. He had the usual childhood illnesses but no significant medical problems. He was not on any concomitant medications.

Family and Social History

Mark lives with his biological parents and his younger brother. His parents have been married 15 years. His father is a lawyer who quit his law firm and started an Internet business from his garage. The business has done very well, and he now has over a hundred employees around the world. His mother has a PhD in English literature, but does not work outside the home. The family is well to do, and the parents' marriage is stable. Mark's father frequently has to travel internationally and might be gone for several weeks at a time, leaving the mother as the primary disciplinarian and manager of the household. The parents denied any psychiatric illness in themselves. Their younger son (age 5) had a temperament opposite to Mark's, being very easygoing and compliant. Family history was remarkable only for a possible history of BP in the paternal grandfather. This individual had never been hospitalized, however, and it was not known if he was currently on medication. There was no history of antisocial behavior in the family. The father's cell phone rang twice during the family interview, and he would step out into the waiting area to take the call. He could be heard barking commands to his employees, although he never became verbally abusive. The mother became quite angry when describing Mark's outbursts and behavior. She stated several times that "he just tries to make me mad." She was dismayed by Mark's lack of respect and was at a loss to explain his explosive behavior. The parents were then interviewed together with Mark. As the parents described some of his recent behavioral incidents, Mark would interrupt to tell them that either the event did not happen or it did not transpire in the manner in which they were describing it. He would often interject with irrelevant details such as "I didn't throw a pencil at him; it was a pen." The psychiatrist observed that the mother became visibly angry at these interruptions.

The parents were asked what interventions they had tried to deal with Mark's behavior. At first, they said "everything," but it was clear that lectures and reprimands were the primary mode of punishment. Mark had been grounded on and off for long periods of time. "We've taken everything away from him," the parents said.

Mental Status Examination

At the time of the initial interview, Mark is an 8-year-old boy who appears slightly small for his age. He was very relaxed during the interview and had an excellent vocabulary. His speech had normal rate and rhythm with no evidence of pressured speech. He evidenced no major concerns and continued to minimize the events that had occurred at school and home. He did acknowledge that he occasionally would get very angry—he described these incidents as feeling like he had "smoke coming out of my ears." He stated that they would last about 5 minutes, though they could go longer if people continued to "hassle him." His mood was neither elevated nor depressed and his affect was appropriate. There was no evidence of irritability or elation during the interview. His thought was logical, coherent, and goal directed, though he lacked considerable insight about the impact of his behavior on others. It was also clear that he recalled his behavior in a very biased way. In all conflicts he was the victim, and he saw the children at school as "being against him." He denied any auditory or visual hallucinations. There was no evidence of flight of ideas. He denied depressive mood and any suicidal ideation. He denied being angry or homicidal at any particular person.

Treatment Course

The appointment with the psychiatrist had been made after an aggressive outburst at school, and 3 weeks had passed since that incident. The parents reported, in fact, that there had been no aggressive outbursts since the appointment had been made. The psychiatrist told the parents that he did not see any evidence of BP and that it would be premature to treat Mark for such a condition. In terms of Mark's medication regimen, the potential risks of combining clonidine and stimulants were discussed with the parents. They felt strongly that both the Adderall and clonidine had provided significant benefit. Given that Mark's blood pressure was stable, it was agreed that no immediate changes to the medication would be made. The psychiatrist pointed out that the parents needed to develop greater consistency in the way they handled Mark's aggressive outbursts and to use positive reinforcement for good behavior. An appointment was made with the clinic psychologist.

The psychologist set up a behavior management program similar to that used for Caitlin's behavior in Chapter 2. The three goals were (1) don't lose temper and don't hit, (2) do things first time asked, and (3) think about your behavior. The third goal was instituted because the psychologist noted that Mark had a very distorted way of assessing social interactions. Consistent with Dodge's theory, Mark interpreted facial expressions from peers as hostile and saw events such as being bumped in the line at school as aggressive acts. Not only was he not troubled by his aggressive behavior, he somewhat enjoyed his reputation as a "tough guy." The sessions consisted of half an hour with the parents reviewing the behavior management principles and debriefing any aggression that had occurred since the last visit, while the second half of the visit was spent with Mark alone. Significantly, the psychologist did not use an open-ended approach. He would tell Mark that he had heard the details of his misbehavior from the parents and that they weren't going to argue about it. Instead, the focus would be solely upon what he could have done differently. Mark's hostile attributions toward other children were challenged, and attempts were made to get him to try to empathize with victims and to see how his aggressive behavior was inhibiting his peer relationships.

Treatment Course, Continued

There appeared to be a modest success with this approach. Mark also attended his social skills group, and he made a number of friends from this group. Teachers, however, continued to report oppositional behavior in the classroom. One day on the playground, a peer did not give a Frisbee back to Mark as requested and Mark exploded. He pushed the peer to the ground and began punching him. The teachers had to pull him off the peer and while Mark was flailing at the peer, he also hit the teacher. Mark was taken to the office and his parents were called. When they arrived, they were informed that Mark had been expelled from the private school and could not return. An emergency appointment was scheduled with both the psychiatrist and psychologist.

The psychiatrist reviewed Mark's behavior over the last several months. It was agreed that while the behavior management plan was helpful at first, there had been a deterioration in Mark's behavior. Mark had been more aggressive at home and school even before this major incident. On interviewing Mark, there was still no evidence of depressive or manic symptoms. He was quite calm in the office and again did not seem to fully recognize the seriousness of his behavior. Use of both SGAs and divalproex was discussed with the parents. They noted that there was a strong history of atherosclerotic disease on the father's side and that they were concerned about the possible effect of SGAs on lipids. They opted for a trial of divalproex. Mark now weighed 60 pounds (27.3 kg), so divalproex was started at 125 mg twice a day. This was gradually increased to 250 mg twice a day based on blood levels. At this dose, Mark's divalproex serum level was 84.

The psychologist met with the family. It was agreed that Mark would be grounded for 1 month in which he could not watch TV or play videogames. He was required to write a letter of apology to the teacher as well as to the peer. The psychologist again spent considerable time getting Mark to focus on his misattribution of hostility because the child held on to the Frisbee. When the parents were meeting alone with the psychologist, the mother burst into tears. She stated that she could not take it anymore and that "this child is driving me crazy." The psychologist inquired about depressive symptoms and found that the mother was indeed depressed three to five times a week. Sleep and appetite were adequate and there was no suicidal ideation. The psychologist agreed to see the mother alone for a brief period of individual therapy.

At the follow-up with the psychiatrist, no adverse events in relation to the divalproex were reported. Mark was transferred to a public school. Mark qualified for special education based on his Other Health Impaired (OHI) status, as he had no learning disabilities. This allowed school staff to pull him out to the counselor's office for "cool-down periods" when he was upset. He continued to argue with his teachers at his new school, but there were no further major aggressive outbursts or fights. The parents agreed that the divalproex was attenuating the aggressive behavior. They continued to implement the behavior management program. In the mother's individual therapy, it was discovered that the father's frequent absences were a major strain in the marriage. The mother also felt an enormous amount of guilt that her child had these aggressive outbursts. She was convinced that he was deliberately doing this to her because she had failed as a mother in some way. The psychologist focused very strongly on the fact that this was not the case and that there was a neurobiological component to Mark's outbursts. It was agreed that the father would come for the next session with the psychologist.

The summer arrived and Mark had been quite stable with no explosive outbursts at home or school. He was eating and sleeping well, and it was suggested by the psychiatrist that the clonidine might no longer be needed. Mark was tapered off the clonidine over a period of about 3 weeks; his behavior remained stable. The father increased his involvement with the family. Over the next several years, Mark continued to show a pattern of 2 to 3 months of good behavior followed by brief periods of deterioration. The number of sessions with the psychologist would increase during these times. Mark was changed to long-acting Adderall XR and to the Depakote ER, but otherwise there were no other major medication changes. His parents had considerable worry about his entering middle school, but this transition initially appeared to go well. Toward the end of sixth grade, a peer made fun of him in an art class. He picked up a pair of scissors, pointed them at the peer, and said, "I'm gonna kill you." He was immediately placed in in-school suspension. Again there was consultation with both a psychiatrist and the psychologist. Since this was a one-time incident (despite its seriousness) and the year had generally gone well, no medication changes were made.

Mark made it through junior high school without any further suspensions. His social skills improved, although he continued to dominate and bully his peers to some degree. He was not well liked by his teachers as he continued to be oppositional and rude. In the summer between eighth and ninth grade, the parents requested a trial of Strattera, as they felt this medication might be more convenient to use; the psychiatrist also wondered if the Strattera might have some beneficial effects on anger. Entering ninth grade, Mark was now 125 pounds (56.8 kg) and 54 inches tall. The Adderall was discontinued and the Strattera started at 25 mg twice a day; it was gradually increased to 50 mg twice a day, and the parents felt that it controlled his symptoms of ADHD as well as the stimulant. In ninth grade, Mark's behavior at school remained stable, but his behavior at home began to deteriorate. He became jealous of his younger brother and more verbally abusive toward his mother in particular. When Mark was 14 years old, the psychological evaluation was repeated. Full Scale IQ was found to be 113, and all achievement testing was at expected levels for this IQ. The psychologist performed the Rorschach, the Thematic Apperception Test, the Incomplete Sentences Blank, and the Children's Depression Inventory (CDI). The CDI was in the normal range. The test responses indicated that he was irritable and oppositional; it showed a strong sense of entitlement and the lack of sensitivity for the feelings of others. The objective testing, in particular, showed continued difficulties with making hostile attributions. Mark's reality testing was only marginally adequate, and the testing suggested that Mark would jump to erroneous conclusions in an attempt to integrate unrelated ideas in an arbitrary manner. He also tended to project grandiose and idiosyncratic ideas onto external reality. In spite of these findings, there continued to be no evidence of any overt manic symptoms. Rather, these findings reflected the underlying thought processes that were leading to his social problems.

Mark continued on the Depakote ER and Strattera. It was sometimes difficult to get blood levels of valproate because Mark was afraid of needles (ironic, given his tough persona). During his sophomore year of high school, the psychiatrist received an urgent phone call. The mother called the psychiatrist from her cell phone outside the house. She had been getting ready to take Mark to school when she told him he could not wear a T-shirt with a particularly gruesome picture on it. Mark became enraged, kicked a hole in the wall of the living room, and threatened his mother. The father was abroad on business. The mother became very frightened and ran from the house, and was now afraid to reenter it. The psychiatrist advised her to go and open the door slightly. If Mark was calm, she should go in and bring him to the office, but if he remained agitated, she should call the police.

As it turned out, Mark had calmed down, and the psychiatrist saw him that day. In contrast to other events of this sort, Mark was remorseful and the psychiatrist made him apologize to his mother. Mark was told if any such incident occurred again it would result in psychiatric hospitalization or the police being called. The psychiatrist made clear that under no circumstances would any such behavior ever be justified. Serious consideration was given to adding an SGA to his medication regimen. However, the parents wanted to see if Mark could get back on track without it. Sessions with the psychologist were rescheduled again.

There were no further aggressive outbursts of this magnitude and initiation of an SGA was not needed. However, the family's home life continued to be seriously affected. The father reacted to the incident by refusing to speak to Mark for several months despite the psychologist urging that this was not the most productive way to handle the situation. The family attended a school play in which Mark's younger brother had a part. At one point during the performance, Mark said, "Boy, these guys suck," loud enough for most people in the audience to hear.

At the session with the psychologist, the parents stated they were at their wit's end. They had looked into sending Mark to a boarding school that specialized in kids with behavior problems, but that specifically excluded children with major mental illness. The psychiatrist and psychologist consulted with each other. They agreed that Mark's behavior was having a very negative impact on family life. They also saw some merit in making clear to Mark that this behavior was unacceptable. They recommended that he attend the boarding school for a year and if his behavior there was good, he could return to the family the following school year. The psychiatrist wrote a letter for Mark's admission truthfully stating that the patient had not been diagnosed with BP. The psychiatrist continued to manage the medication while Mark was at the school, about 300 miles away.

Mark was quite successful at school although he did not like living there. He returned home for his junior year of high school. He remained on the Strattera and the Depakote. No further aggressive outbursts have occurred, though he remains oppositional and he tends to test limits. He did very well on his Scholastic Aptitude Test (SAT) and is currently making plans to attend college. The psychiatrist told the family that if Mark remains free of aggressive outbursts for the next year, consideration could be given to taking him off the Depakote.

The advantage of working with a family like Mark's is that like Caitlin's family, they are compliant with treatment and have resources to bring to bear on their problem. For many children with ADHD and IED, this is not the case and a different approach is needed.

The Case of Taylor

Chief Complaint

ADHD and aggression.

History of Presenting Illness

Taylor is a 6-year-old boy who is the older of two siblings. Taylor's mother reported that he first showed symptoms of inattention and hyperactivity at age 2. His mother described him as "like his father off medication." He had minor problems at day care, but his kindergarten teacher had serious concerns about his inability to focus, stay still, and complete work. A structured interview showed that Taylor met criteria for seven of the nine inattention symptoms and eight of the nine impulsivity–hyperactivity symptoms of ADHD. The mother also reported that he defied adults' requests and was easily annoyed by others. He tended to be physically aggressive toward his younger sibling and threw temper tantrums two to three times a day at home.

In addition to his problems with attention, Taylor had a history of speech problems. Taylor's mother reported that he seemed to comprehend everything that was said to him, but it was difficult for people outside the family to understand his speech. He had been receiving speech therapy from the local school district since the age of 3, and the mother reported that this had substantially improved his ability to make himself understood.

Taylor had previously been seen by a child psychiatrist, who had started him on Adderall XR 5 mg/day; later, the psychiatrist added Tenex 1 mg at bedtime. The psychiatrist had prescribed Tenex primarily for temper tantrums, and while the mother reported a modest response of the tantrums to the Tenex, she was uncomfortable with having the child on two medications.

Taylor's mother denied that he showed any depressive symptoms. She did note that he could get silly at times and would laugh for no reason. She denied any difficulties with sleep or appetite. She denied that he showed any visual or auditory hallucinations. There was no evidence of any manic excitement or flight of ideas. There was no history of self-abusive behavior or suicidal ideation.

Past Psychiatric and Medical History

No history of psychiatric hospitalizations. Taylor had not taken any psychotropic medications other than those noted above. In the last month of pregnancy, the mother was placed on bed rest to prevent premature placental detachment. There were no problems during the birth itself. Motor milestones were all within normal limits, but Taylor was slow to use words and complete sentences. As noted, his speech was difficult to understand. At the time of this assessment, his height was 47.5 inches, and his weight was 56 pounds (25.5 kg).

Family and Social History

Taylor lived with his 4-year-old brother Tim and his mother. Tim also had ADHD, but his symptoms were well controlled on Focalin XR 5 mg once a day. His mother worked as a health care aide in a nursing home; she was required to work erratic shifts. Many times she had to work the 3 to 11 shift and she depended on her mother for child care when the day care was not open. The parents were separated 1 year before the assessment. The mother had no knowledge of the father's whereabouts, and he was not involved in any way with the children's upbringing. He did not pay child support. The mother reported that the father had a history of ADHD and had taken Adderall at various points during their marriage. The mother also reported that Taylor's paternal uncle had a history of BP, although she did not know any details about the clinical course.

During the parent interview, the assessing psychiatrist noted a number of concerns. The mother described numerous aggressive interactions between the boys. She seemed quite nonchalant about these and several times smiled inappropriately when describing how Taylor would jump on top of Tim. She would comment that teachers and other personnel at school were not helpful. She stated that she often refused to come to the phone when the school would call her at work because of some serious misbehavior in the classroom. She told the examiner, "they should just understand that he has ADHD." She stated that she would spank the boys on regular occasions, particularly when she was tired or was "just plain fed up with it all." The spanking occurred on the bottom and no instrument was used. She denied ever leaving bruises. At the time of the interview, the mother looked quite fatigued, having worked the previous evening.

Mental Status Examination

Taylor is a 6-year-old boy who appears his stated age. His speech was difficult to understand, but he responded to all commands well. His drawing of a person was age appropriate. He could write his name and simple words and do elementary arithmetic. His mood was neither elevated nor depressed, and his affect was appropriate. It was difficult to assess his thought processes due to his limited speech, but his play in the waiting room and in the examiner's office appeared age appropriate with no unusual themes.

Treatment Course

It was noted that the Tenex had been added to the stimulant before the Adderall dose had been maximized for the child's weight. Therefore, the Tenex was discontinued and the Adderall XR was increased to 10 mg/day. Due to the many social issues, it was suggested to the mother that she return to see the psychiatry resident for several sessions of behavior therapy. The mother somewhat passively agreed but did not make the appointment when she checked out at the front desk. At a follow-up visit 1 month later, the mother reported that the child was much improved with less aggression and better academic performance in school. This was confirmed by a SNAP rating from the school that showed an inattention rating of 1.0, an impulsivity–hyperactivity rating of 0.6, and an ODD rating of 0.9. The mother stated that she could not attend the behavior therapy sessions due to her changing work schedule.

During the half-hour medication follow-up visit, about 10 minutes were taken to describe the behavior chart (see Figure 2.4) and several goals were set for Taylor. These included not beating his brother, not losing his temper, and doing things the first time asked. The mother was skeptical about whether she could set aside sufficient money to pay the required allowance if Taylor earned it. Because the child was doing well overall, it was determined to release the child to routine follow-up. The mother was asked to call for refills for the Adderall and to return in 3 months.

At the 3-month follow-up the child was doing well, and no changes to the Adderall dose were made. Three months later, the mother reported that while Taylor was doing well at school, he was inattentive and impulsive in the afternoon after 3 P.M. It was noted that his language difficulties were causing problems with peers. The Adderall XR 10 mg was increased to 15 mg/day. His weight at this time was still 56 pounds.

Four months later, the family returned and the mother reported that class work was good. The mother reported that she was using the behavior chart and stated that she was not spanking as much. The mother now had a boyfriend who had his own children, and there were frequent conflicts between her children and the boyfriend's children.

At the next follow-up visit, there were a number of concerning events. The mother had moved to a different school district and did not tell the new school that Taylor had been in special education. The mother stated that she did not want to "bias" new teachers; she also did not tell them that he had ADHD and problems with aggression. However, due to his ongoing speech difficulties, his need for special education became readily apparent. The new school reported that Taylor had serious problems finishing his work and interrupting the teacher. Taylor began wetting himself both at home and school during the daytime. The pediatrician had ruled out any urinary infection or other urological cause. The child was being teased a great deal, but the mother denied that he had been aggressive at school. On mental status examination, he was noted to be mildly dysphoric. Behavior and individual psychotherapy with one of the residents was again recommended. Once again, the mother found that her schedule did not permit this. The Adderall XR was increased to 20 mg/day; the mother was informed that this was the maximum dose.

The mother returned for the next routine 3-month follow-up and reported that there had been a marked deterioration. Approximately a month before the appointment, Taylor had attacked his younger brother, Tim, and left bruises on him. Taylor became suddenly enraged because his brother would not give him the videogame console quickly enough. The school had called child protective services, who referred the family for counseling. The mother had not called at the time of the incident but waited for the routine follow-up appointment to report this to the psychiatrist. Child protective services did not find any evidence of ongoing abuse. The mother was quite exasperated in the interview, saying that Taylor was always losing his temper and attacking his younger brother. Taylor had even hit her several times. He had hit several children at school, and other parents were complaining. For example, he hit one peer at school after the peer jostled him in line by accident. The mother stated in a very casual and yet ominous manner that Taylor told her he heard voices in his head. On mental status examination, Taylor denied any hallucinations at present. He could not say exactly when he heard the voices. He was also vague on the content—describing them either as "noises" or "a man saying to be bad." He denied any visual hallucinations. His play in the office remained age appropriate. His mood was mildly irritable, but there was no evidence of elation, pressured speech, flight of ideas, or any other symptoms of mania. The mother stated that in between aggressive outbursts, Taylor's mood appeared normal. The mother had broken up with her boyfriend, and so the household again consisted of only herself and the boys. Child Protective Services had referred the family for counseling, but did not provide the services themselves. They had closed the case and it was clear there would be no further pressure on the mother to attend therapy. The psychological evaluation performed by the school focused primarily on speech language issues. It could add little to elucidate this new complaint of "hearing voices." The mother had very limited health insurance that did not cover a psychological evaluation, and she clearly could not afford to have it done privately.

At this point, the psychiatrist took a step back to look at a number of options. It was determined that a three-step process was required: (1) to try to clarify the diagnosis by means of clinical interview, (2) to determine what could be done pharmacologically, and (3) to find out what additional services might be available through the school. Given the family history of BP, was it now appropriate to give Taylor this diagnosis? He showed partially treated ADHD, a single episode of severe aggression (and many episodes of minor aggression), some possible psychotic symptoms, and very poor awareness of his behavior, even for a child with ADHD. Nonetheless, direct mental status examination did not yield any evidence of psychosis, and his mood was neither elevated nor irritable in between aggressive outbursts. There was no hypersexuality, decreased need for sleep, racing thoughts, or pressured speech. One could simply retain the diagnosis of ODD, yet this diagnosis by itself no longer captured the clinical severity. Did he now meet criteria for CD? When he injured his brother, the attack was impulsive and irrational, and while this technically meets criteria for the CD item "starts physical fights," it is questionable whether it qualitatively met the criteria. Is this type of aggression really the same as that in a child who attacks a peer on the playground in order to force him to hand over his lunch money? More problematic for a diagnosis of CD, he did not meet any other criteria (except perhaps bullying at school). There was no lying, stealing, staying out without permission, fire setting, and so on. Even his bullying at school was fairly ineffective; the pattern was very much like that at home (i.e., sudden emotional, irrational outbursts that led to hitting). IED is a useful diagnosis in this situation because it captures the explosive outbursts that are not better accounted for by either ADHD or ODD.

As noted in the earlier review of the psychopharmacology of aggression and the CMAP treatment guidelines (Figure 3.1), use of an SGA is indicated in ADHD and comorbid aggression when the ADHD is already well controlled and a behavioral program has been added but not found to fully resolve the aggressive symptoms. It could be argued that a behavioral program had not been fully implanted in this case. However, the CMAP guidelines point out that in severe situations, SGA and behavioral treatment should begin immediately. In this situation, given the mother's inability (or unwillingness) to participate in behavior therapy in the office, what was the best course?

Treatment Course, Continued

Reviewing the medication, it was noted that Taylor was on the maximum dose of Adderall XR. Given the length of time he had been on the medication, it seemed highly unlikely that these quasi-psychotic symptoms were related to the Adderall. The mother confirmed quite emphatically that if he missed a dose of Adderall, his behavior was considerably worse. One option would be to change his stimulant medication, but given the history of good response to the medication in the school, this was not deemed to be desirable. Furthermore, the aggression and other symptoms appeared to be unrelated to the ADHD but rather more to the comorbidity of the ODD. Given the seriousness of the aggression and the potential danger to the child's younger brother, the decision was to start a low dose of Risperdal, 0.5 mg twice a day. Baseline laboratory tests including cholesterol and triglycerides were ordered.

A release of information was obtained to allow the psychiatrist to contact the school counselor. The school counselor reported that Taylor had not shown any psychotic symptoms in school but had been aggressive with other children. These temper outbursts followed very minor frustrations. He was continuing to receive speech therapy. He did not qualify for other services since he was classified for special education only as a "speech-impaired student." An OHI form was completed to qualify Taylor for special services based on the ADHD. The school counselor agreed to see Taylor on a weekly basis to work on anger management. He also attended a "lunch bunch" group for children who were having behavioral problems. Children in this group were in a behavior management program where they earned points for good behavior in the classroom and playground. At the end of the week, they could exchange these points for small toys from the school store. The counselor agreed to contact the psychiatrist if any further psychotic-like symptoms occurred.

A follow-up was scheduled for 3 weeks after the initiation of the Risperdal; however, the mother failed to show up for this appointment. Her phone was disconnected, but contact was made with her when she called for a refill. The appointment was rescheduled, and the mother did report that there had been improvement in Taylor's aggressive behavior. There had been no further attacks on the younger brother. However, the mother had not obtained the laboratory work, once again citing her work schedule. A refill of the Risperdal for 1 month was given, but the mother was told the medicine would have to be discontinued if she did not obtain the laboratory work by the next appointment in 1 month. It was noted that Taylor had gained 2 pounds since beginning the Risperdal. With a follow-up call from the office to encourage her, the laboratory work was obtained. The child's fasting glucose, triglycerides, total cholesterol, and low density/high density cholesterol ratio remained in the normal range. The plan was to keep Taylor on the Risperdal for 1 year and then attempt to wean him off it if the aggressive outbursts did not reoccur.

Severe aggression is even more difficult to manage in cases where the child or adolescent has suffered abuse or neglect. Impulsive aggression is one of the principal reasons that foster placements break down; John's case is a prime example of this phenomena.

The Case of John

Chief Complaint

Physically attacking others.

History of Presenting Illness

John is an 11-year-old boy who was admitted to a residential treatment center for children with severe emotional disturbance. When John was 7 years old, he and his sister had been taken into state custody because John had been physically abused and abandoned by his mother. His mother had a history of severe substance abuse and multiple psychiatric hospitalizations. The physical abuse consisted of slapping and striking with objects, which had left bruises on John and his sister. As far as could be determined, John had not been sexually abused. When John was taken into custody at the age of 7, he was first placed in a children's shelter. His behavior in the shelter was very disruptive, and it was clear to the child protective services staff that an ordinary foster home would not be able to meet John's needs. He was placed in a therapeutic foster home for 18 months, but his foster parent stated that John was extremely aggressive and nearly impossible to control. John alleged that the foster parent was physically abusing him, and these allegations were confirmed. Hence, John was removed from that foster home. He was placed in another therapeutic foster home where he remained for 1 year. At the age of 9, he had several severe aggressive outbursts that resulted in psychiatric hospitalization for 2 weeks. He was placed on psychotropic medication during this hospitalization, but a copy of the discharge summary was not available. For the next year, he was placed in a group home that specialized in more difficult children. However, severe aggressive outbursts continued, and John had three further placements in foster homes that broke down because of outbursts toward other children in the foster home, his foster parents, and peers at school. Whenever placed in foster homes, John would attend local schools, but he would refuse to do work or cooperate. At several of his schools, he destroyed school property, and he had been placed on in-school suspension multiple times.

In the 2 weeks since he had been admitted to the facility, John did not had any major problems. He appeared to be in a "honeymoon" period, but the morning of the interview he had engaged in a major argument with the staff over not wanting to tie his shoes. John was already telling them that he did not want to go to school. The staff reported that they did not observe any symptoms of depression. John was eating and sleeping well and had a good energy level for sports. The staff also had not observed any signs of posttraumatic stress disorder (PTSD). John did not report nightmares, and there was no evidence that he experienced any type of flashback.

Past Psychiatric History

Upon admission to the residential treatment center, John was taking Adderall XR 20 mg once in the morning, Depakote ER 750 mg at bedtime, and Seroquel 150 mg at bedtime.

His state caseworker did not have any information on who had prescribed these medications or the specific indications. Laboratory work was ordered on admission; results showed a valproate level of 96 μg/liter. John's triglycerides, total cholesterol, and high-density and low-density cholesterol were all within normal limits. There were no other clinically significant laboratory findings. A psychological evaluation performed in the last month showed a Full Scale IQ of 83, and reading and mathematics achievement at the high-4th-grade level, despite his being in the sixth grade.

Past Medical History

According to the caseworker, John had a history of seizures. She could not, however, locate any medical records documenting this. As far as the caseworker knew, none of his previous placements had reported any seizure-like activity. The caseworker, who was new to the case, had a vague recollection of the outgoing caseworker saying that a doctor had reported he thought the aggression was due to seizures.

Mental Status Examination

John is an 11-year-old boy who appears his stated age. He made poor eye contact with the examiner and was difficult to engage. His vocabulary was limited, and he spoke slowly. There were no signs of pressured speech. He was alert, and oriented to person, place, and time. His facial expression appeared irritated and downcast, but he denied depression when directly asked. His mood was not elated, and his affect was somewhat blunted. His intellectual functioning was below average. His thought was logical and goal directed but somewhat concrete for his age. His concerns in the interview focused almost entirely on what was going to happen that day. He was eager to end the interview so that he could return to the daily activity. He denied that he thought much about his past and specifically denied any types of intrusive memories, flashbacks, or sense of a foreshortened future. His insight was extremely limited, and he blamed others for his aggressive outbursts, stating that "they always started it." He denied suicidal or homicidal ideation, as well as any auditory or visual hallucinations.

Treatment Course

In view of his stable behavior since admission, it was decided not to make any changes in his medication. He was assigned to a cabin with a very intensive behavior management program, and he participated in therapy three times a week. John continued to have contact with his foster parents from his last therapeutic foster home. The long-term plan was to stabilize John's behavior and return him to this foster home, as the foster parents had established a bond with John. One week after his psychiatric evaluation, the staff reported that John had a major aggressive outburst in which he hit a peer and required restraint for 30 minutes. The psychiatrist noted that John's Seroquel had been administered as a single evening dose, thus leading to the possibility that the medication was being fully metabolized by the end of the day. The Seroquel dosing was changed to 100 mg twice a day. Due to lack of improvement, the dose was further increased at the next visit to 200 mg twice a day.

The next visit with the psychiatrist occurred approximately 6 weeks into John's stay. The patient had hit a staff member and tried to choke another peer. He endorsed daily anger and rage and stated that he "just wants to get out of here." When this was explored, John stated that he wanted to return to the foster home and was completely oblivious to the fact that he had severe problems there. He stated that he did not like the rules at the residential treatment center and "just wanted to do what he wanted." After discussion with the staff, it was noted that John's medication history was quite unclear and the efficacy of his various medications not well established. It was decided to hold the Adderall for 1 week. Input from staff and teachers was sought as to whether there was any increase in hyperactive or impulsive behavior in John off the stimulant. John attended a specialized classroom in the facility that had only six students. At the end of the week, neither the staff nor the teachers noted any change in his behavior off the Adderall and so it was discontinued.

The Seroquel was increased to 200 mg in the morning and 300 mg at bedtime. The valproate level was maintained at 100 µg/liter. The therapist noted that John was extremely difficult to engage in therapy. John would resist coming to therapy, stating that he was bored and that he did not want to talk about his past. He also did not reveal much through drawings or other types of play. At the next follow-up visit, it was reported that John had 20 incidents in the last 30 days, including 10 incidents of physical aggression that required multiple restraints. The situation was no better a month later, and it was determined that the SGA needed to be changed. Over a week, he was tapered off the Seroquel and was titrated to a dose of 10 mg of Abilify in the morning. Over the next 2 months, there was a gradual improvement in the aggressive outbursts. However, while John was having only 7 major events a month, these continued to be very severe ones involving physical attacks on others. There was no evidence of extrapyramidal symptoms on physical exam, so the Abilify was increased to 15 mg a day. The psychiatrist received a phone call the following week stating that John's behavior had deteriorated significantly. Consideration was given to returning to the previous dose of Abilify, but after discussion with the staff it was agreed that his behavior on that earlier dose was still very problematic. Therefore, the Abilify was discontinued, and he was started on Risperdal. He showed no improvement on a low dose of Risperdal 1.5 mg twice a day, so the dose was gradually increased over the next 2 months. This period was characterized by periods of several days in which John's behavior would be appropriate, followed by runs of extreme aggressive behavior. The aggressive episodes continued to be generated by varying minor frustrations. The Risperdal was increased to 3 mg twice a day.

A staff conference was held with the teacher, child care workers, and psychiatrist. It was noted that while the Adderall had not appeared to be beneficial when John was admitted, he continued to exhibit a great deal of inattention and impulsivity in both the classroom and cabin. It was felt that a trial of an alternative stimulant would be indicated. He was started on Concerta 36 mg in the morning. The case was reviewed again a month after the Concerta had been started—the school behavior had improved in terms of his attention span but the aggression was unchanged. Therefore, it was decided to utilize an alternative mood stabilizer. John was tapered off the Depakote and started on lithium 300 mg twice a day; this was titrated to lithium 300 mg in the morning and 600 mg at bedtime on the basis of plasma lithium levels. He obtained a lithium level of 0.8 mEq/liter. White blood cell count and thyroid-stimulating hormone remained within normal limits. Of concern, it was noted that his total cholesterol had risen to 178 µg/dl, with the upper limit of normal being 170. All of his other measures of lipid metabolism remained within normal limits.

After many weeks of sessions, John's therapist decided to shift the approach to John's immediate behaviors, as there seemed to be no evidence that John was suffering from the intrusive memories or flashbacks of PTSD. John did seem motivated to return to his foster home. The therapist held joint sessions with the foster parents and John so that the foster parents could reinforce the message that John could come home when his behavior improved. This also provided a way to gently confront John about the fact that he had had problems while in the foster home and that these behaviors would need to change as well. The therapist spent considerable time debriefing the aggressive outbursts with John, helping him to understand how he had misinterpreted situations. The negative consequences of his aggressive behavior were emphasized. A theme of the therapy became how John had to control himself "even when things were unfair" since John clearly believed that whenever someone had "done something to him," it was okay for him to retaliate.

Over the next several months, John's behavior gradually improved. At the most recent follow-up, he was still on Concerta 36 mg in the morning, lithium 900 mg/day, and Risperdal 3 mg twice a day. His weight had increased considerably, but he had also grown taller and entered puberty. His body mass index (BMI) had not increased in any clinically significant way. At his most recent follow-up with the psychiatrist, it was noted that he had only six minor incidents in the last 30 days, and these did not involve physical aggression. He was doing well in school. He was on track to earn a lengthy Christmas pass with his foster family, and the caseworker was looking forward to uniting them sometime in the spring of the following year.

This case illustrates a number of important principles and controversies in the treatment of children with severe aggression. Did John have PTSD? No evidence of this could be found on direct interview or mental status. Many therapists would argue that the PTSD was suppressed. Certainly, one would not expect a child to speak openly about abuse in an initial interview with a psychiatrist, but for John, themes of past abuse did not emerge even after months of therapy. This is not to say that John's abuse did not harm him psychologically—his hostile attributions, his belief that aggression is the proper response when aggrieved, and his dysregulated affect most likely grew directly from the early abuse and neglect he suffered. Conceptualizing this pattern as PTSD would be an error. It might have led the therapist to "force" John to talk about his abusive past, and this would clearly have done more harm than good. For the psychiatrist, a PTSD diagnosis might have led to treatment with SSRIs, which, as we saw in the case of Mark, might have led to more aggressive behavior.

In terms of medication, several principles were applied. One medication at a time was changed—the psychiatrist cycled through different SGAs until one was found that reduced aggression most fully. The severity of the symptoms called for a concomitant mood stabilizer, thus the gradual transition from the divalproex to lithium. The change in stimulant from amphetamine to methylphenidate might have been made earlier in the course of treatment, given that ADHD was such a prominent part of the picture. Some clinicians might argue that since the pharmacological regimen was similar to that used to treat children with BP, why not diagnose John with that disorder? Nowhere in his course did John ever evidence flight of ideas, grandiosity, elation, decreased need for sleep, psychosis, or increase in goal-directed activity. This brings us to the issue of severe mood dysregulation (Leibenluft et al., 2003) and BP, the topic of the next chapter.

Chapter 4

Bipolar Disorder

An Epidemic of Bipolar Disorder?

Clinicians have seen a major change in diagnostic practices over the last decade regarding the classification of mood lability and aggression. According to the National Ambulatory Medical Care Survey (Moreno et al., 2007), outpatient visits to physicians for youth carrying a diagnosis of bipolar disorder (BP) rose from 25 per 100,000 population in 1994–1995 to 1003 per 100,000. This is a 40-fold increase compared to a 185% increase in adults. Inpatient admissions of children and adolescents for BP showed a near sixfold increase (Blader & Carlson, 2007). Moreno et al. (2007) noted some interesting differences between adults and youth: two-thirds of youth with BP were male and a third had a diagnosis of ADHD, while two-thirds of adults with BP were female and the prevalence of ADHD was only 3%. Descriptions of childhood mania go back to the 19th century (Greves, 1884). A fascinating review (Glovinsky, 2002) of the history of BP in children yielded this quote from a clinician (Sadler, 1952) regarding adult manic patients he had followed since childhood:

> Many children who puzzled me twenty-five years ago, and whose condition I diagnosed merely as nervous irritability, high tension, and overactivity, I have since observed, as they have grown up, to have developed into definite cycloid personalities—manic–depressives.... These youngsters are often emotionally unstable throughout childhood, and the majority of these cycloid deviates belong to the extrovert or ambivalent type of personality. ... Early in childhood they tend to develop this "roller coaster" type of disposition. (p. 452)

Clearly, BP is not a "new" diagnosis. Senior clinicians in the field know that we have always dealt with children who are mood labile, aggressive, and out of control in very disruptive and sometimes dangerous ways. In the psychodynamic classic *When We Deal with Children* by Fritz Redl, the case of Johnny is presented (Redl, 1966):

> Johnny is a restless lad of thirteen and lives in small cottage with eleven other boys ... all are "livewires" with quite emphatic needs for motion, noise and activity. ... Johnny has her

[the house mother] stumped. His behavior is getting worse; he seems to be on a constant binge of triumphant clowning, he has to giggle and act silly all the time, is very mean and exploitative of the younger and weaker members of the group. (p. 237)

The chapter goes on to discuss Johnny's psychodynamic formulation (based on his history of rejection) and how to adjust the "therapeutic milieu" of the house to deal with him. Who doubts that today Johnny would be diagnosed with ADHD and most likely BP as well? In the 1960s to early 1980s, severe mood lability and aggression were explained in the context of "borderline personality disorder" and along the lines of object relations theory (Rinsley, 1983). In this era, children and adolescents could be admitted to hospitals and residential treatment centers for months or years at a time and exposed to intensive individual and milieu therapy. Because children had to have a DSM-IV diagnosis, they were simply diagnosed with conduct disorder. Even at that time, most felt this did not describe the severity of the syndrome, so these patients were sometimes diagnosed as having "borderline traits" since technically the DSM did not permit the diagnosis of a personality disorder in those under 18 years of age.

Thinking in the field underwent a tectonic shift with the publications of the Massachusetts General Group in the mid-1990s. Wozniak et al. (1995) identified 43 children in a psychiatric outpatient clinic who met their criteria (K-SADS) for mania; all but one of these children also met criteria for ADHD. They were compared with 164 nonmanic ADHD children and 84 controls. There were a total of 206 (42 manic and 164 nonmanic) ADHD subjects, which yields a prevalence of mania of 20% among the ADHD sample in this study. There were only two children with euphoric mania; and 77% showed "extreme and persistent mania." That is, they did not cycle or have any prolonged periods of euthymia. Eighty-four percent showed "mixed mania" in which symptoms of mania and depression co-occurred. Parents reported the mean age of onset of the manic symptoms to be 4.4 years, while the ADHD symptoms had been present since age 2. Biederman et al. (1996) studied a second sample of 120 children with ADHD and found 29 children (21%) who met criteria for BP. Child Behavior Checklist (CBCL) scores of the children with ADHD/mania were elevated over the children with ADHD only on nearly all the subscales. Of note, it was the aggression subscale that most differentiated the manic/ADHD group from the ADHD-only group (Biederman et al., 1995c). This again raises the issue of the differential diagnosis of aggression in children with ADHD. While highly controversial at the time (Biederman, 1998; Klein et al., 1998), this work must now be viewed as ground-breaking. It represents a major advance over the psychodynamic theorizing that had dominated the treatment of severely aggressive and mood-labile children in the 1980s.[1] Thus, there is no need to further rehash debates about "whether or not" bipolar is often comorbid in ADHD; rather we turn to the challenging task of differentiating BP (or more specifically mania) from oppositionality and aggression.

---

[1]Sometimes my fellow senior clinicians lament the passing of those days, when we could keep children in the hospital for weeks and years, "really get to understand" them, and help them "make real change." Now, we allegedly "treat everything with medication." My own recollections of this era are far less rosy—I remember children being restrained for hours while they screamed. This was viewed as a good thing, as the child was "working through" the separation-individuation experience, with the odd assumption that we would do it better than the child's parents had.

Phenomenology of BP in Children and Adolescents

How does BP present in children and adolescents? The field has struggled with this question since the Massachusetts General data was first published, the key issues revolving around the nature of cycling in the pediatric BP patient. Since the days of Emil Kraepelin in the late 19th century, manic episodes have been seen as distinct periods with a relatively acute onset. In classic "manic–depressive illness," periods of mania and depression were seen as separated by significant periods of euthymia. The Massachusetts General Group reported that their subjects with mania were rarely euthymic. The concept of "chronic mania" was criticized (Klein et al., 1998). This led to a substantial body of work using structured interviewing and life-charting methods to determine exactly how frequently children and adolescents "cycle." Furthermore, these studies sought to define the key symptoms of mania in children (Kowatch, Youngstrom, Danielyan, & Findling, 2005b). Seven studies were reviewed and the number of manic symptoms from DSM-IV (or its predecessors) were subjected to meta-analysis (Ballenger, Reus, & Post, 1982; Bhangoo et al., 2003; Faedda, Baldessarini, Glovinsky, & Austin, 2004; Findling et al., 2001; Geller, Tillman, Craney, & Bolhofner, 2004; Lewinsohn, Klein, & Seeley, 1995; Wozniak et al., 1995). Often the studies varied as to whether euphoria and/or grandiosity were viewed as cardinal symptoms (i.e., the diagnosis depended on them). Not surprisingly, when they were required, over 85% of those with pediatric mania were euphoric or grandiose (Geller et al., 2004). In contrast, when they were not required (i.e., irritability alone was sufficient for a diagnosis of mania), only 13–33% of manic subjects were found to be euphoric (Ballenger et al., 1982; Wozniak et al., 1995). The rates of other core symptoms of mania in children were increased energy (76–96%), distractibility (71–92%), pressured speech (89–90%), racing thoughts (51–88%), decreased need for sleep (53–66%), poor judgment (38–89%), flight of ideas (46–66%), and hypersexuality (31–45%). Rates of psychosis in children with mania ranged from 24–62% across these studies. Clearly, this indicates that clinicians should look for severe symptoms when diagnosing mania; extreme levels of hyperactivity or aggression by themselves do not make a diagnosis of mania.

Do children and adolescents with mania cycle? Research nurses questioned the families of 26 children with BP closely about the number and length of manic or depressive episodes (Geller et al., 1995). One child reportedly had 104 episodes in a year, each of these episodes lasting from 4 hours to a whole day. Another subject had daily episodes of agitation or depression for a whole year. Only 2 subjects had episodes that lasted longer than 2 weeks as their only episodes. Findling et al. (2001) identified 90 youth ages 5–17 years with BP and used life charting to determine their clinical course. Strikingly, only 2 of the subjects showed interepisode recovery, defined as a 2-month period free of symptoms (50% were rapid cyclers). Therefore, whether a child has "chronic" mania or is an "ultra-radian rapid cycler" seems to be a distinction without a difference. Furthermore, it is becoming clear that interepisode recovery is rare even in adult patients. Retrospective studies in adults of the age of the first episode of mania clearly show childhood onset in the majority of cases, and such onset is associated with greater severity of illness (Perlis et al., 2004; Sachs, Baldassano, Truman, & Guille, 2000). It is striking that general psychiatry is coming to the view of BP as a chronic condition with high levels of depression and/or mixed states and very limited periods of recovery, given that this view of mania in childhood was so controversial a decade ago.

TABLE 4.1. Criteria for the Broad Phenotype of Juvenile Mania: Severe Mood and Behavioral Dysregulation

Inclusion criteria

- Age 7–17 years, with the onset of symptoms before age 12.
- Abnormal mood (specifically, anger or sadness) present at least half of the day most days and of sufficient severity to be noticeable by people in the child's environment (e.g., parents, teachers, peers).
- Hyperarousal, as defined by at least three of the following symptoms: insomnia, agitation, distractibility, racing thoughts or flight of ideas, pressured speech, intrusiveness.
- Compared to his/her peers, the child exhibits markedly increased reactivity to negative emotional stimuli that is manifest verbally or behaviorally. For example, the child responds to frustration with extended temper tantrums (inappropriate for age and/or precipitating event), verbal rages, and/or aggression toward people or property. Such events occur, on average, at least three times a week for the past 4 weeks.
- The symptoms noted in the previous three items are currently present and have been present for at least 12 months without any symptom-free periods exceeding 2 months in duration.
- The symptoms are severe in at least one setting (e.g., violent outbursts or assaultiveness at home, at school, or with peers). In addition, there are at least mild symptoms (distractibility, intrusiveness) in a second setting.

Exclusion criteria

- The individual exhibits any of these cardinal bipolar symptoms: elevated or expansive mood, grandiosity or inflated self-esteem, episodically decreased need for sleep.
- The symptoms occur in distinct periods lasting more than 4 days.
- The individual meets the criteria for schizophrenia, schizophreniform disorder, schizoaffective illness, pervasive developmental disorder, or posttraumatic stress disorder.
- The individual has met the criteria for substance use disorder in the past 3 months.
- IQ <80.
- The symptoms are due to the direct physiological effects of a drug of abuse or to a general medical or neurological condition.

Note. From Leibenluft, Charney, Towbin, Bhangoo, and Pine (2003). Copyright 2003 by The American Psychiatric Association. Reprinted by permission.

The debate on the phenomenology of BP in childhood is not closed, however. In a very influential review, Leibenluft, Charney, Towbin, Bhanghoo, and Pine (2003) distinguished between a narrow phenotype of mania in which it would be required that the child show elated mood (and not irritability) and a broad phenotype that they have termed *severe mood dysregulation* (SMD). Table 4.1 shows their proposed criteria for the broad phenotype—these would cover at least some of the children with IED that we discussed in Chapter 3. Such an approach might also provide more specific criteria for the diagnosis of BP "not otherwise specified" (NOS), which is now so commonly used in child and adolescent mental health. The Leibenluft group has published family history and physiological data suggesting that SMD and the narrow phenotype of mania are distinct entities (Brotman et al., 2006, 2007; Dickstein et al., 2007; Rich et al., 2007); it remains to be seen if such criteria will influence the writing of DSM-V.

As noted earlier, Biederman et al. (1995c) first reported that the ADHD children they found to meet criteria for mania on the K-SADS also showed a particular pattern on parent Child Behavior Checklist (CBCL) ratings. While children with ADHD alone were in the clinical range (a score 2 standard deviations above the mean for the child's age and gender) only on the Attention Problem (AP) scale, children with ADHD and mania were also elevated on the Aggressive Behavior (AGG) and Anxious/Depressed (AD) scales. Other studies have found that children with ADHD/BP show elevations on these three scales relative to those with ADHD alone (Carlson & Kelly, 1998; Geller, Warner, Williams, & Zimerman, 1998b; Mick, Biederman, Pandina, & Faraone, 2003); this pattern has been seen also in the children of mothers with BP (Wals et al., 2001). Recently, the genetic architecture of the CBCL mania proxy has been examined (Hudziak, Althoff, Derks, Faraone, & Boomsma, 2005). CBCL ratings were taken from several thousand monozygotic (MZ) and dizygotic (DZ) twin pairs. The sample of subjects who met the cutoff on only the CBCL-AP scale were about 4–5% of the sample, consistent with the prevalence of ADHD. Those who met the criterion for CBCL-BP (above the 2 standard deviation clinical cutoff on AGG, AP, and AD) were about 0.8% of the sample at age 7, rising to 1.2% of the sample at age 12 (in males). The CBCL-BP group constituted about 15% of the girls with ADHD and 20–25% of the boys with ADHD. The ADHD and ADHD-BP groups showed different patterns of inheritance. Consistent with other twin studies, ADHD showed high genetic effects (~0.75) with unique environmental effects accounting for the remaining variance. In contrast, ADHD-BP also showed strong genetic effects (~0.66), but these were contributions from both unique (~0.15) and common environmental effects (~0.30). This is consistent with family studies showing ADHD-BP to be a different genetic subtype than those with ADHD alone (Faraone, Biederman, Mennin, Wozniak, & Spencer, 1997b). This is *not* to say the CBCL alone can diagnose mania or BP. Rather, this specific pattern of severe aggression and mood lability is not a diagnostic "grab bag" and has an underlying genetic structure.

Theories about the Comorbidity of BP and ADHD

The overlap between ADHD and BP is highly asymmetrical–in clinical samples, about 20% of children with ADHD will meet criteria for BP while about 50% of adolescents with BP and nearly all of preadolescents with BP will meet criteria for ADHD (Kowatch et al., 2005b; Singh, DelBello, Kowatch, & Strakowski, 2006) (see Figure 4.1). Singh et al. (2006) reviewed 17 studies examining this overlap to explore four reasons for the high degree of comorbidity.

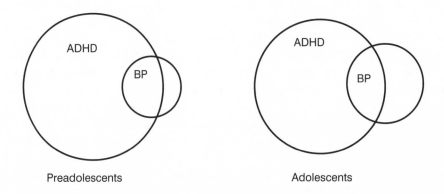

FIGURE 4.1. The asymmetrical overlap of ADHD and BP as a function of age.

BP Symptom Expression Leads to an Overdiagnosis of ADHD in BP (or Vice Versa)

In other words, because the disorders share similar criteria, is overlap an artifact? Children diagnosed with ADHD and BP retain the BP diagnosis even when overlapping criteria are subtracted out (Milberger, Biederman, Faraone, Murphy, & Tsuang, 1995). As noted by Kowatch et al. (2005b), children with ADHD/BP clearly show the core mania symptoms beyond the ADHD symptoms themselves. ADHD symptoms do not resolve when BP patients are euthymic (DelBello et al., 2004). Artifactual overlap does not appear to be the explanation for the ADHD-BP comorbidity, though it is a danger for clinicians who do not utilize the diagnostic criteria appropriately.

ADHD Is a Prodromal Manifestation of BP

ADHD is much more common in adults with BP who report a childhood onset of BP (Perlis et al., 2004; Sachs et al., 2000). ADHD is much more common among the children of parents with BP relative to parents without BP, even when controlling for parental ADHD (Chang, Steiner, & Ketter, 2000; Henin et al., 2005). There seems to be support for the idea that early-onset BP is linked with ADHD, but this should not be interpreted as establishing that *all* children with ADHD have a form of BP since clearly the vast majority of children with ADHD do not go on to develop an affective disorder.

ADHD and Associated Factors (Stimulant Administration) Lead to the Onset of BP

A child who is acutely manic should always undergo mood stabilization before ADHD is treated with stimulants (Biederman et al., 1999b). Can stimulants induce mania in an at-risk child? Carlson, Loney, Salisbury, Kramer, and Arthur (2000) followed 75 boys with ADHD into adulthood; 23% of the group were felt to be at high risk for mania due to high levels of aggression and mood lability. As children, those with and without putative manic symptoms responded equally well to methylphenidate, and there was no association between childhood treatment history and BP diagnosis at adult follow-up. While none of the children in the MTA study met criteria for BP, a small subset ($n = 13$) had severe mood lability suggestive of hypomania. This subset had an equally robust response to methylphenidate relative to those without such mood lability, with no evidence that the stimulant worsened mood (P.S. Jensen, personal communication). Thus the rise in BP diagnoses over the last decade cannot be attributed to the rise in the treatment of ADHD with stimulants, and it is incorrect to say that stimulants commonly "precipitate" or "unmask" mania.

ADHD and BP Share an Underlying Biological Etiology

In a family history study, the first-degree relatives of children with ADHD alone (400 relatives of 125 subjects) and ADHD/BP (51 relatives of 15 subjects) and controls (368 relatives of 120 subjects) were interviewed to determine the prevalence of both ADHD and BP (Faraone et al., 1997b). ADHD was more prevalent among the relatives of children with ADHD and ADHD/BP than among relatives of controls, but rates of BP were elevated fivefold *only* among the relatives of the children with ADHD/BP. This indicates that ADHD by itself is not a risk factor for BP in the absence of a family history of BP. More interestingly, ADHD and BP tended to occur in the same relative (cosegregation). It was not the case that the father with BP married a mother with ADHD and they produced a child with ADHD/BP. Rather, one of the parents was likely to have *both* ADHD and BP. The fact that ADHD/BP and ADHD alone "breed true" in different families strongly suggests that the ADHD associated with BP is a different genetic subtype from that of ADHD without BP. This is a key point for clinicians. What appears to explain the high comorbidity of ADHD with BP is that early-onset BP is linked to a particular form of ADHD. This ADHD-proto-BP is clinically indistinguishable from ADHD simplex when it first emerges (and is stimulant responsive), but the life course is vastly different, with the manic symptoms emerging 2–4 years after the onset of the ADHD.

Diagnostic Issues

I have never seen a case of "acute" onset of mania in late childhood or early adolescence (though I have seen such onset in the 17- to 23-year-old group). By this, I mean it is rare to see a healthy, well-adjusted child who does not have ADHD or ODD who suddenly, over the course of days or weeks, develops full-blown mania. There seem to be two major clinical courses of pediatric BP. Some children have both severe ADHD and mood symptoms during the preschool years (Danielyan, Pathak, Kowatch, Arszman, & Johns, 2007). When these children also have developmental problems (speech–language issues, socialization problems), the clinician must struggle to determine whether pervasive developmental disorders (PDD) are, in fact, the primary issues (or are yet another serious comorbidity). We examine this issue in Chapter 8. The more common course is for the child to present with ADHD (and often ODD). Medications for ADHD are prescribed, and generally there is improvement. But over several years, there is a complaint that "the medications aren't working as well," and mood/aggression symptoms become more prominent. Different ADHD mediations are tried; alpha-agonists may be added for aggression. Finally, the decision is made to try more serious pharmacology (often in response to a major incident, such as a major aggressive outburst). It is usually at this point that the clinician first raises the possibility of BP.

The key for the clinician is to not "jump the gun" in this process. We should refer again to Table 2.1 to review the principles for assessing mood lability and irritability in children with ADHD. As Carlson (2007) pointed out, the differential diagnosis is not *between* ADHD and BP (the child clearly has ADHD), but rather the question is whether the aggression and mood lability meet the criteria for BP. As shown in Table 4.2, severe ADHD, ADHD with ODD/IED, and ADHD/BP are all characterized by increases in motor activity, distractibility, and excessive talking, so these factors cannot be used to distinguish the conditions. Caretakers often view children with ADHD (combined type) as energetic, but those with ADHD/BP show markedly increased in energy ("they never wear out," "everyone else in the family is exhausted"). When it comes to irritable mood, children with ADHD/BP will have a more chronic abnormal mood state, the

TABLE 4.2. When Does a Child with ADHD Cross the Threshold into Mania?

	"Severe" ADHD	ADHD + IED/ODD/CD	ADHD and BP
Motor activity	Increased	Increased	Increased
Distractibility	Increased	Increased	Increased
Excessive talking	Increased	Increased	Increased
Energy	Increased	Increased	Markedly increased
Anger outbursts	None	Intense, but time limited	Prolonged, affective storms, "walking on egg shells"
General mood	Euthymic	Irritable only when frustrated	Pervasive abnormal mood
Sleep	Erratic bedtime and wake-up time, sleeps 8–10 hours	"Night owl," particularly in adolescents—sleeps 8–10 hours	Sleeps 6 hours a night or less
Core mania symptoms			
Pressured speech	Absent	Absent	Present
Flight of ideas	Absent	Absent	Present
Grandiosity	Absent	No remorse, arrogant	"Full of self"
Sexuality	Absent	Early sexual activity	Abnormal sex acts
Judgment/risks	Immature	No future orientation	Dangerous acts
Elation/silliness	Limited	Absent	Present
Psychosis	Absent	Absent	Often present

rage outbursts are prolonged (often requiring restraints by caretakers), and they rarely exhibit a euthymic baseline (at least not until treated). Sleep can be disturbed in all children with ADHD (trouble going to bed and a tendency to sleep late), but only those with ADHD/BP show a true *decreased need* for sleep.

Finally, it is the core symptoms of mania that truly distinguish BP from ODD or mood dysregulation (Geller et al., 1998b, 1998c, 2004). What is the difference between excessive talking and pressured speech? Children with ADHD often engage in more random speech at inappropriate times (talking in class or church). Yet, when they must engage in goal-directed speech, they often are less talkative (such as during the clinician interview). In contrast, children with BP talk over the examiner, use more words, and clearly have an increased *rate and volume* of speech. Patients with ADHD/ODD/IED are often perceived as arrogant and lacking remorse, but the BP patient lacks any realistic awareness of his or her capabilities. While frank delusions of grandeur are rare in children and teens, beliefs that one can do whatever one wants are often a key symptom. A child with ODD knows he will fail a test (and doesn't care), while one with BP may be fully convinced she will make an A even though she has not studied or been to class. Children and teens with BP often hold completely unrealistic fantasies about what will happen in the future and plan their lives around them. Children with ADHD often tend to initiate sexual activity earlier than non-ADHD peers, but there is nothing hypersexual about their behavior. Children with BP engage in age-inappropriate sex play and obsession with pornography (especially on the Internet). Psychosis, when present, clearly places the child in the BP spectrum.

Pharmacological Treatment of ADHD and BP

Thankfully for clinicians and families, there has been an explosion of research on both classic mood stabilizers, such as lithium and divalproex, and SGAs in the treatment of childhood and adolescent mania. While the use of these medications in the under-18 age group is still clearly off-label, these well-conducted studies involving hundreds of subjects give us much more confidence in our treatment strategies. Nearly all the studies involve comparison of monotherapy to placebo, but some dual pharmacology and comparative studies are beginning to emerge. There was high comorbidity of ADHD in nearly all these samples. The first double-blind, placebo-controlled trial of lithium in adolescents was in 25 subjects with BP who had developed substance abuse problems after the onset of their mania (Geller et al., 1998a). After 6 weeks, the lithium group had significantly improved functioning as well as fewer positive urines for drugs of abuse. Kowatch et al. (2000) randomized children and adolescents to lithium, divalproex, or carbamazepine for 6–8 weeks of monotherapy, with no placebo control. All three drugs reduced manic symptoms equally and produced equal degrees of overall clinical response (lithium 42%, divalproex 46%, carbamazepine 34%). Very few of the subjects were in remission at the end of the study, however, suggesting monotherapy of BP with these agents was not sufficient.

Several recent controlled trials of divalproex have yielded conflicting results. Kowatch, Findling, Scheffer, and Stanford (2007) randomized 154 children and adolescents with BP to either placebo, lithium, or divalproex for 8 weeks. Divalproex was significantly superior statistically to placebo in reducing manic symptoms, while there was only a trend for lithium to be effective. In contrast, divalproex ER was not superior to placebo in a 4-week trial in 150 adolescents with BP (Wagner et al., 2007). Youths (n = 56) ages 5–17 years with BP not otherwise specified or cyclothymia (but who did not meet full criteria for BP I or II) and who had one parent with BP were randomized to either divalproex or placebo for up to 5 years (Findling et al., 2007a). Not surprisingly, the study had a high dropout rate and there was no difference between placebo and divalproex in the discontinuation rate. At the 1-year point, only 20% of the sample was still in the study. While there were modest improvements in mood for both groups, they did not differ significantly in mania ratings.

Results were also disappointing for oxcarbazepine (Wagner et al., 2006b) and topiramate (DelBello et al., 2005), neither of which showed superiority over placebo in the treatment of pediatric mania. The former study was hampered by a high placebo response rate, while there was a trend for topiramate to be effective.

In contrast to the modest results of anticonvulsant medications, SGAs have been shown to have a robust antimanic effect in older children and teens with BP. These studies are shown in Table 4.3. As can be seen, effects were present in most studies as early as the first week; remission rates were 40–50% for all of these agents. Attention must be drawn to the marked weight gain induced by olanzapine, which led to the publication of an accompanying editorial in the *American Journal of Psychiatry* stating that "the substantial weight gain associated with olanzapine perhaps suggests a preference to treat first with a more weight-neutral agent" (McClellan, 2007, p. 1462). Controlled studies of risperidone in the treatment of pediatric mania have not been published, though multiple open trials suggest its effectiveness (Biederman et al., 2005; Frazier et

TABLE 4.3. Studies of the Efficacy of Second-Generation Antipsychotics in the Treatment of Child and Adolescent Mania

Study	Age (years)	n	Medication	Dose	Duration	Results
DelBello, Findling, Earley, Acevedo, & Stankowski (2007)	10–17	277	Quetiapine	400 or 600 mg/day	3 weeks	Remission rates: placebo—30%, 400 mg—50%, 600 mg—50%. Different from placebo at day 4. Quetiapine groups had 1.7 kg weight gain versus 0.4 kg on placebo. Increases in triglycerides, glucose, prolactin noted.
Chang et al. (2007)	10–17	296	Aripiprazole	10 or 30 mg/day	4 weeks	Higher remission rates (45%) in 30 mg group at week 4 compared to 10 mg groups (20%). Low rates of extrapyramidal symptoms, effect present at week 1. Minimal weight gain.
Tohen et al. (2007)	13–17	161	Olanzapine	2.5–20 mg/day	3 weeks	Remission rates: 35% on olanzapine versus 11% on placebo. 3.7 kg weight gain on olanzapine. Very significant changes in prolactin, glucose, total cholesterol, hepatic enzymes on olanzapine versus placebo.
Risperidone package insert	10–17	169	Risperidone	0.5–2.5 or 3–6 mg/day	3 weeks	Significant reductions in Young Mania Rating Scale scores on risperidone versus placebo. Doses higher than 2.5 mg/day do not result in higher efficacy.

al., 1999, 2006a, 2006b). As shown in Table 4.3, risperidone is FDA approved for treatment of mania in patients ages 10–17.

Lamotrigine is an anticonvulsant that has been shown to improve maintenance of adult patients with BP and is approved by the FDA for this purpose (Bowden et al., 2003; Calabrese et al., 2003). While it has never been shown to be effective for acute mania, studies show it may be helpful as an adjunct in the treatment of rapid-cycling (Calabrese et al., 2000) and BP depression (Frye et al., 2000; Frye, Altshuler, Szuba, Finch, & Mintz, 1996). A small open trial of lamotrigine was conducted with 20 adolescents with BP depression (Chang, Saxena, & Howe, 2006). Patients were tapered off any antidepressants, but 35% were on other mood-stabilizing medication and 65% had comorbid ADHD. Lamotrigine was gradually titrated over several weeks to a mean dose of 131.6 mg/day. After 8 weeks, there were significant declines in clinician ratings of both mania and depression; 16 patients responded and 11 achieved remission. Since many children and adolescents have mixed mania and rapid cycling, it is possible that lamotrigine will be a useful adjunct, although clinicians must be aware of the risk of Stevens–Johnson syndrome (SJS), a potentially fatal allergic reaction (see Appendix II).

Comparative and combination trials in the treatment of pediatric BP are just beginning to emerge. Biederman et al. (2007a) pooled data from identically designed 8-week open label treatment studies of aripiprazole (n = 19), risperidone (n = 37), olanzapine (n = 17), ziprasidone (n = 21), and quetiapine (n = 22) in the treatment of BP. While each of these were separate studies, the patient groups were similar in age (mean age ~10 years) and baseline clinical severity. All subtypes of BP (including "not otherwise specified") were included. Each agent produced highly significant reductions in mania ratings relative to baseline. When comparing agents, aripiprazole was superior to ziprasidone and quetipine; risperidone was superior to olanzapine, although considerable caution should be exercised here as the studies were not blinded and dosing levels were not designed to be equivalent for each drug. See Appendix II (and Table A6) for discussion of the safety parameters in this study. The authors suggested that overall, risperidone and aripiprazole had an advantage over the other agents. Combining quetiapine with divalproex was superior in treating pediatric BP relative to quetiapine alone (DelBello, Schwiers, Rosenberg, & Strakowski, 2002). Fifty adolescents with BP were randomized to quetiapine (400–600 mg/day) or divalproex (serum level 80–120 µg/ml) for 28 days in a double-blind fashion. The SGA was superior to divalproex in reducing mania ratings and induced a higher remission rate. The difficulty of getting children with BP to achieve remission was illustrated by Findling et al. (2006a), who treated 139 children and adolescents ages 5–17 *concurrently* with lithium and divalproex; 79 subjects dropped out of the study, mostly due to noncompliance or medication intolerance. (Two-thirds of these subjects were taking stimulants for ADHD.) Nineteen subjects deteriorated clinically, leaving only 60 subjects who achieved remission. These subjects were randomized to have either lithium or divalproex removed in a double-blind fashion. There was a marked deterioration in both groups when dual psychopharmacology was discontinued. *This shows that while monotherapy of a mood stabilizer for BP is a useful goal, it is not sufficient for the vast majority of children with this serious disorder.*

Can stimulants be safely combined with mood stabilizers in children with comorbid ADHD and BP? Scheffer, Kowatch, Carmody, and Rush (2005) treated 40 children and adolescents with ADHD and BP with open label divalproex for 8 weeks. Thirty-two subjects achieved clinically significant reduction of their mania symptoms, but only two had resolution of their ADHD. (This also clearly indicates that the ADHD is not an epiphenomenon of the mania.) These subjects underwent a placebo-controlled crossover trial of mixed-salts amphetamine; the stimulant was clearly superior to placebo in reducing inattention symptoms with no evidence that it destabilized mood. As noted earlier, Carlson et al. (2000) demonstrated that boys with ADHD who were at high risk for BP could be safely treated with stimulants. Recently, Findling et al. (2007b) performed a double-blind, placebo-controlled crossover trial of methylphenidate in 19 children with ADHD/BP who were euthymic on mood stabilizers (primarily lithium or divalproex). The stimulant was robustly effective for ADHD, and the patients maintained a euthymic mood. Clinicians face two possible situations in dealing with patients with suspected BP: the child not yet on ADHD medication and the child who presents with a destabilized mood and is currently taking a stimulant or other agent for ADHD.

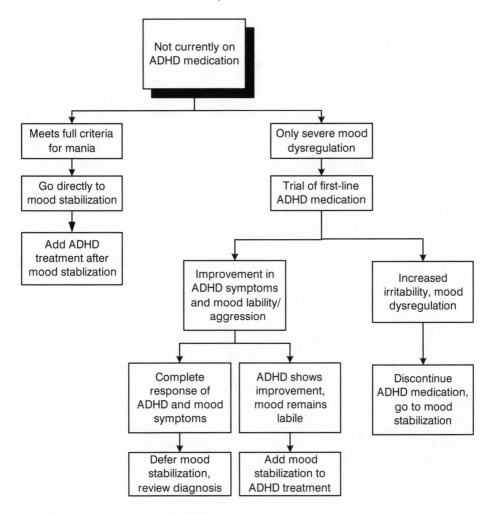

FIGURE 4.2. Decision tree regarding treatment of ADHD in the child with BP not yet on ADHD pharmacotherapy.

Figure 4.2 deals with the child not yet on medication for ADHD. If the child meets full criteria for mania (either of the euphoric or irritable type) and particularly if there are psychotic or major explosive outbursts, then the priority must be mood stabilization. In the vast majority of cases, mood stabilization alone may not treat symptoms of ADHD and this should be pursued once any psychosis has resolved and the child's mood has settled. If the child has primarily mood dysregulation and aggression and the BP diagnosis is more equivocal, then consideration should be given to treating the ADHD first. If mood does become destabilized, the ADHD medication should be discontinued and mood stabilization pursued. If there is remission not only of the ADHD symptoms but the mania symptoms as well, then treatment with mood stabilizers should be deferred; indeed the diagnosis of BP should be reviewed for accuracy at this point. In the majority of these cases of BP not otherwise specified, ADHD symptoms will respond, but the child's mood remains highly labile. In these cases, mood-stabilizing treatment should be added to the ADHD medication.

Figure 4.3 addresses the more thorny issue of how to handle a child with symptoms of mania or severe mood dysregulation when he or she is already on a treatment for ADHD. Here, the key question to ask parents is whether they believe the ADHD medication is helpful. In particular, when the child misses a dose of the stimulant, is there a marked increase in impulsivity and hyperactivity? If the family definitely feels that the ADHD medication is helpful, then it is often prudent to continue the treatment and add mood stabilization. In contrast, if the family no longer sees or has never seen improvement with the ADHD treatment (or is unsure), then the ADHD treatment should be discontinued for 24–72 hours (longer in the case of medication like atomoxetine) and the symptoms of both ADHD and mania observed. If there is an immediate deterioration, the ADHD treatment should be resumed and the mood stabilizers added to it. In contrast, if there is no deterioration or an improvement in mood, the ADHD treatment should be discontinued and the physician should go directly to mood stabili-

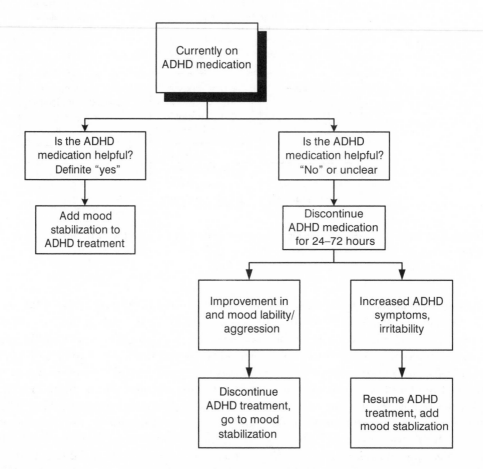

FIGURE 4.3. Decision tree regarding treatment of ADHD in the child with BP currently on ADHD pharmacotherapy.

zation. (This does not preclude the physician reintroducing the ADHD treatment once the child's mood is under control.)

Figure 4.4 addresses mood stabilization itself. This scheme is based on published BP treatment algorithms (Kowatch et al., 2005a), updated with information from recent studies. Physicians may elect to begin monotherapy with either a classic mood stabilizer (lithium or divalproex) or with an SGA. (It must be noted that SGAs must also now be regarded as mood stabilizers; the term no longer applies only to lithium or anticonvulsants.) SGAs should be first line when psychotic symptoms are present. Multiple SGAs should be tried to find one that is most effective for the child. Risperidone, quetiapine, and aripiprazole are generally in the first wave of agents that should be tried, followed by olanzapine (not used first line due to weight gain). Ziprasidone is used second line because of the lack of compelling data for its efficacy in pediatric BP and concerns regarding electrocardiogram (EKG) effects (Appendix II, p. 13). If the child has remission, the continuation phase can begin. If there is only a partial response, a classic mood stabilizer should be added. If remission is not then achieved, then treat with an SGA, lithium, and valproate in combination. Alternatively, the clinician may discontinue the classic mood stabilizer and undertake a trial of lamotrigine. The titration should be gradual, and the serious risk of SJS considered (see Appendix II). If lamotrigine is only partially effective, consideration can be given to adding back the lithium or valproate (in the latter case, the dose of valproate should be reduced and levels monitored carefully).

Table 4.4 shows the medications used in the 121 children and adolescents with BP in our database. Over 70% remain on stimulants and the remaining patients are on other agents for ADHD. Consistent with the above data, the vast majority of patients are on SGAs (82%). Aripiprazole, risperidone, and quetiapine are used about equally; use of ziprasidone and olanzapine is rare. This is most likely due to the need for EKG monitoring in the case of the former and weight issues with the latter. About 12% were on lithium and a quarter on anticonvulsant mood stabilizers. Only 16 (13.2%) were on one medication, 45 (37.1%) were on two medications, 28 (23%) took three medications daily, and another quarter were on four or more medications. The most common combination was a stimulant and an SGA (21.5%), followed by the combination of a stimulant, an SGA, and a mood stabilizer.

Psychosocial Interventions for ADHD and BP

Where to begin? Families with a child with ADHD and BP often feel they are under siege, as the child's functioning is impaired in so many areas (i.e., school, home, and peers). Often a parent suffers from BP or some other serious mental disorder. If the stressors of poverty or marital problems are added, these situations become very volatile. Sadly, due to the chaos in their lives, these families often have difficulty setting aside the time and resources to attend the interventions they need. This leaves a disturbing number of children with ADHD/BP receiving only psychopharmacological treatment. In adults with BP, intensive family-focused psychotherapy is superior to supportive care in achieving end-of-year recovery (64% vs. 52%), shorter time to recovery, and longer periods of being clinically well (Miklowitz et al., 2007). While few controlled trials of psychosocial interventions have been done in pediatric BP, the emerging data

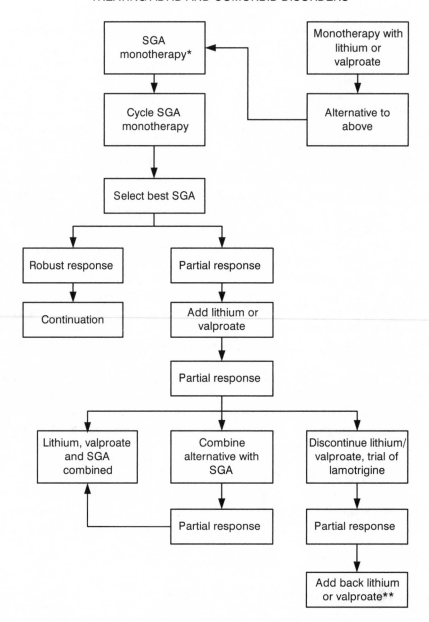

FIGURE 4.4. Algorithm for treatment of BP in children with ADHD. *Risperidone, quetiapine, and aripiprazole should be considered for initial use; olanzapine and ziprasidone, second line. **Extreme caution should be used when combining valproate and lamotrigine.

TABLE 4.4. Medications Used in Children with Comorbid ADHD and BP

Medication type	n (121)	%
Alpha-agonist	7	5.8
SGA	99	81.8
Aripiprazole	22	18.1
Ziprasidone	0	0
Risperidone	28	23.1
Quetiapine	39	32.2
Olanzapine	4	3.3
SSRI	7	5.8
Bupropion	10	8.3
Lithium	15	12.3
Anticonvulsant mood stabilizer	31	25.6
Stimulant	88	72.7
Atomoxetine	10	8.3

Note. SGA, second-generation antipsychotic; SSRI, selective serotonin reuptake inhibitor.

yield similar results. Multifamily group therapy leads to greater knowledge about affective disorders and increased positive family interactions, although negative interactions were not decreased (Fristad, Goldberg-Arnold, & Gavazzi, 2003). An open trial of an adolescent version of the family-focused treatment combined with pharmacotherapy (Miklowitz et al., 2007) in 20 patients with BP showed improvements in mania symptoms and behavior after 21 sessions (Miklowitz et al., 2004).

Mani Pavuluri and David Miklowitz have developed a child- and family-focused cognitive-behavioral therapy (CFF-CBT) designed for treatment of children with BP and their families (Pavuluri et al., 2004a). The program uses the acronym RAINBOW for elements of the program as shown in Box 4.1. Children and families participate in 12 sessions with each session having two to seven topics to cover. The manual is available from the online version of the article in the *Journal of the American Academy of Child and Adolescent Psychiatry* (*www.jaacap.com*). The philosophy of the program is shown in Figure 4.5. The sessions are divided into three phases focusing on different aspects of the disorder. Symptoms are addressed first, with a therapeutic alliance established and the need for predictable routine emphasized. The role of medication is addressed, as well as what medication cannot address. In the second phase, greater understanding of BP by the family is sought, and reference is made to what is hypothesized about the pathophysiology of the disorder. CBT begins in earnest in the next phase, where the *A, I,* and *N* of the RAINBOW become the focus. Finally, environmental stressors are addressed in the third phase, with emphasis on developing good peer relationships. In their open label pilot study, 34 patients stable on medication showed significant reductions in a wide variety of symptoms (Pavuluri et al., 2004a).

The Plan B program (Greene & Ablon, 2006), described in Chapter 3, also works well for children with ADHD/BP as they are highly prone to severe, explosive rages (affective storms). Often, parents of young children with ADHD/BP need to be taught safe techniques for physically redirecting or restraining them during these outbursts in

---

BOX 4.1. The RAINBOW Program for Children with BP and Their Families

R—Routine. Encouraging families to develop a predictable, stable routine; an emphasis is placed on good sleep hygiene.

A—Affect regulation. Parents are encouraged to be positive role models in controlling their tempers and speaking in a level tone of voice. An actual picture of a rainbow is used to help parents and children visualize how to avoid both depressed and manic states.

I—I can do it! The child is encouraged to develop a list of positive self-statements; parents and children write positive scripts about each other's behavior to avoid excessive reactivity.

N—No negative thoughts and live in the "now." Teach families to debrief anger outbursts and move on. The psychoeducational component of RAINBOW teaches families how to differentiate helpful from unhelpful thoughts.

B—Be a good friend and Balanced lifestyle for parents. A major focus is on the development of peer activities. Parents are taught to focus on their own activities, making pie charts that divide up the time they spend at work versus with the children.

O—Oh, how can we solve this problem? Actively teaching problem solving.

W—Ways to get support. During therapy, parents and children draw a support tree that includes ways to get support from extended family and the community. The focus is on reducing the isolation of these families.

Fran Pavuluri et al. (2004a). Copyright 2004 by Wolters Kluwer. Reprinted by permission.

---

order to reduce the chance of injury or of using excessive force. We now review three cases where intensive pharmacotherapy and/or psychosocial interventions were needed to deal with difficult children and teens with ADHD and BP.

The Case of Steve and Sam: Identical Twins with ADHD and BP

Chief Complaint

Sam and Steven are 7-year-old identical twins referred by their pediatrician for aggressive outbursts, extreme silly and inappropriate behavior, and severe insomnia.

History of Presenting Illness

Sam and Steven are 7-year-old identical twins, who had been followed by their pediatrician for ADHD since the age of 4. Both boys had been expelled from their after-school program when they both climbed to the top of the basketball pole and attempted to leap off onto a thin gymnastics mat below. Several times in the previous 3 months, the boys had left the after-care program without permission to wonder up and down the busy street outside. The staff at the day care felt they could no longer assure the boy's safety. The pediatrician referred them to a counselor so that the parents could enhance their behavior management skills. During this initial evaluation, the counselor came to the psychiatrist who was housed in the same clinic and asked for an immediate emergency evaluation. Since the psychiatrist's scheduled evaluation had canceled, the psychiatrist went to the counselor's office to assess the situation. Even before entering the office, the psychiatrist could hear wild laughing and screaming. Upon opening the door, the psychiatrist saw both the mother and father sitting on the floor, a twin in the lap of each one, as they attempted to restrain them. Sam was butting his head against his father's chest, while Steve was singing loudly and intermittently laughing. Toys were strewn about the office and the counselor's lamp had been broken.

The psychiatrist asked the mother to bring Sam into his office, while the father was asked to take Steve into the waiting area, where a video was playing. The psychiatrist obtained a history on both boys from the mother. Their clinical courses were identical, though the mother stated that Sam generally had quantitatively more severe symptoms.

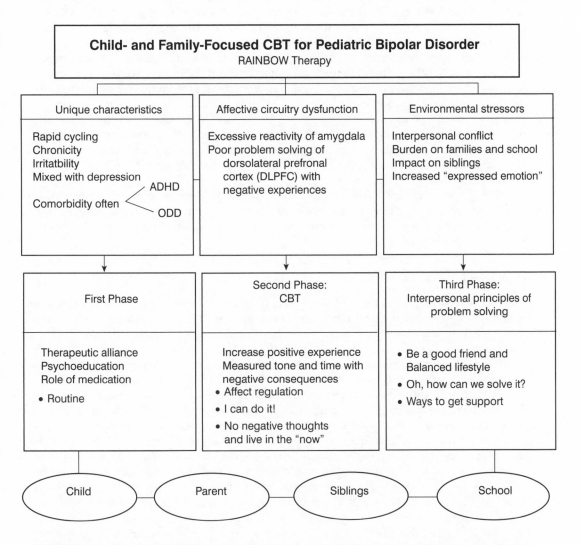

FIGURE 4.5. The RAINBOW model for child- and family-focused cognitive-behavioral therapy (CFF-CBT) for pediatric bipolar disorder. From Pavuluri et al. (2004a). Copyright 2004 by Wolters Kluwer. Reprinted by permission.

Both boys were severely hyperactive from the time they had learned to walk. As toddlers, they were frequently climbing on furniture and running away from her at stores. They would refuse to remain in their car seats, and the mother had received several tickets from the police when one or both of the boys had managed to be out of their car seats while the car was moving. From the age of 2 years on, both boys frequently threw serious tantrums. Sam, in particular, developed the habit of banging his head, and this had remained an ongoing problem. Babysitters and relatives would not stay with the boys, as the slightest frustration led to a prolonged tantrum. Both boys were severely inattentive, and from early childhood could never focus on any play activity for more than a few minutes at a time. Even television shows would not hold their interest. At preschool, the boys were constantly out of their seats, talking out, engaging in dangerous behavior on the playground, and being very aggressive with peers.

Neither boy showed evidence of any delays in language or motor coordination. Both boys were very verbal and talked at an early age. When not having tantrums, both boys were described as "always happy," "like a tornado," and "always smiling and laughing." Their energy level was always high and they frequently engaged in silly and inappropriate joking behavior. They frequently made jokes about breasts, genitalia, and buttocks. It was impossible to get them to take a timeout either at home or school. They were friendly with everyone, but when frustrated by peers they would react angrily and frequently hit other children in school. They played so roughly with their toys that none lasted for very long. The mother denied any auditory or visual hallucinations in the boys. They spoke very rapidly, and she could not reason with them about anything. They appeared to have no awareness of the seriousness of their misbehavior and had no fear of any dangerous situation. As they were fearless, they never showed any evidence of anxiety and the mother denied that they had ever shown any depressive symptoms.

Both boys were very affectionate and bonded well with their parents and older sibling (a 9-year-old sister). They enjoyed the company of other children, but their behavior was frequently overwhelming to peers. There was no evidence of any abnormalities in social interactions suggestive of a PDD.

Past Psychiatric History

The parents had brought the twins to their pediatrician at the age of 3 with concerns about their behaviors. Just after their fourth birthday, the pediatrician initiated a trial of Ritalin 5 mg twice a day for both boys. This appeared to have a modest effect on their behavior. However, as each boy weighed only 36 pounds at the time, it was decided not to increase the dose any further. When they entered kindergarten and had severe difficulties, the Ritalin was increased. This appeared to have no effect and the parents noticed that the boys seemed even more active in the evening when the medication wore off. The boys were started on Adderall XR 5 mg/day, and this was gradually increased over their kindergarten year to 15 mg (the dose they were taking at the time of the psychiatric assessment). During their first-grade year, the parents noted that their sleep was increasingly impaired. This is viewed as a side effect of the stimulant, but it became apparent that the twins were sleeping as little as 5 to 6 hours a night. They frequently would not go to bed until midnight and would be running around the house yelling and screaming for much of the night. The pediatrician added clonidine at bedtime, which was gradually increased to 0.2 mg at bedtime. The parents took the twins to a pediatric neurologist. Neurological examination was within normal limits, and there was no history of any seizure-like symptoms. Nonetheless, an EEG was ordered, and this showed no abnormalities. During the examination, the neurologist noted several behaviors in both boys that he felt were tic-like in nature. He added Risperdal 1 mg at bedtime to the boys' medication regimen.

At school, both boys did very well academically despite the whirlwind of their misbehavior. Their arithmetic and reading abilities were at or above those of their classmates.

Past Medical History

The twins were born at 28 weeks, and they each weighed about 4 pounds. They had breathing difficulties and were slow to feed at first, but had no major perinatal complications such as intracranial bleeding or lung disease. They made good progress in the nursery and went home after 7 weeks. Their infancy was unremarkable; motor and social milestones were all within the normal range. They showed a normal bonding and social ability with parents. The extreme motor activity was the only unusual finding in their preschool years. They had no other concurrent medical illnesses.

Family and Social History

The parents were in their mid-30s and had been married for 12 years. The father worked as an air-conditioning technician, and the mother had worked as a secretary until the birth of the twins. She attempts to work part time but has difficulties because she is constantly being called by the school regarding the twins' misbehavior. The parents described their marriage as stable, although there was constant conflict over the best way to handle the boys. The mother felt that the father sometimes avoided being at home. He often had several beers with his colleagues after work, and he would come home at 8:00 or 9:00 P.M. He was never intoxicated, however, and there was no evidence of any alcohol abuse. Their 9-year-old daughter had no psychiatric problems and was well behaved at school. She frequently had to assist her mother in managing the twins' behavior.

Mental Status Examination

The boys were interviewed separately. Sam was a 7-year-old boy who appeared his stated age. His speech was pressured, and he interrupted the examiner constantly. He could not sit in his chair and answer questions directly but had to be on the floor playing with toys and manipulating objects in the office. He could not even draw a person without stopping to ask irrelevant questions of the examiner. He made good eye contact and smiled broadly throughout the interview. He rhymed words in a silly manner and then laughed at his own jokes. His mood was clearly elevated, and his affect was labile. His thought processes were illogical, and there was evidence of flight of ideas. His reality testing was impaired as he exhibited the strong belief that he could jump off the roof of the house and not be hurt. He denied any suicidal or homicidal ideation. He did not appear to be internally distracted, and he denied that he ever heard voices or saw things.

Steve's mental status examination was quite similar to that of his brother. He also showed pressured speech and flight of ideas. His level of motor activity was not quite as pronounced as that of his brother, and he was able to answer more questions directly.

Both boys weighed 42 pounds at the time of the assessment. Sam's blood pressure was 80/55, while Steve had a systolic blood pressure of 79. It was difficult to hear his diastolic pressure. Both boys had pulses in the 100s.

Treatment Course

The parents were uncertain if the Adderall was being effective for the boys' severe hyperactivity. The possible interaction of the Risperdal and clonidine was discussed with the parents, particularly in view of the low blood pressures that were obtained. Because it was uncertain if the stimulant was being effective, it was decided to discontinue it. It was also decided to stop the clonidine as the psychiatrist felt that the poor sleep was part of the manic syndrome. The Risperdal was increased to 1 mg twice a day in the hope of achieving full mood stabilization. Several days later, the psychiatrist received a phone call informing him that both boys were drooling and seemed to be excessively sluggish mentally. The Risperdal was discontinued, and they were started on Seroquel 25 mg twice a day. After several weeks off the Adderall, the teacher reported that their hyperactivity and impulsivity remained a significant problem. However, the parents felt the Adderall really had not been that effective. It was elected to begin a trial of Concerta 18 mg in the morning, in combination with the Seroquel 25 mg twice a day. Several weeks went by, and the psychiatrist had not heard from the family when they came for the follow-up visit. The psychiatrist discovered that the parents had restarted the clonidine on their own. The boys' blood pressures were stable and improved over the previous readings. The parents were again warned about possible interactions between Seroquel and clonidine, and psychoeducation was undertaken to help them understand that the poor sleep was due to the mania. The parents were, however, quite insistent that the boys would not sleep if they did not have the clonidine. The boys' Seroquel dose was changed to 25 mg in the morning and 25 mg mid-afternoon at school. This was done to prevent any additive effect of Seroquel and clonidine being given together at night. Since the ADHD symptoms had not fully improved, the Concerta was increased to 27 mg in the morning. At the follow-up 1 month later, the parents reported considerable improvement. There had been no further risk-taking behavior and the activity level had declined to a manageable level. In the office, both boys could now sit quietly and play with toys on the floor while the psychiatrist spoke with the parents. Their speech was significantly less pressured, and they were able to answer questions appropriately. And while they were still "night owls," they were sleeping at least 7 hours a night.

About 4 months went by, with the boys exhibiting generally stable behavior. When the psychiatrist arrived at the clinic one morning, he found the mother and both boys already waiting. They had an appointment for 3 P.M., but Sam had been up all night the night before. The mother was sitting on the floor of the waiting room, and to the horror of other parents, she was restraining Sam, who was again head-butting her. The psychiatrist took the mother and twins into the office and learned that the mother had discontinued her sessions with the counselor when she thought the medication was working well. She acknowledged that Sam had missed a few doses of Seroquel. Both boys' vital signs were stable. Steve was actually doing quite well, so it was elected to increase Sam's Seroquel to 25 mg in the morning and 50 mg at mid-afternoon. The psychiatrist consulted with the counselor, and an appointment was made for the family later in the week.

The counselor undertook a course of sessions using the RAINBOW model. The counselor had an intern from a local university master's level program working with him. The intern took the boys off to work on play skills. The intern was instructed to gradually wean them away from videogames and crashing trucks together to do more calming activities such as board games and playing cooperatively with each other. The counselor asked both parents to come to the session. A behavior management plan was implemented. The parents at first resisted, saying these schemes had not worked in the past, but the need for a predictable routine was emphasized. They were counseled that since the mood stabilization had been achieved, the behavior management program would be much more likely to succeed. They were encouraged to enroll the boys in soccer. Since both boys were so verbal and expansive in their mood, it was also suggested that they be enrolled in a local children's theater provided their behavior was not disruptive to the production.

At school, an admission, review, and dismissal (ARD) committee was held; both boys qualified for special education based on their ADHD status. They could be pulled out of the mainstream classroom for brief periods of time when their behavior became too erratic, and they were allowed to complete their work in a quiet room. With these interventions, their behavior was improved, although they were far from complete remission. They continued to have one to two aggressive outbursts a week at home, but they were no longer aggressive at school. While they did well in the children's theater program, they were unable to stay on the soccer team as they would act silly and run around the field rather than focus on the game. After the initial 10 sessions of the RAINBOW program, the counselor attempted to see them at least twice a month to maintain their gains. The psychiatrist saw them every 3 months. Vital signs remained stable, there was no abnormal weight gain, and their serum lipids and glucose remained within normal limits. The psychiatrist continues to speak with the family about reducing the evening clonidine.

The above case illustrates how the combination of treatment for ADHD and monotherapy with an SGA can be quite effective. The concomitant use of psychotherapy focusing on peer relationships, affect regulation, and parent training was critical to achieving success in this case. In other cases, the medication regimen may need to be much more complex, as shown below.

The Case of David: Severe Mood Dysregulation ("Mood Disorder Not Otherwise Specified"), Obsessions, and Obesity

Chief Complaint

Needs a psychiatrist who can prescribe medication.

History of Presenting Illness

David is an 8-year-old boy whose family had moved to the city recently; they were in need of a psychiatrist to continue their child's medication for mood disorder not otherwise specified and anxiety disorder. In addition, David had not adjusted to the move very well. He was very aggressive at both home and school, and while he was naturally big and muscular for his age he had gained even more weight on an SGA. As a result, even when David was not particularly angry, he frightened both peers and teachers because of his size. He had overturned a desk in school when told that he had not done a problem correctly. He had pushed a boy down on the playground, and while he had not intended to hurt him, the momentum with which he pushed the child resulted in an injury. He was suspended from school for 3 days. The parents stated that David was in a bad mood nearly all the time. He only seemed happy when playing his computer games; otherwise, he sat in a chair with an angry look on his face and would refuse any suggestions to do fun things at home. He was particularly irritable and aggressive with his sister, hitting her several times a week. The family went out of their way to avoid upsetting David. David was highly impulsive, often saying things before he thought about it, but he was not hyperactive. The parents also felt some of the decline in his activity level was due to his weight gain. David would argue with both his parents and his teachers; he not only did not show respect for them but seemed to be unaware of any need to do so. He expected to interact with adults as peers. He often stated that he knew the answers to problems when he clearly did not.

On his current medications (see below) David did not exhibit any rapid speech, elated mood, inappropriate sexual behavior, or other risk-taking behaviors. The parents denied any psychotic symptoms.

Past Psychiatric History

David first began experiencing symptoms of ADHD in kindergarten. He was also noted by his kindergarten teacher to be highly oppositional, behavior that he also displayed at home. He would not remain in the reading circle and never wanted to do the activity the class was engaged in. His behavior was in striking contrast to that of his younger sister, who was an excellent student in her prekindergarten program. The parents took David to their pediatrician, who started him on Adderall 10 mg XR in the morning. He had a robust response to the Adderall, and this was continued over the course of the kindergarten year. David grew quickly, and the dose was gradually increased to 40 mg XR in the morning. In first and second grade, David's behavior began to deteriorate again, and he became increasingly irritable and aggressive. He would scream, "I hate you" at teachers, and his parents noted that his mood became worse and worse. The pediatrician referred them to a child psychiatrist, who initially made a diagnosis of mood disorder not otherwise specified. The psychiatrist prescribed Risperdal 1 mg twice a day. in combination with the Adderall. Over the course of the second-grade year, it was noted that David's weight gain was substantial, leading to gradual increases in both medications, such that by the age of 8, David was taking 60 mg of Adderall XR in the morning and 2 mg of Risperdal twice a day.

When David entered the third grade, a number of obsessive behaviors were noted by his parents and teachers. He would write the same word on his paper multiple times. He would insist that the pencils in his desk line up exactly with each other. He would talk obsessively about video game characters, often telling the same story to his parents over and over again. The psychiatrist added Celexa 20 mg in the morning, reasoning that these symtoms were suggestive of obsessive–compulsive disorder. The obsessive symptoms did seem to decline, and there were no reports of increased manic behavior. At this point in his second-grade year, the parents moved to a new city. At the time of his presentation to the new psychiatrist, his medications were Adderall XR 60 mg a day, Celexa 20 mg a day, and Risperdal 2 mg three times a day. His weight was 75 pounds and his height was 48 inches, placing him in the 90th percentile for weight. The parents reported that they were concerned about his behavior and felt that the current medication regimen was not effective.

Past Medical History

David had asthma, for which he used an inhaler on an as-needed basis. He had never been hospitalized for an asthma attack. Developmental milestones were all within normal limits. At a previous school David had undergone psychological testing that showed an IQ in the average range and achievement that was consistent with his intellectual functioning. There was no evidence of any learning disabilities.

Mental Status Examination

David was a moderately obese 8-year-old boy. His motor activity in the office was reduced, rate of speech was within normal limits, and his vocabulary was appropriate. He related well to the examiner but generally did not elaborate on any answers to questions and minimized his problems considerably. He claimed not to be aware of the fact that he had been suspended. His mood was neither elevated nor depressed, but his affect was appropriate to thought content. His thought was logical and goal directed, and there was no evidence of flight of ideas. He denied any auditory or visual hallucinations. His intellectual functioning was average. He did not see his strong interest in computer characters or the need to align his pencils as problematic in any way. He showed no insight whatsoever into his behavior. He denied suicidal or homicidal ideation.

Treatment Course

As David was clearly not in remission, it was elected to make some changes to the medication regimen. The parents were quite certain that the Adderall was effective. They stated that when other physicians had attempted to reduce the dose or if they accidentally missed a dose, David was much more irritable, impulsive, and explosive. The psychiatrist raised the question of the Celexa and whether it was an appropriate medication for a child with BP. The parents were made aware of the mood destabilizing effects of antidepressants. It was decided to taper David off the Celexa and transition him from Risperdal to Abilify. It was hoped that the Abilify would be more weight neutral. A follow-up appointment was scheduled for 2 weeks, and a list of local therapists who worked with children with BP was given to the family. Roughly a week after the initial evaluation, the parents called to state that the obsessions had gotten markedly worse and that their child was far more aggressive on the Abilify. The parents had discontinued the Abilify on their own and restarted the Risperdal. Because they wanted David to "catch up" on his dose, they gave him 4 mg at one time. The parents described stiffness and drooling. The parents were directed to their family physician, who was able to see them and give David a shot of diphenhydramine. The extrapyramidal symptoms resolved. The psychiatrist pointed out that the parents had said the Risperdal had not been effective, so rather than restart the Risperdal, a trial of Seroquel was undertaken. Seroquel was started at 25 mg twice a day and gradually increased to 100 mg twice a day. However, after about 2 weeks on this dose, the parents again restarted the Risperdal on their own at a dose of 2 mg twice a day. They also had restarted the Celexa.

This case points out some of the difficulties in establishing a therapeutic alliance with families of children with severe BP. Well-meaning parents of children with BP frequently alter their child's regimen without discussing it with the physician. While the physician should always discourage this practice, it generally does little good to insist that they use a medication regimen with which they are not comfortable. The physician must seek a balance between being flexible with parents and setting limits so that the child is not endangered.

Treatment Course, Continued

The patient was now back on his original doses of Adderall XR 60 mg in the morning, Risperdal 2 mg twice a day, and Celexa 20 mg in the morning. The parents stated that while this was not satisfactory, it was still better than what the new psychiatrist had tried so far. Having cycled through several SGAs, the psychiatrist determined that it was not useful to try any other SGAs. Due to David's weight problem, olanzapine was not considered. After discussion with the parents, it was decided to add Depakote to David's regimen. The dose was titrated up to 375 mg/day; therapeutic levels were achieved, but the parents noted further increase in appetite. They also did not notice any change in David's explosiveness and irritability. The trial of Depakote was deemed a failure, and he was tapered off this medication. David's mood symptoms were further explored, in particular his dark, pessimistic, and irritable mood. David did not show any evidence of MDD. He had no suicidal ideation, he rarely cried, and never made negative comments about himself. He did state that he thought he would never have any friends or be able to control his temper. Thus, given the dysphoric nature of David's mood symptoms, it was decided to undertake a trial of Lamictal. David was started on 25 mg a day of Lamictal, and this was gradually increased over the course of several months to 100 mg in the morning and 100 mg in the evening. In general, the parents reported improvement; his aggressive outbursts in particular declined markedly. He was not suspended at all during his third- and fourth-grade years. He stopped hitting his sister though he continued to say very mean things to her.

Throughout this period, David continued to gain weight. At a follow-up session, the psychiatrist found that the parents had increased the Risperdal to 4 mg twice a day. Since this coincided with the period that the Lamictal had been at therapeutic levels, it confounded the situation somewhat. It was also of concern to the psychiatrist that this high dose of Risperdal would not only increase weight gain but was now at a level where it might be functioning as a typical antipsychotic. Potential risks of tardive dyskinesia were discussed with the parents. The parents acknowledged the risks but felt that David was functioning so much better, they did not want to make any changes to the medication regimen. Their desires were documented in the chart, and they were told that no further increase in Risperdal would be permissible (i.e., the psychiatrist would not refill any higher dose of this medication). On physical exam, David did not show any evidence of extrapyramidal symptoms and his Abnormal Involuntary Movement Scale (AIMS) score was zero.

The weight gain remained a serious issue. At the age of 10, David's BMI was 31. David's trigylcerides were 205 µg/dl (upper limit of normal, 129) and his total cholesterol was 195 µg/dl (upper limit of normal 170). The family joined a local gym and tried to encourage David to use the exercise machines and swim; they also substantially changed their home diet and avoided eating at fast-food restaurants. David was seen in individual therapy by a psychologist. David was very difficult to work with, however, as he exhibited extreme lack of insight. He simply stated that he had nothing to talk about and everything was fine. The psychologist counseled the parents on behavior management techniques and they proved to be quite knowledgeable about these. Indeed their daughter's excellent behavior showed their competence as parents. David showed no interest in sports or other activities with other children. He showed no desire for peer relationships and mainly wished to play his computer games. His academic performance remains adequate. Thus, while David's behavior is stable, there are considerable concerns for both his physical health and psychological adjustment in the long term.

The Case of Sally: Status Manicus?

Chief Complaint

Sexually inappropriate behavior.

History of Presenting Illness

Sally is a 10-year-old girl who was taken into state custody by child protective services (CPS) because of neglectful supervision by her mother. CPS had a long history of involvement with the family. Her biological father had been accused of sexually molesting her when she was 6 years old; he had also sexually abused his older daughter. He was prosecuted, spent 1 year in jail, and was prohibited from returning to the household. CPS suspected that the father was sneaking back to the house to visit the mother and that the mother left the children unattended while she met the father outside the house. CPS received another referral from a neighbor of the family who reported that Sally had attempted to engage in sex play with her daughter. When CPS arrived to investigate, the house was in a shambles and the mother was not present. Sally, her 12-year-old sister, and her 5-year-old brother were at home alone. The children had missed multiple days of school. The 5-year-old reported to the caseworker that Sally had touched him on his private parts. The children were taken to a shelter and when the mother was located, she was found to be intoxicated. She admitted to having been with the biological father of the children, and she tested positive for marijuana.

The children were removed from the home and placed in the local children's shelter. Sally's brother and sister adjusted well to life in the shelter, but Sally presented serious problems to the shelter workers. She was aggressive and threw temper tantrums at the slightest frustration. She talked nonstop and often would not answer questions but would converse about some totally unrelated subject. She only slept 3 to 4 hours a night at the shelter. She told the shelter workers that her mother had a vibrator and Sally enjoyed using it herself. The next night Sally was found trying to sneak into a peer's room, and it was decided that she was a danger to the other children at the facility. She was transferred to a residential treatment center for intensive intervention.

Past Psychiatric History

Upon arrival at the residential treatment center, Sally was taking Focalin XR 30 mg/day and Seroquel 25 mg in the morning and 50 mg at night. These medications had been prescribed at a local community mental health center where Sally's mother had taken her. It was unclear how compliant the family had been with these medications. No medical records were available to document any treatment prior to this. The caseworker revealed that Sally had significant difficulties at school and produced a psychological evaluation from the school district that showed a Full Scale IQ of 88. It was noted, however, that Sally's Verbal IQ was 80 and her Nonverbal IQ was 110, a clinically significant difference. She also was significantly delayed in reading, for which she had received special education support at school. Prior to Sally being taken into custody, the school had plans to move her to a special self-contained behavior unit because of her severe disruptive behavior at school. The school also reported that Sally had been sexually inappropriate with peers during recess.

Past Medical History

Sally was generally in good health but suffered from severe enuresis, which had never been treated.

Mental Status Examination

Sally was a very cute, engaging 10-year-old girl who was small for her age. Her activity level was extremely increased during the interview. At times, she stood on her head in the chair, or rolled around on the floor, and she required constant redirection. Her speech was pressured, and she talked nearly nonstop. It was virtually impossible for the examiner to get her to answer specific questions. When she was asked what kinds of things she was good at, she replied, "I am strong, bong, wong," and then laughed for several seconds. Her mood was extremely elated and her affect labile. Her vocabulary was appropriate for age; she was alert and oriented to person, place, and time. Her intellectual functioning was judged to be average, consistent with her psychological testing. Her thought processes were illogical and exhibited significant flight of ideas. She reported that she heard voices at various times. The voices were multiple people telling her it was okay to do bad things. She denied any suicidal or homicidal ideation. She had very limited insight, and at times during the interview she denied that she had any problems.

Treatment Course

The staff of the residential treatment center also reported severe anger outbursts. She was being restrained one to three times a day and had already been suspended from the campus school. Given the severe manic symptoms, there were concerns about the very high dose of Focalin she was taking. The psychiatrist elected to discontinue this medication. The staff did not report any increase in hyperactivity and indeed reported that there was a very slight improvement in her ability to sit still and answer questions. The Seroquel was gradually increased to 150 mg twice a day; however, there was no reduction of her manic symptoms. At her weight of 75 pounds, the psychiatrist did not feel further dose titration would be appropriate. The Seroquel was discontinued and she was given a trial of Abilify 5 mg in the morning, which was gradually increased over several weeks to 10 mg. The hallucinations stopped, and Sally was somewhat more logical in her thought processes, but she remained aggressive and oppositional. In between aggressive outbursts, her affect remained silly and inappropriate. Depakote ER 250 mg was added to the Abilify, and this was increased to a dose of 750 mg at bedtime in order to achieve a therapeutic level of 92 µg/liter. This regimen was maintained through the first 3 months of Sally's stay in the residential treatment center. Staff continued to report severe manic behavior including getting up in the middle of the night and trying to enter other children's rooms. Trazodone 50 mg at bedtime was added to assist with sleep difficulties.

On examination, Sally's affect remained extremely labile. A urologist had examined her and not found any physiological reason for her enuresis. The urologist prescribed DDAVP as the principal treatment. Given that Sally had not responded to the combination of the Abilify and Depakote, several options were explored. One possibility was to continue to cycle the SGAs. She had not had trials of Risperdal or Geodon. The staff did feel that there had been about a 20% improvement in her symptoms overall and she had not voiced any psychotic symptoms in many months. Thus, there was a reluctance to abandon the Abilify, and given the highly euphoric nature of Sally's symptoms, a trial of lithium was initiated. The dose was ultimately increased to 750 mg a day and she achieved a serum level of 0.9 mEq/liter. The staff did note a marked improvement in her manic symptoms on this combination. She was more settled both at home and at school, and the number of restraints declined. Unfortunately, there was a marked increase in her enuresis. Her sheets were drenched every morning. The increase in bedwetting paralleled exactly the initiation of the lithium and it had to be discontinued as she was already on a maximum dose of DDAVP. There was an immediate increase in her aggressive outbursts and labile mood. At this point, the seriousness of her symptoms were discussed with her caseworker. A trial of Lamictal was suggested and the risks of SJS were laid out. Over several weeks, she was gradually titrated to a dose of 50 mg twice a day. Because of the increasing severity of her behavior, the Abilify was increased to 20 mg once a day.

After 4 weeks on this regimen, staff and teachers noticed a marked improvement. Her serious behavioral incidents declined from one to three a day to one to two a week. She began to progress in the cabin behavior management program, earning "green pins" in substantial numbers. She remained very active and her mood continued to be mildly elevated, but her thought processes became more logical. She began to participate more meaningfully in psychotherapy. Given the hypersexuality caused by mania, it was not felt wise to focus on her past sexual abuse, although it was surely a contributing factor. Sally knew her brother and sister were in a foster home, and she was motivated to join them. Again using the RAINBOW model, there was a greater focus on ways to control her anger and see things from others' point of view. She received special education support for her reading difficulties. As her mood continues to stabilize, consideration might be given to another trial of medication for ADHD, as inattentiveness and impulsivity remain problematic.

In each of these three cases, severe symptoms of mood lability, aggression, or psychosis presented serious challenges. Careful use of a medication algorithm (Figures 4.2–4.4) led to implementation of medication regimens that stabilized mood and reduced aggression. Complete remission was rarely obtained, but sufficient symptom reduction occurred that social functioning was substantially improved. Psychosocial interventions helped these children to develop positive skills to employ once their symptoms were causing less impairment. This completes our review of "overt" symptoms, such as oppositional behvior, aggression, and mood lability. The next two chapters shift to the less well studies "internalizing" disorder of depression and anxiety.

Chapter 5

Depressive Disorders

The Hidden Comorbidity

Much of the discussion of ADHD and comorbid disorders in the last decade has sur-rounded the contentious issues of aggression and BP, which we dealt with in the two previous chapters. Severe aggression and mood lability are far more likely to present as emergencies, thus demanding attention from the clinician. Depression may present as emergent in the face of suicidal ideation, but until then it may remain hidden from clinical view. Regrettably, this is true in terms of research findings—in comparison to the volumes written on aggression and BP in ADHD, relatively few studies have focused on depression in patients with ADHD. Clinical and epidemiological studies have shown substantial overlap between ADHD and depression, but the degree of overlap is highly variable. Up to a third of children with ADHD may meet criteria for depression, while 25–50% of children with depression have ADHD (Angold & Costello, 1993; Pliszka et al., 1999). Eleven percent of the MTA sample meet criteria for major depressive disorder (MDD; MTA Cooperative Group, 1999b), while 40% of a sample of girls with ADHD were significantly depressed (Biederman et al., 1999a). On the other hand, some stud-ies show no overlap at all between ADHD and depression (McGee et al., 1990). Why the disagreement? Some of the principal reasons why researchers and clinicians struggle with this issue follow.

Parent and Child Disagreement on Presence or Absence of Depressive Symptoms

Since parents and children have such low agreement on the presence of depressive symptoms (Bird et al., 1992), studies will vary greatly on the prevalence of depression depending on whether the diagnosis was based on reports of parent, child, or both. Cli-nicians tend to develop a "gut" feeling for which interview is more reliable in individual cases. Attempts can be made to get information from outside the family; however, if the depressive symptoms are not visible to the parent, they are less likely to be visible to teachers or youth leaders.

Child's Ability to Verbalize Symptoms

Research on child depression has taken the adult criteria of DSM-IV and applied them to children and adolescents with little modification, thus depression research has lacked a developmental focus. Based on clinical experience, the manner in which children express depression varies greatly across different ages. Withdrawal and lethargy occur in infants ("anaclitic" depression), while protesting and clinging (often due to disruption in the caretaker relationship) predominate in toddlerhood. Preschoolers may begin to articulate an abnormal mood state—they will use one word (often "bad") to express a wide range of negative mood states (e.g., sadness, boredom, anger, or physical discomfort). Only by the early school years can children discriminate "sad" and "mad," but they often need help from adults in doing so. The process is further hampered if the child has ADHD and is not used to reflecting on his or her own feelings. Take this interview with a fidgety 6-year-old being evaluated for ADHD and possible depression:

> INTERVIEWER : Are you feeling happy today?
>
> CHILD : Yes.
>
> INTERVIEWER : Do you ever feel sad?
>
> CHILD : Yes.
>
> INTERVIEWER : What makes you feel that way?
>
> CHILD : When Joey takes my toys.
>
> INTERVIEWER : What other things make you sad?
>
> CHILD : When my sister hits me.
>
> INTERVIEWER : Does she hit you a lot?
>
> CHILD : Yeah.
>
> INTERVIEWER : Does she hit you every day?
>
> CHILD : No (*beginning to fidget off the couch*).
>
> INTERVIEWER : Did she hit you today or yesterday?
>
> CHILD : No, it was a long time ago.
>
> INTERVIEWER : Most days, do you feel happy or sad?
>
> CHILD : Sad, 'cause Joey won't give back my hotwheels.

Young children tie their feelings to immediate events and are unable to quantify how long they have felt a certain emotion. Information about the amount and timing of symptoms needs to be gathered from parents.

Irritability versus Sadness (Mad or Sad?)

As in the above example, young children are easily confused between "sad" or "mad." Asking a child to list some of the things that make them "sad" is helpful, because if every single event is a frustrating one (e.g., losing a privilege, fighting with a sibling, receiving a timeout, getting homework), the clinician should be suspicious about whether the child is really describing anger. Attention to the child's facial expression and tone of voice are key. Are these nonverbal signs consistent with sadness, or does the child manifest a mainly angry affect? If the child reports events in his or her life such as a missing parent, a sibling's illness, or being called names and furthermore if the child's face is downcast or he or she is tearful, then a sad mood is more likely the right call. Older children and teens have less difficulty making the sad–mad distinction, but the parent interview may add another source of confusion. The child may have opposi-tional behavior and anger outbursts that the parent describes as depression. This may occur for two reasons: (1) the parents have educated themselves about depression and have read that "irritability" is a sign of depression and apply this concept too broadly or (2) the parents ask themselves, "Why is our child acting this way?", and conclude that depression is an an overall explanation. If the parent describes only oppositional behavior and temper outbursts, with no prolonged irritability or neurovegetative signs, then a diagnosis of depression would not be appropriate. This is particularly true if there is a complete absence of depressive symptoms in the child interview. Chapter 2 (Figure 2.2) discussed the differential diagnosis of irritability, as it is important to note that irritability by itself does not discriminate children with ADHD from those with ADHD/MDD (Diler et al., 2007).

The Either–Or Dilemma

In many research studies, a symptom of depression is regarded as present if either the parent or the child endorses it. The question becomes whether one should "add" the different symptoms to get a diagnosis of MDD. For instance, the child may say that she is sad and has trouble sleeping. The parent may deny that the child is sad but state that the child has threatened self-harm, doesn't eat well, and makes negative comments about herself. If the clinician adds these symptoms, then the child clearly meets crite-ria for MDD. In interviews such as the K-SADS, a more subtle approach is followed— separate ratings are assessed for the parent and child for each depressive symptom. The clinician integrates the two interviews, determining the presence or absence of the symptoms based on synthesis of the two sets of interviews, rather than simple addition of symptoms. This is the approach that the interview in Appendix I uses, the final diag-nosis being based on parent report (for number and timing of symptoms) and child report (for current mood state, depressive cognitions, and suicidal ideation).

Categorical versus Dimensional Approaches to Measuring Depression

DSM-IV is by definition categorical. The diagnosis of MDD is made when a child has a pervasive depressed or irritable mood *and* meets four of the seven "B" criteria (neu-rovegetative signs, suicidal ideation, etc.). If a child falls just below those criteria but has impairing symptoms, he or she is often diagnosed as having "depressive disorder not otherwise specified." In contrast, there is a continuous range of depressive symptoms in children that can be assessed by rating scales. A child with ADHD can have a higher than normative number of depressive symptoms without meeting criteria for MDD or dysthymia per se. While there is, in fact, good correspondence between parent-rated CBCL depressive symptoms and interview-derived diagnosis of depression (Biederman, Mick, & Faraone, 1998), Blackman, Ostrander, and Herman (2005) found that a third of their sample of children with ADHD were in the clinical range on the self-rating Chil-dren's Depression Inventory alone. Only 10% of the sample met criteria for depression on *both* the self-rating and the clinician-structured interview. To avoid overdiagnosis by using self-ratings alone, the interview in Appendix I uses a hybrid approach, combining the quantitative number of symptoms reported by the child with the structured MDD criteria assessed through parent report.

Overlap of Some MDD Criteria with ADHD (Psychomotor Agitation, Poor Concentration)

It is possible that an artificial overlap of ADHD and MDD could occur because some symptoms are common to both disorders. For instance, a child with ADHD might be irritable (due to comorbid ODD), have poor concentration, and appear agitated. If these are subtracted from the list of MDD criteria, the child might no longer meet criteria for the depressive disorder. Biederman, Faraone, Mick, and Leleon (1995a) controlled statistically for this overlap in their sample of over 400 consecutively referred clinic children, and the overlap of ADHD and MDD was not significantly reduced.

Are Children with ADHD and Depression Simply "Demoralized"?

Another source of artifactual overlap is that patients with ADHD may experience a lifetime of frustrations and negative interactions that cause them to "give up," become pessimistic, and develop low self-esteem rather than develop a true depressive episode (Biederman et al., 1998). It has been shown, however, that when children with ADHD have comorbid depression, the ADHD and MDD have independent courses: ADHD severity is not related to severity of MDD and MDD often remits even if the ADHD does not (Biederman et al., 1998). All this is inconsistent with the idea that the comorbidity of ADHD and depression is due to diagnostic criteria overlap.

How Do Depression and ADHD Affect Each Other?

In children with ADHD and MDD, the mean age of onset of ADHD (~4 years) was significantly earlier than that of MDD (~8 years) (Biederman et al., 1995a). Data from a large epidemiological study of depressed adolescents showed that the disruptive behavior disorders preceded the onset of the affective disorder in 72% of the cases (Rohde, Lewinsohn, & Seeley, 1991). In the Isle of Wight study over three decades ago (Rutter, Tizard, & Whitmore, 1970), children with "conduct disorders" were compared to those with "emotional disorders" as well as to a group of children with "mixed disorders." Children in the "mixed" category had symptoms of both conduct and emotional problems; given the British diagnostic system of the time, a large number of the children with CD would have met criteria for ADHD. When the "mixed" children were compared to the other groups, they appeared much more similar to the "pure" CD group than to the "emotional disorder" group in terms of symptom severity, family variables, and the degree of reading disorders (Biederman et al., 1995a).

How does ADHD affect the expression of depression (Kovacs, Feinberg, Crouse-Novack, Paulauskas, & Finkelstein, 1984; Kovacs, Paulauskas, Gatsonis, & Richards, 1988)? Comorbid ADHD does not affect recovery rates from depression (Kovacs, Akiskal, Gatsonis, & Parrone, 1994). There are conflicting findings as to whether the co-occurrence of ADHD in MDD increases the risk for suicide completion over MDD-only youth. Suicide completers were found to have an 18% prevalence of ADHD compared to a 5% rate in suicidal inpatients, though the difference did not reach statistical significance (Brent et al., 1988). Further studies did not show any relationship between ADHD and suicide attempts or completions (Brent et al., 1993b, 1993c). In contrast, the combination of impulsive–aggressive personality disorder and MDD does substantially increase the risk of suicide (Brent et al., 1993a, 1994; Kovacs, Goldston, & Gatsonis, 1993). Thus, the risk of suicide in the child with ADHD/MDD is *not* increased over the risk in a child with MDD alone, but a child with "triple" comorbidity (ADHD/MDD/CD) *is* at such increased risk (James, Lai, & Dahl, 2004). More recently, Biederman et al. (2008a) completed a 5-year follow-up of girls with ADHD and matched controls; the sample had a mean age of 12 years at the time of the baseline assessment and 18 years at follow-up. In this study, there was a strikingly high rate of MDD in the females with ADHD (65%) versus the controls (21%). Both ADHD and MDD produced independent degrees of impairment in a wide range of areas of functioning. Comparing girls with MDD alone to those with ADHD/MDD, the comorbid group has an earlier onset of depression, longer depressive episodes, more psychiatric hospitalizations, and more suicide attempts.

Blackman et al. (2005) compared their sample of depressed and nondepressed children with ADHD to healthy controls on a variety of measures. Depressed children with ADHD were not different from nondepressed subjects in terms of hyperactivity, conduct problems, or aggression, but they did have greater problems with social competence. Parents and teachers of depressed children with ADHD rated them as having poorer social skills than nondepressed children with ADHD, and the depressed children rated themselves as less popular. As discussed in Chapter 2, ODD/CD is often a gateway to depression (Burke et al., 2005). In younger children with ADHD, those with and without comorbid ODD/CD do not differ in depressive symptoms (although children with ADHD have elevated depressive symptoms compared to controls). However, as children age those with ADHD/ODD show greater depression than children with ADHD alone (Ostrander, Crystal, & August, 2006). An intriguing pathway may link ODD, family environment, and self-esteem in the development of depression (Drabick, Gadow, & Sprafkin, 2006; Ostrander et al., 2006). In children with ADHD, family environments characterized by low cohesion, high family conflict, and low marital satisfaction were related to the development of *both* ODD and depression (Drabick et al., 2006). About half of the depression in younger children with ADHD was predicted by parent/teacher appraisal of low social competence, while depression in older children with ADHD was better predicted by the child's own sense of low social competence (Ostrander et al., 2006). Before flushing this relationship out further, we need to look at some of the family history studies of depression and ADHD.

Family Studies

In addition to the higher than expected prevalence of depression in patients with ADHD, there is a much greater than expected rate of ADHD among children of depressed parents, as shown in Figure 5.1. As can be seen, 5 out of 8 studies (Beardslee et al., 1988; Biederman et al., 2001, 2006; Grigoroiu-Serbanescu et al., 1991; Hammen, Burge, Bur-

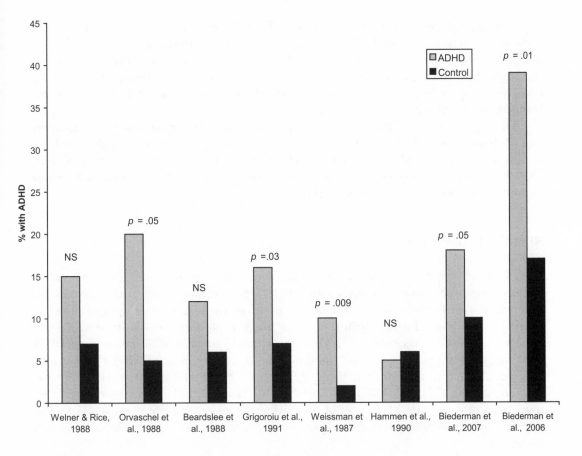

FIGURE 5.1. Prevalence of ADHD in the children of depressed parents. Adapted from Faraone and Biederman (1997). Copyright 1997 by Wolters Kluwer. Reprinted by permission.

ney, & Adrian, 1990; Orvaschel, Walsh-Allis, & Ye, 1988; Weissman et al., 1984; Welner & Rice, 1988) show depressed parents to have a higher prevalence of ADHD among their children than control parents. Pooling data from studies up to 1991, Faraone and Biederman (1997) found that 12.4% of children of depressed parents had ADHD, compared with 6.6% of the children of nondepressed parents, a significant difference. The last two studies in the figure (Biederman et al., 2001, 2006) involved the same sample; the later study followed up the subjects 5 years later. These two studies also examined disruptive behavior disorders without separating out ADHD from ODD/CD.

The patterns of genetic risk for ADHD and MDD were assessed by examining the rate of both ADHD and MDD in the relatives of boys with ADHD alone, boys with comorbid ADHD/MDD, and healthy controls (Biederman et al., 1992). Both MDD and ADHD were elevated in the relatives of the boys with ADHD, but the disorders did not cosegregate in relatives, indicating that comorbid ADHD/MDD in boys was not a separate genetic subtype. A different genetic pattern emerged when a similar study was done with girls (Mick, Biederman, Santangelo, & Wypij, 2003). In girls with both ADHD and MDD, the two disorders did tend to cosegregate, indicating a distinct genetic subtype. This would mean that genes and environment play different roles in MDD and ADHD depending on gender. In boys, ADHD and MDD share familial factors, and perhaps some environmental factor leads to the development of ADHD alone versus ADHD/MDD. In girls, those with ADHD alone and ADHD/MDD are genetically distinct from the beginning, much as ADHD/BP is distinct from ADHD alone. Nonetheless, there is no clinical way to distinguish patients with ADHD who will develop MDD in the future from those who never will.

These gender factors complicate our picture of how MDD develops in the children and adolescents with ADHD. The studies reviewed in the previous section of the role of family environment and social competencies in mediating depressive symptoms were conducted mostly with boys. The family studies suggest there are different pathways to depression for boys and girls with ADHD.

Stimulants and MDD

Does treatment of ADHD with stimulants lead to MDD? Is this the reason that MDD is more prevalent among patients with ADHD? Two animal studies have raised the concern that early stimulant exposure may increase the risk of developing comorbid depression (Bolanos, Barrot, Berton, Wallace-Black, & Nestler, 2003; Carlezon, Mague, & Andersen, 2003). A recent case-control, retrospective study of adolescents with ADHD used survival analyses to examine whether time from the onset of ADHD to the first pharmacological treatment influenced the long-term risk of comorbid MDD (Daviss, Birmaher, Diler, & Mintz, 2008). The later in childhood stimulant treatment had been initiated, the *greater* the likelihood of the patient experiencing the onset of MDD, the opposite pattern from what one would expect if stimulants primed a child for a depressive episode.

Pharmacological Treatment of ADHD and MDD

The psychopharmacology of MDD in children and adolescents and its possible relationship to suicidal ideations has been extensively reviewed (Bridge et al., 2007; Hammad, Laughren, & Racoosin, 2006b; Hughes et al., 2007). Table 5.1 shows the pooled

TABLE 5.1. Meta-Analysis of Response Rates and Rates of Suicidal Ideation during Treatment with Antidepressants for Child and Adolescent MDD

	Disorder		
	MDD ($n = 3.480$)	OCD ($n = 718$)	Anxiety ($n = 1,162$)
Treatment response	61%	52%	69%
Placebo response	50%	32%	39%
p	.001	.001	.001
Treatment suicidal ideation	3%	1%	1%
Placebo suicidal ideation	2%	0	0
p	.08	.57	.21

Note. Adapted from Bridge et al. (2007). Copyright 2007 by the American Medical Association. Adapted by permission.

response rates of antidepressant medications versus placebo in over 5,000 child and adolescent patients. The number needed to treat to benefit (NNT) was 10, meaning that one would need to treat 10 patients with MDD with an antidepressant to feel 95% certain that one patient benefited from the drug over placebo. Safety issues regarding the use of antidepressants for children are further discussed in Appendix II. Overall, we can clearly see that depressed children respond better to antidepressants than placebo, but it should be noted that while many depressed children respond to placebo, up to one-third of depressed children and adolescents fail an initial trial of an antidepressant. In contrast, initial treatment of ADHD is highly effective, and placebo response is very limited. Therefore, when the clinician is dealing with a child with comorbid ADHD/MDD, a decision must be made as to which of the two conditions should be the initial focus of psychopharmacology. The Children's Medication Algorithm Project (CMAP; Pliszka et al., 2006) struggled with this issue and developed the algorithm shown in Figure 5.2. The key aspect of the algorithm is to assess the relative severity of both the ADHD and the MDD in the child with comorbidity. If the depression is severe with marked neurovegetative signs or suicidal ideation is present, then treatment of the MDD becomes imperative. Following the MDD algorithm, this would mean initia-

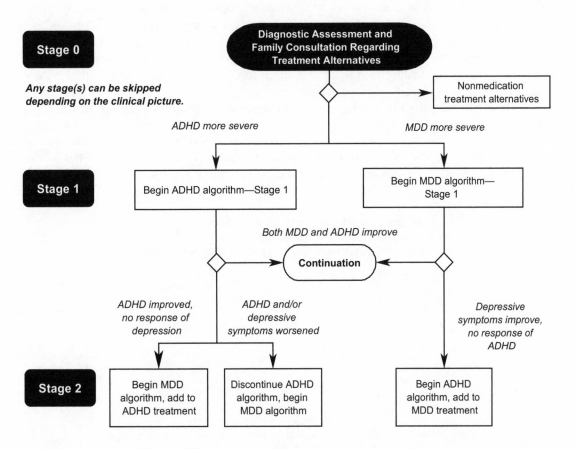

FIGURE 5.2. CMAP algorithm for the pharmacological treatment of ADHD and comorbid MDD. *See Hughes et al. (2007).

tion of a selective serotonin reuptake inhibitor (SSRI) for the depressive symptoms. The clinician should progress through this algorithm, which generally recommends sequential trials of two SSRIs followed by a trial of a non-SSRI (such as bupropion or venlafaxine) (Hughes et al., 2007). The presence of ADHD does not appear to moderate the response of depression to the antidepressant (Emslie et al., 2002), but comorbidity in general tended to predict a lowered response to an antidepressant (Curry et al., 2006). Once the episode of MDD has resolved, the physician should assess whether the ADHD has also resolved. If fact, this is unlikely to occur, as successful treatment of a depressive episode has not been shown to lead to the remission of ADHD symptoms (Findling, 1996). At this point, treatment of ADHD can begin. Typically, a stimulant is added to the antidepressant, but while atomoxetine has no efficacy in depression it has been combined with fluoxetine to treat ADHD in those with comorbid ADHD/MDD (Kratochvil et al., 2005).

In other situations, the MDD is of moderate severity (i.e., less pervasive sadness, limited neurovegetative signs, and no suicidal ideation). If the parents are asked, "What is causing you the most problems, the depression or the ADHD?" and the answer is unequivocally the ADHD, then treatment of the ADHD should begin first. Fifteen patients with comorbid ADHD/MDD entered a feasibility study of the CMAP depression algorithm (Emslie et al., 2004b). Stimulants were started as initial treatment in 9 of these 15 subjects. Six subjects continued only on a stimulant (i.e., their depression resolved after treatment of the ADHD), while seven subjects had an SSRI added to their stimulant treatment. Thus, if MDD symptoms do not resolve with treatment of the ADHD, a course of psychotherapy or the addition of an antidepressant should be the next step.

Table 5.2 shows the medications used for patients with ADHD and comorbid depression in our clinic (excluding those with BP or IED). The vast majority are on stimulants, with SSRIs being the second most commonly prescribed medication. Bupropion is the second most commonly prescribed antidepressant, perhaps due to its effects on both ADHD and depressive symptoms (Daviss et al., 2001). Interestingly, other antide-

TABLE 5.2. Medications Used in Clinic for Treatment of ADHD and Depression (Dysthymia, MDD, and Depression NOS Combined)

Medication type	n (95)	%
SGA	12	12.6
Mood stabilizer	2	2.1
SSRI	36	37.9
SNRI	2	2.1
Bupropion	15	15.7
Other antidepressant	3	3.2
Atomoxetine	5	5.3
Stimulants	76	80.0

Note. Those with a diagnosis of BP or IED are excluded. SGA, second-generation antipsychotic; SSRI, selective serotonin reuptake inhibitor; SNRI, serotonin–norepinephrine reuptake inhibitor.

pressants such as venlafaxine or duloxetine were rarely used, suggesting the clinicians found that the use of SSRIs led to sufficient improvement in depression that moving to these alternative agents was not found to be necessary.

Psychosocial Interventions for ADHD and MDD

The efficacy of both interpersonal (IPT) and cognitive-behavioral therapy (CBT) for the treatment of MDD has been extensively documented (AACAP, 2007). A course of one of these therapies may be used first line in the treatment of depression before antidepressant treatment is initiated. Combining CBT with medication may afford the most efficacious and safest treatment (March et al., 2004; TADS Team, 2007) (see Appendix II). The CBT manual from the Treatment for Adolescents with Depression Study (TADS) is in the public domain and can be downloaded (*trialweb.dcri.duke.edu/tads/index.html*). It should always be borne in mind that CBT has little or no effectiveness for childhood ADHD per se (Abikoff et al., 1988; Abikoff, 1991; Abikoff et al., 1985), and that it may be quite difficult to get an inattentive patient to use the cognitively demanding strategies of CBT even when the focus is depression. There is no data on how ADHD may moderate the response of an ADHD patient to these therapies.

To apply CBT to depressed children and adolescents with ADHD, one must rely on practical clinical experience to modify the approaches. CBT is generally packaged into 8–10 sessions with the sessions grouped into phases—recognizing negative, self-defeating cognitions, formulating new or alternative cognitions, and practicing the more adaptive behaviors these new cognitions can generate (Reinecke, Dattillio, & Freeman, 2006). In CBT with depressed children who don't have ADHD, the depressive cognitions tend to be highly self-critical (e.g., "I'm no good," "my parents divorced because of me," "the teacher is gonna hate my project, so what's the use?"). These cognitions can certainly occur in children and teens with ADHD, but there is often an added complication. Patients with ADHD may have unrealistic views of their competency and underestimate the difficulty of tasks (e.g., "It's easy," "I can do my homework before class tomorrow") (Hoza et al., 2004; Hoza, Pelham, Dobbs, Owens, & Pillow, 2002). When they come up against cold reality, they experience intense anger and dysphoria; their depression takes the form of a hostile, bewildered state (e.g., "the teacher's picking on me," "the work is always stupid," "the coach doesn't like me"). Often, the comorbid depression emerges when adolescents find they cannot do whatever they want, that parents and teachers will set limits, and that things are not going to be as easy as they thought. Table 5.3 suggests some ways to modify CBT for the patient with ADHD and depression.

Chapter 2 discussed using behavioral therapy to reduce oppositional and noncompliant behavior, but as Drabick et al. (2006) noted, harsh and inconsistent parenting is related to depression as well as to ODD/CD. Thus, it is often necessary to combine parent management training with CBT in children with the triple comorbidity of ADHD, ODD, and depression; reduction in family tension may have a strong therapeutic effect on the child's mood. IPT is a desirable component when specific environmental stressors (e.g., loss of parent through death or separation, abuse issues, illness in family) are present. Therapists should always bear in mind that children with ADHD tend not to

TABLE 5.3. Modifications of CBT for the Patient with ADHD and Comorbid Depression

Phase of therapy	Issues	Interventions
Early: Recognize negative cognitions	"Adults are always unfair." "Teachers pick on me." "Other kids are mean to me." "I can't do _____ because _____." "If I can't have fun right now, I get depressed."	Review specific conflicts with parent, teacher; help the child see how his/her attitudes made him/her behave in a way that was not helpful (arguing, talking back) and how that affected his/her feelings. Discuss lack of anticipation of workload for activities rather than lack of ability. Examine patient's need to have fun all of the time—how it sets him/her up for disappointment.
Middle: Develop new cognitions	"Sometimes parents and teachers are right." "Stuff isn't easy; you disappoint yourself if you think it is." "Things will be fun later; you don't have to do them right now."	Practice not feeling embarrassed or humiliated when the child must accept an adult's view of matters. Even smart people need to plan and things aren't easy for them either.
Late: Practice new behaviors	"Listen to adults before jumping to conclusions, be mature, accept judgments." "Set aside time to get work done; you'll feel better if you get things done and then you can relax." "Don't expect to have fun all the time."	Engage parents—help with organizational skills, accepting parents' help. Schedule time with friends, videogames, anticipate having fun later.

be introspective and are easily bored by lengthy discussions of "issues"; they are very uncomfortable with an overly passive therapy style.[1] Shifting from an open-ended interpersonal therapy style to a more directive CBT style is frequently key.

The Case of Kellie

Chief Complaint

"I think my meds are making me depressed."

History of Presenting Illness

Kellie is a 15-year-old girl with a history of ADHD, inattentive type, since age 9. At that time, she had been started on Focalin 5 mg twice a day with a good response. In seventh grade, she was changed to Focalin XR 20 mg once each morning and continued to do well. Kellie had always been a good student with no behavior problems. During her sophomore year of high school, her parents noted that she seemed more withdrawn and

---

[1]A psychotherapy trainee brought a videotape of a session with a child with ADHD; the therapist was using a very unstructured approach. At one point, the child said he was upset because he had failed a spelling test. After a few seconds of silence, the therapist brought his fingers together and said, "Help me understand why you might have had such difficulty with the test." The child replied, "I didn't know the answers."

quiet; she also became very sensitive and would burst into tears at the slightest criticism. Her grades dropped, and she was forced to quit the cheerleading team. The family came in for a follow-up appointment with the concern that perhaps the medication was making her moody. The parents were interviewed first. In terms of ADHD, there were no complaints from school similar to the ones that had led to Kellie's referral in elementary school. Teachers had not noticed anything in the classroom beyond Kellie getting behind on major projects, although one teacher noted that Kellie participated much less in class than usual.

Kellie's mother reported that Kellie was having crying spells three to five times a week, usually precipitated by requests to check her work ("You think I'm stupid") or minor suggestions about her wardrobe or appearance ("I know I'm ugly"). There was no particular timing to these events. They did not consistently occur at midday (when the medication would be expected to be peaking), nor did they appear to be occurring in the evening (when the medication would have been wearing off). Kellie's mother noted that she was staying up later at night to try to get homework done and that she was very moody in the morning when her mother woke her up. She had gained some unwanted weight since quitting the cheerleading team. The mother did not note any suicidal ideation in Kellie. She had been complaining of neck pain and stomachaches, but her family physician said her physical and X-rays were normal. The mother had no reason to suspect substance or alcohol abuse. The mother denied that Kellie showed any temper outbursts, periods of excessive energy or elation, aggression, or psychosis. Her speech rate was average and had not undergone any changes in recent months.

Kellie was interviewed alone. She report feelings of sadness every day, lasting several hours at least each day. The feelings had started about 2 weeks after the start of 10th grade; she was not sure what brought them on. Kellie denied any family stressors; her parents' marriage was stable and she got along well with them. She disliked herself intensely, feeling she was letting down classmates and her family. She had trouble sleeping, felt very tired most days, and was thinking more slowly. She had lost interest in subjects—when she failed English she was relieved because it required her to quit cheerleading. She had become convinced that she was not very attractive and kids were laughing at her when she did her routines. She had passive thoughts of wishing she were dead but never had any active suicidal ideation. She denied alcohol or substance abuse (though she occasionally took a drink with her friends). She wasn't sure if her medication was working and suspected it was making her moody. She had never had a boyfriend per se, but many boys at school had asked her out. On the Mood and Feelings Questionnaire (MFQ), she endorsed 21 items as being "true," suggesting significant depressive symptoms.

Past Psychiatric and Medical History

She had been followed in the psychiatry ADHD clinic since the age of 9. Her course was unremarkable, with visits consisting of routine follow-ups for monitoring progress, which was usually good. Occasional and expected dose adjustments had been made over the years. She had no history of any other significant medical illness.

Family and Social History

Kellie's mother had a history of depression and had responded well to a course of Zoloft. Her mother had never been treated for ADHD but reported she was always a poor student in high school and dropped out of college after 1 year. People were always surprised to learn this since Kellie's mother was so well spoken. Kellie's mother's depression was related to her perceived lack of accomplishment.

Mental Status Examination

Kellie is a pleasant 15-year-old girl who looked mature for her age. Her vocabulary was advanced, and her speech rate and volume were average. She became tearful at several points in the examination. Her intellectual functioning was at least average if not above average. Her mood was moderately depressed, and her affect was appropriate to thought content. Recent and remote memory was intact. Thought processes were logical and goal directed; there were no hallucinations or delusions. There was no flight of ideas. She was preoccupied with negative views of herself and a sense that things would not be getting better. At the time of the interview, she had no suicidal ideation.

The initial dilemma to be addressed was whether Kellie's stimulant medication was inducing a depressed mood. Mood lability and irritability are very rare side effects of stimulant medications (see Appendix II). Furthermore, Kellie had been on Focalin for many years with no evidence of such an effect. Kellie's sad moods were fairly persistent and had no relationship to the time course of the action of the Focalin. Nonetheless, the degree of the concern that the Focalin was causing the problems was great enough that the clinician felt this had to be addressed before treatment of a mood disorder should proceed.

Treatment Course

It was decided to discontinue the Focalin for a 1-week trial period. Kellie's mother gave rating scales to teachers in two of her daughter's classes; both Kellie and her mother were asked to observe any increase or decrease in symptoms of inattention. They were also asked to report any mood changes. A follow-up appointment was arranged for the next week. At that appointment, teacher ratings were compared to ratings that had been obtained earlier in the school year. Both teachers noted a further decline in Kellie's productivity in the past week and that Kellie had been tardy to class for the first time that school year. The mother clearly noted increased inattentiveness and distractibility at home. Most important, Kellie did not notice any improvement in her depressed mood. There was also no change in sleep or appetite, ruling out the possibility that these symptoms were secondary to the stimulant. Therefore, the clinician concluded that they were part of a depressive syndrome. The Focalin XR was restarted at the previous dose of 20 mg once a day. Treatment options for the depression were discussed with both Kellie and her mother; this included a discussion of the risk of suicidal ideation with antidepressant medication. While Kellie's mother had responded positively to antidepressants, she was reluctant to start her daughter on such medication. Kellie was also reluctant, feeling that she ought to be able to control her moods better. It was decided that Kellie would receive five to eight sessions of CBT, and an appointment was made with the clinic psychologist.

At the first session of therapy, Kellie's mood history and any recent stressors were discussed. It was confirmed that there appeared to be no acute psychosocial stressors, and that the prominent negative cognitions were low self-esteem, excessive self-criticism (particularly around body image issues), and a sense that she was not smart enough or talented enough to do the work. Kellie's high level of internal tension was also noted. The therapist began with some basic relaxation techniques—Kellie was encouraged to take a moment at various points in the day and imagine a family vacation to Florida that she had found particularly relaxing. The therapist and Kellie drew up a list of her accomplishments and her abilities. Kellie was encouraged to engage in "self-talk" relating to these abilities whenever she felt discouraged or self-critical. She was encouraged to find some other form of exercise to replace the cheerleading practice. Kellie had a good relationship with the therapist and found many of these suggestions helpful. It was difficult, however, to attend all the scheduled sessions because of homework and the parents' work schedules. At a 4-week follow-up appointment, Kellie reported to the psychiatrist that her mood was "about 50% better." She was encouraged to continue the sessions.

The psychiatrist did not hear from Kellie or her mother for about another 2 months. The mother then called and requested an urgent appointment, because Kellie had reported that she wanted to kill herself. Kellie was seen the next day and reported that she had an increase in her depressed mood after she received another failing grade in English. She now reported being sad every day and having increased difficulty sleeping. The CBT techniques that she had learned did not seem to be as effective in keeping her depressed mood away. At this point, the mother and Kellie agreed that an antidepressant trial was appropriate. Given the fact that the mother had had a positive response to Zoloft, this antidepressant was chosen for the initial trial. She was started on 50 mg in the morning, and this was increased after 4 to 5 days to 100 mg in the morning. The psychiatrist had no openings in the next 2 weeks, so an appointment was scheduled for 3 weeks. The mother was asked to call the office during each of the intervening weeks if any suicidal ideation was present. The mother was told to secure any firearms, knives, or medications at home.

Kellie reported marginal progress at 3 weeks. She denied any suicidal ideation but stated that she continued to feel sad nearly every day. The mother thought that Kellie was sleeping better. Appetite remained unchanged, and there were no other noticeable side effects of the Zoloft. The dose was increased to 150 mg a day and another follow-up was scheduled in 3 weeks. At this appointment, Kellie reported that her mood was substantially improved. At this session, she was again smiling and appeared to have regained much of her original personality. The mother reported that Kellie had more energy to do work and had turned around several grades, although it appeared likely that she would have to repeat some classes in summer school. Kellie was encouraged to continue therapy; the therapist offered to meet with her for one to three booster sessions every few months or so in order to maintain the gains she had made. Kellie successfully completed English in summer school and she was eligible to try out for the cheerleading team again in her junior year.

In Kellie's family history, it is notable that her mother suffered not only from major depression, but also possibly from ADHD, which had gone unrecognized during the mother's childhood. This is consistent with the concept of segregation of ADHD and depression in females noted by Mick et al. (2003). Kellie's course of MDD was fairly straightforward and did not complicate the management of her ADHD. In Kellie's case, it was relatively easy to separate ADHD and MDD symptoms. Let us now examine a case where this process is much more difficult.

The Case of Ryan: ADHD, Depression, Irritability, and Cannabis Abuse

Chief Complaint

Irritability.

History of Presenting Illness

Ryan is a 15-year-old boy with a history of ADHD and ODD since the age of 6. At the time of his presentation to the clinic, he was taking Concerta 72 mg/day. Ryan had been living with his aunt and uncle for the last 3 years because his mother had been incarcerated due to a drug conviction. The aunt and uncle sought consultation because of Ryan's chronic irritability and negative attitude. Over the last year, Ryan had become increasingly uncooperative and verbally abusive. He would often respond with a stream of curse words whenever he was asked to do something. He had missed multiple days of school and would frequently seclude himself in his room to watch television. Any attempt to cheer him up led to arguments. He always appeared unhappy and would rarely interact with his cousins. Occasionally, his aunt and uncle would get very frustrated with him and remind him that they took him in and were trying to help him out. Such conversations often led to Ryan making statements such as "Well then, maybe I should just kill myself." During one of his classes at school, Ryan drew a picture of coffins and guns. For several days, he insisted on going to school dressed entirely in black. This raised the concern of the school counselor, who met with Ryan several times. Ryan stated that he was not "crazy," but did agree that he was in a "shitty mood" nearly all the time. The counselor notified the aunt and uncle, which led them to seek psychiatric consultation.

The aunt and uncle clearly felt that the stimulant medication was effective. They noted that occasionally Ryan would get angry and refuse his morning dose, which would inevitably lead to the school calling because Ryan had had a particularly bad day. They reported that Ryan had always been difficult to manage ever since he had entered their household, but he had always been a generally happy child. In the last year, they had noted this extreme change in mood. They denied that Ryan ever expressed any sadness, nor did he have any crying spells. Ryan had always slept poorly, he was difficult to get to bed, and recently he had been staying up until 3 or 4 in the morning. He would watch television or play videogames, so it was very difficult to get him to go to school the next day. He needed to sleep until 2 or 3 in the afternoon on weekends and if they woke him early, he was particularly irritable. Ryan regularly made vague threats of self-harm, and when angry, he had made small cuts on his arms and wrists. The uncle felt this was a manipulative gesture. Ryan often had difficulty coming home on time, and the aunt and uncle suspected that he was hanging out with the "wrong crowd."

Despite his verbal outbursts, Ryan had never been physically aggressive toward other people, except for occasional scuffles with peers. He did slam doors and had used a pencil to poke multiple holes in the walls of his room. The aunt and uncle described Ryan as "lazy," and they laughed when asked if Ryan had ever shown any periods of unusual high energy or elation. He moved very slowly and at times appeared to be simply staring off into space.

Past Psychiatric and Medical History

Ryan had been treated with a variety of stimulants since first being diagnosed with ADHD at age 6. The aunt and uncle were unaware of the details of his early treatment. Ryan's mother had told them that everything seemed to work for "a little while." Ryan had never been treated with antidepressant medication or mood stabilizers, and he had never required psychiatric hospitalization. Ryan had been sent to a therapist when he was 12 years old. The focus of this treatment was feelings of abandonment Ryan allegedly felt due to his mother's absence. Ryan resisted talking about this, which the therapist interpreted as resistance, but after several months Ryan still refused to talk about it at all. Ryan's past medical history was unremarkable.

Family and Social History

The aunt reported that Ryan's mother (her sister) probably had ADHD as a child but was never diagnosed or treated. She had repeated behavior and learning problems throughout her school years, becoming pregnant with Ryan at age 15. The aunt had never learned who the father was, as her sister would not say. By age 18, Ryan's mother had a significant substance abuse problem including frequent alcohol use, regular use of marijuana, and inappropriate use of prescription painkillers. CPS became involved, and while there was no history of physical abuse or overt neglect, it was agreed that Ryan should live with his aunt and uncle. Not long after this, the mother was arrested for possession of a large amount of marijuana. Because she had several convictions for driving while under the influence of alcohol, she was required to serve a 5-year prison term and after that she disappeared. Ryan's mother had a history of frequent suicide attempts; one overdose attempt resulted in her being in an intensive care unit for several days.

Mental Status Examination

Ryan is a 15-year-old boy who appeared his stated age. He was wearing a dirty sweatshirt and worn jeans. He slumped into his chair and stretched out his legs, then pulled his hat down over his eyes. He was minimally cooperative with the examiner, but did answer specific questions without a great deal of elaboration. His speech rate and volume were average. His mood was severely irritable, and his affect was quite intense. Even simple questions would generate an answer such as "Well, what do you think?" Intellectual functioning was average. Thought processes were logical and goal directed. Thought content focused on the fact that everything was "fucked." He viewed all of his teachers as "stupid" and his aunt's and uncle's rules as completely unfair and idiotic. He did not spontaneously bring up his mother and causally dismissed any suggestion that this was a current factor in his life. He spoke admiringly of Kurt Cobain (a singer who committed suicide), but denied any suicidal ideation, as well as any hallucinations or delusions. On the mood and feeling questionnaire, he endorsed 30 items, suggesting significant depression. While he was not suicidal at the time of the interview, he did report suicidal ideation in the last 2 weeks.

Treatment Course

The diagnosis was reviewed with the aunt and uncle, making note of the pervasive irritability, pessimism, suicidal ideation, insomnia, and self-abusive behavior. A diagnosis of depression not otherwise specified was made. Prozac 20 mg/day was added to the Concerta, and a follow-up appointment scheduled within 2 weeks. Ryan and his family were referred to a therapist who was skilled in both CBT and parent training. The therapist noted that the aunt and uncle had difficulty setting limits with Ryan. The aunt's and uncle's own two daughters had not presented any behavioral problems, so it had never been necessary for them to set strong limits. The therapist began to speak with them about putting Ryan on an allowance and setting consequences when he left the house without permission.

At the 2-week follow-up, the aunt and uncle reported a modest improvement in Ryan's irritability. There had not been any increase in suicidal ideation or acts of self harm. Ryan agreed that he felt less cranky and that he was not snapping at his aunt and uncle as much. His academic performance remained poor, and he continued to go out at night without permission. A month later, the aunt and uncle reported that they had accidentally given Ryan 108 mg of Concerta that morning. They had received a call from the school telling them that Ryan had an exceptionally good day and for the first time had completed all of his work in class without any difficulties. The psychiatrist reviewed Ryan's weight, which was 147 pounds (66.8 kg), and noted that Ryan had not had any side effects from this increased dose. The psychiatrist gave permission to the family to continue the 108 mg of Concerta/day.

At the next monthly follow-up, the aunt and uncle reported that they had discontinued the session with the psychologist. They did not want to see daily report cards or do any other aspects of behavior management. It was too cumbersome, and furthermore it just seemed to make Ryan more irritable. They stated that overall, they saw a significant improvement on the medication and wished to continue the current regimen. They were released to routine care, although the psychiatrist suggested that he would prefer that they continue with some sort of psychosocial intervention. Several months went by with the aunt and uncle requesting routine refills and reporting to the office staff that everything was going well. They came in for a routine follow-up at the beginning of Ryan's 11th-grade school year. They reported that Ryan had gradually become more irritable and oppositional but continued to state that he felt much better. He stated that he had not had any suicidal ideation in the last 6 months. The aunt and uncle wondered if the Prozac was still working. During the interview, Ryan appeared mildly agitated. While he said everything was fine, he fidgeted in his seat and his rate of speech was considerably higher than it had been at the previous session. He had done a number of foolish acts including riding his skateboard on a freeway access ramp. The psychiatrist became concerned that Ryan was having some activation with the Prozac and that a possible hypomanic phase was emerging. Given that Ryan denied all depressive symptoms, it was decided to take him off the Prozac to get a new baseline. Roughly 2 weeks after discontinuing the Prozac, Ryan had a marked *increase* in his irritability and was referred to the counselor's office for an anger outburst at a teacher. The Prozac was restarted. He remained on the Concerta throughout this period as the aunt and uncle felt strongly about its benefit.

At the next follow-up, Ryan continued to show increased agitation. His eyes appeared dilated and he tended to look right through the examiner. On questioning, Ryan admitted that he had begun using marijuana. He used it primarily on the weekends when he was with friends. The psychiatrist was concerned that Ryan was under the influence during the session. Drug testing was ordered and was positive for cannabis. Extensive discussion was held with the aunt about the risks of combining his psychotropic medications with illegal substances. The aunt felt that Ryan's functioning was far superior on the medicine than off, and she did not even think he could remain in the home if he was completely off medication. The psychiatrist agreed to continue the medicine, but Ryan would have to undergo regular drug testing and resume therapy.

Ryan began sneaking out through a window at night to meet with friends in order to smoke marijuana. The police raided a party that Ryan was at, and he was arrested for possession of marijuana. As a condition of his probation, he was required to enter a 30-day inpatient rehabilitation program. Ryan returned to follow up with the psychiatrist after being released from rehabilitation. Now that he was off marijuana, his affect had normalized. His speech rate and volume were appropriate, and his thought processes were more logical. He resumed working with the therapist. This time, the therapist explored Ryan's cognitions. They discussed his tendency to go into an irritable funk in response to frustrations. This was based on thinking that everything should go his way. Considerable effort was focused on getting Ryan to see how unrealistic this was and how his reactions made things worse. The therapist discussed with him how avoiding chores and homework and arguing with his aunt about trivial matters took up more time than doing the act itself. The inevitable punishments led him to become irritable and angry at the world and to feel as if his situation was hopeless. His desire to *always* feel "good" also led to his marijuana use. This focus on Ryan's cognitions was coupled with an attempt to reengage his aunt and uncle in limit setting. Fortunately, his probation officer was available to help with this process, making it clear to Ryan that he needed to stay "clean" and keep his curfew. As the therapy progressed, the focus shifted to helping Ryan develop more of a future orientation. He successfully completed his probation, and his general attitude at home improved. Plans were made to discontinue the Prozac in 6 months to a year if he remained drug free and euthymic.

In Ryan's case, there were no signs of mania (except when under the influence), and there was no history of aggressive outbursts or severe mood lability. His mood was persistently irritable with associated lethargy, low motivation, and self-abusive behavior. There was not the clear correlation between starting the antidepressant and mood improvement that was seen in Kellie's case; there was even a question as to whether the Prozac was inducing activation. Stopping the SSRI was the key to showing that this was not the case. It is unlikely that success would have been obtained in this case without the concurrent therapy and the support of the probation officer.

We now move on to anxiety disorders, where we encounter many of the same dilemmas, with the added complexity of the many manifestations of anxiety disorders.

Chapter 6

Anxiety Disorders

The comorbidity of anxiety in children and adolescents with ADHD has been studied more than that of depression. Yet many of the same dilemmas we encountered in Chapter 5 apply here as well. This includes the definition of anxiety in children, the disagreement among informants about the nature of the anxiety symptoms, and the decision about whether to intervene with the anxiety or ADHD symptoms first. Anxiety disorders are also highly heterogeneous, covering simple phobias, generalized anxiety, physical tension, separation fears, and full-blown panic attacks. Obsessive–compulsive disorder is also part of the anxiety spectrum, but because of its relationship to tic disorders we address it in the next chapter. We also return here to the discussion of post-trauma symptoms, this time focusing on the anxiety component rather than on the impulsive–aggressive aspect as we did in Chapter 3.

Assessment of Anxiety in Children with ADHD

Anxiety is a high-arousal negative state that occurs in response to a perceived threat. The threat may be physical (a hurricane is approaching), social (meeting someone new), or performance related (an upcoming examination). Anxiety is adaptive if it causes us to take action against a threat (evacuating the coast or studying for the examination), but becomes symptomatic if it is so severe that the person is persistently in a negative state (always worrying) or avoids situations to the point that it is self-defeating. In the interview about anxiety symptoms, the clinician asks both the parent and the child if the child is anxious (nervous, scared) about a variety of situations (school, social situations, world events, health, objects, and animals) and if the anxiety impairs function. In addition, anxiety is generally associated with physical symptoms such as muscle tension, poor sleep, internal feelings of restlessness, sweating, racing heart, and shortness of breath. When the symptoms of physical arousal are extreme and uncontrollable, a panic attack is said to occur.

As with depression, parent and child agreement about the symptoms of anxiety is quite poor (Bird et al., 1992). Two studies showed little or no overlap between the child and parent report of being anxious (Diamond, Tannock, & Schachar, 1999; Vance et al., 2002a). It is unclear why parents report anxiety and the child denies it. Some parents use the terms *restless* and *anxiety* interchangeably, or they assume their child's hyperactivity is the result of internal tension. If all the examples parents give of their child's anxiety reflect motor activity, this may be the case. Many children with ADHD become oppositional just prior to difficult tasks, such as homework or chores; anticipating this conflict, the parent may say the child is "anxious" about it. In these situations, the child will deny all anxiety. The parent report should not be dismissed, however, as there may be something about this negative affectivity that predicts response to treatment.

In other situations, parents may be unaware of their child's anxiety; showing them the child's self-ratings or discussing the anxiety symptoms with both the parent and child together may be helpful in making the parent aware. Interestingly, young children often have an easier time describing being scared of things or events than they do describing sad feelings. The content of the child's anxiety should be about unrealistic fears, self-esteem, or performance issues. If the child is only "worried" about getting bad grades, being grounded, or other direct consequences of ADHD behavior, then an anxiety disorder is less likely. Finally, symptoms of anxiety should be frequent (at least three to five times a week, lasting for enough time to affect behavior), not simply transient feelings.

Prevalence of Anxiety Disorders in Children with ADHD

A substantial body of research shows that anxiety disorders occur in persons with ADHD far above average levels. As noted in Table 6.1, estimates of the prevalence of anxiety disorders in children with ADHD have ranged from 25 to 50%, compared to a prevalence of about 6–20% in the general pediatric population (Costello, Egger, & Angold, 2004).

Thus, the odds ratio for anxiety disorders in children with ADHD relative to the general population is 2.1–4.3 (Angold et al., 1999). Children with anxiety disorders also have higher than expected rates of ADHD (Last, Hersen, Kazdin, Finkelstein, & Strauss, 1987), as do adults with panic disorder (Fones, Pollack, Susswein, & Otto, 2000; Safren, Lanka, Otto, & Pollack, 2001). Adults with ADHD also show high rates of anxiety disorders relative to the general population (Biederman et al., 1993).

How Do ADHD and Anxiety Affect Each Other?

How does the comorbidity of anxiety affect the presentation of ADHD symptoms? A number of studies have examined this issue by comparing children with ADHD and an anxiety disorder (ADHD/ANX) to those with ADHD alone on a variety of cognitive, behavioral, and psychosocial measures. Pliszka (Pliszka, 1989, 1992) assessed children with ADHD and ADHD/ANX in an observation room where the subjects had to perform mathematics problems while the rates of off-task, fidgeting, vocalizing, and out-of-seat behaviors were assessed by a rater blind to diagnosis. The children with ADHD/ANX showed lower rates of these impulsive-hyperactive behaviors relative to those with ADHD. Compared to those with ADHD/ANX, the ADHD-only group showed more

TABLE 6.1. Overlap of Anxiety Disorders and ADHD

Study	ADHD children with anxiety	Anxious children with ADHD
Children		
Anderson, Williams, McGee, & Silva (1987)	26%	24%
Bird, Canino, & Rubio-Stipec (1988)	23%	21%
Pliszka (1989)	28%	—
Last et al. (1987)		
Separation anxiety	—	23%
Overanxious	—	15%
Newcorn et al. (2001)	33%	—
Biederman et al. (1992)	29%	—
Adults		
Biederman et al. (1993)		
Generalized anxiety disorder	43%	
Social phobia	32%	
Multiple anxiety disorders	50%	
Fones et al. (2000)		
Panic disorder		23.5% (childhood history) 9.4% (adult ADHD)

impulsive responding on a memory task (Pliszka, 1989), poorer performance on a measure of response inhibition (Pliszka, Borcherding, Spratley, Leon, & Irick, 1997), and more errors of commission on the continuous performance task (Pliszka, 1992). In contrast, children with ADHD/ANX showed poorer working memory compared to controls and those with ADHD alone (Tannock, Ickowicz, & Schachar, 1995). Manassis, Tannock, and Barbosa (2000) compared four groups of children (ADHD, ADHD/ANX, ANX only, and controls) on a dichotic listening task that measures sensitivity to the emotional content of words. In this task, words relating to sadness are detected preferentially in the left ear (negative emotion is processed more strongly by the right hemisphere). All four groups showed the expected lateralization of detecting sad words on the left, but this effect was significantly greater in the ADHD/ANX group. The ADHD/ANX group again did not show response inhibition deficits relative to controls on the stop signal task. In a more recent study of a new sample of these four groups, Manassis, Tannock, Young, and Francis-John (2007) found that children with ADHD/ANX had more impaired academic achievement than those with ADHD or ANX alone, although they did not find the differences in working memory found in the earlier study (Tannock et al., 1995). It should be noted that these cognitive differences between ADHD and ADHD/ANX, while interesting from a theoretical perspective, are quite subtle and not useful for diagnostic purposes.

Studies have been inconsistent as to whether children with ADHD and ADHD/ANX differ in terms of the presence of other disruptive behavior disorders. One study found a lower rate of CD (Pliszka, 1989), whereas other studies have shown no difference in the rate of ODD or CD (Biederman, Faraone, Keenan, Steingard, & Tsuang, 1991; Pliszka, 1992). Still, other studies have shown increased rates of ODD/CD in the

ADHD/ANX group relative to those with ADHD alone (Newcorn et al., 2001; Tannock, 2000). The subgroup of children with dual comorbidity (ADHD/ANX + ODD/CD) is particularly interesting as they may show differences from children with ADHD/ANX but no ODD/CD. Newcorn et al. (2001) examined continuous performance test errors in children with ADHD in the MTA study, stratified by comorbidity. The ADHD/ANX group showed decreased impulsivity and dyscontrol errors relative to the other ADHD groups, and this effect was moderated by gender: only girls with ADHD/ANX showed this pattern. Subjects with ADHD/ANX *and* ODD/CD were as impulsive on this measure as those with ADHD alone. Teachers also rated children with ADHD/ANX as less impulsive than either the ADHD only or dual comorbid group. On the other hand, parents rated children with ADHD/ANX + ODD/CD as *more* impulsive and hyperactive than those with ADHD alone.

Children with ADHD/ANX may have higher rates of stressful life events than those with only ADHD (Biederman et al., 1991), but they are not different in terms of school performance or learning disabilities (Tannock, 2000). Maternal anxiety during the prenatal period is associated with higher than expected rates of ADHD (Volkow, Wang, Fowler, & Ding, 2005). There is also evidence that children with ADHD/ANX are physiologically different from those with ADHD alone. Compared with those with ADHD, children with ADHD/ANX show a greater increase in diastolic blood pressure when moving from a sitting to standing position (Vance, Costin, & Maruff, 2002b). This would be consistent with an earlier study assessing urinary norepinephrine and its metabolites in children with ADHD and ADHD/ANX and controls (Pliszka, Maas, Javors, Rogeness, & Baker, 1994). Both ADHD groups showed evidence of increased noradrenergic activity relative to controls, but there was evidence that the ADHD/ANX group showed increased acute release of norepinephrine (as well as increased epinephrine) during a stressful task compared with ADHD subjects. This raises the intriguing question of whether the comorbidity of anxiety superimposes a more active noradrenergic state on a noradrenergic system already made dysfunctional by the ADHD.

Future studies will need to separate those with ADHD/ANX from those with ADHD/ANX and ODD/CD. These two groups appear different from a cognitive perspective (Newcorn et al., 2001), the former perhaps being less impulsive and the latter being more so. Anxiety disorders are equally prevalent among children with combined or inattentive type of ADHD, so the subtype of ADHD does not account for this distinction (Power, Costigan, Eiraldi, & Leff, 2004).

What Causes the Increased Risk of Anxiety in ADHD?

Genetics is involved in the etiology of both ADHD and anxiety disorders (Foley, Pickles, Maes, Silberg, & Eaves, 2004; Hudziak, Derks, Althoff, Rettew, & Boomsma, 2005). Family studies have attempted to disentangle the seperate genetic factors by examining the rates of both ADHD and anxiety disorders in the relatives of children with ADHD and ADHD/ANX (Biederman et al., 1992; Perrin & Last, 1996). Relative to a control sample, ADHD was found to be elevated in the relatives of both ADHD and ADHD/ANX subjects, but elevated rates of anxiety were found only in the relatives of the ADHD/ANX group (Biederman et al., 1992). ADHD and anxiety disorders did not cosegregate in the relatives of the children with ADHD/ANX; that is, they had some relatives with *only* ADHD while other relatives had *only* anxiety. This means ADHD/ ANX is not a genetic subtype distinct from ADHD alone: rather ADHD and anxiety are inherited independently. Later studies were consistent with this pattern (Perrin & Last, 1996). It may be that in some families, there is assortive mating (i.e., a higher likelihood that persons with ADHD will have children with persons with anxiety disorders). This would be one explanation for the higher than expected co-occurrence of anxiety disorders and ADHD. Anxiety cannot be viewed as merely secondary to ADHD because relatives of ADHD/ANX children often had anxiety disorders without having ADHD (Biederman et al., 1992).

How Does the Presence of Anxiety Affect the Treatment of ADHD?

Early studies suggested that children with ADHD who showed high levels of anxiety showed a poorer response to stimulant medication compared to those with ADHD alone (Pliszka, 1989; Taylor et al., 1987). Pliszka (1989) randomized a large number of children with ADHD and ADHD/ANX to a 4-week, double-blind, placebo-controlled trial of methylphenidate. Response to medication was assessed by teacher and parent rating scales as well as by weekly observations in a laboratory setting where behavior was assessed by blinded raters. Response was defined as behavior rating scale scores on one of the weeks of the stimulant being at least one standard deviation improved over the scores during the placebo week. Based on this criterion, 87% of the children with ADHD were considered responders compared to 31% of the subjects in the ADHD/ ANX group. The ADHD alone group also showed more robust reductions of off-task behaviors in the observation room. Based on this, Pliszka (1989) concluded that children with ADHD/ANX responded less robustly to stimulants than those without anxiety, although there was no evidence that methylphenidate worsened symptoms of either ADHD or anxiety in those with ADHD/ANX.

Later, more extensive studies did not confirm this finding. Diamond et al. (1999) randomized 91 children with ADHD and ADHD/ANX to an acute controlled trial of methylphenidate followed by a 4-month extended trial. Subjects with and without anxiety responded equally well to the stimulant, and side effects were similar in the two groups. As noted earlier, there was little correspondence between the parent and child reports of anxiety, but response to methylphenidate was equally good regardless of whether the anxiety diagnosis was based on parent or child report. Anxiety was not a predictor of nonresponse in children with ADHD who had comorbid tics (Gadow, Nolan, Sverd, Sprafkin, & Schwartz, 2002). The most definitive study on this matter was the MTA study, where children with ADHD underwent a 5-week, double-blind placebo-controlled crossover study of methylphenidate. Again, the children with ADHD/ANX showed as positive a response to methylphenidate as those without anxiety. Subjects in the MTA study were also randomized to community treatment, intensive behavioral intervention, medication management, or a combination of the medication and behavioral intervention. Interestingly, those subjects with ADHD/ANX (but not ODD/CD) had a more robust response to the behavioral intervention by itself relative to nonanxious children with ADHD. The subgroup with dual comorbidity (ADHD + ODD/CD) was more likely to benefit from the combination treatment of the behavioral intervention and medication relative to the children with ADHD alone. In a further analysis of the MTA treatment outcome data, March et al. (2000) showed that it was parent-reported anxiety alone that was a moderator; there was no relationship between the child's self-report of anxiety and treatment outcome. Parent-reported anxiety was strongly related to the comorbidity of ODD/CD and to the phenomenon of "negative affectivity," rather than fears and phobia. Thus, March et al. (2000) hypothesized that the strong behavioral management focus of the MTA psychosocial intervention was helpful for children with ADHD/ANX and ODD/CD because it helped the parent manage such negativity. March et al. (2000) cautioned that children with ADHD who self-report intense anxiety might benefit from cognitive therapy (see below). Nonetheless, two major clinical issues appear to have been resolved by the MTA study: (1) children with ADHD/ANX respond as well to stimulants as those without anxiety and (2) children with ADHD/ANX might benefit more strongly from the addition of a psychosocial intervention to their pharmacological intervention.

Treatment of the ADHD should generally be the first step when comorbid anxiety is present, as shown in Figure 6.1 (Pliszka et al., 2006). The CMAP algorithm shows two pathways to treat this combination: stimulants followed by a trial of an SSRI or monotherapy with atomoxetine. If the anxiety resolves after treatment of the ADHD with stimulants, there is no need to go on to a pharmacological intervention for the anxiety.

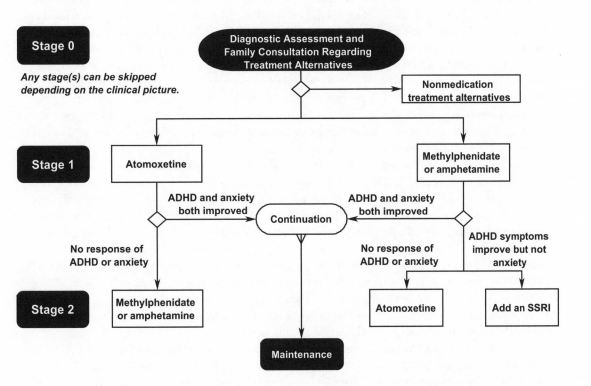

FIGURE 6.1. Algorithm for the treatment of ADHD with comorbid anxiety.

128 TREATING ADHD AND COMORBID DISORDERS

Treating Anxiety in the Child with ADHD

Cognitive-behavioral therapy (CBT) has been shown to be a highly efficacious treatment for anxiety disorders of childhood (Compton et al., 2004). In CBT, the child and family are educated about the disorder, taught relaxation techniques, shown how to engage in cognitive restructuring (developing mental techniques to deal with fears and anxieties in a more adaptive manner), and helped to find ways to use mental imaging to expose oneself to fearful situations in a virtual manner so as to gradually extinguish the fear. In most of the CBT studies cited in the above review, only a small percentage of the subjects (8–15%) met criteria for ADHD in addition to their anxiety disorder diagnosis. None of these studies were powered to determine if ADHD was a moderator of outcome of anxiety to CBT treatment. Manassis et al. (2002) divided their sample of anxious children (8% of whom had ADHD) into high- or low-hyperactivity groups based on parent rating. A median split was used so many of the highly "hyperactive subjects" did not have ADHD. Parent report of activity level did not relate to outcome after CBT treatment. This suggests ADHD is not a bar to CBT in anxious children, although it should again be noted that CBT is not an effective treatment for ADHD (Abikoff & Gittelman, 1985). Some highly distracted children with ADHD may not be able to be actively involved in CBT until their inattention is treated with medication.

How and when should anxiety be treated pharmacologically in the presence of ADHD? Numerous studies have established the efficacy of SSRIs in the treatment of a variety of child and adolescent anxiety disorders (Birmaher et al., 2003; Birmaher, Yelovich, & Renaud, 1998; Rynn, Siqueland, & Rickels, 2001; Walkup et al., 2001), but since SSRIs do not treat ADHD, they must be combined with a stimulant. Abikoff et al. (2005) treated 32 children with ADHD/ANX with methylphenidate and found that 26 (81%) responded with respect to ADHD but remained anxious. Twenty-five children were then randomized to either placebo or fluvoxamine (while remaining on methylphenidate) for 8 weeks; at the end of the study period, there was no difference between the treatment groups in terms of anxiety. Thus, the efficacy of this approach remains to be established.

Alternatively, atomoxetine may treat both ADHD and anxiety. A large sample ($n = 162$) of children with ADHD/ANX were randomized to receive either atomoxetine or placebo for 12 weeks in a double-blind, placebo-controlled, parallel-groups design (Geller et al., 2007a). An ADHD rating scale and an anxiety scale were used to assess the different comorbid symptoms over the course of the trial. *Both* ADHD symptoms and anxiety showed significant reductions on atomoxetine relative to placebo; clinicians also rated those children on atomoxetine as showing greater global improvement. CMAP is neutral in terms of which approach should be selected first. However, if the child's ADHD is more severe relative to the anxiety, then a stimulant trial might be the first choice. In contrast, the child with more severe anxiety might benefit from starting directly on an atomoxetine trial.

Table 6.2 shows the medication used in our clinic to treat children with ADHD and comorbid anxiety alone, excluding those with affective disorder or IED. While stimulants were satisfactory for the vast majority of children, over a third of the patients required treatment with an antidepressant (most commonly an SSRI).

TABLE 6.2. Medications Used in Children with ADHD and Comorbid Anxiety

Medication type	n (87)	%
Alpha-agonist	1	12.6
Buspirone	1	2.1
Benzodiazepine	2	37.9
Miscellaneous antidepressant	5	2.1
Bupropion	1	15.7
SNRI	1	3.2
SSRI	30	34.4
Atomoxetine	3	5.3
Stimulants	65	80.0

Note. SNRI, serotonin–norepinephrine reuptake inhibitor; SSRI, selective serotonin reuptake inhibitor.

PTSD and ADHD, Revisited

In Chapter 3 we discussed explosive, aggressive behavior in children who had experienced abuse. There, we focused on children who were irritable and aggressive but did not show other cardinal signs of PTSD, such as flashbacks, nightmares, disassociation, or foreshortened sense of the future. Caution was raised against assuming that aggression or symptoms of ADHD were in fact an expression of PTSD. In that subset of patients, we focused on the treatment of aggression and the use of SGAs and mood stabilizers. We now shift to a different subset of patients with ADHD, who have experienced abuse and *do* show overt symptoms of PTSD. It is highly unlikely that symptoms of ADHD are an expression of PTSD (Wozniak et al., 1999), so if both sets of symptoms are present, generally both diagnoses should be made. There are exceptions to this—if onset of the child's symptoms of inattention occurred well after age 7 and were clearly temporally related to the trauma, then a diagnosis of ADHD would not be appropriate. Careful interviewing in these cases is needed. Is the child's inattention due to internal distraction by memories of the trauma? Do the ADHD symptoms completely resolve when the child is away from all reminders of the trauma? If the answer to these questions is affirmative, then PTSD is probably the only diagnosis. If the trauma occurred before age 7, the PTSD may well have had concurrent onset with the ADHD, and there is no way to argue that the ADHD is "real" or "secondary to" PTSD. So, how then is the clinician to determine the treatment course?

As with the CMAP algorithm for treating ADHD and comorbid depression (Hughes et al., 2007c), the decision should rest on the severity of the PTSD symptoms (see Figure 6.2). If the ADHD is causing the most impairment (e.g., failing grades, constant conflict with caregivers) and the PTSD is of mild severity (e.g., intrusive memories, anxiety, nightmares, but no flashbacks or dissociative episodes), then pharmacological treatment of the ADHD should be pursued while the PTSD is addressed concurrently through psychosocial interventions. For children who show more prominent PTSD symptoms (e.g., daytime flashbacks, inability to go to places that remind them of

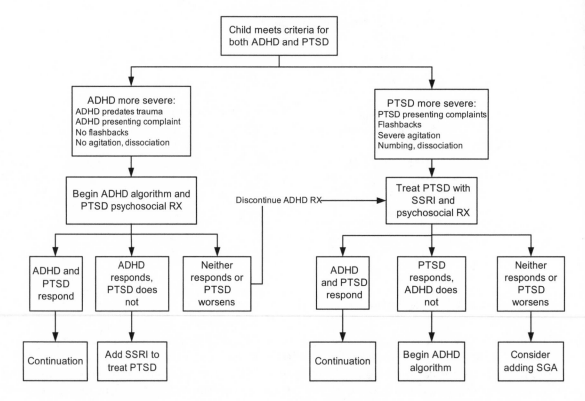

FIGURE 6.2. Algorithm for the treatment of ADHD with comorbid PTSD.

the trauma, being awakened by nightmares, chronic irritability), then treatment of the PTSD should begin first. Generally, this will involve a psychosocial intervention with or without concurrent treatment with an SSRI (Donnelly, 2003). Once the PTSD symptoms are brought under control, the ADHD algorithm can be utilized if the inattention and impulsivity–hyperactivity symptoms continue to impair the child's functioning. The third arm of the algorithm is for those children with severe PTSD comorbid with ADHD *and* aggressive outbursts. These children often display self-abusive behavior and severe flashbacks of a hallucinatory nature (e.g., seeing or sensing the abuser in the room at night). Such children will need complex psychopharmacology, perhaps the addition of an SGA to the SSRI if the PTSD does not fully resolve. ADHD treatment can be pursued when this process is complete.

Not only are there no data on the treatment of children with comorbid ADHD and PTSD, but the entire literature on the pharmacological treatment of PTSD is sparse, consisting of a handful of open trials of clonidine, nefazodone, imipramine, propranolol, and citalopram (Connor & Meltzer, 2008; Donnelly, 2003). Guidelines for the pharmacological treatment of PTSD in adults recommend the use of SSRIs as the first line of treatment. A review of this literature showed that multisite randomized controlled trials found sertraline, fluoxetine, and paroxetine superior to placebo in reducing a wide range of PTSD symptoms in adults (Friedman & Davidson, 2007). In children, much more work has been done to evaluate psychosocial interventions (particularly CBT) in the treatment of PTSD. As reviewed by Danielson et al. (2006), CBT was modified for the treatment of PTSD and consisted of: (1) coping skills training, (2) gradual exposure and cognitive and affective processing, (3) behavioral management skills training, and (4) psychoeducation regarding exposure to traumatic events and personal safety. The Medical University of South Carolina provides Web-based training for clinicians holding a master's degree or higher (*tfcbt.musc.edu*). Several large-scale randomized controlled trials show that this CBT approach is superior to standard community care in reducing symptoms of PTSD in children exposed to sexual and physical abuse (Cohen, Deblinger, Mannarino, & Steer, 2004; Danielson et al., 2006; Deblinger, Mannarino, Cohen, & Steer, 2006; Deblinger, Stauffer, & Steer, 2001; Deblinger, Steer, & Lippmann, 1999).

The Case of Karen: Anxiety and Negative Affectivity

Chief Complaint

Anxiety and irritability.

History of Presenting Illness

Karen is a 9-year-old girl who is brought by her parents for a second opinion with regard to her medication management. Karen had been on Luvox 100 mg/day for the past 6 months for an anxiety disorder, and her parents were unsure whether the medication was helping or not. The parents had taken Karen to a child and adolescent psychiatrist at the beginning of her fourth-grade year because of her frequent somatic complaints. These complaints were generally present only on school days and led to Karen making multiple requests that she stay home. Karen's pediatrician could find no physical cause for these complaints. The parents had experienced marital difficulties in the last year and there had been several months in which the father resided temporarily outside the home. The parents had considered separation but were now going to marital counseling with the goal of improving their marriage. The psychiatrist had told Karen's parents that he felt this turmoil contributed to Karen's anxiety.

The new psychiatrist proceeded with the structured interview. In the ADHD section of the interview, the parents endorsed seven of the nine inattention symptoms and three of the nine hyperactive-impulsive symptoms. It was also determined that Karen showed five of nine ODD symptoms, but no aggressive or CD symptoms. When the psychiatrist remarked on this, the mother recalled that the first-grade teacher commented on Karen's inattentiveness in class, but thought this was simply due to immaturity. The parents stated that since their child was "not hyperactive," they never seriously considered an ADHD diagnosis. The parents denied that Karen showed any prolonged depressive symptoms. Her sleep, appetite, and energy level were all age appropriate. She had never expressed any suicidal ideation but did make comments indicative of low self-esteem. Karen thought that she was not as pretty as other girls in the class and that the other girls did not like her. The mother did report that Karen tended to be shy around other children and sometimes did not respond to friendly overtures.

The psychiatrist then proceeded with the structured interview regarding the anxiety symptoms. Curiously the parents denied that Karen showed excessive concern with performance, nor did she worry excessively about events in the world. They did not describe Karen as a "worrier." The psychiatrist asked them to describe in more detail what they viewed as the symptoms of their daughter's anxiety. They again brought up the somatic complaints related to school, going to church, and doing homework. Karen was not self-confident and regularly said, "I can't do it" whenever a new challenge presented itself. Karen was very picky about certain details in her life and would get upset if things were not done to her liking. She always insisted on wearing certain articles of clothing even if the weather was not appropriate. Her dolls had to be arranged in certain ways in her room. She only ate certain foods, and these had to be arranged on her plate in a very particular way. In spite of this, the parents denied that Karen showed any classic symptoms of obsessive–compulsive disorder. She did not show any hand-washing obsession with germs or cleanliness (indeed, she was very sloppy about most things), nor did she have any obsessive thoughts. While Karen never showed any aggression or rage attacks, she would become very intense and argumentative over trivial issues.

Karen was an adequate student but she received negative marks on her conduct folder for being rude to the teacher. No one had ever suggested that Karen had any cognitive deficits or learning disabilities.

Past Psychiatric and Medical History

Other than treatment with the Luvox, Karen had not had any other mental health intervention. The mother's pregnancy and Karen's birth were unremarkable, and Karen's developmental milestones were appropriate. She had the usual childhood illnesses, and was not taking any other medication.

Family and Social History

As noted, the parents had experienced marital difficulties, but there was no history of physical or verbal abuse in the family. The parents felt they had been able to keep the details of their marital struggles from Karen. Karen was an only child. The father worked as a hospital administrator, and the mother worked part time in an office. The mother described herself as being "uptight" but had never had treatment for an anxiety disorder. Karen's paternal uncle and his sons had been treated for ADHD.

Mental Status Examination

Karen is a 9-year-old girl who appeared her stated age. She made good eye contact with the examiner and did not appear to be anxious during the interview. Her speech rate and volume were appropriate. She interrupted the examiner at times with questions about books and objects in the office, making numerous requests to touch them or play with them. Her intellectual functioning was average to above average, and her vocabulary was age appropriate. Her mood was neither elevated nor depressed, and her affect was appropriate to thought content. Karen denied feeling anxious or sad when directly asked. Scores on her self-ratings of depression and anxiety were also low. She then said that there were lots of things that she "didn't like." She stated that she wanted to be in a different classroom with a close friend of hers. She was upset that her mother would not allow her to wear the clothes she liked. As she spoke about these things, her jaw set and she clearly showed that she could be very stubborn. She denied any suicidal ideation. There were no auditory or visual hallucinations.

Treatment Course

The psychiatrist met with the parents and raised the issue of ADHD as a possibility. He also expressed a degree of uncertainty about the anxiety diagnosis. He asked the parents how effective they felt the Luvox has been. They stated that it seemed Karen was some-what less argumentative and her anger was under better control. They were less certain whether the number of somatic complaints had declined. In general, they estimated that she had "about a 20% improvement." Nonetheless, they felt anxiety was Karen's main problem. Given that Karen had been on the Luvox for 6 months at a reasonable dose, the psychiatrist recommended a trial of a different agent for anxiety. Karen was tapered off the Luvox and placed on Celexa 10 mg once a day. Rating scales were given to Karen's teacher.

The family returned a month later. No adverse events had been reported with the Celexa but the parents were vague as to whether it was any more helpful than the Luvox. It seemed to them that Karen's anger was improved on the Celexa relative to the previous medication, but they could not quantify this change. The teacher rating scale was consistent with the parents' report of inattentive symptoms. Nonetheless, the teacher had written on the rating scale that Karen could do her work if she wanted to and just had "a little bit of an attitude problem." Karen's stubbornness and somatic complaints continued. Karen and her family came for a monthly follow-up and the Celexa dose was increased to 20 mg/day because progress continued to be slow. At the next follow-up the parents brought her report card, which had shown a marked decrease in her grades. At this point, discussion of her ADHD symptoms was renewed and the parents agreed to a trial of a stimulant medication. Karen was begun on Adderall XR 5 mg in the morning, and this was gradually increased to 15 mg in the morning over a 4-week period. The teacher reported marked improvement in Karen's ability to concentrate in class, and her grades improved somewhat. The parents, however, noted an increase in her irritability. Furthermore Karen's weight decreased and she began to bite her fingernails excessively.

After discussion, the psychiatrist and the family agreed that the addition of the Adder-all was minimally helpful. One possibility was a trial of another stimulant (in the meth-ylphenidate class), but the psychiatrist was also concerned by the vagueness of the anxiety symptoms. Karen continued to deny anxiety when asked directly and the parents continued to report anxiety but always in the context of Karen being asked to do something she didn't want to. The psychiatrist explored the family's child-rearing style and found a marked lack of consistency in setting limits and following through on consequences. Indeed, because her parents viewed her symptoms as arising from anxiety, they tended to respond to Karen's emotional upsets by trying to reason with her and expressing sympathy. The psychiatrist advised them to switch tactics and set up a behavior management program (similar to the one devised for Caitlin in Chapter 2). Karen's three goals were (1) do things first time asked, (2) don't lose temper, and (3) talk about your feelings, don't scream. An allowance system based on the number of points she earned each week was implemented. Following the CMAP algorithm for ADHD/ANX the psychiatrist tapered her off the Celexa, discon-tinued the Adderall, and started a trial of Strattera, gradually increasing the dose over 3 weeks to 25 mg twice a day.

At a 2-month follow-up the parents reported, to their surprise, that Karen's behavior improved at both home and school. She was more even tempered, had a happier expres-sion on her face, and was more compliant. Karen strongly endorsed the behavior plan; she enjoyed keeping track of her allowance and having her own money to spend. The family was released for routine follow-up.

Karen's case clearly illustrates the type of "negativity affectivity" that was associated with better response to behavior management in the MTA study (Barry et al., 2004). The anxiety was reported only by the parent and this seemed to reflect Karen's difficult, emotionally high-strung temperament. Was this a true anxiety disorder? Perhaps not if the DSM nomenclature is applied strictly, but the parents' perception of their child's feelings did suggest that a combined medication-behavioral treatment was most effective.

The Case of Darren: Acute PTSD

Chief Complaint

"Panic attacks."

History of Presenting Illness

Darren is a 10-year-old boy who had been followed in the ADHD clinic since the age of 8 when he was first diagnosed with ADHD. He had been treated with Vyvanse 50 mg each morning and had done well on this medication. At most of his follow-up visits, his teacher ratings were in the normal range, his grades were good, and he did well in sports. At some visits, his parents remarked that he had intense nightmares after watching certain cartoons. He was mildly afraid of dogs, but none of these minor anxieties interfered with his functioning. In the summer after his fifth-grade year, the family took a rafting trip. The river was running somewhat faster than usual, but there appeared to be no danger. Darren's family was one of two that set off with the guides on the raft; everyone was wearing life jackets. About 30 minutes into the trip, the raft hit very heavy rapids and capsized, dumping all the passengers into the raging water. Darren's father was able to hang on to his wife and Darren's younger sister, and an eddy took them to the shore. Darren was swept downstream with the rest of the passengers, being submerged several times. A boy his age in the other family was swept along with him. As they both came up, the other child struck a rock and was killed. Darren saw the body as they were both swept onto the bank of the river. Darren had broken his arm.

   The fracture was not complicated and healed well with no deformity. For the first 2 weeks after the accident, Darren did not appear to be affected. He did not talk about it and seemed more concerned about not being able to play baseball because of his cast. By the third week, however, he began to have nightmares about the accident in which he saw the other boy. He began to sleep in his parents' room. He refused to go to the local water park (which had been one of his favorite places), and this gradually developed into a general fear of swimming pools. One evening his mother turned on the bath water and opened the faucet quickly, sending a rush of water into the tub. Darren was nearby and began screaming and breathing rapidly. This escalated into a full-blown panic attack. He was taken to the local emergency room and given a low dose of Ativan. The parents spoke to the psychiatrist on call, and an appointment was made for the next day.

Past Psychiatric and Medical History

None other than the history of ADHD.

Family and Social History

A paternal great-uncle had been treated at the VA hospital for PTSD after the Vietnam War. Darren's family was intact with no other psychosocial stressors. Darren's sister did not appear to have any emotional sequelae from the accident.

Mental Status Examination

Darren is a 10-year-old boy who appeared his stated age. He had a cast on his left arm. He was tearful during the interview and stated that he did not want to talk about the accident. His mood was severely depressed/irritable, and his affect was intense but appropriate to thought content. Thought processes were somewhat illogical as he reported that he might have another accident soon. With careful interviewing, Darren revealed that he had constant intrusive thoughts of the accident, but no overt flashbacks. He had no suicidal ideation. He denied any auditory or visual hallucinations.

Treatment Course

Darren had been off his ADHD medication on the days that he took pain medication for his arm. His parents had not noticed any change in the anxiety symptoms on the days he was off stimulant medication, but they did note an increase in distractibility on those days. The psychiatrist advised them to continue the Vyvanse. It was recommended that Darren begin Zoloft; the parents were warned to watch for agitation or any suicidal ideation. The Zoloft was started at 25 mg in the morning, increasing over 3 weeks to 100 mg/day. He was also referred to a therapist with reassurance that the therapist would not force him to talk about the accident. The therapist began with relaxation techniques, suggesting to Darren that he focus on playing baseball whenever "bad" feelings emerged. Because of the intensity of his anxiety, the therapist did not go beyond such techniques in the first month of treatment. Darren's nightmares continued and the psychiatrist prescribed Klonopin 0.25 mg at bedtime for a month. Gradually, Darren was able to push the memories out of his mind when watching TV or playing baseball. His parents had to be careful that movies or shows did not contain any content that would remind him.

After about seven sessions of therapy, the therapist shifted from relaxation techniques to desensitization techniques. Darren was first asked to recall the fun he had swimming in a neighborhood pool before the accident. His parents were asked to replay videos of a poolside birthday party when he was 8 years old. The parents bought a small portable pool and Darren was encouraged to lie in it until he was comfortable with water. Over the course of the summer, Darren was able to ride in the family car as they passed the neighborhood pool, but he was not able to go within the grounds. The therapist advised the parents against pushing Darren to do this in any way. The family practiced turning on the bath water while Darren was downstairs, and then over the course of several weeks they would turn on the water as he stood progressively closer to the bathroom. At each step of this process, Darren practiced his relaxation techniques. He gradually lost his fear of running water in the bathtub; furthermore, this sound no longer triggered intrusive memories. The therapist began to work on other, more frightening intrusive memories, especially Darren's memory of the other child in the raft. Darren did not exhibit any inappropriate guilt about the incident. He did not evidence any desire that he had died rather than the other child, nor did he think that he could have done anything differently. He was bothered by memories of the other child's body floating in the river. The therapist explored Darren's beliefs about the afterlife. Darren's family was moderately religious, and the therapist expected Darren to say that the child had gone to heaven. Darren stated, however, that he thought the child had become a ghost and was beginning to haunt him. Prior to the accident Darren had frequently read ghost and horror stories and had some degree of belief that they might be real. The therapist held a family session, and together they reassured Darren that ghosts did not exist. This made it easier for Darren to use his relaxation techniques whenever these very intrusive thoughts appeared. Altogether, Darren had about 20 sessions of therapy in which these techniques were used. He remained on Zoloft for a year and a half. After he had been symptom free for 6 months, the psychiatrist tapered him off the antidepressant over a 6-week period. His symptoms of PTSD did not reoccur.

Darren's emotional development had been unremarkable prior to the accident, and the trauma that he suffered was acute and dramatic. As a result, he developed a classic case of PTSD that was superimposed on the ADHD. The two disorders did not interact with each other in terms of their treatment, although it is unlikely that Darrin could have participated in the cognitive exercises if his ADHD had not remained well controlled by his stimulant medication. In children who experience chronic abuse, the picture can be quite different.

The Case of Ellen: Chronic PTSD

Chief Complaint

Aggression and possible psychosis.

History of Presenting Illness

Ellen is a 13-year-old girl who had been in the custody of CPS for 6 years. She had been living in a foster home when she became markedly aggressive toward her foster mother, knocking her down after the foster mother tried to physically redirect her. Ellen had walked away while the foster mother had been speaking to her. This incident came at the end of a 3-month period in which Ellen's behavior had become increasingly unmanageable both at home and at school. Ellen had a history of severe physical and sexual abuse, beginning when she was at least 5 years of age and continuing until the time she was removed from the care of her biological mother. While the sexual abuse had occurred at the hands of the mother's boyfriend, both the mother and her boyfriend had been physically aggressive with Ellen, leaving multiple bruises on her. Since going into custody, Ellen had been difficult to manage and had failed multiple foster placements. At one foster placement, she had accused her foster father of touching her inappropriately, but CPS did not validate this complaint. Three weeks prior to hitting her current foster mother, she had been taken to a local community mental health clinic, where the psychiatrist had placed her on Celexa 20 mg in the morning for symptoms of depression. Because of her history, Ellen was transferred to a residential treatment center (RTC).

Since admission to the RTC, Ellen had displayed multiple aggressive outbursts every day. Her mood was chronically irritable; she was withdrawn from peers and showed little interest in the cabin activities. She had trouble sleeping and came out of her room several times at night. She told the night staff that she could sense her mother's boyfriend in the room and asked if she could sleep in the day area. She was extremely suspicious of male staff members. Even though her cabin had an all-female staff, precautions were taken so that Ellen did not interact with male staff by herself, as there were concerns that she would make a false accusation.

Past Psychiatric and Medical History

When Ellen was first taken into custody at age 7, she was noted to be very impulsive and hyperactive. Over time she had been treated with numerous ADHD medications, and at the time of her admission, she was taking Ritalin LA 30 mg once a day. She weighed 108 pounds (49 kg), and her vital signs were within normal limits. She had no other medical problems. A psychological evaluation conducted 2 months prior to admission showed a Full Scale IQ of 87 and reading achievement at the fourth-grade level. (Ellen was nominally in the seventh grade.)

Mental Status Examination

Ellen is a 13-year-old girl who appeared her stated age. Prior to the interview, she was seen arguing with a child-care worker in the hallway. She slumped into her seat and looked away from the examiner. When asked how she was feeling, she replied, "everything's fine," with a very negative tone of voice. Her speech rate and volume were reduced, and she often replied, "I don't want to talk about it" to even very basic questions. Her mood was severely depressed and irritable; her affect was appropriate to thought content, but labile and intense. Thought processes were difficult to assess due to Ellen's lack of spontaneity. There were no loose associations, flight of ideas, or other signs of disorganized thinking during the interview. Ellen acknowledged that she was having flashbacks of her past abuse, but none were present at the time of the interview. She acknowledged that she would have visions of her mother's boyfriend appearing in her room at night, but would not elaborate.

Treatment Course

Ellen began intensive therapy with the cottage therapist, who met with her three times a week. Despite their difficulty with her, Ellen's foster parents desired to remain in contact and hoped that she might eventually return to them. Therefore, weekly family therapy was also scheduled. The psychiatrist elected to continue the current medications: Ritalin LA 30 mg in the morning and Celexa 20 mg once a day. Over the next month, Ellen continued to show significant irritability and aggressive outbursts. Her sleep problems continued, and she began to report flashbacks during the day, particularly during school. The therapist was concerned that some of these school-related flashbacks could have had something to do with her dislike of school. The psychiatrist increased the Celexa to 30 mg once a day. At the next monthly follow-up, it was noted that the number of Ellen's aggressive incidents had increased by 20%. The teacher rating scale showed continuing symptoms of inattention and impulsivity in the classroom.

The therapist was concerned that Ellen was making very little progress in therapy. She continued to refuse to talk about any past issues and mainly wanted to play checkers or other games during the session. She also was reluctant to talk about her current behavior in the RTC and regularly refused to take responsibility for her actions. On interview, the psychiatrist found that Ellen's mood had changed little. She continued to be highly irritable and to report bedtime problems. In view of the mediocre response to treatment, the psychiatrist elected to taper Ellen off her medications to obtain a new baseline. For the first 2 weeks off all medicines, the staff did not report either improvement or deterioration in Ellen's behavior or mood. There was a modest decline in aggressive incidents, and the teacher did report that Ellen seemed less "antsy." The psychiatrist elected to try an alternative SSRI, and Ellen was started on Prozac 20 mg a day. Over the next several weeks, staff reported a slight improvement in Ellen's irritability, and they noted that she would smile from time to time. The nighttime visions continued, even though Ellen was able to remain in her bedroom. One weekend, the on-call psychiatrist received an urgent message. Ellen reported that she was having a hallucination of her mother's boyfriend's voice saying he was coming after her. Ellen was started on Seroquel 50 mg at bedtime, titrating up to 100 mg twice a day. At the next follow-up, Ellen reported that the nighttime visions had stopped;

her aggressive incidents had dropped to about three a week instead of occurring daily. The Seroquel was increased to 300 mg/day and the physical aggression stopped entirely, although Ellen continued to be oppositional.

The monthly follow-up teacher ratings were again reviewed. These continued to show a high level of inattention in the classroom; staff also reported that they had a lot of trouble getting Ellen to focus on her chores. As the hallucinatory activity had ceased, it was elected to begin Ellen on Concerta 18 mg/day. When there was no response to this dosage, it was increased to 36 mg a day and then finally to 54 mg a day. There was no increase in irritability or hallucinatory phenomena, and the teacher reported significant improvement in classroom behavior and educational performance.

The therapist continued to find Ellen extremely resistant in therapy. The psychiatrist noted Ellen had very poor verbal skills and cautioned the therapist about pushing too hard to get Ellen to talk about the past. Ellen did not really understand more advanced cognitive-behavioral techniques, but was able to work with the therapist on ways to keep "bad thoughts" away. The therapist integrated her individual work with the cabin's behavior management program. If her behavior for the day was positive, Ellen could choose a favorite activity to do during therapy, as long as she would talk with the therapist about ways to manage her feelings. This was reinforced in the family work—it was clear that Ellen viewed her anger outbursts as justified by other people's actions. The incident in which she pushed her foster mother was reviewed, and Ellen was encouraged to see how she had reacted inappropriately. She began her weekend passes and did not show any aggressive behavior. At her final follow-up, Ellen did not report any irritable mood or flashbacks. She returned to the foster family and was enrolled in special education to assist her with her reading problems. Ellen and her foster family continued with outpatient care.

How is this case different from that of John (IED) in Chapter 3 or Sally (mania) in Chapter 4? Like them, Ellen clearly showed mood lability and aggression. Recall that John did *not* show any evidence of intrusive memories, flashbacks, or mood disturbance in between his aggressive outbursts. Thus, a diagnosis of PTSD (and treatment with an SSRI) would have been inappropriate. In Sally's case, there were clear-cut symptoms of mania, such as flight of ideas and pressured speech, all of which were absent in Ellen's case. Ellen, in contrast, had overt symptoms of PTSD with a chronic irritable mood that could be connected to her history of past abuse. These symptoms predicted response to an SSRI, but because of Ellen's chronic abuse, her PTSD was resistant to the SSRI alone. The flashbacks had elevated to the level of hallucinatory and dissociative-like states, necessitating the use of an SGA. Note, in particular, that the therapist did not seek to "force" Ellen to "deal" with her past abuse. Perhaps the day will come when Ellen has the cognitive skills and the emotional stability to be introspective about her past. But it is more likely that repression will continue to be a far better strategy, coupled with a focus on building better current relationships.

In the next chapter, we move on to a different type of anxiety disorder, obsessive–compulsive disorder, which is frequently comorbid with tic disorders. The relationship of these two disorders with ADHD is complex.

Chapter 7

Tic and Obsessive–Compulsive Disorders

Obsessive–compulsive disorder (OCD) has always been thought to be one of the anxiety disorders, yet it is qualitatively different from them. The anxiety disorders studied in Chapter 6 are *quantitatively* different from a normal, adaptive behavior. A modest amount of general anxiety keeps us alert and wary to challenges; developmentally appropriate separation fears signal the development of bonding and keep a vulnerable toddler close to caregivers. Most people feel some anxiety after a trauma. It is when these feelings become excessive and interfere with functioning that anxiety becomes an *anxiety disorder*. In contrast, it is difficult to see any adaptive element in the symptoms of OCD. Why would human beings find themselves compelled to count objects, touch things in a certain way, or obsess about sex, violence, dirt, or excrement in an unpleasant manner? Why would a child feel an unstoppable urge to pull all his/her hair out? The anxiety that patients with OCD feel is often *secondary* to the disruption these symptoms produce in their lives. In other situations, it arises only when they are prevented from carrying out their compulsions. Subjective anxiety may not appear at all in an individual with OCD or tics who has poor insight. OCD must also be distinguished from an obsessive personality. Many healthy individuals are fastidious, highly organized, and neat, yet do not engage in strange rituals or obsess about odd topics.

OCD is also distinguished from other forms of anxiety by its motor component. While other anxiety disorders are primarily cognitive (e.g., phobias, internal tension, intrusive memories), persons with OCD commit motor acts (the compulsions) and even their obsessions relate to urges to *do* things (e.g., hurt others, have sex). OCD has a close relationship with tic disorders at a genetic level. People with OCD have a higher than expected number of relatives with tic disorders and vice versa (Pauls et al., 1995; Pauls, Leckman, & Cohen, 1993). Roughly 13–26% of patients with OCD have tic disorders (Geller, 2006), while up to 50% of patients with full-blown Tourette's syndrome have symptoms of OCD (Swain, Scahill, Lombroso, King, & Leckman, 2007). Thus it appears that the OCD and tic disorders are etiologically related to one another (see Figure 7.1). Tics, of course, are motor acts. Patients with tics and OCD often experience

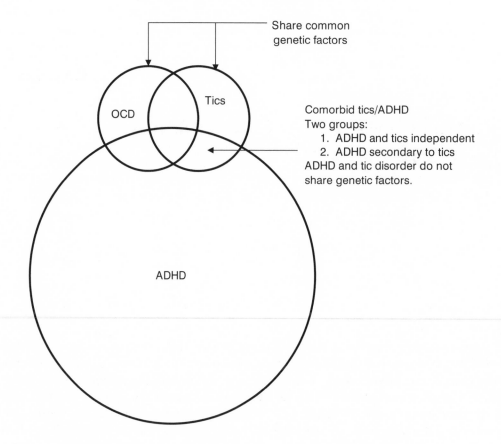

FIGURE 7.1. Understanding the overlap of ADHD, OCD, and tic disorders.

a premonitory urge before the tic appears or the compulsion is performed; both sets of patients must exert major effort to stop the symptoms, and they both experience a sense of relief once the tic or compulsion is released. Patients with Sydenham's chorea often display symptoms of OCD and develop phonic tics, which leads to the hypothesis that OCD and tics are related to the development of auto-antibodies to central nervous system structures in genetically vulnerable individuals after a beta-hemolytic streptococcal infection (Swedo et al., 1998). More recently, it has been suggested that other bacterial and viral illnesses can trigger this autoimmune response (Snider & Swedo, 2004). However, studies to investigate this theory, as well as studies of the efficacy of antibiotic prophylaxis of tics and OCD have not shown a clear pattern (Swain et al., 2007).

Theories of the neurology of OCD and tics have focused on the connections between the motor cortex, caudate nucleus, and thalamus (Leckman, Vaccarino, Kalanithi, & Rothenberger, 2006). There are oscillations of neural activity between the motor cortex and the thalamus that relate to ongoing motor behavior. When a new behavior (or change in a current behavior) is required (usually in response to sensory input), these cortico-thalamic oscillations are interrupted by "bursts" of neuronal activity in the caudate nucleus. In this model, OCD and tics might be two sides of a coin: in tics, there are abnormal interruptions of cortico-thalamic oscillations, while patients with

OCD literally get "caught in the loop" at the neural level and express the same behavior (or thought) over and over again. Since the caudate nucleus and prefrontal cortex are also involved in ADHD (Castellanos, Sonuga-Barke, Milham, & Tannock, 2006), it is not surprising that children with OCD or tics have a high prevalence of ADHD, but the relationship is not straightforward.

The "impulse-control disorders" (ICD) of trichotillomania, skin picking, kleptomania, pyromania, and pathological gambling add another layer of complexity to this issue. Many persons with ADHD are sensation seeking, and their impulsivity leads them to engage unwisely in gambling or shoplifting. In contrast, an ICD involves a highly compulsive and irrational engagement in the activity; the patient is driven to do the activity rather than getting pleasure from it. Comparing patients with OCD to those with trichotillomania or skin picking, Ferrão, Almeida, Bedin, Rosa, and Busnell (2006) found the patients with ICD to have fewer premonitory urges and more sudden onset of the urges. In general, patients with OCD "thought more" about their symptoms than those with ICD, had greater insight, and were more likely to be taking SSRIs.

ADHD and Tics

Simple and transient tics are quite common in the pediatric population, affecting 6–20% of all children (Khalifa & von Knorring, 2005), while full-blown chronic tic disorder or Tourette's syndrome occur in 4–6 per 1,000 children (Khalifa & von Knorring, 2003). Onset of tics is generally at the age of 3–5 years with a peak prevalence at 9–12 years, with only about 20% of children continuing to experience tics in adulthood (Bloch et al., 2006; Swain et al., 2007). The natural course of tics parallels the time that children with ADHD are likely to start and stop stimulant treatment, and this may have led to the false belief that stimulants "unmask" or "cause" tics (see below). As Figure 7.1 shows, the overlap between tics and ADHD is highly asymmetrical. Up to 60% of children with tic disorders have ADHD (Spencer et al., 1998), whereas only about 10% of children with ADHD have a tic disorder (MTA Cooperative Group, 1999a). This raises the question as to whether ADHD and tic disorders are alternate phenotypes of the same underlying disorder (Comings & Comings, 1990) or ADHD with comorbid tics is a different genetic subtype from ADHD alone.

Stewart et al. (2006) addressed this issue by interviewing over 600 relatives of children in four groups: controls ($n = 49$), children with ADHD ($n = 41$), children with tics only ($n = 74$), and children with comorbid ADHD/tics ($n = 75$). As expected, ADHD was elevated in the relatives of children with ADHD, and tics were more prevalent in the relatives of children with tic disorders. The important questions were whether tic disorders would be found at an unexpectedly high rate among the relatives of children with ADHD only *and* whether higher rates of ADHD would be found in the relatives of those with tics only. If both of these findings occurred, it would suggest that the disorders shared a genetic etiology. In fact, ADHD was *not* elevated among the relatives of children who had only tics, but more tics were found among the relatives of patients with ADHD More interesting, comorbid ADHD and tic disorders were more common in all four groups. Thus, ADHD and tic disorders do not directly share genetic factors (or tics would have been elevated in the relatives of patients with tics), but ADHD with comorbid tics may have some overlapping pathophysiology. One possibility is that an aberrant cortical-striatal activity hypothesized to underlie tic disorders might lead to a secondary ADHD.

All of this is key to understanding the root causes of ADHD and tic comorbidity, but how are the comorbid patients different *clinically* from those with ADHD or tics alone? Rizzo et al. (2007) examined the CBCL scores of children with ADHD alone, tic disorders alone, and ADHD with tic disorders, and controls (20 subjects in each group, see Figure 7.2). On the CBCL, a *T* score of 50 is the mean of the general population, and each 10 points represent a standard deviation above or below this mean. Note that for the most part, all three clinical groups are more impaired than the control group, and children with and without tics who have ADHD do not differ in their degree of inattentiveness. The increased impairment in the comorbid ADHD tic group (relative to the tic-only group) is carried by the presence of the ADHD alone, consistent with other studies (Swain et al., 2007). That is, the effect of ADHD in comorbid tics is simply additive—the symptoms of ADHD are not quantitatively or qualitatively different in the child with comorbidity. Despite the great interest in tic disorders as a brain disease, there are surprisingly few neuropsychological differences between children

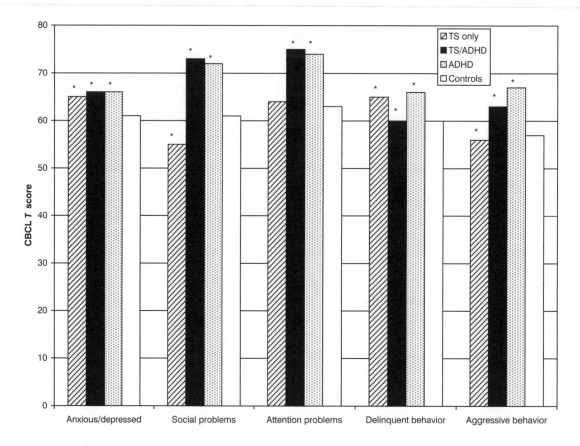

FIGURE 7.2. Child Behavior Checklist (CBCL) total behavior scores in children with ADHD, Tourette's syndrome (TS), comorbid ADHD and TS, and controls. Adapted from Rizzo et al. (2007). Copyright 2007 by Elsevier Limited. Adapted by permission.

with ADHD and comorbid tics and those with ADHD alone. Other than a very modest decrease in Performance IQ, a group of children with ADHD with and without tics did not differ from each other on any other measures of intellectual, academic, or social functioning (Dykens et al., 1990). Greimel, Herpertz-Dahlmann, Gunther, Vitt, and Konrad (2008) did not find any differences between children with ADHD who had tics and those who didn't on several laboratory measures of impulsivity, executive function, and sustained attention. This should caution clinicians against treating ADHD and tic disorders as something very unusual as it may blind them to treatment of the more impairing symptoms of ADHD.

Do Stimulants Cause Tics?

The short answer is no. Certainly, the inducement of tics is not a common side effect of stimulants in patients with ADHD generally. A review of 12 recent randomized, placebo-controlled trials of stimulant medications involving over 1,000 subjects found no evidence that the rate of new-onset tics was higher with stimulants relative to placebo (Roessner, Robatzek, Knapp, Banaschewski, & Rothenberger, 2006). In research spanning over a decade, Kenneth Gadow and his colleagues have shown that children with ADHD and comorbid tic disorders *do not,* on average, experience an increase in tics when treated with stimulants and show a very robust response of their ADHD symptoms (Gadow, Nolan, Sprafkin, & Sverd, 1995; Gadow, Nolan, & Sverd, 1992a; Gadow, Nolan, & Sverd, 1992b; Gadow & Sverd, 2006; Gadow, Sverd, Nolan, Sprafkin, & Schneider, 2007; Nolan & Gadow, 1997; Sverd, Gadow, Nolan, Sprafkin, & Ezor, 1992). Nonetheless, a significant minority of children with ADHD and tics will have an increase in tics if treated with a stimulant. All clinicians have seen individual children who have had a new onset of tics or an aggravation in tics when starting a stimulant. Stimulants may increase minor stereotypies such as fingernail biting, hair twirling, or other habits. While uncomfortable and sometimes requiring a change of medication, these should not be referred to as tics and surely should not be diagnosed as tic disorder or Tourette's syndrome. The natural course of tics is that they emerge at the same time that ADHD treatment is initiated; therefore the coincidence of a tic emerging when a stimulant was started should not be viewed as a cause-and-effect relationship. It may take stopping and restarting a stimulant for two to three trials to definitely conclude that a given child has tics as a side effect of a particular stimulant. If a child develops a mild tic while on a stimulant, it would be appropriate to observe the child for several weeks to see if it resolves on its own.

Behavioral Treatment of Tics

In many clinical situations, the tics are of mild to moderate severity and may not rise to the level where psychopharmacological intervention for the tic per se is required. It is important to note that behavioral treatments are increasingly viewed as viable treatments for tics. Specifically, eight randomized trials have shown that habit reversal training (HRT) is a promising option (Himle, Woods, Piacentini, & Walkup, 2006). HRT involves three components: (1) achieving awareness of premonitory urges, (2) use of relaxation techniques when the urge is building, and (3) making a competing motor response incompatible with the tic. This competing response is repeated several times until the urge dissipates. An example is given in the case of Wayne, later in this chapter.

Pharmacological Treatment of ADHD and Tics

The CMAP algorithm for the treatment of ADHD with comorbid tics is shown in Figure 7.3 (Pliszka et al., 2006). The central tenet of this algorithm is that the ADHD should be the first focus of treatment. Following the main CMAP algorithm, this would involve a stimulant trial. The goal is to find an ADHD treatment that is robust in reducing the symptoms of ADHD but doesn't worsen, and perhaps even simultaneously improves tics. In fact, controlled trials show that methylphenidate and atomoxetine can reduce tic severity in those with comorbid ADHD and tic disorder (Spencer et al., 2008; Tourette's Syndrome Study Group, 2002). There have been case reports of bupropion exacerbating tics (Spencer, Biederman, Steingard, & Wilens, 1993), while clonidine and guanfacine can be efficacious for both tics and ADHD (Connor, Fletcher, & Swanson, 1999; Scahill et al., 2001). Alpha-agonists (at least in their short-acting formulations) do not appear to have the same effect size as stimulants, so clinicians may face a situation where the child requires a stimulant for treatment of his or her ADHD but tics remain a problem or are exacerbated.

The Tourette's Syndrome Study Group (2002) conducted a randomized, double-blind clinical trial involving 136 children with ADHD and a chronic tic disorder. Subjects were randomly administered clonidine alone, methylphenidate alone, combined clonidine and methylphenidate, or placebo in a parallel group design for 16 weeks (weeks 1–4: clonidine/placebo dose titration; weeks 5–8: added methylphenidate/placebo dose titration; weeks 9–16: maintenance therapy). On the primary outcome measure of ADHD (Conners teacher ratings), significant improvement occurred for subjects assigned to clonidine and those assigned to methylphenidate. Compared with placebo, the greatest benefit occurred with the combination of clonidine and methylphenidate. Clonidine appeared to be most helpful for impulsivity and hyperactivity, while methylphenidate was best for inattention. The number of subjects reporting worsening of tics was no different among those treated with methylphenidate (20%), clonidine alone (26%), or placebo (22%). Sedation was common with clonidine treatment (28% reported moderate or severe sedation). There was no evidence of cardiac toxicity, even for the group receiving the combination treatment. This study clearly validates the practice of combining stimulants with alpha-agonists for the treatment of the comorbid condition when ADHD treatment alone does not control both sets of symptoms.

What about the child whose tics do not respond to an alpha-agonist? Four randomized controlled trials have shown that risperidone is superior to placebo for the treatment of tics (Bruggeman et al., 2001; Dion, Annable, Sandor, & Chouinard, 2002; Gaffney et al., 2002; Scahill, Leckman, Schultz, Katsovich, & Peterson, 2003) at doses of 1–3.5 mg/day. The first two studies showed that risperidone was equivalent in efficacy to pimozide, while an additional study has shown risperidone to be superior to pimoxide (Gilbert, Batterson, Sethuraman, & Sallee, 2004). Other SGAs have been reported to be helpful in small open trials (Swain et al., 2007). The risk of weight gain, hyperlipidema, and sedation with SGAs means that only the most severe tics resistant to psychosocial interventions and/or alpha-agonist treatment should be treated with these agents.

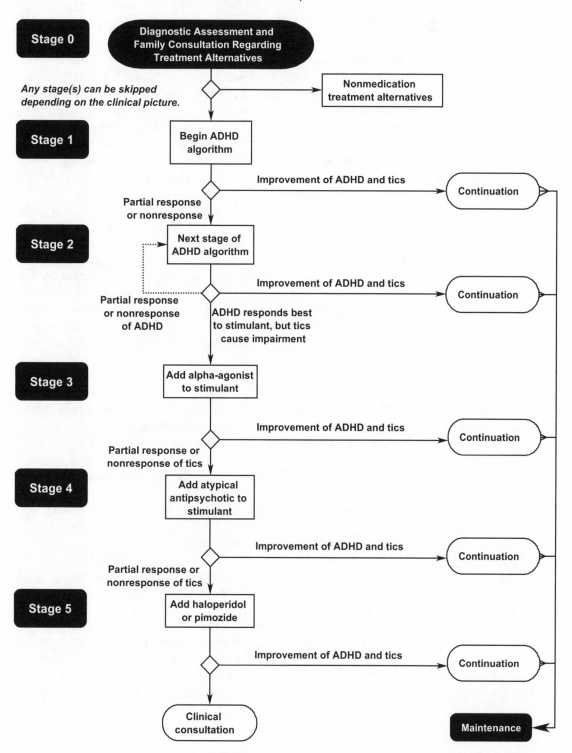

FIGURE 7.3. Algorithm for the pharmacological treatment of ADHD with comorbid tic disorders.

ADHD and OCD

Epidemiology studies have shown that the prevalence of OCD in the general adolescent population ranges from 2 to 4% (Geller, 2006). OCD has an asymmetrical overlap with ADHD, as do tic disorders (see Figure 7.1). OCD does not commonly occur in epidemiological samples of children with ADHD in the community and certainly does not exceed the rates in the general population. The MTA did not mention whether any of the third of patients who met criteria for an anxiety disorder specifically met criteria for OCD. In contrast, 51% of children and 36% of adolescents with OCD also met criteria for ADHD, and this ADHD is not accounted for as an epiphenomenon of the OCD itself (i.e., obsessions distracting the patient) (Geller et al., 1998d, 2002; Geller, 2006). How do OCD and ADHD influence each other? As with tics, the presence of ADHD has no effect on the expression of the OCD symptoms themselves, although children with ADHD/OCD have an earlier age of onset of their OCD compared to those without ADHD (Masi et al., 2006a; Walitza et al., 2008). Compared to those with ADHD alone, children with ADHD/OCD have higher rates of educational dysfunction (Geller et al., 2003c). Masi et al. (2006a) compared children with OCD alone and those with ADHD/OCD in terms of OCD symptoms, psychiatric diagnoses, and social functioning. OCD children with and without ADHD did not differ in prevalence of ordering, aggressive, contamination, or hoarding obsessions. Those with ADHD/OCD had generally poorer social functioning compared to those with OCD only; they also had a higher prevalence of bipolar, tic, and oppositional disorders, but a lower prevalence of depression. Similarly, Sukhodolsky et al. (2005) found children with ADHD/OCD to have poorer social skills both at home and school, less family cohesion, and higher ratings of internalizing symptoms than children with OCD only (who in turn were more impaired on these measures than controls). As with tic disorders, the greater impairment in ADHD/OCD was driven primarily by the presence of the ADHD and other externalizing diagnoses associated with it, rather than any unique interaction of the ADHD and OCD symptomatology.

Why would ADHD be elevated above the general population rates in children with OCD? Family studies have looked at the rate of both OCD and ADHD in the relatives of children with OCD alone and ADHD alone and those with ADHD/OCD compared to controls (Geller et al., 2007b, 2007c). Again, as with tics, the rate of ADHD is elevated in the relatives of patients with ADHD, and OCD is elevated in the relatives of patients with OCD, but ADHD/OCD combined is found only in those patients with ADHD/OCD (cosegregation). Like bipolar or conduct disorder, ADHD with OCD is a distinct familial subtype of ADHD in terms of underlying pathophysiology. The bottom line is that the OCD and ADHD by themselves are independent conditions but ADHD + OCD is a separate familial subtype. Nonetheless, the ADHD in comorbid OCD is clinically indistinguishable from ADHD appearing alone, even though the underlying genetics of the ADHD in the comorbid group differ from the genetics of ADHD occurring alone.

Treatment of OCD

Interestingly, treatment of OCD in children and adolescents is one of the better-researched topics in the mental health field, and this is true for both CBT and psychopharmacology. In terms of medication, there have been 12 double-blind, placebo-controlled, randomized trials of SSRIs for the treatment of OCD (Geller et al., 2003b; Reinblatt & Riddle, 2007). These trials included studies of fluoxetine, paroxetine, sertraline, and fluvoxamine; a meta-analysis showed these agents to have a combined effect size of 0.46 with little difference in clinical efficacy between them. Typically, about half the samples would respond to the SSRI compared to about 25–33% for the placebo group. Paroxetine had less efficacy for OCD symptoms in those with ADHD comorbidity (51%) compared with children with OCD alone (75%) (Geller et al., 2003a). However, Masi et al. (2006a) did not find that children who had OCD with and without ADHD differed in their response to SSRIs in general.

CBT has been a well-established treatment for OCD in children. A typical course of therapy involves the sessions shown in Table 7.1. The Pediatric OCD Treatment Study (POTS) randomized 112 children and adolescents to one of four treatment groups: placebo, CBT alone, sertraline alone, or combination of CBT and sertraline, with 97 of the subjects completing 12 weeks of intervention (Pediatric OCD Treatment Study [POTS] Team, 2004). All three active treatments were superior to placebo; the response rates for the different conditions were 3.6% (placebo), 39.3% (CBT alone), 21.4% (sertraline alone), and 56.3% (combination treatment). Statistically, combination treatment was superior to both CBT alone and sertraline alone, which did not differ from each other. The low rate of sertraline response in the POTS study stands in contrast to the 57% response rate for this agent for the treatment of OCD in an earlier study (March et al., 1998). Furthermore, CBT effectiveness varied by site in the multicenter study, suggesting therapist factors were at play. Thus, clinicians should view with some skepticism the authors' recommendation that CBT should *always* be combined with SSRI treatment of OCD. Nonetheless, it is clear that CBT is a key intervention for OCD, though it is not known if ADHD affects the ability of the child to participate in it. Comorbid tics appeared to predict a poorer response of OCD to sertraline (March et al., 2007).

Even with combined treatment in the POTS, only about 50–60% of patients responded. This brings up the controversial issue of augmenting SSRI treatment with SGAs. Sometimes, this point is moot—as in the treatment of patients with ADHD/OCD

TABLE 7.1. Cognitive-Behavioral Therapy for OCD

The CBT regimen consisted of 14 visits over 12 weeks:

- *Psychoeducation.* Discussing the nature of OCD, emphasizing the patient's ability to gain control.
- *Cognitive training.* Becoming aware of OCD symptoms, gaining insight.
- *Mapping OCD target symptoms.* When did OCD symptoms occur, what triggered them? If no trigger, developing alternative thoughts to counter them.
- *Exposure and response (ritual) prevention.* Exposing self to contaminants (bathroom, toilet, trash can) or throwing away hoarded materials; using relaxation techniques while doing so.

Each session included:

- A statement of goals
- A review of the previous week's progress
- Provision of new information
- Therapist-assisted practice, homework for the coming week
- Monitoring procedures

Sessions 1, 7, and 11 included parents for the entire session.

Note. Data from the Pediatric OCD Treatment Study (POTS) Team (2004).

who also have severe comorbid BP or aggressive symptoms (Masi et al., 2006a) that require the use of these agents. In other cases, the obsessions and compulsions have a "psychotic" feel to them—as in the child who believes holding his arm in a certain position all week will help him hit a home run in the baseball game. Three studies with adults (Erzegovesi, Guglielmo, Siliprandi, & Bellodi, 2005; Hollander, Baldini, Sood, & Pallanti, 2003; McDougle, Epperson, Pelton, Wasylink, & Price, 2000) have shown that risperidone added to an SSRI improves response of OCD symptoms in those who have not responded adequately to the SSRI alone; the presence or absence of tics does not predict response to the SGA (McDougle et al., 2000). When treating OCD with SSRIs or SGAs, the physician must be alert to the problems of suicidality and weight gain, respectively (see Appendix II). Certainly, a trial of CBT or other therapy would be recommended *before* adding an SGA to the medication regimen of a child with OCD. When ADHD is present with OCD, the ADHD should be treated concurrently, typically with a combination of an ADHD medication and an SSRI.

The following cases focus on the more difficult situations of triple comorbidity of ADHD, tics, and OCD.

The Case of Wayne

Chief Complaint

Hair pulling.

History of Presenting Illness

Wayne is a 9-year-old boy brought by his parents because he was not responding for treatment of his hair pulling. Wayne had been pulling the hair out of the back of his head for the last 18 months. For the first 6 months, Wayne's parents had verbally discouraged him from doing it and cut his hair shorter, but the hair pulling persisted. Indeed, it had worsened in the last 6 months, and he began to pull at his eyebrows as well. He would occasionally eat the hairs. Wayne had no particular reason for doing this; he would only say that it felt good to pull his hair. The hair pulling increased when Wayne watched television, read a book, or listened to the teacher in class. In addition to pulling his hair, Wayne had several tics: he twitched his eyebrows, constantly cleared his throat, and would lift his shoulders several times in a row. Other children in his class would laugh at him when he did the latter tic, but this did not deter Wayne. Wayne had been evaluated by a neurologist, who performed an EEG which was within normal limits, as was the standard neurological exam. A diagnosis of tic disorder was made and Wayne was started on Haldol 0.25 mg twice a day. The shoulder shrug improved somewhat after several weeks of treatment, but the hair pulling remained problematic so the neurologist added Zoloft 25 mg in the evening. After 2 months on this medication, no change was noted and the parents sought a second opinion.

Past Psychiatric and Medical History

When Wayne was in the first grade, the teacher reported that he was very inattentive and did not finish his work; he was also slow to learn to read. Teachers in the second and third grades had similar complaints, but Wayne was not hyperactive and seemed to "get by." His parents had to spend large amounts of time in the evening helping him complete schoolwork that he had not finished that day in school. At present, he had several failing grades. Wayne was not oppositional or aggressive, though he would be very stubborn about pulling his hair. The parents had not taken any active steps to modify this behavior, believing the symptoms to be neurological in origin.

Wayne's parents denied that he had ever shown symptoms of depression, and there was no history of suicidal ideation. He ate and slept well, tended to be lazy, but had normal energy. He was not an anxious or fearful child but had a variety of what the parents called "weird habits." When questioned, they reported that Wayne always wanted to sit with his body "symmetrical," that is, each of his arms and legs had to be in the same position. Also he did not want the positions of the superhero figures on his bookshelf to be changed, so the maid had to be extra careful when dusting. Wayne had no history of any significant medical illnesses and weighed about 72 pounds (33.3 kg).

Family and Social History

Both parents were professionals, in good physical and mental health, and enjoyed a stable marriage. Wayne had a 6-year-old sister who did not have any mental health issues. There was no family history of OCD, but the mother recalled that her brother had ADHD and had an eye-blinking tic when he was younger, though it resolved by the time he entered adolescence.

Mental Status Examination

Wayne is a 9-year-old boy who appeared his stated age. He sat very quietly on the couch in the examiner's office, his arms and legs placed symmetrically around him, except when he reached up to pull his hair, roughly every 3 minutes. He shrugged his shoulders and twitched his left eye at about the same frequency. He answered most questions with only one to three words, and there was little spontaneous conversation. He denied depressed mood, but his affect was somewhat blunted. He was oriented to person, place, and time; intellectual functioning appeared average. Thought processes were overall logical and goal directed with no loose associations or flight of ideas. He did state he had to keep his body "lined up" and he just "liked the feeling" of pulling his hair. He stated that he never really tried to stop himself from doing it. He denied suicidal ideation or any type of hallucinations. His insight was poor, as he did not seem aware of how odd some of his behaviors were; he seemed to have no motivation to stop the hair pulling.

Treatment Course

In view of the risk of tardive dyskinesia, the Haldol was discontinued. The parents filled out a behavior rating scale that showed a high level of inattention, so the psychiatrist sent a behavior rating scale to the school. Given the clear-cut compulsions, the Zoloft was gradually increased to 100 mg a day over a 4-week period; there was no sign of agitation or suicidal ideation. The parents and Wayne met with a therapist, who engaged Wayne in HRT. First, the therapist provided psychoeducation, noting that while tics have a neurological origin they could be altered by behavioral techniques. Wayne and his parents were taught several "incompatible" actions for Wayne to use when he had an urge to pull his hair. These included sitting on his hands and using a small "stress" ball to squeeze several times when he got the urge to pull his hair. Unfortunately, Wayne had difficulty recognizing the onset of the urge to pull his hair and did not seem motivated to actively try to do so.

The parents returned for the visit with the psychiatrist. They had not noticed any improvement since the increase in Zoloft and the tics were occurring at about the same level after a brief increase when the Haldol was discontinued. The parents were frustrated by Wayne's inability (or unwillingness) to use the HRT techniques. The teacher rating scale was reviewed; it was consistent with the parents' rating. It was clear that Wayne met criteria for ADHD, inattentive type. There was a possibility that Wayne might have to repeat the third grade, which the teacher thought would be a shame since he clearly knew the work. Given that the Zoloft had not been helpful, he was tapered off it and a stimulant trial was initiated. Given his tics, a much lower starting dose was used—2.5 mg of short-acting Ritalin twice a day. This was increased in weekly increments to 10 mg three times a day. The teacher noted a marked improvement in his classroom work and it seemed to her that he was pulling his hair less. There was no increase in his other tics. To the parents, the hair pulling appeared unchanged—it might have been there was less of it at school because he was more involved in schoolwork. Because Wayne tolerated the stimulant well, he was switched to Concerta 36 mg/day.

The therapist noted that Wayne was more attentive in the sessions. The therapist added a behavior management component. Wayne was not allowed to be alone in his room (where he did a lot of hair pulling) until his hair grew back. He had to play in the living room where his parents could see him. The parents kept a marble jar—each time they saw Wayne pull at his hair they removed a marble; if he used a reversal technique they added a marble. Every day, Wayne earned an allowance based on the number of marbles left in the jar. Wayne could get a new bike when his hair grew back completely.

Wayne passed to the fourth grade, and there was a steady improvement in his hair pulling. The shoulder shrugging and eye blinking remained resistant to HRT treatment. The psychiatrist added Tenex, starting at 0.5 mg in the evening and increasing to 1 mg twice a day over about 2 weeks. The eye blinking resolved and the shoulder shrugging decreased to once an hour rather than constantly. By summer his hair had grown back, but he still had odd obsessions about body symmetry and ordering his possessions. After discussion with the parents, it was decided to undertake a trial of a different SSRI. Wayne was started on Prozac 20 mg/day, again with warnings for the parent to watch for possible suicidal ideation. A month later, the parents reported that he was more flexible about the arrangements of objects in his room, though his desire for bodily symmetry remained. This compulsion, however, did not cause major impairment. Wayne and his family were released to routine follow-up.

The next case illustrates OCD symptoms so severe that psychosis or autism spectrum disorders enter the differential.

The Case of Bobby

Chief Complaint

"Rule out Asperger's syndrome."

History of Presenting Illness

Bobby is a 7-year-old boy referred by his family practitioner because of several highly unusual behaviors. Bobby had severe ADHD, combined type, and was on Adderall XR 30 mg/day, which at least allowed him to remain in the classroom and get a reasonable amount of work done. He engaged in severe skin picking; his arms and legs were covered with sores in various states of healing. He would pick off a scab as soon as it began to heal. He had numerous scars from old wounds. The family had been reported to CPS several times by well-meaning neighbors and teachers because they thought Bobby was being beaten. He had an intense fear that bees would fly into his ears, so he would not play outside; he had to stay in the classroom during recess at school. Bobby had never been stung by a bee. He engaged in a wide array of odd rituals. He had an obsession with pencils. He would collect them and refuse to allow them to be thrown away, even when they were worn down to the eraser. He would retrieve them from the trash if his mother tried to throw them away. He arranged them in specific patterns in his room, sometimes carrying them around the house in very specific positions. His mother would ask him what he was doing, thinking he was engaging in fantasy play (e.g., pretending the pencils were an airplane), but he would say that he just needed the pencils to be carried this way. This ritual was repeated every day, and if he was prevented from doing it he would become very tearful and upset.

Unless his rituals were interrupted, he was not aggressive or oppositional. He insisted on carrying other objects around when he interacted with peers, thus they viewed him as "a dork" and did not want to play with him. He would also show them his open sores. He had no close friends and only appeared mildly upset about this. His mother did not notice any hallucinatory activity. He had no history of depression or suicidal ideation. When off his Adderall, he was very hyperactive and hypertalkative, but slept normally. There was no evidence of grandiosity, hypersexuality, or other manic symptoms.

Past Psychiatric and Medical History

Bobby's developmental milestones were within normal limits; he was a happy baby who had bonded well with his mother. There were no delays in language or social development, but from the time he could walk he was very hyperactive—he had been removed from two day cares due to his behavior. He contracted meningitis when he was 3½ years of age and was in the hospital. He appeared to recover without sequelae. He had been treated with a variety of stimulant medications and atomoxetine; his physician had returned to Adderall since it seemed to work the best.

Family and Social History

Bobby was being raised by a single mother; she worked as an office assistant at a local school. Bobby had a younger brother who also showed signs of ADHD but no obsessive behavior. Bobby had no contact with his biological father, who had left the household shortly after the younger brother was born. The mother reported she had a history of depression and was treated with Lexapro for it; her own mother had a history of hoarding. Bobby's grandmother would not throw things out, and their house was filled with worthless objects.

Mental Status Examination

Bobby is a 7-year-old boy who appeared his stated age. His arms and legs were covered with sores in different states of healing. His fingernails were bitten off. He made good eye contact and related well to the examiner. His mood was neither elevated nor depressed and his affect was appropriate. Intellectual functioning was average. His thought processes were illogical in several areas. He referred to his pencils as his friends, and while he did not talk to them (and the pencils did not talk to him), he seemed to view them as having magical powers to ward off monsters and bad events. The pencils would only do this if they were arranged or carried in a certain way. He lacked any insight into how false this belief was. He insisted bees were just outside the office door. He denied any suicidal or homicidal ideation and denied visual or auditory hallucinations.

Bobby had no history of impaired social development; friends had stayed away as a result of his obsessions. His speech prosody and eye contact were normal. As a result, autism spectrum disorders were viewed as unlikely. He clearly did have severe OCD and skin picking.

Treatment Course

Bobby was started on Prozac 10 mg/day in addition to his Adderall. It was arranged for Bobby to see a therapist to do HRT. A number of behaviors incompatible with the picking were developed—squeezing the stress ball, tearing pieces of paper, or tapping his finger on his side when he had the urge to pick. There was an attempt to get Bobby to shift his pencil obsession into something more adaptive, such as building with blocks or Legos. His stimulant treatment history was carefully reviewed. Despite the high dose of Adderall (Bobby weighed 52 pounds [23.6 kg]), the mother did not feel the medication increased the skin picking. Since many other stimulants and atomoxetine had been tried in the past, it was decided that changing the ADHD medication would not be a viable strategy. During the therapy sessions, Bobby reported missing his father. It was clear that he had many unresolved feelings about this, but it was not clear whether his feelings of loss were directly related to his obsessions. Nonetheless, the therapist integrated some aspects of interpersonal therapy into the CBT approach.

Bobby made some minor progress. His skin picking decreased, and a few sores were able to heal. His fear of bees was less intense; he was able to go to recess as long as the playground monitor made a survey of the area to prove there were no bees. The Prozac was increased to 20 mg/day. At the next visit, the mother reported that Bobby was more irritable and was having more tantrums. More worrisome, there was no further improvement in the skin picking. The Prozac was discontinued and Zoloft was started, with a gradual increase in dose to 100 mg/day over several weeks. The mother thought that the Zoloft worked "a little better" than the Prozac. The school agreed that he seemed less fearful of bees. The therapist felt he had made limited progress. A behavior management system was attempted to reward Bobby for doing other things in the evening besides arranging pencils. Bobby, however, showed only very limited interest in activities other than the pencils.

The family doctor raised the concern that some of Bobby's sores were becoming infected. This could lead to his developing sepsis (due to the large number of sores) or a treatment-resistant staphylococcus skin infection. Therefore, the psychiatrist decided to add Risperdal 0.5 mg twice a day to his regimen. At the next follow-up in 3 weeks, his skin had improved markedly; many sores were healing. His mother had also found that he was more easily diverted from the pencil arranging. His OCD symptoms remained prominent and he continued weekly psychotherapy for the long term.

In each of these cases, it can be seen that ADHD needed to be controlled in addition to addressing the OCD or tics. Severe or bizarre obsessions are also associated with autism spectrum disorders. In addition, mood lability and self-abusive behavior can severely complicate the situation, making the treatment of comorbid ADHD difficult.

Chapter 8

Intellectual Disability
and Autism Spectrum Disorders

Every parent awaits the birth of a child with high expectations that the baby will be healthy and grow into a bright and happy individual. The realization that the child has a serious delay in intellectual or social development is traumatic, altering the life of the family forever. In the first part of the 20th century, children with mental retardation (the term is soon to be phased out, see Box 8.1) and autism were generally placed in large institutions, often very early in life. This was done quietly, and often the placed child was hardly spoken of at all. Today, such children remain in the family and in the local school, so that the responsibility for their care falls on practitioners in the community. This fact must be borne in mind when discussing figures regarding the prevalence of both intellectual disability (ID) and autism spectrum disorders (ASD). The assessment and management of each of these conditions can fill several books; this chapter focuses on the management of ADHD as well as the other comorbidities we have discussed previously in children with severe developmental disorders.

ADHD and ID

ADHD occurs in children with ID at prevalence rates of 18–40%, compared to 7–10% in the general population (Epstein, Cullinan, & Polloway, 1986; Koller, Richardson, Katz, & McLaren, 1983; Pearson & Aman, 1994). Several large-scale studies looking at the prevalence of ADHD symptoms in those with ID have concluded the increased rate cannot be accounted for by rater bias or by confounding associations with other psychiatric conditions (Hastings, Beck, Daley, & Hill, 2005; Simonoff, Pickles, Wood, Gringras, & Chadwick, 2007). The presence or absence of ADHD is not related to the underlying etiology of the ID. Fragile X syndrome has been thought to be specifically associated with ASD or ADHD. Hagerman, Smith, and Mariner (1983) found that 71% of their sample of 24 fragile X males met criteria for ADHD, but other controlled studies have not shown that ADHD is more prevalent among fragile X patients relative to other ID subjects (Borghgraef, Fryns, Dielkens, Pyck, & Van den Berge, 1987; Dykens, Leckman, Paul, & Watson, 1988; Einfeld, Hall, & Levy, 1991).

BOX 8.1. Defining Intellectual Disability: A Long Journey

What is the most accurate and humane way to refer to individuals whose intellectual development is delayed? Many professionals are not aware of the curious fact that the terms *idiot, imbecile,* and *moron* were once medical/legal terms. Indeed, the term *cretin* or *cretinism* (once used to refer to those with profound intellectual disability) was a version of a French word for "Christian," apparently to remind medieval people that those with ID should still be treated with respect. With time, however, the term became one of general abuse, which curiously appears to affect all terms used to define ID. An idiot was a person with profound ID, while an imbecile was someone with severe ID. The term *moron* was coined in 1910 by— it's hard to believe—the American Association for the Feeble Minded; today, we would refer to such individuals as having mild ID. The above organization changed its name to the American Association on Mental Deficiency and then to the American Association on Mental Retardation (AAMR) after World War II. The term *mental retardation,* once seen as a more humane and precise term, is now being phased out. In the 1960s, my friends and I referred to things as being "retarded" and called each other "retards." Clinicians fell into the habit of referring to patients as "the mentally retarded" rather than as "patients with mental retardation." The term "retardation" clearly has a pejorative sound to the modern ear. The AAMR has changed its name to the American Association on Intellectual and Developmental Disabilities (AAIDD), and the term *intellectual disability* will surely replace *mental retardation* in DSM-V.

We should remind ourselves that a name change alone does not change attitudes. Each term developed by professionals invariably has become misused. Will the next generation of children say to each other, "You are so ID"? We should also be careful that we do not use name changes to disguise the seriousness of the problems we face. As noted in the text, there has been a decline in the number of children diagnosed with ID and an increase in ASD diagnoses. Is this just to avoid the stigma of having a child with an intellectual developmental delay?

Stimulant Treatment of ADHD in the Child with ID

Over the last 15 years, at least 20 randomized controlled trials have examined the effects of methylphenidate in children with ADHD who have comorbid ID (see Handen & Gilchrist, 2006, for a review). The response rate to methylphenidate (45–66%) significantly exceeds that of placebo and is only slightly below the response rate for typically developing children with ADHD. Some studies have shown that an IQ above 50 predicts a better response to stimulant (Aman, Kern, McGhee, & Arnold, 1993; Aman, Marks, Turbott, Wilsher, & Merry, 1991) and that very low IQ levels (severe, profound) predict a poorer response (Aman, Buican, & Arnold, 2003). There is evidence that children with ADHD and ID are at a higher risk for both tics and social withdrawal than typically developing children (Handen, Feldman, Gosling, Breaux, & McAuliffe, 1991). It is not possible to predict, clinically, which individual child will develop side effects, so a "start low, go slow" approach is appropriate when treating ADHD in this population. At the same time, therapeutic nihilism would not be justified. While there are no studies of amphetamine or atomoxetine in the treatment of children with ADHD and ID, there is no reason to suggest (based on clinical experience) that they are not useful or harmful in this population.

Overview of ASD

While we use the term ASD in this chapter, DSM-IV defines five "pervasive developmental disorders" (PDD): autistic disorder, Asperger's disorder, Rett's disorder, childhood disintegrative disorder, and PDD not otherwise specified (PDD-NOS). A child with autistic disorder must have impairment in social interaction and language and also show abnormal stereotyped patterns of behavior. Onset must be before age 3. ID is present in at least the majority of patients with autism (40–55%; Johnson & Myers, 2007), and high-functioning autistic individuals of normal intelligence rarely can use their talents in a socially adaptive way. Specific genetic conditions such as fragile X, tuberous sclerosis, Angelman's syndrome, Smith–Lemli–Opitz syndrome, or other specific chromosome abnormalities are present in at most 10% of patients with autism (Abrahams & Geschwind, 2008). Nonetheless, genetics plays a role in most cases of autism, as the rate of concordance of the disorder in monozygotic twins is 70–90% compared with a 0–10% rate in dizygotic twins (Abrahams & Geschwind, 2008). A number of environmental factors are thought to be involved in the etiology. However, much misinformation on this topic, particularly with regard to vaccinations, makes the debate about the

---

BOX 8.2. Theories of ASD

ASD has a strong genetic basis (Abrahams & Geschwind, 2008) and are elevated by a factor of 25 in the relatives of those with the disorders. Their heritability (the percentage of variance in the symptoms of ASD that can be attributed to genetics) is nearly 90%, particularly if one includes milder ASD-like social skills and communication problems. Specific genetic syndromes like tuberous sclerosis are associated with ASD. Persons with autism show a particular pattern of excessive brain growth early in life (and actual macrocephaly in some cases), followed by arrested brain growth and possible degeneration (Courchesne et al., 2007). Abrahams and Geschwind (2008) reviewed loci (>30) on multiple chromosomes that have been found to be altered in ASD relative to controls. Recently, parental age was shown to be a risk factor for ASD (Croen, Najjar, Fireman, & Grether, 2007; Reichenberg et al., 2006). If the incidence of ASD is indeed rising, then the tendency of baby-boomer parents to delay childbirth is one major societal shift that could account for it (spontaneous genetic mutations rise with age). Despite popular beliefs that some environmental toxin (particularly vaccines) might be at work, there is no evidence to support this view (Institute of Medicine, 2004; Stehr-Green, Tull, Stellfeld, Mortenson, & Simpson, 2003). If some toxin was involved, why would ASD be rising after several decades of programs to clean the environment? Why did it not peak in the early twentieth century, when people were exposed to many more toxins? (Compare pictures of Pittsburgh in the 1920s to those taken today.)

One of the tragedies of ASD is that the infant often appears to be developing normally when he/she stops relating, cooing, and playing—or worse, regresses. This trauma is perhaps even worse than that of parents who have known their child will not develop typically from birth, as in the case of Down syndrome. The parent of the child with ASD may feel his/her child is "still in there"—if the toxin could just be removed or the allergy uncovered. Considerable progress will be made in the next decade to uncover the genetics of ASD and it is hoped that this will truly lead to new treatments.

prevalence of autism heated (see Box 8.2). Autism was viewed as a very rare disorder in the 1960s and 1970s (5 per 10,000), but recent estimates are 60 per 10,000 (1 child in 166; Newschaffer et al., 2007). What must be borne in mind is that these figures now include those with Asperger's (who previously had no diagnostic home). There has also been a marked decrease in the diagnosis of ID, resulting in the phenomenon of "diagnostic substitution" rather than an actual increase in ASD (Johnson & Myers, 2007). Since most patients are now treated in the community, physicians and mental health professionals are more likely to deal with such cases in their office, leading to the need for clinicians to upgrade their skills in terms of dealing with ASDs.

Individuals with Asperger's disorder have intact language and basic communication skills but, like individuals with autism, show impaired social skills and stereotyped behavior. A flat, odd tone of voice, poor eye contact, and a lack of awareness of others' feelings often characterize Asperger's. While males are more affected by autism and Asperger's, Rett's disorder is found only in females; it is also distinguished by a characteristic deceleration of head growth between the ages of 5 and 48 months despite normal head circumference at birth. Severe or profound ID is almost always present, gait and trunk movements become poorly coordinated, and language and social interactions are extremely impaired. Rett's is the only ASD to be linked to a single chromosomal abnormality—an X-linked mutation in the MECP2 gene, one of many that regulate brain growth (Abrahams & Geschwind, 2008). In childhood disintegrative disorder, head circumference is normal, and in contrast to autistic disorder, development in language and social interaction is normal for the first 2 years of life. Then, before age 10, the child experiences loss of *previously* acquired skills in at least two of the following areas: language, social skills, bowel or bladder control, play, or motor skills.

ADHD and ASD

When is it appropriate to diagnose ADHD in the presence of an ASD? Children with ASD, particularly those with severe autism, chronically attend to inappropriate (and meaningless) stimuli and rarely focus on normal stimuli. The whole array of symptoms under the inattention cluster of the ADHD criteria are difficult to apply to those with ASD. What is a "careless" mistake for an autistic child? Failure to listen to directions may be due to the communication deficits. What children with autism organize their behavior or keep track of their things? A lack of social relatedness means the clinician cannot judge their failure to comply with requests as signs of distractibility. If they are drawn from goal-directed activity to something in their environment (e.g., spinning objects), this may not be due to distractibility but to a "stereotyped and restricted pattern of interest." For children with Asperger's, the symptom of inattention can be treated in much the same way as it is in children without an ASD, as their adequate language skills mean they can be expected to complete most schoolwork and a teacher can more reliably report lack of focus or distractibility.

It is quite possible for such a child with autism to meet criteria for ADHD, impulsive–hyperactive type. As can be seen, *general* increased motor activity is not a symptom of ASD. A child might have a *specific* stereotypy (e.g., finger flapping), but if this is the only motor symptom present then the hyperactivity criteria of ADHD are not met. If, on the other hand, the child is climbing on furniture or impulsively running into the street, these gross-motor activities are not stereotypies and should not be regarded as part of the ASD. Similarly, being "on the go" or "driven like a motor" are purely ADHD symptoms unless they are present only during the performance of a stereotypy. Yelling out, loud laughter, and labile mood are also possible signs of ADHD in a child with ASD. Clinically significant symptoms of ADHD affect up to 40–60% of children with ASD (Hazell, 2007; Research Units on Pediatric Psychopharmacology (RUPP) Autism Network, 2005a, b).

Pharmacological Treatment of ADHD in the Child with ASD

Stimulants

In the last decade there has been growing a body of evidence for the effectiveness of stimulants, primarily methylphenidate, in the treatment of ADHD symptoms in children with ASD. Two small double-blind placebo-controlled crossover studies in small samples of children with ASD showed that methylphenidate reduced teacher ratings of inattention and hyperactivity without increasing stereotypies or other core symptoms of autism (Handen, Johnson, & Lubetsky, 2000; Quintana et al., 1995). The issue was studied in depth by the Research Units in Pediatric Psychopharmacology (RUPP) Autism Network (Research Units on Pediatric Psychopharmacology Autism Network, 2005). A sample ($n = 72$) of children with ASD (primarily autism and Asperger's) received a test dose of methylphenidate; 66 of those who tolerated it were enrolled in a 4-week double-blind crossover study of placebo and three different doses of methylphenidate. Adverse events (though none serious or life threatening) led to discontinuation of medication in 18% of the participants. Overall, 49% of the subjects were considered methylphenidate responders, with effect sizes of 0.2 to 0.4 (depending on the dose). These effects and this response rate are clearly lower than those found in children with ADHD without ASD. This confirms the clinical experience that while stimulants are helpful in reducing inattention and hyperactivity in children with ASD, one must expect more treatment failures than in more typically developing children with ADHD.

Atomoxetine

Two small studies have examined the effect of this agent in the treatment of ADHD in children with ASD. Twelve children with ASD underwent a 10-week open-label trial of atomoxetine at a mean dose of 1.9 mg/kg/day (Troost et al., 2006). There was a significant 44% reduction in symptom severity as rated by the ADHD rating scale, but five of the subjects discontinued the study because of gastrointestinal side effects. This suggests, as with stimulants, that one may expect more side effects than in non-ASD children with ADHD. Posey et al. (2006b) treated 16 young children (mean age 7.7 years) with an open-label trial of atomoxetine at a mean dose of 1.2 mg/kg/day for 8 weeks; only 2 discontinued and the effect was robust (effect size 1–1.9) on ratings of ADHD symptoms. Effect sizes can be quite large in open-label studies, however, as baseline is compared to endpoint and the effects of time and expectations are not controlled. Arnold et al. (2006) undertook a double-blind, placebo-controlled crossover trial of atomoxetine in 16 children (7 with autism, 1 with Asperger's, 8 with PDD-NOS). Atomoxetine was significantly superior to placebo in reducing hyperactivity, but not inattention; overall 9/16 were responders during the atomoxetine phase while only 4/16 responded in the placebo phase.

Alpha-Agonists

Jaselskis, Cook, Fletcher, and Leventhal (1992) performed a double-blind placebo-controlled crossover study of clonidine in eight male autistic children (ages 5–13) who had high levels of inattention, impulsivity, and hyperactivity and who had failed previous trials of stimulants, antidepressants, and neuroleptics. The children received 6 weeks of placebo and clonidine with a 2-week washout period in between; the dose of clonidine was 0.15 to 0.20 mg/day in divided doses. The most significant effect was a 33% reduction in teacher ratings of irritability on active drug relative to placebo. Clonidine was significantly better than placebo in reducing ratings of ADHD behaviors on both the parent and teacher Conners scales. Clinician ratings, however, did not distinguish placebo from clonidine. After the study, six of the subjects continued on clonidine, but the medication lost its effectiveness in two-thirds of these children. Hypotension and irritability prevented dose increases. A trial of the clonidine transdermal patch in children with autism showed no advantage over placebo after either 2 or 4 weeks of treatment (Frankenhauser, Karumanchi, German, Yates, & Karumanchi, 1992), with sedation presenting as a significant problem.

Guanfacine was studied in an open-label trial of 25 children with ASD at doses of 1–3 mg/day; all of the subjects had failed a trial of methylphenidate (Scahill et al., 2006). After 8 weeks of treatment, there were significant reductions in hyperactivity, irritability, social withdrawal, and stereotypies. While sedation was common (~28%), there were no clinically significant changes in blood pressure, pulse, or EKG indices. About half the sample was rated as "much" or "very much" improved.

The clinician should feel comfortable using the standard medications for ADHD (stimulants, atomoxetine, alpha-agonists) in the child with ASD who has significant inattention or impulsivity–hyperactivity. In the most problematic cases of ASD, children can show a wide range of comorbid psychiatric symptoms in addition to ADHD, including obsessive behaviors and stereotypies, aggression, and self-injurious behavior (SIB), and severe mood lability or bipolar disorder. A wide variety of medications have been brought to bear on these questions, but psychosocial interventions are key as well.

Psychosocial Interventions for ASD

Over the last three decades a variety of intensive behavioral, speech–language, and social skills approaches have been developed for children with autism, while specific treatments for Asperger's are less well elaborated. A complete description of these methods would be beyond the scope of this chapter, but the American Academy of Pediatrics guidelines on the management of ASD (Myers & Johnson, 2007) offer an excellent summary. Several major thrusts of treatment are most commonly used.

Applied Behavior Analysis

Applied behavior analysis (ABA) involves the use of intensive (up to 40 hours a week) behavior management, which consists of teaching and reinforcing new, needed skills such as maintaining eye contact, imitating, using words to make requests, and so on. Features of the environment that may be reinforcing negative behaviors such as stereotypies are identified and eliminated. Perhaps the most well-studied of therapies for autism, ABA has been shown to induce sustained gains in IQ, language, academic performance, and adaptive behavior (Bregman, Zager, & Gerdtz, 2005; Eikeseth, Smith, Jahr, & Eldevik, 2002; Howard, Sparkman, Cohen, Green, & Stanislaw, 2005; Lovaas, 1987; Matson, Benavidez, Compton, Paclawskyj, & Baglio, 1996). ABA principles are often used to structure specialized classroom situations for autistic children.

Structured Teaching

The Treatment and Education of Autistic and related Communication-handicapped Children (TEACCH; Mesibov, Shea, & Schopler, 2005) program emphasizes organization of the physical environment, making the child's routine predictable, and using visual schedules and cues. It has less emphasis on directly modifying the child's behavior as in ABA, and the data for its efficacy is less well developed. However, a 4-month study of this approach did show that children with autism enrolled in a TEACCH program made greater gains than those in a standard day treatment program (Ozonoff & Cathcart, 1998).

Developmental Models

These models focus more on the social relatedness problems of children with autism and are thus even less behaviorally based. Greenspan and Wieder's (1997) developmental, individual-difference, relationship-based (DIR) model and Gutstein and Sheely's (2002) relationship-development intervention (RDI) both focus on playtime or other social activities designed to enhance the child's attachment to others. Theoretically this is thought to come closer to addressing a core deficit in autism.

Beyond these specific therapies, children with autism often benefit from speech and language therapy to boost these skills or provide alternative means to communicate (signing, using pictures). Social skills training may be particularly useful for older children with Asperger's and autism.

Pharmacological Treatment of ASD

Medication treatment of specific symptoms is an adjunct to the varied psychosocial interventions for ASD.

Second-Generation Antipsychotics

SGAs have been shown to be very effective in reducing some of the most severe autistic behaviors such as SIB and stereotypies. Lott, Kerrick, and Cohen (1996) found highly significant reductions in aggression and SIB in 33 adults with PDD in an institutional setting who were treated with risperidone. Of particular interest, patients on risperidone were much more likely to become employed, and earnings for the group increased by 37% after 6 months of risperidone treatment. Thus, the patients' quality of life improved, a fact to be borne in mind when balancing the risks of weight gain or hypercholesterolemia. Staff injuries secondary to resident aggressive outbursts also declined markedly. More recently, both risperidone (Table 8.1) and other SGAs (Table 8.2) have been studied in the treatment of severe behavioral dysfunction in children and adolescents with ASD (but see Box 8.3 for a study with findings against the trend in these tables). The best controlled studies have been done with risperidone. In particular, the RUPP studies (McCracken et al., 2002) showed that it had a robust effect on irritability, stereotypies, and global improvement, with a near immediate deterioration in symptoms when it was discontinued (Research Units on Pediatric Psychopharmacology Autism Network, 2005). Quetiapine appeared not to be very helpful in ASD accord-

TABLE 8.1. Studies of Risperidone in Children and Adolescents with ASD

Study	Medication and dose	Number and age of subjects	Design	Results
McCracken et al. (2002)	Risperidone 0.5–3.5 mg/day	101 children, mean age 8.8 ± 2.7 years	8-week, double-blind, placebo-controlled parallel groups	Risperidone superior to placebo in reducing irritability, 75% much improved on active drug compared with 11% on placebo; drowsiness, weight gain (2.7 kg) most common side effects.
RUPP Autism Network (2005b)	Risperidone discontinuation study	63 children from above study	Children completed 4-month open-label RX with risperidone, then randomized to placebo or active drug	62.5% of children on placebo deteriorated, compared to only 12.5% on risperidone.
Shea et al. (2004)	Risperidone, mean dose 1.2 mg/day	79 children, mean age 7.5 years	8-week, double-blind, placebo-controlled parallel groups	53% of risperidone group much improved versus 18% on placebo, 2.7-kg weight gain on active drug versus 1.0 kg on placebo.
Nagaraj, Singhi, & Malhi (2006)	Risperidone 1 mg/day	40 children aged 2–9 years	Randomized to placebo or risperidone for 6 months	17/19 showed significant improvement in drug group versus none in placebo group. Risperidone was associated with increased appetite, weight gain, mild sedation (20%), and cases of transient dyskinesias in three children.
Luby et al. (2006)	Risperidone 0.5–1.5 mg/day	24 preschoolers ages 2.5–6 years	Randomized to placebo or risperidone for 6 months, risperidone more impaired at baseline.	No difference in drug versus placebo on outcome measure, marked increase in weight, leptin, and prolactin.

TABLE 8.2. Studies of Other Second-Generation Antipsychotics in Children with ASD

Study	Medication and dose	Number and age of subjects	Design	Results
Hollander et al. (2006)	Olanzapine, mean dose 10 + 2.04 mg/day	11 children, ages 6–14 years	8-week, double-blind, placebo-controlled parallel groups	Trend toward effectiveness of olanzapine (3/6 improved) versus placebo (1/5), 3.4-kg weight gain on olanzapine.
Malone, Carter, Sheikh, Choudhury, & Delaney (2001)	Olanzapine (7.9 mg/day) versus haloperidol (1.4 mg/day)	12 children, mean age 7.9 years	Randomized to either drug for 6 weeks of open-label treatment	5/6 responders in olanzapine group, 3/6 in haloperidol group, marked weight gain in olanzapine group.
Martin, Koenig, Scahill, & Bregman (1999)	Quetiapine, mean dose 225 mg/day	6 children, ages 6–15 years	Open-label treatment	Poorly tolerated, 1 child with seizure.
Findling et al. (2004)	Quetiapine, mean dose 292 mg/day	9 adolescents, ages 12–17 years	Open-label treatment	Only 2 of 9 judged to be responders.
Corson, Barkenbus, Posey, Stigler, & McDougle (2004)	Quetiapine, mean dose 249 mg/day	20 patients, ages 5–28 years	Open-label treatment, 4–180 weeks	40% judged to be responders.
Hardan et al. (2005)	Quetiapine, mean dose 477 mg/day	10 patients, ages 5–19 years	Open-label treatment	6/10 judged to be responders.
Valicenti-McDermott & Demb (2006)	Aripiprazole 10 + 6.9 mg/day	32 children, various ages	Chart review, uncontrolled	56% improvement rate, 7 discontinuations due to adverse events.
Stigler et al. (2006)	Aripiprazole 1.25–15 mg/day, mean dose 7.5 mg/day	13 children, mean age 8.9 years	Open-label treatment, 14 weeks	12/13 subjects "much" or "very much" improved, mean weight gain 1.2 kg.
McDougle, Kem, & Posey (2002)	Ziprasidone, mean dose 59 mg/day	12 patients, mean age 11.6 years	Open-label treatment, average duration 14 weeks	6/12 judged to be responders, patients lost weight after having been on other SGAs.

ing to case series published so far, but early studies may not have used adequate doses. More controlled studies are needed with the SGAs other than risperidone.

Naltrexone

Naltrexone is a potent opiate antagonist that began to be used in the treatment of individuals with autism because of the theoretical role of the endogenous opiates in attachment and SIB (Herman, Hammock, Arthur-Smith, Kuehl, & Appelgate, 1989). It has been found to reduce SIB in small samples of severely disturbed patients (Barrett, Feinstein, & Hole, 1989), but a double-blind placebo-controlled trial in adults with ID was negative (Willemsen-Swinkels, Buitelaar, Nijhof, & van Engeland, 1995). Other small studies of this agent in the treatment of children with autism have shown more

---

**BOX 8.3. Treating Aggression in Patients
with ID Using SGAs: A Cautionary Note**

The widespread use of SGAs in the treatment of aggression and other severe behavior disorders was called into question by a recent controlled trial performed in the United Kingdom and Australia (Tyrer et al., 2008). Nonpsychotic patients with ID and aggressive behavior were randomized to receive placebo ($n = 29$), risperidone ($n = 29$), or haloperidol ($n = 28$) for 12 weeks. Ratings of aggression and global improvement were obtained at 4, 12, and 26 weeks; the Modified Overt Aggression Scale (MOAS) was obtained weekly during the first 12 weeks. Surprisingly, there was no difference between any of the three groups in either aggression or side effects. To quote the authors, "We conclude that the routine prescription of antipsychotic drugs early in the management of aggressive challenging behavior, even in low doses, should no longer be regarded as a satisfactory form of care" (p. 62). So, should we severely limit the use of antipsychotics in the ID and ASD population? It is important to examine Figure 1 of this study (p. 61), which shows a dramatic drop in MOAS scores in all three groups in the *first week* of the study, despite the fact that these were chronically impaired individuals. Since the median MOAS score dropped by more than half even for the placebo group in 7 days, one has to question whether some major Hawthorne effect was at work. Furthermore, the variance in the ratings was very large (MOAS scores ranging from 0 to 14.5), requiring some statistical adjustments (logarithmic transformations) to analyze the data. Despite the big drop in MOAS scores, the global improvement ratings showed that only about a quarter of the sample was markedly improved, suggesting some sort of disconnect between clinician and caregiver ratings. The study should make us think more carefully about using SGAs in patients with ID and aggression, but it is not definitive.

---

effects on hyperactivity than on SIB (Campbell et al., 1990, 1993; Kolmen, Feldman, Handen, & Janosky, 1995).

Symons, Thompson, and Rodriguez (2004) reviewed 27 studies (both controlled and open label) examining the effect of naltrexone on SIB in patients with both ID and ASD. Roughly 80% of the subjects were judged to have a reduction in SIB; about 47% had their SIB rates reduced by more than half. Common side effects included mild sedation, loss of appetite, vomiting, or increased liver functions. Thus, the evidence on naltrexone is mixed. Clinical experience suggests that a trial of it should last 2–3 months (assuming there are no uncomfortable side effects) before concluding that it is not effective. Quantitative measures of SIB (hours needed wearing protective helmet, number of times per day SIB occurs, etc.) are helpful in objectifying the outcome. Total daily amounts of naltrexone are generally 50 mg/day in children and 100 mg/day in adults, divided into two doses.

Selective Serotonin Reuptake Inhibitors

A number of years ago, it was discovered that about 25% of individuals with autism have elevated serotonin in their platelets (Cook, 1990). While this fact did not turn out to be of any clinical relevance, it led to an interest in serotonergic drugs for the treatment of people with autism. In fact, the evidence for the efficacy of SSRIs in autism is spare.

In a small open trial of ($n = 15$) adults with ID, paroxetine was not successful in reducing either aggression or SIB (Davanzo, Belin, Widawski, & King, 1998). Clomipramine was similarly unimpressive in an open trial with eight children with autism (Sanchez et al., 1996); indeed, six of the children worsened during the trial. In the largest study to date (McDougle et al., 1996), 30 adults with autism were randomized to placebo or fluvoxamine. Fluvoxamine was superior to placebo in reducing repetitive thoughts and behavior and aggression, and increasing language use and social relatedness. A similar trial of fluvoxamine in children was far less successful (McDougle, Kresch, & Posey, 2000). Only 1 of 18 children with an ASD randomized to the active drug group showed improvement, with agitation, insomnia, and aggression being common side effects. Hollander et al. (2005) enrolled 39 children (ages 5–16 years, mean age 8.2 years) in a double-blind crossover trial of placebo and fluoxetine. Each treatment phase was 8 weeks long with a 4-week washout between phases. Fluoxetine was superior to placebo in reducing repetitive behaviors, with no significant side effects. In a review of case series of sertraline, paroxetine, citalopram, and escitalopram in the treatment of ASD, case reports indicated that the majority of children with ASD improved, but again, aggression and agitation were not uncommonly noted (Posey, Erickson, Stigler, & McDougle, 2006a).

The Case of Donald

Chief Complaint

Hit a classmate.

History of Presenting Illness

Donald is an 11-year-old boy who was referred by the school because of a series of altercations during the first 6 weeks of sixth grade (middle school). He became very agitated in his social studies class when the teacher interrupted his answer to a question about the causes of World War I. Donald spoke for nearly 5 minutes on the details of trench warfare, naming cities, battles, and generals. When the teacher tried to redirect him, he began screaming at her that this was very important. He finally calmed down in the principal's office but continued to insist on his "right" to answer the question the way he wanted to. Several days later, when he was waiting for the school bus he told the students standing in line they had to stand "no less than one foot" away from him, both in front and in back. The student next to him began laughing and Donald punched him without warning. He was given in-school suspension.

The parents attended the evaluation together and reported these incidents without much emotion. The father was an engineer who worked at home on a contract basis; he was also responsible for managing the household. The mother was an attorney who did not do any courtroom work; instead she was responsible for reviewing legal documents and records in land disputes, which required combing through hundreds of pages of old land titles and contracts. She worked in an office in the basement of the firm and had refused offers of a more spacious office closer to colleagues. Donald was their only child. Initially, the parents implied that Donald's problems with aggression and oppositionality had started only in middle school, but as the interview progressed they reported that Donald had been "different" since preschool. He was asked to leave several day-care centers due to hyperactivity and anger outbursts; this was part of why the father had decided to work at home. Donald read very early; he was sounding out words by his fourth birthday and reading far above his age level when he entered kindergarten. His parents stated that he always wanted to read the same book over and over again. The kindergarten teacher remarked that Donald was always out of his seat and very stubborn. He always wanted to "reserve" certain toys for himself, and he was not well liked by the other children. In first grade, he excelled academically but the teacher again reported that he needed redirection to stay in his seat and not interrupt her. He frequently got his conduct folder marked—the parents saw this as "normal" boy behavior. As he progressed in elementary school, his academic performance declined, although he always made B's and C's. Mathematics was his weakest subject. Donald disliked sports, as he had poor motor coordination. When he was in the Cub Scouts, Donald attempted to redirect the group to activities he was interested in.

When Donald was in the fifth grade, his teacher continued to report the following symptoms: distractibility, needing constant reminders to stay on task, impulsively blurting out, and argumentativeness. Donald was viewed as very strange and nerdy by his peers. He developed a strong interest in military history and could list the battles of World Wars I and II by name, often listing the names of generals, casualty figures, and so on. His peers (even those who enjoyed playing "army") were bored and annoyed by his renditions. This was all seen as his "just being Donald." His parents had not anticipated any major problems when he moved to middle school but Donald was unhappy from the first day. He did not like changing classes and was very annoyed by the array of rules, and his disorganization problems multiplied. While Donald always had a tendency to be irritable and have a short temper, the recent incident was the first time he had been physically aggressive.

The parent ADHD rating scale showed highly elevated scores on the inattention, impulsivity–hyperactivity, and ODD subscales.

The parents denied that Donald showed any depression or anxiety. He was a very picky eater but slept well and had good energy. There was no history of psychosis, suicidal thoughts, or self-injurious behavior.

Past Psychiatric and Medical History

Donald had never received any mental health treatment. His medical history was unremarkable, as he had only suffered the usual childhood illnesses. There was no history of seizures or head injury.

Family and Social History

The parents denied any psychiatric disorder in themselves or their siblings. The mother recalled that an uncle had been sent away to a state institution as a child and the family never talked about it. As a result, she had no details about this. The mother worked long hours; the father communicated with his colleagues mostly by e-mail. The father and Donald both enjoyed playing Internet fantasy games. The family did not socialize much with people in the neighborhood and claimed there were no children in the area that Donald could play with.

Mental Status Examination

Donald is an 11-year-old boy who appeared his stated age. When the examiner went to shake hands with him, he did not notice the gesture and kept walking past the examiner to sit in the chair farthest away from the examiner's desk. His eye contact was poor and despite the fact that he was alone in the room with the examiner, he raised his hand before speaking.

He was very distracted by nearly everything in the room. His tone of voice was very nasal, and his voice had little range or expression of affect. He was alert, oriented, and had a superior vocabulary but used a number of words out of context. His intellectual functioning was above average. His mood was neither elevated nor depressed, but his affect was restrained and inappropriate to thought content. His thought processes were at times illogical—he would launch into a discussion of the color of the books on the shelf. He spontaneously remarked that the examiner resembled a monk. When the examiner mentioned that his parents had mentioned his interest in military history, Donald launched into a discussion of the tides preceding D-day, which he had just read about. The examiner asked him about why the war was fought and Donald was confused—he could not even guess. He denied suicidal ideation or hallucinations but stated that he sometimes felt like killing people when they did not agree with him—but he stated this without any affect and appeared not to realize the impact of such a statement on others.

Treatment Course

The psychiatrist shared the results of Donald's mental status with the parents. They were surprisingly unconcerned by his threats and mentioned that Donald did often make threats toward others and even toward them. They did not take these things seriously as Donald had not been aggressive in the past. They did not have any weapons at home. The psychiatrist told the parents that some of Donald's interactions were atypical enough that Asperger's syndrome should be considered but that the psychiatrist was not prepared to diagnose this based on one interview. Given that Donald had a long history of symptoms of ADHD, the psychiatrist suggested that this be the initial focus of treatment. The parents were also referred to a therapist to help with behavior management and to assist Donald in peer relations. Given the suspicion of ASD, Donald was started on a low dose of Ritalin LA, 10 mg in the morning. Rating scales were sent to the school, but these showed no change after a week on medication and the dose was increased to 20 mg a day (Donald's weight was 85 pounds [38.6 kg]). Both parents and teacher noted an improvement in his ability to focus, but there was little change in social skills. His dose was further increased to 30 mg in the morning, which seemed to provide additional improvement.

Donald remained stable for about 2 months. He then got into a conflict with a teacher over the school's requirement that he use the proper stairway (the school's stairs were divided into up and down sections). When the teacher insisted he use the correct stairway, he threatened to strangle her. He was suspended and was seen the next day in the psychiatrist's office. He showed no remorse for the statement and continued to perseverate about his "right" to use whatever stairway he wanted to. As he spoke he became agitated, remarking that the school had set the stairways up that way just to "get him in trouble." He denied hallucinations, and there were no overt delusions. The psychiatrist was concerned that the stimulant might have induced abnormal thinking, but the parents reported that overall he was improved in terms of his grades and completed work. Given the seriousness of the aggression and the quasi-paranoid thinking, it was recommended that Donald begin Seroquel 25 mg twice a day, increasing to 50 mg twice a day after a week. The parents called about 5 days later to report that, in fact, Donald appeared more irritable. They discontinued the Seroquel on their own, and the psychiatrist agreed with this.

The psychiatrist referred them to a psychologist in the community who specialized in the evaluation of ASD. Unfortunately, this professional was not on the parents' insurance plan and they could not afford to pay out of pocket. They contacted the school, and he was scheduled for evaluation in about 9 weeks' time. The patient's therapist agreed that Donald showed many Asperger's features, as she had found it very difficult to get Donald to understand why his behavior was inappropriate. The parents came in for a session by themselves; the therapist joined by teleconference. The therapist reported many other obsessive thoughts and behaviors. Donald kept a list of all his action figures with each of their attributes and spent much time updating it. He reported intense anger and despair when any criticism was offered. Given the negative response to the SGA, it was decided to cautiously start Donald on an SSRI. He was started on Prozac 5 mg/day, increasing to 10 mg/day after 1 week. Two weeks later, there were no adverse events reported (no appearance of suicidal ideation), but no positive effect on behavior. However, at 4 weeks Donald smiled more in the interview, was less argumentative, and was less obsessive about irrelevant topics. Teachers reported that Donald was not challenging them on rules or lecturing about odd topics in class. The parents also reported that he was more flexible with them at home.

The school psychological evaluation did not diagnose Asperger's despite high ratings on the parent Gilliam Asperger's Disorder Scale (Gilliam, 2001); teacher ratings on this scale did not match the parent rating and focused primarily on oppositional behavior. Nonetheless, Donald had rated himself as depressed on the Child Depression Inventory (despite denying depression in the office), and he was given an Emotionally Disturbed (ED) categorization, which did qualify him for special education. He became eligible to meet with a support counselor at the school at times of high stress. Donald progressed through the remainder of the school year without further aggressive outbursts.

There are a number of interesting features to the case. The parents were older than average, socially isolated, but very talented in an idiosyncratic sort of way. The mother's uncle had a history suggestive of a severe developmental disorder. One of the dilemmas that this case illustrates is whether to use an SSRI or SGAs in the treatment of the ASD symptoms. This patient showed both illogical thinking and stereotypical obsessions, but he also exhibited impulsive aggression. This led to the decision to treat with SGAs first. When the expected improvement did not occur (and indeed there was worsening of mood), there was an immediate shift to an SSRI, which attenuated the rigidity and obsessive nature of Donald's personality style.

The final case of the chapter and the book is chosen to illustrate the severe challenges that some children with ADHD and autism can present and how far we have to go in developing treatments for these individuals.

The Case of Peter

Chief Complaint

Severe hyperactivity and self-injurious behavior.

History of Presenting Illness

Peter is a 15-year-old-boy who had been in state custody since the age of 4. He was nonverbal and carried a diagnosis of severe mental retardation. He had also been diagnosed with ADHD and autism at about age 6. Since entering state custody, he had been in multiple residential and foster placements; very few of these lasted very long because of the severe nature of his behavior. He was admitted to the current residential treatment facility because his foster mother had reported severe self-abusive and aggressive behavior. He would drop to the ground without warning, occasionally banging his head on the floor. He would slap himself and would suddenly attack his foster mother or the other foster children in the home for no apparent reason. Prior to admission to the residential treatment center, he had been hospitalized at a psychiatric facility. The hospital psychiatrist placed him on clonidine 0.1 mg four times a day, Focalin XR 30 mg in the morning, Depakote ER 1,000 mg at bedtime, and Zyprexa 20 mg at bedtime. No discharge summary or past records accompanied Peter on his admission. The residential treatment center (RTC) nurse reported that he began having difficulties almost from the moment that he arrived. The child-care staff noted that he was extremely hyperactive. He would run around the cottage, jump onto furniture, and might suddenly dart out the door without warning. He was in a cottage with other seriously autistic individuals, and yet he was more difficult to manage even for this experienced staff. Similar to what had been reported by the foster parent, he regularly banged his head and slapped himself.

Peter did have some minimal ability to perform activities of daily living. He was toilet trained, dressed himself if his clothes were laid out, fed himself without difficulty, and would manipulate objects. He showed an unusual interest in electrical sockets and would attempt to insert various objects into them. The staff was greatly concerned that he might electrocute himself. He could sit down and build with Legos, putting them together in an elaborate design, which nonetheless did not bear any relationship to a real object. He was completely nonverbal, did not make eye contact, and did not appear to recognize any of the staff members individually. He did respond to his name. At times, he would suddenly make a series of odd noises that would have a musical quality. He also showed an abnormal interest in the ceiling fans and would become agitated if they were not turned on all the time.

Past Psychiatric and Medical History

Peter had 10 caseworkers over the course of his life, and it was difficult to develop a coherent history. Review of records showed that he had several EEGs in the past, all of which were within normal limits. Physical examinations had not shown any unusual abnormalities; there was no evidence of any obvious medical stigmata suggestive of any type of congenital syndrome. It was known that his mother had been a chronic substance abuser and used cocaine during his pregnancy. However, his birth was apparently without any complications. Peter was in and out of foster homes during the first 3 years of life and was taken into permanent state custody when his mother was sent to prison for a drug offense. There were no other known relatives who were involved in Peter's life. All of Peter's language and social developmental milestones were delayed. All laboratory work from the psychiatric hospital was within normal limits.

Mental Status Examination

Peter is a 15-year-old-boy who appeared slightly younger than his stated age. He was brought to the medical office in the residential treatment center by the child-care staff. As he approached the office, he was making a "hoot-hoot" sound suggestive of an owl. He was extremely physically active. One staff person needed to stand at the door to keep him from running out while the other was stationed within the office to prevent him from climbing onto an examiner's desk. He was nonverbal and did not make eye contact. Several times during the session he slapped himself. His mood was severely irritable, and his affect was highly labile. Thought processes could not be assessed but, based on his behavior, appeared to be highly disorganized and illogical.

Treatment Course

Given the severe nature of the behaviors in spite of the extensive psychiatric medication regimen, it was determined that significant changes were needed. He was first tapered off the clonidine by giving him 0.5 mg three times a day for 3 days, then 0.5 mg twice a day for 2 days, then discontinuing it. The Focalin was held for 72 hours, and the staff was queried as to whether they saw any change in his hyperactivity. When they responded in the negative, it was discontinued. The valproate level on admission was 80 µg/ml, which was therapeutic. His aggressive and self-injurious behavior continued, and it was decided to discontinue the Zyprexa and begin him on Seroquel 100 mg twice a day. Seroquel was increased fairly rapidly to the dose of 300 mg twice a day. Staff reported a modest improvement in his self-injurious behavior. Instead of slapping himself almost continuously, these events declined to 3–4 times per day. Nonetheless, he remained extremely hyperactive. At school, the teachers were unable to get Peter to focus on any of the rehabilitative activities in the classroom.

A genetics evaluation was within normal limits with no evidence of any specific chromosomal syndrome. Physical examination and laboratory work were all within normal limits at the residential treatment center, and the center pediatrician did not recommend any further medical evaluation.

Peter remained on Seroquel 600 mg/day and Depakote ER 1,000 mg/day while the psychiatrist undertook trials of various ADHD medications. In succession over 3 months, he was given trials of Adderall XR, Concerta, and Strattera. All of these were started at low doses and gradually titrated up. He did not show any marked decrease in hyperactive behavior on any of these agents. At times, staff felt that the stimulant actually aggravated the hyperactivity and impulsivity, but this was difficult to pin down. The psychiatrist concluded that there had been adequate trials of multiple ADHD agents without significant benefit, and it was decided not to pursue this line of therapy any further.

Given that Peter's agitation and hyperactivity appeared to fall more into the bipolar spectrum, it was decided to undertake sequential trials of different SGAs. He was tapered off the Seroquel over about a week, and Risperdal was gradually titrated to 4 mg/day. The incident reports showed a marked increase in self-injurious behavior and physical restraints, so Peter was transitioned over to Abilify, which was gradually increased over 2 months to 30 mg/day. School let out and Peter was placed in the residential treatment center's summer program, which he appeared to enjoy. He remained relatively stable on Depakote and Abilify. When school resumed in the fall, his problematic behavior continued. He often refused to get on the bus and was sent home from school for throwing food in the lunch room. The school brought a behavioral specialist from the state capital to consult on Peter's behavior. Attempts were made to help Peter communicate using signing and other visual cues.

One afternoon, Peter thrust his head through a window and caused a laceration that required 10 stitches to treat. The psychiatrist added lithium, and the dose was gradually titrated up until Peter had a serum level of 1.2 mEq/liter. Unfortunately, he now seemed more confused; staff reported that he was bumping into things and appeared less well coordinated. The lithium was discontinued.

Given that the valproate levels were therapeutic, the psychiatrist determined that this medication had reached maximum benefit. It was gradually discontinued, and a trial of Lamictal was initiated. Peter was gradually titrated to 100 mg twice a day, over about a 9-week period. Unfortunately, the staff did not report any major changes in behavior, and this medicine was also discontinued. At a case conference, past medications were reviewed, and the consensus was that he was better on Depakote relative to the other mood stabilizers. He was retitrated to a dose of 1,000 mg/day of Depakote ER. Next, a trial of naltrexone was initiated for self-injurious behavior; the dose was titrated to 50 mg twice a day. Review of the incident reports showed there was about a 10 to 15% decrease in number of self-injurious acts after he had been on this medicine for about 2 months. Nonetheless, his self-injurious behavior remained a serious problem.

Peter was maintained on Abilify 30 mg/day, Depakote 1,000 mg/day, and naltrexone 100 mg/day, but after about 4 months there was a gradual deterioration in Peter's condition. His head banging increased as did some apparent confusion. The psychiatrist was concerned that Peter might be showing early signs of neuromalignant syndrome (NMS), but his creatinine phosphokinase levels were within normal limits. He did not show any hyperthermia or elevated blood pressure. He became so agitated that the residential treatment facility requested that CPS remove him to a more restrictive setting. However, he had been at nearly every other RTC in the state, and all of them refused his admission. All of the private psychiatric hospitals in the city also refused his admission due to his low level of functioning. One evening, his head banging became severe, and he began running around the room, making incoherent noises and attacking staff physically when they tried to intervene. He was taken to the local emergency room, where his physical examination was within normal limits, as were all laboratory values. He was sedated, and a magnetic resonance image (MRI) of the brain was obtained. This did not show any abnormality. He was given Ativan in the emergency room to sedate him, and he returned to the facility.

The psychiatrist filled out commitment papers so that Peter could be transferred to the state hospital. At the state hospital, the naltrexone was discontinued, he was placed on propranolol 40 mg three times a day and his Abilify was discontinued. He was started on Seroquel, and over the 3 months that he remained at the state hospital, the dose was increased to 1,100 mg/day. While this was an unusually high dose, such dosages were often seen in the state hospital, particularly with adult patients. His behavior stabilized and he returned to the RTC. The psychiatrist ordered blood pressure checks twice a day for 2 weeks, and these were within normal limits. Peter's behavior was more manageable on this regimen. He had been placed on a waiting list for admission to a state school for the mentally retarded, and it was hoped he could remain reasonably stable until this admission. About 2 months after his return from the state hospital, the staff reported that Peter was again showing an increase in hyperactivity, aggression, and self-injurious behavior. He abruptly began refusing all medications. He, in effect, took himself off the very high dose of Seroquel, as well as the propranolol and Depakote. He had to be placed on one-to-one with staff. Ultimately, he was transferred to the state school, where a new psychiatrist will undertake his treatment.

The facility Peter went to has been in existence since 1895, though obviously much upgraded. The 19th-century wards are long gone, and it has pleasant living facilities and a very low patient-to-staff ratio. Nonetheless, it is sad that with all our advances in diagnosis and pharmacological agents, Peter essentially ends up where many patients did over a century ago. My hope is that in reviewing these cases throughout the book, you will feel more confident to help as many of the children and adolescents with ADHD and comorbidity as our present knowledge permits, while realizing how much we need to learn.

Structured Clinical Interview for Parents

This questionnaire helps us gather information about your child and family that will be helpful in determining the type of treatment which would be most likely to help with the problems your child is experiencing. Please fill out all of the questions as completely as possible.

I. IDENTIFYING INFORMATION

Child's name _____
               Last   First   Middle

Address _____
           Street   City   State   ZIP

Date of birth ____/____/____ Current age _____

Ethnicity: White Hispanic African American Asian Other

Grade _____ School _____ District _____

Legal guardian bringing child for treatment _____

Relationship to child _____

II. PARENTS (If parents are separated, please circle parent child lives with most of the time.)

Mother _____ Home phone: _____ Work phone: _____

Father _____ Home phone: _____ Work phone: _____

(cont.)

III. MARITAL HISTORY

	Date of marriage	Date divorced/ widowed (if applicable)	Name of stepparent
Child's biological/adoptive parents	_____	_____	_____
Mother's 2nd marriage	_____	_____	_____
Father's 2nd marriage	_____	_____	_____
Mother's 3rd marriage	_____	_____	_____
Father's 3rd marriage	_____	_____	_____

If parents are separated, does the noncustodial parent want to be involved
in the treatment of the child?   Yes   No

If yes: Do you think the noncustodial parent will object to medication or counseling
for your child?   Yes   No

Mother's/stepmother's educational level:	Father's/stepfather's educational level:
1. Less than 7th grade	1. Less than 7th grade
2. 8–9th grade	2. 8–9th grade
3. 10–11th grade	3. 10–11th grade
4. High school graduate	4. High school graduate
5. Partial college (at least 1 year)	5. Partial college (at least 1 year)
6. Standard college degree (i.e., 4 years)	6. Standard college degree (i.e., 4 years)
7. Graduate degree beyond college	7. Graduate degree beyond college
Current occupation _____	Current occupation _____

IV. BROTHERS AND SISTERS OR OTHER FAMILY MEMBERS IN CHILD'S MAIN RESIDENCE

1. _____ Age ( ) _____
2. _____ Age ( ) _____
3. _____ Age ( ) _____
4. _____ Age ( ) _____
5. _____ Age ( ) _____
6. _____ Age ( ) _____
7. _____ Age ( ) _____

(cont.)

V. CHILD'S PROBLEMS

Please briefly describe your child's problems. _____

_____

_____

_____

_____

_____

_____

_____

_____

_____

_____

_____

VI. CHILD'S HEALTH HISTORY

A. Mental Health Treatment

Please list any medications your child is on now or has been on in the past for behavioral or emotional problems.

Medicine	Doctor	Dates taken	Results		
			Good	Fair	Poor
			Good	Fair	Poor
			Good	Fair	Poor
			Good	Fair	Poor

Has your child been in therapy or counseling before?   Yes   No

Therapist/clinic	When?	No. of times seen	Results		
			Good	Fair	Poor
			Good	Fair	Poor
			Good	Fair	Poor

Has your child been in a psychiatric (mental) hospital before? Yes   No

Hospital	When?	Doctor	Results		
			Good	Fair	Poor
			Good	Fair	Poor
			Good	Fair	Poor

(cont.)

B. Medical History

Please list any serious illness, operations, or hospitalizations.

Child's age when ill   Type of illness/injury   Treatment

_____

_____

_____

_____

_____

_____

_____

C. Difficulties during Pregnancy or Childbirth

Did you have any difficulties during your pregnancy or during your child's birth? If yes, please describe.

_____

_____

_____

VII. DEVELOPMENT

At what age did your child:

Hold his/her head up _____   Smile _____   Sit up _____

Take first steps _____   Walk _____   Run _____

Babble, coo _____   Say first words _____   Use sentences _____

Toilet trained _____   Was toilet training easy/hard? _____

Slept through the night _____   Was he/she a "fussy" or "easy" baby? _____

Did he/she suffer from colic? If yes, please describe. _____

_____

As an infant or toddler did your child have trouble attaching or bonding to either parent? If yes, please describe. _____

_____

_____

Did (or does) he/she have any speech delays or problems? _____

_____

_____

Does he/she have problems with poor motor coordination (being clumsy)? _____

If yes, please describe: _____

_____

(cont.)

174

Does your child have a main best friend?	Yes	No
Does your child have a steady group of friends?	Yes	No
Does your child have trouble making friends?	Yes	No
Does he/she have trouble keeping friends?	Yes	No
Does your child have friends who get him/her in trouble?	Yes	No
Is he/she a leader or a follower?	Yes	No
Do neighbors tell their children not to interact with your child?	Yes	No
Do other children think your child is "weird" or "odd"?	Yes	No
Do other children think your child is mean?	Yes	No
Does he/she play mostly with younger children?	Yes	No
Do teachers or day-care workers say your child doesn't get along with other children?	Yes	No

VIII. CHILD'S SCHOOLING

Please list the schools your child has attended since kindergarten.

Grade school		Teacher reported behavior or learning problems?		In special education?	
K.	_____	Yes	No	Yes	No
1.	_____	Yes	No	Yes	No
2.	_____	Yes	No	Yes	No
3.	_____	Yes	No	Yes	No
4.	_____	Yes	No	Yes	No
5.	_____	Yes	No	Yes	No
6.	_____	Yes	No	Yes	No
7.	_____	Yes	No	Yes	No
8.	_____	Yes	No	Yes	No
9.	_____	Yes	No	Yes	No
10.	_____	Yes	No	Yes	No
11.	_____	Yes	No	Yes	No
12.	_____	Yes	No	Yes	No

IX. CHILD'S ACTIVITIES

Bedtime on school days _____   Weekends/holidays _____   Sleeps by self? _____

Typical bedtime behavior: Goes to bed easily   Argues/resists   Scared/needs reassurance

Wets bed? Yes   No   Nightmares? Yes   No

Sleepwalking? Yes   No   Loud snoring? Yes   No

(cont.)

Wake-up time on school days _____   Wake-up time on weekends _____

Hours of sleep/night _____

Average hours of television watched on school nights _____   Weekends _____

What sports is the child involved in? _____

_____

_____

What other structured activities (scouts, church, etc.) is the child involved in? _____

_____

_____

Describe the child's computer/Internet usage. _____

_____

_____

_____

Child and Adolescent Clinician Interview

Child's name _____ Age _____ Date of interview ___/___/_____

Examiner _____ Date of birth ___/___/___

Informant _____

Instructions

1. Have parent fill out rating scales:
   a. ADHD Rating Scales (parent/teacher)
   b. Child Mania Rating Scale Questionnaire
   c. Aggression Questionnaire

2. Interview parent alone first, without the child. Review rating scales, assess details of problems. If developmental problems endorsed, administer screening scales for autism spectrum diorder.

3. Interview child alone. Obtain the following rating scales from child (> 7 years):
   a. Depression Scale
   b. Anxiety Scale
   c. CRAFFT

4. Integrate data and debrief parent.

Chief complaint _____

Brief overview of history _____

_____

_____

_____

_____

_____

Obtain medical and developmental milestones from New Patient Questionnaire.

(cont.)

I. DISRUPTIVE BEHAVIOR DISORDERS

Attention-Deficit/Hyperactivity Disorder (ADHD)

Parent Rating Scale

     Inattention   _____ of 9 symptoms rated > 1

     Impulsivity/hyperactivity   _____ of 9 symptoms rated > 1

     Age of onset _____   Yes   No   Present nearly every day > 6 months

Teacher Rating Scale

     Inattention   _____ of 9 symptoms rated > 1

     Impulsivity/hyperactivity   _____ of 9 symptoms rated > 1

     _____ Teacher rating not available

Oppositional Defiant/Conduct Disorder (ODD/CD)

Parent Rating Scale

     Oppositional defiant   _____ of items 9 rated > 1

     Conduct disorder   _____ of items 13 rated > 1

Teacher Rating Scale

     Oppositional defiant   _____ of items 19–22 rated > 1

     Conduct disorder   _____ of items 23–28 rated > 1

     _____ Teacher rating not available

Yes   No   Parent history reliable   Yes   No   Parent provides examples of behavior

Yes   No   Clinical judgment confirms diagnosis. If no, please document why not below.

If aggressive behavior is present, have parent fill out Aggression Questionnaire.

_____

_____

II. MOOD DISORDERS

Review Child Mania Rating Scale, Mood and Feelings Questionnaire, and Anxiety Scales. Discuss with parent and assess as below.

Mood state during current episode of illness	Euthymic Depressed Euphoric Irritable Mixed	Does your child have times when he/she is sad? How about irritable, grouchy, or miserable all the time? Does your child have times when he/she is so happy you think something is wrong with him/her? How about extremely silly or giddy?
Severity of mood disturbance	Mild Moderate Severe	

(cont.)

How long do the moods last?	Minutes Hours All day	How often does this happen?
How often do the moods occur?	Once a month Once a week 3–5 times/week Daily	When these episodes occur, how long do they last? Do they keep him/her from doing activities or meeting responsibilities? How long have these things been going on?
How long has the current episode lasted? Fill in one:	_____ days _____ weeks _____ months _____ chronic; age of onset _____	If child is irritable: Is he/she only irritable when he/she is being punished or can't have his/her way?

Associated Symptoms of Major Depression

Pleasure loss	Yes No	Excessive pessimism	Yes No
Appetite loss	Yes No	Psychomotor agitation	Yes No
Appetite increase	Yes No	Psychomotor retardation	Yes No
Weight loss	Yes No	Energy loss/fatigue	Yes No
Weight gain	Yes No	Low self-esteem	Yes No
Trouble falling asleep	Yes No Bedtime: Falls asleep:	Poor concentration (If child has ADHD, does sadness impair concentration over baseline?)	Yes No
Awakening during night	Yes No	Abnormal guilt	Yes No
Early morning awakening	Yes No Wake-up time:	Circadian rhythm reversal	Yes No

Associated Symptoms of Mania

Increased energy	Yes No	Grandiosity	Yes No
Distractibility	Yes No	Sexual interest	Yes No
Hypertalkative	Yes No	Decreased need for sleep Hours of sleep per night	Yes No
Pressured speech/push of speech	Yes No	Delusions of grandeur/paranoia	Yes No
Intrusiveness	Yes No	Flight of ideas	Yes No

(cont.)

179

Current suicidal ideation?   No   Yes

Current suicidal plan?   No   Yes

Current suicidal intent?   No   Yes

If Yes, describe current suicidal ideation. _____

_____

_____

Past suicide attempts/gestures: None

Date	Age at time	Method	Outcome

Past Episodes of Depression or Mania

_____ The current episode is the first and only episode in the child's life (present 1 year or less).

_____ The abnormal mood state has been chronic (more than a year) and appeared to begin when the child was age _____.

_____ The mood state has been getting progressively worse and is now the worst it has ever been.

_____ The mood state has been getting better and was at its worst when the child was age _____.

_____ The child has had several discrete abnormal mood states separated by periods when he/she was doing well.

Type of episode	Age at episode	Approximate length
Depression/mania/anger/mixed		
Depression/mania/anger/mixed		
Depression/mania/anger/mixed		
Depression/mania/anger/mixed		

(cont.)

III. ANXIETY DISORDERS

Generalized Anxiety Disorder	Yes No	Is the anxiety associated with:		Frequency	< once/month Monthly
Worries excessively about schoolwork	Yes No	Restlessness	Yes No		1–3 times/month Weekly Daily
Blames self for things that are not his/her fault	Yes No	Tiredness	Yes No		
Worries excessively about how he/she does at sports/games	Yes No	Poor concentration	Yes No	How long?	Minutes Several hours All day
Worries excessively about bad things happening in the world	Yes No	Irritability	Yes No	Duration	1–3 weeks 1 month 2–6 months > 6 months
Worries excessively about upcoming events	Yes No	Muscle tension	Yes No		
Worries excessively about getting sick or dying	Yes No	Sleeplessness	Yes No	When did current episode begin?	
Very scared of meeting new people or social situations	Yes No				

No trauma/PTSD reported _____

Has the child suffered a severe trauma? If Yes, ask about posttraumatic stress disorder.	
Recurrent and intrusive recollections of the event and/or repetitive play with theme of trauma	
Recurrent, distressing dreams of the event	
Acting or feeling as if the traumatic event were recurring (i.e., flashbacks)	
Intense distress when exposed to reminders of the trauma	

No separation probems reported _____

Does the child have separation difficulties? If yes, ask about separation anxiety.	
Extremely upset when separated	
Excessive worry about losing or harm befalling loved one	
Excessive worry about an event which will lead to separation	
Refusal to go to school or elsewhere because of fear of separation	

(cont.)

Physiological reactivity when exposed to reminders of the event	
Posttraumatic stress disorder— Avoidance	
Efforts to avoid thoughts, feelings, conversations about the trauma	
Efforts to avoid activities or places associated with the trauma	
Lack of recall of all or part of the trauma	
Decreased interest in activities	
Detachment or estrangement from others	
Restricted range of affect	
Sense of foreshortened future	
Posttraumatic stress disorder— Physiological	
Difficulty falling asleep	
Irritability or outburst of anger	
Difficulty concentrating	
Hypervigilance	
Exaggerated startle response	

Refusal to be alone without attachment figures nearby	
Refusal to go to sleep without attachment figures in room or nearby	
Frequent nightmares with theme of separation	
Repeated complaints of physical complaints when separation occurs	
Is duration of symptoms at least 4 weeks?	

No OCD-like symptoms reported _____

Does the child have rituals/ compulsions? If yes, ask about OCD.	
Fears of becoming aggressive toward others	
Unwanted guilt-ridden sexual thoughts	
Religious obsessions	
Obsessions of germs/disease	
Obsessions of cleanliness, dirt	
Obsessions about being on time, being late	
Obsessions about following rules	
Hand washing	
Checking locks, ovens, etc.	
Arranging objects in certain ways	

No panic symptoms reported _____

Does the child have severe panic (anxiety) attacks? If yes, ask about panic attacks.	
Palpitations, pounding heart	
Sweating	
Trembling or shaking	
Sensations of shortness of breath (SOB) or smothering	
Feelings of choking	
Chest pain or discomfort	
Nausea or abdominal distress	
Feeling dizzy, unsteady, faint	
Derealization	
Fear of going crazy	

(cont.)

Obsessively counting objects		Fear of dying	
Ritualistic actions		Paresthesias	
Compulsive praying		Chills or hot flushes	
Saying repetitive words to self		Agoraphobia	

Does the child have tics? No/Yes If yes, list: _____

_____

IV. SUBSTANCE ABUSE

No substance abuse reported _____

Substance	Ever in life	Last time of use	Frequency and pattern of use
Alcohol			
Marijuana			
Stimulants, speed			
Cocaine			
Opiates			
Hallucinogens			
Other			

V. DEVELOPMENT/AUTISM SPECTRUM DISORDERS
Review infancy and early childhood milestones.

Note any developmental delays from chart or parent questionnaire.

_____

_____

Note: Items below are for screening. If concern is elicited, more intensive evaluation is required.

Autistic/PDD behaviors _____ No autistic behaviors reported		**Asperger's behaviors (language must be present)** _____None	
Poor eye contact		Flat tone of voice all the time	
Lack of language development		Tone of voice doesn't match emotion	

(cont.)

Language random, not used to communicate		Very wordy, uses words that are odd	
Makes meaningless sounds		Talks excessively and annoyingly about one interest	
Obsessions with objects		Usually good memory for facts	
Obsessions with sameness		Peers think he/she is "weird"	
Toe walking or hand flapping		Doesn't see what others are feeling	
Repeats what is said (echolalia)		Doesn't realize when he/she hurts others' feelings	
Does not use pronouns (I, you, me)		Can't figure out why others are mad	
Does not have social bond with parents/ siblings		Always does the "wrong" thing at social gatherings	
Does not have social bond with others, ignores people		Clumsy, poor motor skills	
Ritualistic actions		Doesn't like to be touched, hugged	
Pica, eats odd objects		No good at make-believe (for younger child)	
Other odd behaviors or movements		Doesn't understand jokes or tells meaningless jokes	

Psychosis screen	Full assessment	Parent	
Hears voices Yes No	Talks to people who are not there, talks to self abnormally	Yes	No
	Literally believes he/she is someone else	Yes	No
Sees things Yes No	Claims to hear voices talking to him/her	Yes	No
	Claims his/her mind is being controlled by others	Yes	No
Paranoid Yes No	Claims to get messages from TV/radio	Yes	No
	Believes important people(e.g., the president) know him/her	Yes	No
Talks to self Yes No	Involved in "Satan worship" or strange religious activities	Yes	No
	Paranoid, thinks people are plotting to get him/her	Yes	No
Abnormal speech Yes No	Has developed strange or bizarre ideas about the world	Yes	No
If Yes to any of the above, ask detailed questions at right.	Claims to have visions or see things no one else can	Yes	No
	Speech makes no sense at all	Yes	No
	Very strange or bizarre fanatasy life, inappropriate for age	Yes	No

(cont.)

VI. FAMILY HISTORY

	Father	Mother	Sibs	Pat. GM	Pat. GF	Pat. Uncle	Pat. Aunt	Pat. Cousin	Mat. GM	Mat. GF	Mat. Uncle	Mat. Aunt	Mat. Cousin
Depression													
ADHD													
Alcoholism													
Drug abuse													
Criminal behavior/history													
Schizophrenia													
Mania													
OCD													
Tics													
Anxiety													

VII. PAST PSYCHIATRIC HISTORY

Psychotropic Medication: None

Medication	Indication	Dose/ directions	Start date	Stop date	Side effects?	Effective?

Psychiatric hospitalization: None

Hospital	Nature of problem	Date of hosp.	Outcome

(cont.)

CHILD INTERVIEW

I. Open-ended interview. Establish rapport (5 minutes). Review ADHD, ODD, CD, and aggression items from parent interview.

II. Administer Mood and Feelings/Anxiety Questionnaire. Discuss items endorsed as positive by child.

Depression/Anxiety Self-Ratings: Completed   Not done/Invalid

Current suicidal ideation?	No	Yes	In past
Current suicidal plan?	No	Yes	In past
Current suicidal intent?	No	Yes	In past

If yes or in past to any of the above, describe. _____

_____

III.   Substance abuse (> age 10 years). Administer CRAFFT.

No substance abuse reported _____

Substance	Ever in life	Last time of use	Frequency and pattern of use
Alcohol			
Marijuana			
Stimulants, speed			
Cocaine			
Opiates			
Hallucinogens			
Other			

CRAFFT (for those who endorse any use)

Have you ever ridden in a CAR driven by someone (including yourself) who was high or had been using alcohol or drugs? Yes   No

Do you ever use alcohol or drugs to RELAX, feel better about yourself, or fit in? Yes   No

Do you ever use alcohol or drugs while you are by yourself, ALONE? Yes   No

Do you ever FORGET things you did while using alcohol or drugs? Yes   No

Do your family or FRIENDS ever tell you that you should cut down on your drinking or drug use? Yes   No

Have you ever gotten into TROUBLE while you were using alcohol or drugs? Yes   No

(cont.)

CHILD AND ADOLESCENT MENTAL STATUS EXAMINATION

I. Appearance

Maturity: ____ appropriate ____ immature ____ overly/pseudo mature

Dress: ____ appropriate ____ unkempt ____ provocative ____ meticulous

Speech: ____ articulate ____ poorly articulated

Speech rate: ____ appropriate ____ slowed ____ rapid

Activity: ____ appropriate ____ decreased ____ increased

II. Mood and Affect

Depression: ____ none ____ mild ____ moderate ____ severe

Elation: ____ none ____ mild ____ moderate ____ severe

Irritability ____ none ____ mild ____ moderate ____ severe

Affect: ____ appropriate ____ blunted ____ flat ____ labile ____ intense

III. Orientation

Person: ____ yes ____ no

Place: ____ yes ____ no ____ not applicable for age

Time: ____ yes ____ no ____ not applicable for age

IV. Intelligence

____ below average ____ average ____ above average

Basis of estimate: ____ prior testing ____ vocabulary

V. Thought Processes/Cognition

Loose associations: ____ present ____ absent ____ unsure/no inquiry

Auditory hallucinations: ____ present ____ absent ____ unsure/no inquiry

Visual hallucinations: ____ present ____ absent ____ unsure/no inquiry

Paranoia: ____ present ____ absent ____ unsure/no inquiry

Ideas of reference: ____ present ____ absent ____ unsure/no inquiry

Delusions (grandiose): ____ present ____ absent ____ unsure/no inquiry

Delusions (persecution): ____ present ____ absent ____ unsure/no inquiry

Intrusive thoughts: ____ present ____ absent ____ unsure/no inquiry

Thoughts incoherent: ____ yes ____ no

VI. Suicidal Ideation

____ none ____ suicidal plan, no intent to carry out

____ wishes he/she were dead ____ clear intent to harm/kill self

____ suicidal thoughts, no plan

VII. Homicidal Ideation

____ none

____ thoughts of harming others, no threats

____ general threats to harm others

____ plan to harm specific individuals

(cont.)

187

DIAGNOSES

Axis I   **Axis II**   **Axis III**

_____   _____   _____

_____   _____   _____

_____   _____   _____

Axis IV (Psychosocial Stressors) _____

Axis V (GAF) _____

Impression/formulation: _____

_____

_____

_____

_____

Risks/benefits/side effects of medications discussed as follows: _____

_____

Medication	Dosage	No. of pills	Refills

Treatment plan: _____

_____

_____

_____

_____

_____

____ Referral for psychotherapy   ____ School consultation

                                              _____
                                              Clinician signature

                                              _____
                                              Clinician printed name

Brief Update on Child
and Adolescent Psychopharmacology

This appendix provides an overview of the pharmacological treatment of ADHD itself; it also covers important safety issues regarding the major medications discussed in the book. Chapters 2–8 focused on the efficacy of the agents, but the physician must always weigh the cost and benefits that accompany the use of any given medication. This is particularly true for mood stabilizers and SGAs, which can be very helpful for multiple conditions, yet can be the source of significant health problems for the child in the long term if used too liberally or without adequate monitoring.

Stimulants: Clinical Use

Two major reviews have recently examined the voluminous literature regarding the efficacy of stimulant medications in the treatment of ADHD (e.g., Biederman & Spencer, 2008c; Pliszka, 2007b), and the American Academy of Child and Adolescent Psychiatry (AACAP) has recently updated its practice parameters regarding their clinical use (Pliszka, 2007a). The effect size for the stimulant medications relative to placebo is close to 1.0, making them among the most efficacious medications in all of health care, rivaling the antibiotics in this regard. Interestingly, they were also in clinical use before the invention of antibiotics (Bradley, 1937). There are now several long-acting formulations of both methylphenidate (Tables A.1 and A.2) and amphetamine (Table A.3) in addition to the immediate-release versions.

Despite the many studies comparing each class of stimulant to placebo, there has never been a large-scale randomized controlled trial comparing methylphenidate directly to amphetamine that would determine if there is any clinically meaningful difference between the two classes in terms of either efficacy or safety. Arnold (2000) reviewed studies (all with small samples of subjects) in which subjects underwent a trial of both amphetamine and methylphenidate. This review suggested that approximately 41% of the subjects with ADHD responded equally to both methylphenidate and amphetamine, while 44% responded pref-

TABLE A.1. Dosing of Methylphenidate in the Treatment of ADHD

Starting dose	Maximum dose	Total daily dose of methylphenidate IR[a]	Concerta 12 hours	Metadate and Ritalin LA 8 hours	Focalin XR
< 23 kg		5 mg			
23–30 kg		10 mg	18 mg q A.M.	10 mg q A.M.	5 mg q A.M.
31–44 kg		20 mg	18 mg q A.M.	10 mg q A.M.	5 mg q A.M.
> 45 kg	< 23 kg	30 mg	36 mg q A.M.	20 mg q A.M.	10 mg q A.M.
		40 mg	54 mg q A.M.	30 mg q A.M.	15 mg q A.M.
	24–45 kg	50 mg	54 mg q A.M.	30 mg q A.M.	20 mg q A.M.
	46–55 kg	60 mg	72 mg q A.M.	40 mg q A.M.	30 mg q A.M.
	Adult sized	80 mg	108 mg q A.M.	60 mg q A.M.	40 mg q A.M.

Note. IR, immediate release; XR, extended release; LA, long acting; q A.M. , every morning.
[a]Dosing in this column must be divided twice (A.M. and noon) or three times (A.M. , noon, and 4:00 P.M.)

erentially to one of the classes of stimulants. This suggests that the initial response rate to stimulants may be as high as 85% if *both* stimulants are tried (in contrast to the finding of 65–75% response when only one stimulant is tried). There is, however, no way to determine a priori if a child is going to be an amphetamine or methylphenidate responder. Clinicians should gain experience with all of these agents. Of course, parental preference may play a role, but there is no evidence that any one of the stimulant preparations should be regarded as first line in all cases.

Table A.1 indicates the general dose *range* for methylphenidate for a child based on weight. Increasingly though, mg/kg dosing has given way to a fixed titration schedule (Pliszka, 2007b) in which one starts with a low dose and steps through (in stages of about 1 week) each dose running down the column in Table A.1 until one reaches the maximum dose for a child of that size. The titration should stop if side effects make the child uncomfortable. Equivalent doses of the methylphenidate preparations are shown across the rows, but the physician should bear in mind that the child may respond uniquely to different formulations of even the same stimulant. It is advisable to start a titration of any stimulant formulation at the lowest dose. The methylphenidate transdermal patch (Daytrana) has a unique dosing that is shown in Table A.2. The number of milligrams of methylphenidate in the patch does not directly relate to the doses of methylphenidate given by mouth. The patch is not more efficacious than methylphenidate by mouth—thus its use tends to be mainly for children who refuse medication by mouth, a fairly small group.

Dosing of amphetamine preparations is shown in Table A.3. The principles of titration are similar to that of methylphenidate; the physician should begin with the lowest dose in each weight category and titrate in weekly steps until the symptoms resolve, side effects interfere, or the maximum dose is reached.

TABLE A.2. Daytrana (Methylphenidate Transdermal System) Dosing

	Week 1	Week 2	Week 3	Week 4
Patch size	12.5 cm²	18.75 cm²	25 cm²	37.5 cm²
MPH mg/9 hr	10 mg (1.1 mg/hr)	15 mg (1.6 mg/hr)	20 mg (2.2 mg/hr)	30 mg (3.3 mg/hr)

Note. Always start with the smallest patch; titrate up on a weekly basis. Milligrams of methylphenidate/9 hours does not correspond directly to an oral methylphenidate dose. Once the patch is off, it must be discarded. Medication tapers down gradually when the patch is removed.

TABLE A.3. Dosing of Amphetamine in the Treatment of ADHD

Starting dose	Maximum dose	Adderall Dexedrine Dextrostat	Adderall XR Dexedrine spansule	Vyvanse
< 23 kg		2.5 mg q A.M.		
23–30 kg		2.5 mg b.i.d.	5 mg q A.M.	20 mg q A.M.
31–44 kg		5.0 mg b.i.d.	10 mg q A.M.	30 mg q A.M.
> 45 kg	< 23 kg	7.5 mg b.i.d.	15 mg q A.M.	30 mg q A.M.
		10.0 mg b.i.d.	20 mg q A.M.	50 mg q A.M.
		12.5 mg b.i.d.	25 mg q A.M.	60 mg q A.M.
	24–45 kg	15.0 mg b.i.d.	30 mg q A.M.	70 mg q A.M.
	46–55 kg	20.0 mg b.i.d.	40 mg q A.M.	80 mg q A.M.
	Adult sized	30.0 mg b.i.d.	60 mg q A.M.	100 mg q A.M.

Note. q A.M. , in the morning; b.i.d., twice a day.

Stimulants: Side Effects

Stimulants are commonly associated with short-term side effects such as loss of appetite, insomnia, and headaches. These side effects are usually time limited and, if they do not resolve, can be managed by changing stimulant class, adjusting the dose, or using adjunctive pharmacotherapy (Biederman et al., 2008c; Pliszka, 2007a). There have been concerns about the long-term effects of stimulants on growth (Swanson et al., 2007c), substance abuse (Volkow & Swanson, 2008), and cardiovascular functioning (Vitiello, 2008). Data from the MTA study showed that continuous stimulant use is associated with about a 2 cm (0.8 inch) reduction in expected growth after 3 years of treatment (Swanson et al., 2007b), and this effect was persistent (but not progressive) at 6–8 years (Elliott & Swanson, 2007). Children with ADHD who entered the MTA study with a history of stimulant treatment were already shorter than those who were treatment naive, and naive subjects who started stimulants grew less than those who were never treated with medication. There was not any evidence of catch-up growth in the later teen years. The Preschool ADHD Treatment Study (PATS) also showed that young children with ADHD treated with stimulants had lower than expected gains in height after one year of treatment (Swanson et al., 2006). In contrast, a group of children who were treated with stimulants but had drug holidays lasting, on average, 31% of the time showed no effect of either methylphenidate or amphetamine on growth (Pliszka, Matthews, Braslow, & Watson, 2006). Thus, drug holidays may attenuate the growth effect consistent with earlier studies (Klein, Landa, Mattes, & Klein, 1988). *Parents do need to be informed that long-term stimulant use can reduce ultimate height to some degree, and height should be assessed two to four times a year and plotted on a growth chart* (Pliszka, 2007a). The physician and the family must determine if the loss of 1 inch of height warrants discontinuing (or never starting) stimulant medication. Given the robust effect of stimulants on symptoms of ADHD, the answer to this question is most likely "yes," but the parent should have all the facts. If a child on stimulant medication drops a full decile on his or her growth chart, consideration should be given to more aggressive drug holidays, changing stimulants, or a trial of a nonstimulant.

There has always been concern in the lay media regarding the prescription of a controlled substance for children, and whether this predisposes a child with ADHD to the use of illegal substances. The issue can be difficult to study, as ADHD itself (particularly when comorbid with CD) is a risk factor for substance abuse (Chapter 2). Early studies suggested that early treatment of ADHD might protect against the development of substance abuse (Biederman, Wilens, Mick, Spencer, & Faraone, 1999c; Wilens, Faraone, Biederman, & Gunawardene, 2003). Recently, several long-term follow-up studies (Biederman et al., 2008d; Mannuzza et al., 2008; Molina et al., 2007) did not find this to be the case. At the same time, these studies did *not* find that stimulant treatment of ADHD increased the risk of substance abuse. Thus, while clinicians can reassure parents that treatment of ADHD with medication will not make their child more likely to abuse substances, medications by itself will not prevent such an occurrence.

There has been recent controversy over the cardiovascular risks of stimulants after the American Heart Association (AHA) issued a press release on April 21, 2008, which appeared to recommend that an electrocardiogram be *mandatory* before a child with ADHD could be prescribed a stimulant (Vetter et al., 2008). In March of 2006, the Pediatric Advisory Committee of the Food and Drug Administration also addressed the risk of sudden death occurring with agents used for the treatment of ADHD (Villalaba, 2006). The FDA review of events related to sudden death revealed 20 sudden death cases with amphetamine or dextroamphetamine (14 child, 6 adult), while there were 14 pediatric and 4 adult cases of sudden death with methylphenidate (MPH). The rate of sudden death in the general pediatric population has been estimated at 1.3 to 8.5 per 100,000 patient-years; for those with a history of congenital heart disease, the rate can be as high as 6% by age 20 (Liberthson, 1996). Villalaba (2006) estimated the rate of sudden death in treated ADHD children for the exposure period January 1, 1992, to December 31, 2004, to be 0.2/100,000 patient-years for MPH, 0.3/100,000 patient-years for amphetamine, and 0.5/100,000 patient-years for atomoxetine (the differences between the agents are not clinically meaningful). Thus, the rates of sudden death of children on ADHD medications *do not* appear to exceed the base rate of sudden death in the general population. Given this data, the rationale behind the recommendation in the original AHA statement was not clear. A review of over 50,000 youth treated with stimulants did not find an excess of cardiac deaths or hospitalizations for a cardiac compliant, though children on multiple medications were more likely to have cardiac-related ER visits (Winterstein et al., 2007). EKG screening of thousands of subjects for atomoxetine clinical trials did not reveal any clinical significant abnormalities (Prasad, Furr, Zhang, Ball, & Allen, 2007). The original AHA statement led to much debate and was revised and clarified on May 16, 2008, as follows, "Acquiring an ECG is a Class IIa recommendation. This means that it is *reasonable* for a physician to *consider* obtaining an ECG as part of the evaluation of children being considered for stimulant drug therapy, but this should be at the physician's judgment, and it is *not mandatory* to obtain one." Thus, physicians should screen children for heart disease and perform a physical examination on children who will be prescribed stimulants, but EKGs should be obtained only on those in whom the physician suspects underlying heart disease.

Atomoxetine

Atomoxetine is a noradrenergic reuptake inhibitor that is superior to placebo in the treatment of ADHD in children, adolescents, and adults (Michelson et al., 2001, 2002, 2003; Swensen, Michelsen, Buesching, & Faries, 2001). Its effect size was calculated to be 0.7 in one study (Michelson et al., 2002). Atomoxetine can be given daily or twice a day, with the second dose given in the evening. This medication may have less pronounced effects on appetite and sleep than stimulants, although it may produce relatively more nausea or sedation. Michelson et al. (2002) showed that while atomoxetine was superior to placebo at week 1 of the trial, the greatest effects were observed at week 6, suggesting the patient should be maintained at the full therapeutic dose for at least several weeks in order to obtain the drug's full effect.

In children and young adolescents, atomoxetine is initiated at a dose of 0.3 mg/kg/day and titrated over 1–3 weeks to a maximum dose of 1.2–1.8 mg/kg/day. Adult-sized adolescents should start with atomoxetine 40 mg daily and titrate to 80–100 mg daily over 1–3 weeks if needed. There is no evidence that increasing the dose in nonresponders up to 3.0 mg/kg/day was beneficial (Kratochvil et al., 2007). The American Academy of Pediatrics (2001), an international consensus statement (Kutcher et al., 2004), and the Texas Children's Medication Project (Pliszka et al., 2006) have all recommended stimulants as the first line of treatment for ADHD, particularly when no comorbidity is present. Direct comparisons of the efficacy of atomoxetine to that of MPH (Michelson, 2004; Newcorn et al., 2008) and amphetamine (Wigal et al., 2004) have shown a greater treatment effect of the stimulants. Newcorn et al. (2008) directly compared MPH and atomoxetine to placebo in a 6-weeek controlled trial. While both drugs were superior to placebo, the methylphenidate produced significantly more improvement statistically than atomoxetine. Of the 70 subjects who did not respond to methylphenidate, 30 (43%) subsequently responded to atomoxetine whereas 29 (42%) of the 69 patients who did not respond to atomoxetine had previously responded to the stimulant.

Side effects that occurred more often with atomoxetine than placebo include gastrointestinal distress, sedation, and decreased appetite. These can generally be managed by dose adjustment, and while some attenuate with time, others such as headaches may persist (Greenhill, Newcorn, Gao, & Feldman, 2007). If discomfort persists, the atomoxetine should be tapered off and a trial of a different medication initiated. On December 17, 2004, the FDA required a warning be added to atomoxetine because of reports that two patients (an adult and a child) developed severe liver disease (both patients recovered). In clinical trials of 6,000 patients, no evidence of hepatotoxicity was found. Patients who develop jaundice, dark urine, or other symptoms of hepatic disease should discontinue atomoxetine. Routine monitoring of hepatic function is not required during atomoxetine treatment. In September 2005, the FDA also issued an alert regarding suicidal thinking with atomoxetine in children and adolescents (Food and Drug Administration, 2005). In 12 controlled trials involving 1,357 patients on atomoxetine and 851 on placebo, the average risk of suicidal thinking was 4 per 1,000 in the atomoxetine-treated group versus none in those on placebo. There was one suicide attempt in the atomoxetine group but no completed suicides. A boxed warning was added to the atomoxetine labeling. This risk is quite small, but it should be discussed with patients and family, and children should be monitored for the onset of suicidal thinking, particularly in the first few months of treatment.

Alpha-Agonists

The alpha-agonist clonidine has long been used for treating ADHD. Connor et al. (1999) performed a meta-analysis of 11 studies of clonidine that suggested it possessed efficacy in the treatment of ADHD. Recently, a 16-week, randomized, double-blind, placebo-controlled clinical trial was conducted in 122 children with ADHD (ages 7–12 years). They were randomly assigned to clonidine, MPH, clonidine in combination with MPH, or placebo (Palumbo et al., 2008). Medications were adjusted to optimal doses for 4 weeks and then continued for 8 weeks. Teacher ratings of ADHD behaviors were the primary outcome measure. MPH was superior to placebo in improving classroom behavior, while clonidine by itself was not. (The positive effect of clonidine on teacher ratings of attention attenuated by the end of the study.) The combination appeared to be superior to either medication

TABLE A.4. Dosing of Immediate-Release Alpha-Agonists

Week	Dosage (mg) of alpha-agonist (weight < 45 kg)		Dosage (mg) of alpha-agonist (weight > 45 kg)	
Baseline	Clonidine	Guanfacine	Clonidine	Guanfacine
1–2	0.05 q h.s.	0.5 q h.s.	0.1 q h.s.	1.0 q h.s.
3–4	0.05 b.i.d.	0.5 b.i.d.	0.1 b.i.d.	1.0 b.i.d.
5–6	0.05 t.i.d.	0.5 t.i.d.	0.1 t.i.d.	1.0 t.i.d.
7–8	0.05 q.i.d.	0.5 q.i.d.	0.1 q.i.d.	1.0 q.i.d.

Note. q h.s., at bedtime; b.i.d., twice a day; q.i.d., four times a day; t.i.d., three times a day.

alone, but this effect was not statistically significant. In contrast to teachers, parents did report that clonidine was superior to placebo (even more so than MPH), but there also was a high rate of sedation. There were no significant findings on EKG or other cardiovascular measures, though generally more adverse events were reported with clonidine (80%) versus MPH (50%) (Daviss et al., 2008). The combination did not appear better than MPH alone overall for ADHD, suggesting that the combination should be reserved for those with comorbid tics (Chapter 7).

The closely related alpha$_{2a}$ agonist guanfacine was superior to placebo in reducing ADHD symptoms in children with comorbid ADHD and tics (Scahill et al., 2001). In general, guanfacine has less sedation than clonidine. Dosing of both clonidine and guanfacine is shown in Table A.4. An extended-release guanfacine has recently been studied in a large-scale double-blind, placebo-controlled trial in the treatment of ADHD (Biederman et al., 2008b). Children with ADHD ages 6–17 years were randomly assigned to one of four treatment groups of guanfacine extended release: 2 mg/day ($n = 87$), 3 mg/day ($n = 86$), or 4 mg/day ($n = 86$), or placebo ($n = 86$), for 8 weeks. All three dosages were significantly better than placebo in reducing symptoms of ADHD, but not different from each other. An effect was apparent at week 2, but was maximal at week 6. The percentage of children rated by clinicians as "much" or "very much" improved (i.e., clinical responders) was 25.6% (placebo), 56% (1 mg), 50% (2 mg), and 55.6% (4 mg). Two-thirds of the sample on guanfancine reported sedation at least once during the study, but only about 7% of the subjects discontinued the medication due to sedation. There were no significant changes on EKG in the guanfacine group relative to placebo. Guanfacine extended release has not been compared with the immediate release form nor directly to stimulants. It is anticipated that guanfacine extended release will be available in 2009.

Other Agents for ADHD

A number of controlled studies have shown that tricyclic antidepressants are superior to placebo in the treatment of ADHD, although the effect size is less than that of stimulants (Daly & Wilens, 1998). Their use is severely limited because of the requirement to obtain EKG monitoring due to a number of cases of sudden death that occurred with desipramine (Riddle et al., 1991; Riddle, Geller, & Ryan, 1993). Bupropion is an antidepressant that affects primarily the norepinephrine and dopamine systems; it too shows modest efficacy in the treatment of ADHD (Conners et al., 1996). Dosing of bupropion ranges from a starting dose of 3 mg/kg/day to a maximum dose of 6 mg/kg day or 300 mg/day, whichever is smaller. While data are limited, bupropion has found use in the subset of children with ADHD and comorbid depression (Daviss et al., 2001). As noted in Chapter 5, treatment guidelines have recommended SSRIs as first-line agents for the treatment of depression, with stimulants for ADHD often added to the SSRI (Hughes et al., 2007). Nonetheless, the use of bupropion in children with ADHD and MDD remains an option for this group, particularly if SSRIs have not been helpful.

Second-Generation Antipsychotics

It should now be clear to the reader that SGAs are used for a wide range of symptoms, including psychosis, aggression, mood instability, mania, and severe PTSD. They can be likened to a bulldozer—they move a lot of material, but can be very destructive. Their significant side-effect profile must always be borne in mind by the clinician.

Neuromotor Symptoms

In youth with psychosis randomized to both first-generation antipsychotics (FGAs) and SGAs, the rates of extrapyramidal symptoms (EPS) for each agent were 67% (haloperidol), 56% (olanzapine), and 54% (risperidone), though the EPS were more severe with the FGA (Sikich, Hamer, Bashford, Sheitman, & Lieberman, 2004). In a review of longer-term studies of SGA use in children, EPS were found to occur at rates of 8–26% (Correll & Kane, 2007), and combining SSRIs with SGAs may increase this risk (Correll, 2008). Akathisia can be mistaken for hyperactivity, though a careful titration (particularly of high-potency agents like aripiprazole and risperidone) can avoid this side effect. Withdrawal from an SGA can also induce a dyskinesia. This can also be avoided by careful tapering of the dose (Correll, 2008). A meta-analysis consisting of 10 studies, lasting at least 11 months, of nearly 800 pediatric patients found tardive dyskinesia to have an annualized incidence of 0.4% (Correll & Kane, 2007).

Neuromalignant syndrome (NMS) is a potentially fatal syndrome usually involving antipsychotic treatment. A child may develop muscle rigidity, elevated heart rate and blood pressure, fever, and elevated creatinine phosphokinase levels. It is more likely to occur in children on multiple psychotropics, and may present with agitation and confusion before the physiological symptoms appear. Physicians on call to psychiatric hospitals need to be particularly alert to NMS. An agitated child already on several medications may receive emergency doses of an SGA—yet staff report more agitation and "psychosis" when the child goes into delirium. The treatment for NMS is to stop the SGA. The physician must question staff carefully about the child's mental status, obtain vital signs, and examine the child for rigidity. When in doubt, hold the next dose of SGA and obtain creatinine phosphokinase. If the vital signs are unstable, the child may need to be sent to the emergency center.

Weight Gain and Adverse Metabolic Effects

Children are more likely than adults to gain weight while taking an SGA (Correll & Carlson, 2006). Taking a stimulant in combination with an SGA does not appear to reliably attenuate the weight gain (Aman, Binder, & Turgay, 2004). Combining SGAs and mood stabilizers can aggravate an increase in weight (Correll, 2007). In adults, the link between SGA use and diabetes is well established and there have been case reports of this occurring in children (Correll & Carlson, 2006). Children should have height, weight, and body mass index (BMI) calculated at each visit. Blood pressure should be assessed quarterly. Fasting blood glucose, lipids, and liver function tests should be performed every 6 months. Table A.5 shows laboratory and growth parameters that should trigger concern about metabolic

TABLE A.5. Warning Signs for Adverse Metabolic Effects in Children Treated with SGAs

- BMI > 85th percentile for age
- Waist circumference > 90th percentile for age
- Total cholesterol > 170 mg/dl
- Low-density-lipoprotein cholesterol (LDL) > 130 mg/dl
- High-density-lipoprotein cholesterol (HDL) < 40 mg/dl
- Triglycerides > 110 mg/dl
- Fasting blood sugar   100–125 mg/dl (needs glucose tolerance test)

syndrome (and risk for future cardiac disease). If the child shows these signs, the physician should review whether the SGA is truly needed. If the child must remain on the SGA, then a weight loss and exercise program should be pursued, with a referral to the child's primary care physician for further intervention.

SGAs (particularly risperidone) may also induce prolactin-related side effects (Correll, 2008), and ziprasidone may be more prone to increase the QTc interval on EKGs (Blair, Scahill, State, & Martin, 2005; Correll, 2008). One death of a child on ziprasidone has been reported (Scahill, Blair, Leckman, & Martin, 2005). As shown in Table A.6, our clinic has placed SGAs into two tiers; olanzapine and ziprasidone have been placed in a second tier due to the respective risk of weight gain and effects on QTc on the EKG.

Divalproex

Divalproex should be started at a dose of 15 mg/kg/day or 1,250mg/day (whichever is smaller). At baseline, a complete blood count (CBC), liver function tests, and platelet counts should be obtained. Dosages of divalproex should be adjusted on a weekly basis until 12-hour postdose serum concentrations reach 75 to 115 mg/ml. After therapeutic serum levels have been achieved, it may take as long as 4 weeks for the drug to achieve maximum effectiveness. Side effects are nausea and gastrointestinal upset, and mild weight gain. Hepatic failure has not occurred in children over the age of 10 (Dreifuss, Langer, Moline, & Maxwell, 1989). Polycystic ovary disease and menstrual difficulties in young women is a definite concern (Joffe et al., 2006), so adolescent girls should be asked to report any menstrual irregularities and inform their gynecologist that they are on divalproex.

Lithium

The prelithium laboratory workup in children is similar to that in adults: electrolytes, thyroid function, hematology studies, and EKG. Adolescents weighing at least 54.5 kg can be started on 300 mg three times a day as adult patients would be. Children weighing 35–50 kg can be started on 300 mg twice a day. Blood levels should be checked weekly until therapeutic levels (0.5 to 1.2 mEq/liter) are obtained. Lithium toxicity (over 3 mEq/liter) can be life threatening, but even levels over 1.6 mEq/liter can result in neurological problems. Adolescents who engage in strenuous activities and perspire heavily need closer monitoring of levels, as lithium is extensively excreted in sweat, leading to a decline in lithium levels (Jefferson, Greist, & Ackerman, 1987). Lithium levels and thyroid function should be checked every 6 months.

Nausea (24%), vomiting (48%), tremor (16%), and polyuria were the most frequent side effects to lithium noted in children (Campbell et al., 1995). Lithium has been used in

TABLE A.6. Dosing of SGAs

First-tier SGAs. These agents have shown efficacy in controlled trials of either aggression or mania and have been extensively used in children and adolescents.

Risperidone	*Preadolescents*	*Adolescents*
Weeks 1–2	0.5 q h.s.	1 mg q h.s.
Weeks 3–4	0.5 mg b.i.d.	1 mg b.i.d./t.i.d.
Weeks 5–6	1 mg b.i.d./t.i.d.	2 mg b.i.d./t.i.d.

Watch for extrapyramidal symptoms, elevated prolactin, breast discharge.

Quetiapine	*Preadolescents*	*Adolescents*
Weeks 1–2	25 mg q d.	50 mg b.i.d.
Weeks 3–4	25 mg b.i.d./t.i.d.	200 mg b.i.d.
Weeks 5–6	50–200 mg b.i.d.	300 mg b.i.d.

Aripiprazole	*Preadolescents*	*Adolescents*
Weeks 1–2	10 mg q A.M.	10 mg q A.M.
Weeks 3–4	15 mg q A.M.	15–30 mg q A.M.

Second-tier SGAs. Olanzapine (Zyprexa) shows efficacy in pediatric mania, but has more severe metabolic side effects. Ziprasidone requires EKG monitoring and has only very limited efficacy data.

Ziprasidone	*Preadolescents*	*Adolescents*
Weeks 1–2	20 mg q P.M.	40 mg b.i.d.
Weeks 3–4	20 mg b.i.d.	60 mg b.i.d.
Weeks 5–6	40 mg b.i.d.	80 mg b.i.d.

EKG required pretreatment and after dose adjustments.

Olanzapine	*Preadolescents*	*Adolescents*
Weeks 1–2	2.5 mg q h.s. or A.M.	5 mg q h.s. or A.M.
Weeks 3–4	5 mg q h.s. or A.M.	10 mg q h.s. or A.M.
Weeks 5–6	10–15 mg q h.s. or A.M.	20 mg q h.s. or A.M.

Severe weight gain.

Note. For all SGAs: Monitor weight, BMI, glucose, and lipid measures every 6 months. q h.s., at bedtime; q A.M., in the morning; q P.M., in the afternoon; q d., daily; b.i.d., twice a day; t.i.d., three times a day.

children ages 4 to 6 years (Hagino et al., 1995), but severe side effects (including ataxia) were found. Divalproex might be a better choice in this age group. DeLong and Aldershof (1987) report that they successfully maintained children and adolescents on lithium without long-term problems for up to 10 years. Since their report, no further case reports of untoward effects of lithium have emerged, but there have not been any well-controlled long-term studies either.

Lamotrigine

As noted in Chapter 4, the anticonvulsant lamotrigine is finding growing use in child and adolescent disorders, particularly for BP depression, despite a lack of controlled data. Certainly lamotrigine should be used only as a second- or third-line treatment, when SGAs, divalproex, or lithium have failed to stabilize mood. The most serious concern with lamotrigine is rash and possible Stevens–Johnson syndrome (SJS). SJS is a severe allergic-type reaction in which the immune system attacks the skin and mucous membranes of the body; severe blisters, fluid loss, skin loss, and scarring can occur. The disorder can be fatal. Mac-

TABLE A.7. Dosing of Lamotrigine (Not on Valproate)

	Children (divide b.i.d.)	Adolescents
Weeks 1–2	0.3 mg/kg/day	25 mg daily
Weeks 3–4	0.6 mg/kg/day	25 mg b.i.d.
Week 5	Add 0.6 mg/kg/day to previous dose	50 mg b.i.d.
Weeks 6–7		100 mg b.i.d.

Note. After week 6, get level and adjust. b.i.d., twice a day.

kay, Wilton, Pearce, Freemantle, and Mann (2008) examined the outcome of 11,316 epilepsy patients (adults and children) treated with lamotrigine. Rash occurred in 201 (1.9%) of the patients and led to discontinuation of the drug. The incidence of rash was higher in children (ages 2–12), with 47 patients out of 1,598 developing a rash in the first month of treatment. SJS was reported in 12 patients (5 younger than 8 years). Nine of the 12 patients were concurrently taking valproate (including all 5 of those younger than 8 years). There were also five cases of erythema multiforme, and 10 cases of other serious hematological or autoimmune illness. So while these events are rare, they can be serious. Careful titration of the lamotrigine to therapeutic dose is critical (see Table A.7), and patients should be advised not to restart the full dose of this medication after a period of noncompliance. Given the risks associated with concurrent valproate and lamotrigine administration, this should be avoided for treatment of purely psychiatric conditions.

Antidepressants

The decision as to whether to start antidepressants in a depressed child or adolescent is one of the most vexing for the physician given the "black box" warning that the Food and Drug Administration has applied to all antidepressants in regard to their use in minors. How does one convey this information to families in order to obtain informed consent? The clinician wishes to appropriately warn the child's family yet not frighten them into not obtaining critically needed treatment. The risk of suicidal ideation in the first 6–10 weeks of antidepressant treatment has been estimated at 3–4% (Bridge et al., 2007; Hammad, Laughren, & Racoosin, 2006a). In contrast, antidepressants produce a mean response rate in anxiety and depressive disorders of 50–60%, (10–20% above the rates produced by placebo). The clinician must always bear in mind that (1) depression and anxiety can respond to nonspecific support and (2) antidepressants are effective, but the "Number Needed to Treat" to be 95% sure that at least one patient has responded to drug over placebo is 10, while the number "Needed to Harm" is 143 (Bridge et al., 2007). This gives families a sense of how to balance risks and benefits.

The equation is made more complex by considering the role of psychotherapy, especially cognitive-behavioral therapy (CBT) in the treatment of depression. In the Treatment for Adolescents with Depression Study (TADS) (March et al., 2004), the rate of response to depression for fluoxetine with CBT was 71.0%; fluoxetine alone, 60.6%; CBT alone, 43.2%; and placebo, 34.8%. In terms of responders, the two fluoxetine groups were statistically superior to CBT and to placebo. Suicidal thinking declined in all four treatment groups, but fluoxetine with CBT showed the greatest reduction. The TADS team concluded that the combination of fluoxetine with CBT offered the most favorable trade-off between benefit and risk for adolescents with MDD. Longer-term response rates showed a similar pattern: 85% for combination therapy, 69% for fluoxetine therapy, and 65% for CBT at week 18;

and 86% for combination therapy, 81% for fluoxetine therapy, and 81% for CBT at week 36 (TADS Team, 2007).

Should a clinician require a patient to engage in CBT (or at least some type of therapy) before starting an antidepressant? Certainly one should always recommend it, but it is a questionable practice to try to hold patients hostage if they do not wish to participate in therapy. In many cases, parents do not have access to therapy, especially CBT (e.g., no insurance, cannot take off work or school, the teen finds it boring and refuses to cooperate). In these cases, the physician may need to document that therapy was suggested but that barriers were too great and the severity of the depression warranted starting the antidepressant. A similar conundrum arises with the package insert regarding how frequently the patient must be seen when starting an antidepressant. Weekly follow-up in the first month of treatment is often not at all practical—the spirit of the recommendation is that patients should have close follow-up in the first 1–2 months of treatment, even if this is by requesting the parent call the office to report that suicidal ideation has not occurred or worsened. If at all possible, follow-up within a month is always desirable.

Once the decision to start an antidepressant is made, which agent should be used first? Fluoxetine has now been shown to be efficacious for the treatment of MDD in multiple trials involving children and adolescents (Emslie et al., 1997, 2002, 2004a; March et al., 2004), while sertraline was modestly effective when data from two depression trials were pooled (Wagner et al., 2003). Citalopram produced a significantly greater decline in depression rating scale scores in children and adolescents with MDD relative to placebo; the response rate to citalopram (36%) was also greater than that to placebo (24%). In contrast, escitalopram was not superior to placebo in a large trial ($n = 262$) of its efficacy in the treatment of MDD, although a post hoc analysis of the subgroup of adolescents (ages 12–17) did show a significant improvement in depression rating scale scores relative to placebo (Wagner, Jonas, Findling, Ventura, & Saikali, 2006a). Venlafaxine was not found to be effective for the treatment of depression in children or adolescents (Emslie, Findling, Yeung, Kunz, & Li, 2007), while the non-SSRIs bupropion and duloxetine have never been the focus of rigorous clinical trials testing their efficacy in the treatment of depression in children

TABLE A.8. Dosing of Antidepressants in Children and Adolescents

	Children's dosage (mg/day)		Adolescent's dosage (mg/day)	
	Starting	Max.	Starting	Max.
SSRI antidepressants				
Citalopram (mg)	10–20	40	10–20	40
Escitalopram (mg)[a]	5–10	20	5–10	20
Fluoxetine (mg)[b]	5–10	60	10–20	60
Sertraline (mg)[c]	25	200	25–50	200
Fluvoxamine[c]	25	200	50	300
Non-SSRI antidepressants				
Venlafaxine (mg)[d]	37. 5	75	37.5	150–225
Bupropion (mg)[e]	As in ADHD dosing			
Duloxetine (mg)[e]	20	40	20	60

[a]Efficacy not proved in clinical trials.
[b]FDA approved for use in pediatric depression.
[c]Not approved by FDA for depression, but positive efficacy trial in MDD, approved for OCD.
[d]Efficacy not shown in clinical trials in children and adolescents.
[e]Not studied for treatment of MDD in children and adolescents.

and adolescents. Studies reviewing the use of SSRIs in anxiety and OCD were discussed in Chapters 6 and 7, respectively. Table A.8 shows the dosing range for these agents. In general, fluoxetine should be preferred as a first-line treatment given its established efficacy, with sertraline and citalopram as "on-deck" SSRIs if fluoxetine should fail.

Children and adolescents with MDD who failed to respond to an adequate trial of an SSRI subsequently had equal response when they were switched to either an alternative SSRI or venlafaxine, but the alternative SSRI group had fewer adverse effects (Brent et al., 2008). This suggests that two SSRIs should be tried before a changing to a non-SSRI (Hughes et al., 2007).

Conclusions

The contemporary physician has many pharmacological tools at his or her disposal for dealing with ADHD, mood lability, aggression, tics, and affective/anxiety disorders. With these new opportunities comes the responsibility to use these agents judiciously and with full awareness of their ability to cause adverse events. Thus, the clinician is constantly balancing benefits and risks. There is no doubt that for the severely impaired child or adolescent, this balance is clearly in favor of treatment with medication. While no direct connection can be made, it is an ominous sign that the decline in antidepressant prescription rates that occurred after the FDA initiated its "black box" warning on these medications (Libby et al., 2007) coincided with an increase in suicide rates for adolescents (Hamilton et al., 2007). Fear of side effects should not be allowed to drive people from needed treatment.

References

Abikoff, H. (1991). Cognitive training in ADHD children: Less to it than meets the eye. *Journal of Learning Disabilities, 24*, 205–209.

Abikoff, H., Ganeles, D., Reiter, G., Blum, C., Foley, C., & Klein, R. G. (1988). Cognitive training in academically deficient ADDH boys receiving stimulant medication. *Journal of Abnormal Child Psychology, 16*, 411–432.

Abikoff, H., & Gittelman, R. (1985). Hyperactive children treated with stimulants: Is cognitive training a useful adjunct? *Archives of General Psychiatry, 42*, 953–961.

Abikoff, H., McGough, J., Vitiello, B., McCracken, J., Davies, M., Walkup, J., et al. (2005). Sequential pharmacotherapy for children with comorbid attention-deficit/hyperactivity and anxiety disorders. *Journal of the American Academy of Child and Adolescent Psychiatry, 44*, 418–427.

Abrahams, B. S., & Geschwind, D. H. (2008). Advances in autism genetics: On the threshold of a new neurobiology. *Nature Reviews Genetics, 9*, 341–355.

Aman, M. G., Binder, C., & Turgay, A. (2004). Risperidone effects in the presence/absence of psychostimulant medicine in children with ADHD, other disruptive behavior disorders, and subaverage IQ. *Journal of Child and Adolescent Psychopharmacology, 14*, 243–254.

Aman, M. G., Buican, B., & Arnold, L. E. (2003). Methylphenidate treatment in children with borderline IQ and mental retardation: Analysis of three aggregated studies. *Journal of Child and Adolescent Psychopharmacology, 13*, 29–40.

Aman, M. G., De Smedt, G., Derivan, A., Lyons, B., Findling, R. L., & the Risperidone Disruptive Behavior Study Group. (2002). Double-blind, placebo-controlled study of risperidone for the treatment of disruptive behaviors in children with subaverage intelligence. *American Journal of Psychiatry, 159*, 1337–1346.

Aman, M. G., Kern, R. A., McGhee, D. E., & Arnold, L. E. (1993). Fenfluramine and methylphenidate in children with mental retardation and ADHD: Clinical and side effects. *Journal of the American Academy of Child and Adolescent Psychiatry, 32*, 851–859.

Aman, M. G., Marks, R. E., Turbott, S. H., Wilsher, C. P., & Merry, S. N. (1991). Clinical effects of methylphenidate and thioridazine in intellectually subaverage children. *Journal of the American Academy of Child and Adolescent Psychiatry, 30*, 246–256.

American Academy of Child and Adolescent Psychiatry. (2007). Practice parameter for the assessment and treatment of children and adolescents with attention-deficit/hyperactivity disorder. *Journal of the American Academy of Child and Adolescent Psychiatry, 46*, 894–921.

American Academy of Child and Adolescent Psychiatry. (2007). Practice parameters for the assessment and treatment of children and adolescents with depressive disorders. *Journal of the American Academy of Child and Adolescent Psychiatry, 46,* 1503–1526.

American Academy of Pediatrics. (2001). Clinical practice guideline: Treatment of the school-aged child with attention-deficit/hyperactivity disorder. *Pediatrics, 108,* 1033–1044.

American Psychiatric Association. (2000). *Diagnostic and statistical manual of mental disorders* (4th ed., text rev.). Washington, DC: Author.

Anderson, J. C., Williams, S., McGee, R., & Silva, P. A. (1987). DSM-III disorders in preadolescent children: Prevalence in a large community sample. *Archives of General Psychiatry, 44,* 69–76.

Angold, A. & Costello, E. J. (1993). Depressive comorbidity in children and adolescents: Empirical, theoretical, and methodological issues. *American Journal of Psychiatry, 150,* 1779–1791.

Angold, A., Costello, E. J., & Erkanli, A. (1999). Comorbidity. *Journal of Child Psychology and Psychiatry, 40,* 57–87.

Angold, A., Costello, E. J., Messer, S. C., Pickles, A., Winder, F., & Silver, D. (1995). The development of a short questionnaire for use in epidemiological studies of depression in children and adolescents. *International Journal of Methods in Psychiatric Research, 5,* 237–249.

Armenteros, J. L., Lewis, J. E., & Davalos, M. (2007). Risperidone augmentation for treatment-resistant aggression in attention-deficit/hyperactivity disorder: A placebo-controlled pilot study. *Journal of the American Academy of Child and Adolescent Psychiatry, 46,* 558–565.

Arnold, L. E. (2000). Methylphenidate vs. amphetamine: Comparative review. *Journal of Attention Disorders, 3,* 200–211.

Arnold, L. E., Aman, M. G., Cook, A. M., Witwer, A. N., Hall, K. L., Thompson, S., et al. (2006). Atomoxetine for hyperactivity in autism spectrum disorders: Placebo-controlled crossover pilot trial. *Journal of the American Academy of Child and Adolescent Psychiatry, 45,* 1196–1205.

Arnold, L. E., & Molina, B. (2007, October 23–28). Six- to eight-year intent-to-treat outcomes and normative comparison group. Presented at the 54th Annual Meeting of the American Academy of Child and Adolescent Psychiatry, Boston, MA.

August, G. J., & Stewart, M. A. (1983). Familial subtypes of childhood hyperactivity. *Journal of Nervous and Mental Diseases, 171,* 362–368.

August, G. J., Winters, K. C., Realmuto, G. M., Fahnhorst, T., Botzet, A., & Lee, S. (2006). Prospective study of adolescent drug use among community samples of ADHD and non-ADHD participants. *Journal of the American Academy of Child and Adolescent Psychiatry, 45,* 824–832.

Ballenger, J. C., Reus, V. I., & Post, R. M. (1982). The "atypical" clinical picture of adolescent mania. *American Journal of Psychiatry, 139,* 602–606.

Barkley, R. A. (1990). *Attention deficit hyperactivity disorder: A handbook for diagnosis and treatment.* New York: Guilford Press.

Barkley, R. A. (1997a). *ADHD and the nature of self-control.* New York: Guilford Press.

Barkley, R. A. (1997b). *Defiant children: A clinician's manual for assessment and parent training* (2nd ed.). New York: Guilford Press.

Barkley, R. A. (2006a). *Attention deficit hyperactivity disorder: A clinical handbook* (3rd ed.). New York: Guilford Press.

Barkley, R. A. (2006b). Comorbid disorders, social and family adjustment, and subtyping. In R. A. Barkley (Ed.), *Attention deficit hyperactivity disorder: Handbook for diagnosis and treatment* (3rd ed., pp. 184–218). New York: Guilford Press.

Barkley, R. A., McMurray, M. B., Edelbrock, C. S., & Robbins, K. (1989). The response of aggressive and nonaggressive ADHD children to two doses of methylphenidate. *Journal of the American Academy of Child and Adolescent Psychiatry, 28,* 873–881.

Barkley, R. A., & Murphy, K. R. (2005). *Attention-deficit hyperactivity disorder: A clinical workbook* (3rd ed.). New York: Guilford Press.

Barrett, R. P., Feinstein, C., & Hole, W. T. (1989). Effects of naloxone and naltrexone on self-injury: A double blind, placebo-controlled analysis. *American Journal of Mental Retardation, 96,* 644–651.

Barry, R. J., Clarke, A. R., McCarthy, R., Selikowitz, M., Johnstone, S. J., & Rushby, J. A. (2004). Age and gender effects in EEG coherence: I. Developmental trends in normal children. *Clinical Neurophysiologies, 115,* 2252–2258.

Beardslee, W. R., Keller, M. B., Lavori, P. W., Klerman, G. K., Dorer, D. J., & Samuelson, H. (1988). Psychiatric disorder in adolescent offspring of parents with affective disorder in a non-referred sample. *Journal of Affective Disorders, 15,* 313–322.

Bell, S., & Eyberg, S. M. (2002). Parent-child interaction therapy. In L.VanderCreek, S. Knapp, & T. L. Jackson (Eds.), *Innovations in clinical practice: A source book* (pp. 57–74). Sarasota, FL: Professional Resource Press.

Bhangoo, R. K., Dell, M. L., Towbin, K., Myers, F. S., Lowe, C. H., Pine, D. S., et al. (2003). Clinical correlates of episodicity in juvenile mania. *Journal of Child and Adolescent Psychopharmacology, 13,* 507–514.

Biederman, J., Wozniak, J., Mick, E., Hammerness, P., Doyle, R., Joshi, G., et al. (2007a, October 23–28). *Comparative efficacy of second generation antipsychotics for pediatric bipolar disorder.* Paper presented at the 54th Annual Meeting of the American Academy of Child and Adolescent Psychiatry, Boston, MA.

Biederman, J. (1998). Resolved: Mania is mistaken for ADHD in prepubertal children, affirmative. *Journal of the American Academy of Child and Adolescent Psychiatry, 37,* 1091–1093.

Biederman, J., Ball, S. W., Mick, E., Monuteaux, M. C., Kaiser, R., Bristol, E., et al. (2007b). Informativeness of maternal reports on the diagnosis of ADHD: An analysis of mother and youth reports. *Journal of Attention Disorders, 10,* 410–417.

Biederman, J., Ball, S. W., Monuteaux, M. C., Mick, E., Spencer, T. J., McCreary, M., et al. (2008a). New insights into the comorbidity between ADHD and major depression in adolescent and young adult females. *Journal of the American Academy of Child and Adolescent Psychiatry.*

Biederman, J., Faraone, S. V., Hatch, M., Mennin, D., Taylor, A., & George, P. (1997). Conduct disorder with and without mania in a referred sample of ADHD children. *Journal of Affective Disorders, 44,* 177–188.

Biederman, J., Faraone, S. V., Hirshfeld-Becker, D. R., Friedman, D., Robin, J. A., & Rosenbaum, J. F. (2001). Patterns of psychopathology and dysfunction in high-risk children of parents with panic disorder and major depression. *American Journal of Psychiatry, 158,* 49–57.

Biederman, J., Faraone, S. V., Keenan, K., Benjamin, J., Krifcher, B., Moore, C., et al. (1992). Further evidence for family-genetic risk factors in attention deficit hyperactivity disorder: Patterns of comorbidity in probands and relatives psychiatrically and pediatrically referred samples. *Archives of General Psychiatry, 49,* 728–738.

Biederman, J., Faraone, S. V., Keenan, K., Steingard, R., & Tsuang, M. T. (1991). Familial association between attention deficit disorder and anxiety disorders. *American Journal of Psychiatry, 148,* 251–256.

Biederman, J., Faraone, S., Mick, E., & Leleon, E. (1995a). Psychiatric comorbidity among referred juveniles with major depression: Fact or artifact? *Journal of the American Academy of Child and Adolescent Psychiatry, 34,* 579–590.

Biederman, J., Faraone, S. V., Mick, E., Spencer, T., Wilens, T., Kiely, K., et al. (1995b). High risk for attention deficit hyperactivity disorder among children of parents with childhood onset of the disorder: A pilot study. *American Journal of Psychiatry, 152,* 431–435.

Biederman, J., Faraone, S. V., Mick, E., Williamson, S., Wilens, T. E., Spencer, T. J., et al. (1999a). Clinical correlates of ADHD in females: Findings from a large group of girls ascertained from pediatric and psychiatric referral sources. *Journal of the American Academy of Child and Adolescent Psychiatry, 38,* 966–975.

Biederman, J., Faraone, S. V., Mick, E., Wozniak, J., Chen, L., Ouellette, C., et al. (1996). Attention deficit hyperactivity disorder and juvenile mania: An overlooked comorbidity? *Journal of the American Academy of Child and Adolescent Psychiatry, 35,* 997–1008.

Biederman, J., Faraone, S. V., Spencer, T., Wilens, T., Norman, D., Lapey, K. A., et al. (1993). Patterns of psychiatric comorbidity, cognition, and psychosocial functioning in adults with attention deficit hyperactivity disorder. *American Journal of Psychiatry, 150,* 1792–1798.

Biederman, J., Melmed, R. D., Patel, A., McBurnett, K., Konow, J., Lyne, A., et al. (2008b). A randomized, double-blind, placebo-controlled study of guanfacine extended release in children and adolescents with attention-deficit/hyperactivity disorder. *Pediatrics, 121,* e73–e84.

Biederman, J., Mick, E., & Faraone, S. V. (1998). Depression in attention deficit hyperactivity disorder (ADHD) children: "True" depression or demoralization? *Journal of Affective Disorders, 47,* 113–122.

Biederman, J., Mick, E., Faraone, S. V., & Burback, M. (2001). Patterns of remission and symptom decline in conduct disorder: A four-year prospective study of an ADHD sample. *Journal of the American Academy of Child and Adolescent Psychiatry, 40,* 290–298.

Biederman, J., Mick, E., Prince, J., Bostic, J. Q., Wilens, T. E., Spencer, T., et al. (1999b). Systematic chart review of the pharmacologic treatment of comorbid attention deficit hyperactivity disorder in youth with bipolar disorder. *Journal of Child and Adolescent Psychopharmacology, 9,* 247–256.

Biederman, J., Mick, E., Wozniak, J., Aleardi, M., Spencer, T., & Faraone, S. V. (2005). An open-label trial of risperidone in children and adolescents with bipolar disorder. *Journal of Child and Adolescent Psychopharmacology, 15,* 311–317.

Biederman, J., Mick, E., Wozniak, J., Monuteaux, M. C., Galdo, M., & Faraone, S. V. (2003). Can a subtype of conduct disorder linked to bipolar disorder be identified? Integration of findings from the Massachusetts General Hospital Pediatric Psychopharmacology Research Program. *Biological Psychiatry, 53,* 952–960.

Biederman, J., Monuteaux, M. C., Spencer, T., Wilens, T. E., MacPherson, H. A., & Faraone, S. V. (2008d). Stimulant Therapy and Risk for Subsequent Substance Use Disorders in Male Adults With ADHD: A Naturalistic Controlled 10-Year Follow-Up Study. *American Journal of Psychiatry, 165,* 597–603.

Biederman, J., Petty, C., Hirshfeld-Becker, D. R., Henin, A., Faraone, S. V., Dang, D., et al. (2006). A controlled longitudinal 5-year follow-up study of children at high and low risk for panic disorder and major depression. *Psychological Medicine, 36,* 1141–1152.

Biederman, J., & Spencer, T. J. (2008c). Psychopharmacological interventions. *Child and Adolescent Psychiatric Clinics of North America, 17,* 439–58, xi.

Biederman, J., Wilens, T., Mick, E., Spencer, T., & Faraone, S. V. (1999c). Pharmacotherapy of attention-deficit/hyperactivity disorder reduces risk for substance use disorder. *Pediatrics, 104,* e20.

Biederman, J., Wozniak, J., Kiely, K., Ablon, S., Faraone, S., Mick, E., et al. (1995c). CBCL clinical scales discriminate prepubertal children with structured interview-derived diagnosis of mania from those with ADHD. *Journal of the American Academy of Child and Adolescent Psychiatry, 34,* 464–471.

Bird, H. R., Canino, G., & Rubio-Stipec, M. (1988). Estimates of prevalence of childhood maladjustment in a community survey in Puerto Rico. *Archives of General Psychiatry, 45,* 1120–1126.

Bird, H. R., Gould, M. S., & Staghezza, B. (1992). Aggregating data from multiple informants in child psychiatry epidemiological research. *Journal of the American Academy of Child and Adolescent Psychiatry, 31,* 78–85.

Birmaher, B., Axelson, D. A., Monk, K., Kalas, C., Clark, D. B., Ehmann, M., et al. (2003). Fluoxetine for the treatment of childhood anxiety disorders. *Journal of the American Academy of Child and Adolescent Psychiatry, 42,* 415–423.

Birmaher, B., Khetarpal, S., Brent, D., Cully, M., Balach, L., Kaufman, J., et al. (1997). The Screen for Child Anxiety Related Emotional Disorders (SCARED): Scale construction and psychometric characteristics. *Journal of the American Academy of Child and Adolescent Psychiatry, 36,* 545–553.

Birmaher, B., Yelovich, A. K., & Renaud, J. (1998). Pharmacologic treatment for children and adolescents with anxiety disorders. *Pediatric Clinics of North America, 45,* 1187–1204.

Blackman, G. L., Ostrander, R., & Herman, K. C. (2005). Children with ADHD and depression: a multisource, multimethod assessment of clinical, social, and academic functioning. *Journal of Attention Disorders, 8,* 195–207.

Blader, J. C., & Carlson, G. A. (2007). Increased rates of bipolar disorder diagnoses among U.S. child, adolescent, and adult inpatients, 1996–2004. *Biological Psychiatry, 62,* 107–114.

Blair, J., Scahill, L., State, M., & Martin, A. (2005). Electrocardiographic changes in children and adolescents treated with ziprasidone: A prospective study. *Journal of the American Academy of Child and Adolescent Psychiatry, 44,* 73–79.

Bloch, M. H., Peterson, B. S., Scahill, L., Otka, J., Katsovich, L., Zhang, H., et al. (2006). Adulthood outcome of tic and obsessive-compulsive symptom severity in children with Tourette syndrome. *Archives of Pediatrics and Adolescent Medicine, 160,* 65–69.

Bolanos, C. A., Barrot, M., Berton, O., Wallace-Black, D., & Nestler, E. J. (2003). Methylphenidate treatment during pre- and periadolescence alters behavioral responses to emotional stimuli at adulthood. *Biological Psychiatry, 54,* 1317–1329.

Borghgraef, M., Fryns, J. P., Dielkens, A., Pyck, K., & Van den Berge, H. (1987). Fragile (X) syndrome: a study of the psychological profile in 23 prepubertal patients. *Clinical Genetics, 32,* 179–186.

Bowden, C. L., Calabrese, J. R., Sachs, G., Yatham, L. N., Asghar, S. A., Hompland, M., et al. (2003). A placebo-controlled 18-month trial of lamotrigine and lithium maintenance treatment in recently manic or hypomanic patients with bipolar I disorder. *Archives of General Psychiatry, 60,* 392–400.

Bradley, C. (1937). The behavior of children receiving benzedrine. *American Journal of Psychiatry, 94,* 577–585.

Bregman, J. D., Zager, D., & Gerdtz, J. (2005). Behavioral interventions. In F.R.Volkmar, R. Paul, A. Klin, & D. Cohen (Eds.), *Handbook of autism and pervasive developmental disorders* (3rd ed., pp. 897–924). Hoboken: John Wiley & Sons.

Brent, D., Emslie, G., Clarke, G., Wagner, K. D., Asarnow, J. R., Keller, M., et al. (2008). Switching to another SSRI or to venlafaxine with or without cognitive behavioral therapy for adolescents with SSRI-resistant depression: the TORDIA randomized controlled trial. *Journal of the American Medical Association, 299,* 901–913.

Brent, D. A., Johnson, B., Bartle, S., Bridge, J., Rather, C., Matta, J., et al. (1993a). Personality disorder, tendency to impulsive violence, and suicidal behavior in adolescents. *Journal of the American Academy of Child and Adolescent Psychiatry, 32,* 69–75.

Brent, D. A., Johnson, B. A., Perper, J., Connolly, J., Bridge, J., Bartle, S., et al. (1994). Personality disorder, personality traits, impulsive violence and completed suicide in adolescents. *Journal of the American Academy of Child and Adolescent Psychiatry, 33,* 1080–1086.

Brent, D. A., Kolko, D. J., Wartella, M. E., Boylan, M. B., Moritz, G., Baugher, M., et al. (1993b). Adolescent psychiatric inpatients' risk of suicide attempt on six-month follow up. *Journal of the American Academy of Child and Adolescent Psychiatry, 32,* 95–105.

Brent, D. A., Perper, J. A., Goldstein, C. E., Kolko, D. J., Allan, M. J., Allman, C. J., et al. (1988). Risk factors for adolescent suicide: A comparison of adolescent suicide victims with suicidal inpatients. *Archives of General Psychiatry, 45,* 451–588.

Brent, D. A., Perper, J. A., Mortiz, G., Allman, C., Friend, A., Roth, C., et al. (1993c). Psychiatric risk factors for adolescent suicide: A case-control study. *Journal of the American Academy of Child and Adolescent Psychiatry, 32,* 521–529.

Bridge, J. A., Iyengar, S., Salary, C. B., Barbe, R. P., Birmaher, B., Pincus, H. A., et al. (2007). Clinical response and risk for reported suicidal ideation and suicide attempts in pediatric antidepressant treatment: A meta-analysis of randomized controlled trials. *Journal of the American Medical Association, 297,* 1683–1696.

Brinkmeyer, M., & Eyberg, S. M. (2003). Parent-child interaction therapy for oppositional children. In A. E. Kazdin & J. R. Weisz (Eds.), *Evidence-based psychotherapies for children and adolescents* (pp. 204–223). New York: Guilford Press.

Brotman, M. A., Kassem, L., Reising, M. M., Guyer, A. E., Dickstein, D. P., Rich, B. A., et al. (2007). Parental diagnoses in youth with narrow phenotype bipolar disorder or severe mood dysregulation. *American Journal of Psychiatry, 164,* 1238–1241.

Brotman, M. A., Schmajuk, M., Rich, B. A., Dickstein, D. P., Guyer, A. E., Costello, E. J., et al. (2006). Prevalence, clinical correlates, and longitudinal course of severe mood dysregulation in children. *Biological Psychiatry, 60,* 991–997.

Brown, T. E. (2001). *The Brown Attention Deficit Disorder Scales.* San Antonio, TX: Psychological Corporation.

Bruggeman, R., van der Linden, L. C., Buitelaar, J. K., Gericke, G. S., Hawkridge, S. M., & Temlett, J. A. (2001). Risperidone versus pimozide in Tourette's disorder: A comparative double-blind parallel-group study. *Journal of Clinical Psychiatry, 62,* 50–56.

Buitelaar, J. K., Van der Gaag, R. J., Cohen-Kettenis, P., & Melman, C. T. (2001). A randomized controlled trial of risperidone in the treatment of aggression in hospitalized adolescents with subaverage cognitive abilities [comment]. *Journal of Clinical Psychiatry, 62,* 239–248.

Burke, J. D., Loeber, R., Lahey, B. B., & Rathouz, P. J. (2005). Developmental transitions among affective and behavioral disorders in adolescent boys. *Journal of Child Psychology and Psychiatry, 46,* 1200–1210.

Calabrese, J. R., Bowden, C. L., Sachs, G., Yatham, L. N., Behnke, K., Mehtonen, O. P., et al. (2003). A placebo-controlled 18-month trial of lamotrigine and lithium maintenance treatment in recently depressed patients with bipolar I disorder. *Journal of Clinical Psychiatry, 64,* 1013–1024.

Calabrese, J. R., Suppes, T., Bowden, C. L., Sachs, G. S., Swann, A. C., McElroy, S. L., et al. (2000). A double-blind, placebo-controlled, prophylaxis study of lamotrigine in rapid-cycling bipolar disorder. *Journal of Clinical Psychiatry, 61,* 841–850.

Caldwell, M. F., Malterer, M., Umstead, D., & McCormick, D. J. (2008). A retrospective evaluation of adjunctive risperidone treatment in severely behaviorally disordered boys receiving psychosocial treatment. *Journal of Child and Adolescent Psychopharmacology, 18,* 34–43.

Campbell, M., Adams, P. B., Small, A. M., Kafantaris, V., Silva, R. R., Shell, J., et al. (1995). Lithium in hospitalized aggressive children with conduct disorder: A double blind and placebo controlled study. *Journal of the American Academy of Child and Adolescent Psychiatry, 34,* 445–453.

Campbell, M., Anderson, L. T., Small, A. M., Adams, P., Gonzalez, N. M., & Ernst, M. (1993). Naltrexone in autistic children: Behavioral symptoms and attentional learning. *Journal of the American Academy of Child and Adolescent Psychiatry, 32,* 1283–1291.

Campbell, M., Anderson, L. T., Small, A. M., Locascio, J. J., Lynch, N. S., & Choroco, M. C. (1990). Naltrexone in autistic children: A double blind placebo controlled study. *Psychopharmacology Bulletin,* 130–135.

Campbell, M., Small, A. M., Green, W. H., Jennings, S. J., Perry, R., Bennett, W. G., et al. (1984). Behavioral efficacy of haloperidol and lithium carbonate: A comparison in hospitalized aggressive children with conduct disorder. *Archives of General Psychiatry, 41,* 650–656.

Cantwell, D. P. (1972). Psychiatric illness in the families of hyperactive children. *Archives of General Psychiatry, 27,* 414–417.

Carey, B. (2007). Debate over children and psychiatric drugs. *The New York Times* (February 15, 2007). Available at *www.nytimes.com/2007/02/15/us/15bipolar.html?_r=1&scp=1&sq=Rebecca +Riley&st=nyt.*

Carlezon, W. A., Jr., Mague, S. D., & Andersen, S. L. (2003). Enduring behavioral effects of early exposure to methylphenidate in rats. *Biological Psychiatry, 54,* 1330–1337.

Carlson, G. A. (2007). Who are the children with severe mood dysregulation, a.k.a. "rages"? *American Journal of Psychiatry, 164,* 1140–1142.

Carlson, G. A. & Kelly, K. L. (1998). Manic symptoms in psychiatrically hospitalized children— what do they mean? *Journal of Affective Disorders, 51,* 123–135.

Carlson, G. A., Loney, J., Salisbury, H., Kramer, J. R., & Arthur, C. (2000). Stimulant treatment in young boys with symptoms suggesting childhood mania: A report from a longitudinal study. *Journal of Child and Adolescent Psychopharmacology, 10,* 175–184.

Castellanos, F. X., Sonuga-Barke, E. J., Milham, M. P., & Tannock, R. (2006). Characterizing cognition in ADHD: Beyond executive dysfunction. *Trends in Cognitive Sciences, 10,* 117–123.

Chang, K. D., Nyilas, M., Aurang, C., Johnson, B., Jin, N., Marcus, R., et al. (2007, October 23–28). *Efficacy of aripiprazole in children (10–17 years old) with mania.* Paper presented at the 54th Annual Meeting of the American Academy of Child and Adolescent Psychiatry, Boston, MA.

Chang, K., Saxena, K., & Howe, M. (2006). An open-label study of lamotrigine adjunct or monotherapy for the treatment of adolescents with bipolar depression. *Journal of the American Academy of Child and Adolescent Psychiatry, 45,* 298–304.

Chang, K. D., Steiner, H., & Ketter, T. A. (2000). Psychiatric phenomenology of child and adolescent bipolar offspring. *Journal of the American Academy of Child and Adolescent Psychiatry, 39,* 453–460.

Coccaro, E. F., Harvey, P. D., Kupsaw-Lawrence, E., Herbert, J. L., & Bernstein, D. P. (1991). Development of neuropharmacologically based behavioral assessments of impulsive aggressive behavior. *Journal of Neuropsychiatry, 3,* 544–551.

Coccaro, E. F., & Kavoussi, R. J. (1997). Fluoxetine and impulsive aggressive behavior in personality-disordered subjects. *Archives of General Psychiatry, 54,* 1081–1088.

Coccaro, E. F., Kavoussi, R. J., Berman, M. E., & Lish, J. D. (1998). Intermittent explosive disorder-revised: Development, reliability, and validity of research criteria. *Comprehensive Psychiatry, 39,* 368–376.

Coccaro, E. F., McCloskey, M. S., Fitzgerald, D. A., & Phan, K. L. (2007). Amygdala and orbitofrontal reactivity to social threat in individuals with impulsive aggression. *Biological Psychiatry, 62,* 168–178.

Coccaro, E. F., Posternak, M. A., & Zimmerman, M. (2005). Prevalence and features of intermittent explosive disorder in a clinical setting. *Journal of Clinical Psychiatry, 66,* 1221–1227.

Coccaro, E. F., Schmidt, C. A., Samuels, J. F., & Nestadt, G. (2004). Lifetime and 1-month prevalence rates of intermittent explosive disorder in a community sample. *Journal of Clinical Psychiatry, 65,* 820–824.

Cohen, J. A., Deblinger, E., Mannarino, A. P., & Steer, R. A. (2004). A multisite, randomized controlled trial for children with sexual abuse-related PTSD symptoms. *Journal of the American Academy of Child and Adolescent Psychiatry, 43,* 393–402.

Comings, D. E., & Comings, B. G. (1990). A controlled family history study of Tourette's syndrome, I: attention-deficit hyperactivity disorder and learning disorders. *Journal of Clinical Psychiatry, 51,* 275–280.

Compton, S. N., March, J. S., Brent, D., Albano, A. M., Weersing, R., & Curry, J. (2004). Cognitive-behavioral psychotherapy for anxiety and depressive disorders in children and adolescents:

An evidence-based medicine review. *Journal of the American Academy of Child and Adolescent Psychiatry, 43,* 930–959.

Conners, C. K. (2008). *Conners 3rd Edition (Conners 3).* North Tonawanda, NY: Multi-Health Systems.

Conners, C. K., Casat, C. D., Gualtieri, C. T., Weller, E., Reader, M., Reiss, A., et al. (1996). Bupropion hydrochloride in attention deficit disorder with hyperactivity. *Journal of the American Academy of Child and Adolescent Psychiatry, 35,* 1314–1321.

Connor, D. F. (2002). *Aggression and antisocial behavior in children and adolescents: Research and treatment.* New York: Guilford Press.

Connor, D. F., Barkley, R. A., & Davis, H. T. (2000). A pilot study of methylphenidate, clonidine, or the combination in ADHD comorbid with aggressive oppositional defiant disorder or conduct disorder. *Clinical Pediatrics, 39,* 15–25.

Connor, D. F., Carlson, G. A., Chang, K. D., Daniolos, P. T., Ferziger, R., Findling, R. L., et al. (2006). Juvenile maladaptive aggression: A review of prevention, treatment, and service configuration and a proposed research agenda. *Journal of Clinical Psychiatry, 67,* 808–820.

Connor, D. F., Fletcher, K. E., & Swanson, J. M. (1999). A meta-analysis of clonidine for symptoms of attention-deficit hyperactivity disorder. *Journal of the American Academy of Child and Adolescent Psychiatry, 38,* 1551–1559.

Connor, D. F., Glatt, S. J., Lopez, I. D., Jackson, D., & Melloni, R. H., Jr. (2002). Psychopharmacology and aggression: I. A meta-analysis of stimulant effects on overt/covert aggression-related behaviors in ADHD. *Journal of the American Academy of Child and Adolescent Psychiatry, 41,* 253–261.

Connor, D. F., & Meltzer, B. M. (2008). *Pediatric psychopharmacology: Fast facts.* New York: Norton.

Cook, E. H. (1990). Autism: Review of neurochemical investigation. *Synapse, 6,* 292–308.

Correll, C. U. (2007). Weight gain and metabolic effects of mood stabilizers and antipsychotics in pediatric bipolar disorder: A systematic review and pooled analysis of short-term trials. *Journal of the American Academy of Child and Adolescent Psychiatry, 46,* 687–700.

Correll, C. U. (2008). Antipsychotic use in children and adolescents: Minimizing adverse effects to maximize outcomes. *Journal of the American Academy of Child and Adolescent Psychiatry, 47,* 9–20.

Correll, C. U., & Carlson, H. E. (2006). Endocrine and metabolic adverse effects of psychotropic medications in children and adolescents. *Journal of the American Academy of Child and Adolescent Psychiatry, 45,* 771–791.

Correll, C. U., & Kane, J. M. (2007). One-year incidence rates of tardive dyskinesia in children and adolescents treated with second-generation antipsychotics: A systematic review. *Journal of Child and Adolescent Psychopharmacology, 17,* 647–656.

Corson, A. H., Barkenbus, J. E., Posey, D. J., Stigler, K. A., & McDougle, C. J. (2004). A retrospective analysis of quetiapine in the treatment of pervasive developmental disorders. *Journal of Clinical Psychiatry, 65,* 1531–1536.

Costello, E. J., Angold, A., Burns, B. J., Stangl, D. K., Tweed, D. L., Erkanli, A., et al. (1996). The Great Smokey Mountain study of youth: Goals, designs, methods, and the prevalence of DSM-III-R disorders. *Archives of General Psychiatry, 53,* 1129–1136.

Costello, E. J., Egger, H. L., & Angold, A. (2004). Developmental epidemiology of anxiety disorders. In T. H. Ollendick & J. S. March (Eds.), *Phobic and Anxiety Disorders in Children and Adolescents.* New York: Oxford University Press.

Courchesne, E., Pierce, K., Schumann, C. M., Redcay, E., Buckwalter, J. A., Kennedy, D. P., et al. (2007). Mapping early brain development in autism. *Neuron, 56,* 399–413.

Croen, L. A., Najjar, D. V., Fireman, B., & Grether, J. K. (2007). Maternal and paternal age and risk of autism spectrum disorders. *Archives of Pediatrics and Adolescent Medicine, 161,* 334–340.

Cueva, J. E., Overall, J. E., Small, A. M., Armentos, J. L., Perry, R., & Campbell, M. (1996). Carbamazepine in aggressive children with conduct disorder: A double blind and placebo controlled study. *Journal of the American Academy of Child and Adolescent Psychiatry, 35,* 480–490.

Curry, J., Rohde, P., Simons, A., Silva, S., Vitiello, B., Kratochvil, C., et al. (2006). Predictors and moderators of acute outcome in the Treatment for Adolescents with Depression Study (TADS). *Journal of the American Academy of Child and Adolescent Psychiatry, 45,* 1427–1439.

Daly, J. M., & Wilens, T. (1998). The use of tricyclics antidepressants in children and adolescents. *Pediatric Clinics of North America, 45,* 1123–1135.

Danielson, C. K., de Arellano, M. A., Ehrenreich, J. T., Suarez, L. M., Bennett, S. M., Cheron, D. M., et al. (2006). Identification of high-risk behaviors among victimized adolescents and implications for empirically supported psychosocial treatment. *Journal of Psychiatric Practice, 12,* 364–383.

Danielyan, A., Pathak, S., Kowatch, R. A., Arszman, S. P., & Johns, E. S. (2007). Clinical characteristics of bipolar disorder in very young children. *Journal of Affective Disorders, 97,* 51–59.

Davanzo, P. A., Belin, T. R., Widawski, M. H., & King, G. (1998). Paroxetine treatment of aggression and self-injury in persons with mental retardation. *American Journal of Mental Retardation, 102,* 427–437.

Daviss, W. B., Bentivoglio, P., Racusin, R., Brown, K. M., Bostic, J. Q., & Wiley, L. (2001). Bupropion sustained release in adolescents with comorbid attention-deficit/hyperactivity disorder and depression. *Journal of the American Academy of Child and Adolescent Psychiatry, 40,* 307–314.

Daviss, W. B., Birmaher, B., Diler, R. S., & Mintz, J. (2008). Does pharmacotherapy for attention-deficit/hyperactivity disorder predict risk of later major depression? *Journal of Child and Adolescent Psychopharmacology, 18,* 257–264.

Daviss, W. B., Patel, N. C., Robb, A. S., McDermott, M. P., Bukstein, O. G., Pelham, W. E., Jr., et al. (2008). Clonidine for attention-deficit/hyperactivity disorder: II. ECG changes and adverse events analysis. *Journal of the American Academy of Child and Adolescent Psychiatry, 47,* 189–198.

Deblinger, E., Mannarino, A. P., Cohen, J. A., & Steer, R. A. (2006). A follow-up study of a multisite, randomized, controlled trial for children with sexual abuse-related PTSD symptoms. *Journal of the American Academy of Child and Adolescent Psychiatry, 45,* 1474–1484.

Deblinger, E., Stauffer, L. B., & Steer, R. A. (2001). Comparative efficacies of supportive and cognitive behavioral group therapies for young children who have been sexually abused and their nonoffending mothers. *Child Maltreatment, 6,* 332–343.

Deblinger, E., Steer, R. A., & Lippmann, J. (1999). Two-year follow-up study of cognitive behavioral therapy for sexually abused children suffering post-traumatic stress symptoms. *Child Abuse and Neglect, 23,* 1371–1378.

DelBello, M. P., Adler, C. M., Amicone, J., Mills, N. P., Shear, P. K., Warner, J., et al. (2004). Parametric neurocognitive task design: A pilot study of sustained attention in adolescents with bipolar disorder. *Journal of Affective Disorders, 82* (Suppl. 1), S79–S88.

DelBello, M. P., Findling, R. L., Earley, W. R., Acevedo, L. D., & Stankowski, J. (2007, October 23–28). Efficacy of quetiapine in children and adolescents with bipolar mania: A 3-week, double-blind, randomized, placebo-controlled trial. Presented at the 54th Annual Meeting of the American Academy of Child and Adolescent Psychiatry, Boston, MA.

DelBello, M. P., Findling, R. L., Kushner, S., Wang, D., Olson, W. H., Capece, J. A., et al. (2005). A pilot controlled trial of topiramate for mania in children and adolescents with bipolar disorder. *Journal of the American Academy of Child and Adolescent Psychiatry, 44,* 539–547.

DelBello, M. P., Schwiers, M. L., Rosenberg, H. L., & Strakowski, S. M. (2002). A double-blind, randomized, placebo-controlled study of quetiapine as adjunctive treatment for adolescent mania. *Journal of the American Academy of Child and Adolescent Psychiatry, 41,* 1216–1223.

DeLong, G. R., & Aldershof, A. L. (1987). Long-term experience with lithium treatment in childhood: Correlation with clinical diagnosis. *Journal of the American Academy of Child and Adolescent Psychiatry, 26,* 389–394.

Diamond, I. R., Tannock, R., & Schachar, R. J. (1999). Response to methylphenidate in children with ADHD and comorbid anxiety. *Journal of the American Academy of Child and Adolescent Psychiatry, 38,* 402–409.

Dickstein, D. P., Nelson, E. E., McClure, E. B., Grimley, M. E., Knopf, L., Brotman, M. A., et al. (2007). Cognitive flexibility in phenotypes of pediatric bipolar disorder. *Journal of the American Academy of Child and Adolescent Psychiatry, 46,* 341–355.

Diler, R. S., Daviss, W. B., Lopez, A., Axelson, D., Iyengar, S., & Birmaher, B. (2007). Differentiating major depressive disorder in youths with attention deficit hyperactivity disorder. *Journal of Affective Disorders, 102,* 125–130.

Dion, Y., Annable, L., Sandor, P., & Chouinard, G. (2002). Risperidone in the treatment of Tourette syndrome: A double-blind, placebo-controlled trial. *Journal of Clinical Psychopharmacology, 22,* 31–39.

Dodge, K. A. (2006). Translational science in action: Hostile attributional style and the development of aggressive behavior problems. *Devopmental Psychopathology, 18,* 791–814.

Dodge, K. A., Harnish, J. D., Lochman, J. E., & Bates, J. E. (1997). Reactive and proactive aggression in school children and psychiatrically impaired chronically assaultive youth. *Journal of Abnormal Psychology, 106,* 37–51.

Dodge, K. A., & Schwartz, D. (1997). Social information-processing mechanisms in aggressive behavior. In D. M. Stoff, J. Breiling, & J. D. Maser (Eds.), *Handbook of Antisocial Behavior* (pp. 171–180). New York: Wiley.

Donnelly, C. L. (2003). Post-traumatic stress disorder. In A. Martin, L. Scahill, D. S. Charney, & J. F. Leckman (Eds.), *Pediatric psychopharmacology* (pp. 580–591). New York: Oxford University Press.

Donovan, S. J., Nunes, E. V., Stewart, J. W., Ross, D., Quitkin, F. M., Jensen, P. S., et al. (2003). "Outer-directed irritability": A distinct mood syndrome in explosive youth with a disruptive behavior disorder? *Journal of Clinical Psychiatry, 64,* 698–701.

Donovan, S. J., Stewart, J. W., Nunes, E. V., Quitkin, F. M., Parides, M., Daniel, W., et al. (2000). Divalproex treatment for youth with explosive temper and mood lability: A double-blind, placebo-controlled crossover design. *American Journal of Psychiatry, 157,* 818–820.

Dougherty, D. D., Rauch, S. L., Deckersbach, T., Marci, C., Loh, R., Shin, L. M., et al. (2004). Ventromedial prefrontal cortex and amygdala dysfunction during an anger induction positron emission tomography study in patients with major depressive disorder with anger attacks. *Archives of General Psychiatry, 61,* 795–804.

Dougherty, D. D., Shin, L. M., Alpert, N. M., Pitman, R. K., Orr, S. P., Lasko, M., et al. (1999). Anger in healthy men: A PET study using script driven imagery. *Biological Psychiatry, 46,* 466–472.

Drabick, D. A., Gadow, K. D., & Sprafkin, J. (2006). Co-occurrence of conduct disorder and depression in a clinic-based sample of boys with ADHD. *Journal of Child Psychology and Psychiatry, 47,* 766–774.

Dreifuss, F. E., Langer, D. H., Moline, K. A., & Maxwell, J. E. (1989). Valproic acid hepatic fatalities: II. US experience since 1984. *Neurology, 39,* 201–207.

DuPaul, G. J., Power, T. J., Anastopoulos, A. D., & Reid, R. (1998). *ADHD Rating Scales–IV: Checklists, norms, and clinical interpretation.* New York: Guilford Press.

Dykens, E., Leckman, J., Paul, R., & Watson, M. (1988). Cognitive, behavioral, and adaptive functioning in fragile X and non-fragile X retarded men. *Journal of Autism and Developmental Disorders, 18,* 41–52.

Dykens, E., Leckman, J., Riddle, M., Hardin, M., Schwartz, S., & Cohen, D. (1990). Intellectual, academic, and adaptive functioning of Tourette syndrome children with and without attention deficit disorder. *Journal of Abnormal Child Psychology, 18,* 607–615.

Edelbrock, C., Costello, A., Dulcan, M. K., Conover, N. C., & Kalas, R. (1986). Parent-child agreement on child psychiatric symptoms assessed via structured interview. *Journal of Child Psychology and Psychiatry, 27*, 181–190.

Eikeseth, S., Smith, T., Jahr, E., & Eldevik, S. (2002). Intensive behavioral treatment at school for 4- to 7-year-old children with autism: A 1-year comparison controlled study. *Behavior Modification, 26*, 49–68.

Einfeld, S., Hall, W., & Levy, F. (1991). Hyperactivity and the fragile X syndrome. *Journal of Abnormal Child Psychology, 19*, 253–262.

Elliott, G., & Swanson, J. M. (2007, October 23–28). Growth and cardiovascular outcomes through 6 and 8 years. Paper presented at the 54th Annual Meeting of the American Academy of Child and Adolescent Psychiatry, Boston, MA.

Emslie, G. J., Findling, R. L., Yeung, P. P., Kunz, N. R., & Li, Y. (2007). Venlafaxine ER for the treatment of pediatric subjects with depression: Results of two placebo-controlled trials. *Journal of the American Academy of Child and Adolescent Psychiatry, 46*, 479–488.

Emslie, G. J., Heiligenstein, J. H., Hoog, S. L., Wagner, K. D., Findling, R. L., McCracken, J. T., et al. (2004a). Fluoxetine treatment for prevention of relapse of depression in children and adolescents: A double-blind, placebo-controlled study. *Journal of the American Academy of Child and Adolescent Psychiatry, 43*, 1397–1405.

Emslie, G. J., Heiligenstein, J. H., Wagner, K. D., Hoog, S. L., Ernest, D. E., Brown, E., et al. (2002). Fluoxetine for acute treatment of depression in children and adolescents: A placebo-controlled, randomized clinical trial. *Journal of the American Academy of Child and Adolescent Psychiatry, 41*, 1205–1215.

Emslie, G. J., Hughes, C. W., Crismon, M. L., Lopez, M., Pliszka, S., Toprac, M. G., et al. (2004b). A feasibility study of the childhood depression medication algorithm: The Texas Children's Medication Algorithm Project (CMAP). *Journal of the American Academy of Child and Adolescent Psychiatry, 43*, 519–527.

Emslie, G. J., Rush, A. J., Weinberg, W. A., Kowatch, R., Hughes, C., Carmody, T., et al. (1997). Double-blind placebo-controlled trial of fluoxetine in children and adolescents. *Archives of General Psychiatry, 54*, 1037.

Epstein, M. H., Cullinan, D., & Polloway, E. D. (1986). Patterns of maladjustment among mentally retarded children and youth. *American Journal of Mental Deficiency, 91*, 127–134.

Erzegovesi, S., Guglielmo, E., Siliprandi, F., & Bellodi, L. (2005). Low-dose risperidone augmentation of fluvoxamine treatment in obsessive-compulsive disorder: A double-blind, placebo-controlled study. *European Neuropsychopharmacology, 15*, 69–74.

Faedda, G. L., Baldessarini, R. J., Glovinsky, I. P., & Austin, N. B. (2004). Pediatric bipolar disorder: Phenomenology and course of illness. *Bipolar Disorders, 6*, 305–313.

Faraone, S. V., & Biederman, J. (1997). Do attention deficit hyperactivity disorder and major depression share familial risk factors? *Journal of Nervous and Mental Disease, 185*, 533–541.

Faraone, S. V., Biederman, J., Jetton, J. G., & Tsuang, M. T. (1997a). Attention deficit disorder and conduct disorder: Longitudinal evidence for a familial subtype. *Psychological Medicine, 27*, 291–300.

Faraone, S. V., Biederman, J., Keenan, K., & Tsuang, M. T. (1991). A family-genetic study of girls with DSM-III attention deficit disorder. *American Journal of Psychiatry, 148*, 112–117.

Faraone, S. V., Biederman, J., Mennin, D., Wozniak, J., & Spencer, T. (1997b). Attention deficit hyperactivity disorder with bipolar disorder: A familial subtype. *Journal of the American Academy of Child and Adolescent Psychiatry, 36*, 1378–1387.

Faraone, S. V., Perlis, R. H., Doyle, A. E., Smoller, J. W., Goralnick, J. J., Holmgren, M. A., et al. (2005). Molecular genetics of attention-deficit/hyperactivity disorder. *Biological Psychiatry, 57*, 1313–1323.

Ferrão, Y. A., Almeida, V. P., Bedin, N. R., Rosa, R., & Busnello, E. D. (2006). Impulsivity and compulsivity in patients with trichotillomania or skin picking compared with patients with obsessive-compulsive disorder. *Comprehensive Psychiatry, 47,* 282–288.

Fergusson, D. M., Horwood, L. J., & Ridder, E. M. (2007). Conduct and attentional problems in childhood and adolescence and later substance use, abuse and dependence: Results of a 25-year longitudinal study. *Drug and Alcohol Dependence, 88* (Suppl. 1), S14–S26.

Findling, R. L. (1996). Open-label treatment of comorbid depression and attentional disorders with co-administration of serotonin reuptake inhibitors and psychostimulants in children, adolescents, and adults: A case series. *Journal of Child and Adolescent Psychopharmacology, 6,* 165–175.

Findling, R. L., Blumer, J. L., Kauffman, R., Batterson, J. R., Gilbert, D. L., Bramer, S., et al. (2003). Aripiprazole in pediatric conduct disorder: A pilot study. *European Neuropsychopharmacology, 12* (Suppl. 4), S335.

Findling, R. L., Frazier, T. W., Youngstrom, E. A., McNamara, N. K., Stansbrey, R. J., Gracious, B. L., et al. (2007a). Double-blind, placebo-controlled trial of divalproex monotherapy in the treatment of symptomatic youth at high risk for developing bipolar disorder. *Journal of Clinical Psychiatry, 68,* 781–788.

Findling, R. L., Gracious, B. L., McNamara, N. K., Youngstrom, E. A., Demeter, C. A., Branicky, L. A., et al. (2001). Rapid, continuous cycling and psychiatric co-morbidity in pediatric bipolar I disorder. *Bipolar Disord, 3,* 202–210.

Findling, R. L., McNamara, N. K., Branicky, L. A., O'Riordan, M. A., Schlucter, M., Lemon, E., et al. (2000). A double-blind pilot study of risperidone in the treatment of conduct disorder. *Journal of the American Academy of Child and Adolescent Psychiatry, 39,* 509–516.

Findling, R. L., McNamara, N. K., Demeter, C. A., Stansbrey, R. J., Gracious, B. L., Whipkey, R. E., et al. (2007b, October 23–28). Methylphenidate in bipolar disorder and co-morbid attention-deficit/hyperactivity disorder (ADHD). Paper presented at the 54th meeting of the American Academy of Child and Adolescent Psychiatry, Boston, MA.

Findling, R. L., McNamara, N. K., Gracious, B. L., O'Riordan, M. A., Reed, M. D., Demeter, C., et al. (2004). Quetiapine in nine youths with autistic disorder. *Journal of Child and Adolescent Psychopharmacology, 14,* 287–294.

Findling, R. L., McNamara, N. K., Stansbrey, R., Gracious, B. L., Whipkey, R. E., Demeter, C. A., et al. (2006a). Combination lithium and divalproex sodium in pediatric bipolar symptom re-stabilization. *Journal of the American Academy of Child and Adolescent Psychiatry, 45,* 142–148.

Findling, R. L., Reed, M. D., O'Riordan, M. A., Demeter, C. A., Stansbrey, R. J., & McNamara, N. K. (2006b). Effectiveness, safety, and pharmacokinetics of quetiapine in aggressive children with conduct disorder. *Journal of the American Academy of Child and Adolescent Psychiatry, 45,* 792–800.

Findling, R. L., Reed, M. D., O'Riordan, M. A., Demeter, C. A., Stansbrey, R. J., & McNamara, N. K. (2007c). A 26-week open-label study of quetiapine in children with conduct disorder. *Journal of Child and Adolescent Psychopharmacology, 17,* 1–9.

Fisher, P., Lucas, C., Shaffer, D., Schwab-Stone, M., Graae, F., Lichtman, J., et al. (1997, Oct14–19). Diagnostic Interview Schedule for Children, Version IV (DISC-IV): Test-retest reliability in a clinical sample. Paper presented at the 44th annual meeting of the American Academy of Child and Adolescent Psychiatry, Toronto,CA.

Foley, D. L., Pickles, A., Maes, H. M., Silberg, J. L., & Eaves, L. J. (2004). Course and short-term outcomes of separation anxiety disorder in a community sample of twins. *Journal of the American Academy of Child and Adolescent Psychiatry, 43,* 1107–1114.

Fones, C. S., Pollack, M. H., Susswein, L., & Otto, M. (2000). History of childhood attention deficit hyperactivity disorder (ADHD) features among adults with panic disorder. *Journal of Affective Disorders, 58,* 99–106.

Food and Drug Administration. (2005, September). Suicidal thinking in children and adolescents [FDA Alert]. Available at *www.fda.gov/cder/drug/infopage/atomoxetine/default.htm.*

Ford, J. D., Racusin, R., Daviss, W. B., Ellis, C. G., Thomas, J., Rogers, K., et al. (1999). Trauma exposure among children with oppositional defiant disorder and attention deficit-hyperactivity disorder. *Journal of Consulting Clinical Psychology, 67,* 786–789.

Ford, J. D., Racusin, R., Ellis, C. G., Daviss, W. B., Reiser, J., Fleischer, A., et al. (2000). Child maltreatment, other trauma exposure, and posttraumatic symptomatology among children with oppositional defiant and attention deficit hyperactivity disorders. *Child Maltreatment, 5,* 205–217.

Frankenhauser, M., Karumanchi, V., German, M., Yates, A., & Karumanchi, S. (1992). A double blind placebo-controlled study of the efficacy of transdermal clonidine in autism. *Journal of Clinical Psychiatry, 53,* 77–82.

Frazier, J. A., Meyer, M. C., Biederman, J., Wozniak, J., Wilens, T. E., Spencer, T. J., et al. (1999). Risperidone treatment for juvenile bipolar disorder: A retrospective chart review. *Journal of the American Academy of Child and Adolescent Psychiatry, 38,* 960–965.

Friedman, M. J., & Davidson, J. R. T. (2007). Pharmacotherapy for PTSD. In M. J. Friedman, T. M. Keane, & P. A. Resick (Eds.), *Handbook of PTSD: Science and practice.* (pp. 376–405). New York: Guilford Press.

Fristad, M. A., Goldberg-Arnold, J. S., & Gavazzi, S. M. (2003). Multi-family psychoeducation groups in the treatment of children with mood disorders. *Journal of Marital and Family Therapy, 29,* 491–504.

Froehlich, T. E., Lanphear, B. P., Epstein, J. N., Barbaresi, W. J., Katusic, S. K., & Kahn, R. S. (2007). Prevalence, recognition, and treatment of attention-deficit/hyperactivity disorder in a national sample of US children. *Archives of Pediatrics and Adolescent Medicine, 161,* 857–864.

Frye, M. A., Altshuler, L. L., Szuba, M. P., Finch, N. N., & Mintz, J. (1996). The relationship between antimanic agent for treatment of classic or dysphoric mania and length of hospital stay. *Journal of Clinical Psychiatry, 57,* 17–21.

Frye, M. A., Ketter, T. A., Kimbrell, T. A., Dunn, R. T., Speer, A. M., Osuch, E. A., et al. (2000). A placebo-controlled study of lamotrigine and gabapentin monotherapy in refractory mood disorders. *Journal of Clinical Psychopharmacology, 20,* 607–614.

Gadow, K. D., Nolan, E., Sprafkin, J., & Sverd, J. (1995). School observations of children with attention-deficit hyperactivity disorder and comorbid tic disorder: Effects of methylphenidate treatment. *Journal of Developmental and Behavioral Pediatrics, 16,* 167–176.

Gadow, K. D., Nolan, E. E., & Sverd, J. (1992a). Methylphenidate in hyperactive boys with comorbid tic disorder: I. Clinic evaluations. *Advances in Neurology, 58,* 271–281.

Gadow, K. D., Nolan, E. E., & Sverd, J. (1992b). Methylphenidate in hyperactive boys with comorbid tic disorder: II. Short-term behavioral effects in school settings. *Journal of the American Academy of Child and Adolescent Psychiatry, 31,* 462–471.

Gadow, K. D., Nolan, E. E., Sverd, J., Sprafkin, J., & Schwartz, J. (2002). Anxiety and depression symptoms and response to methylphenidate in children with attention-deficit hyperactivity disorder and tic disorder. *Journal of Clinical Psychopharmacology, 22,* 267–274.

Gadow, K. D., & Sverd, J. (2006). Attention deficit hyperactivity disorder, chronic tic disorder, and methylphenidate. *Advances in Neurology, 99,* 197–207.

Gadow, K. D., Sverd, J., Nolan, E. E., Sprafkin, J., & Schneider, J. (2007). Immediate-release methylphenidate for ADHD in children with comorbid chronic multiple tic disorder. *Journal of the American Academy of Child and Adolescent Psychiatry, 46,* 840–848.

Gaffney, G. R., Perry, P. J., Lund, B. C., Bever-Stille, K. A., Arndt, S., & Kuperman, S. (2002). Risperidone versus clonidine in the treatment of children and adolescents with Tourette's syndrome. *Journal of the American Academy of Child and Adolescent Psychiatry, 41,* 330–336.

Geller, B., Cooper, T. B., Sun, K., Zimerman, B., Frazier, J., Williams, M., et al. (1998a). Double-blind and placebo-controlled study of lithium for adolescent bipolar disorders with secondary substance dependency. *Journal of the American Academy of Child and Adolescent Psychiatry, 37,* 171–178.

Geller, B., Sun, K., Zimerman, B., Luby, J., Frazier, J., & Williams, M. (1995). Complex and rapid cycling in bipolar children and adolescents: A preliminary study. *Journal of Affective Disorders, 34,* 259–268.

Geller, B., Tillman, R., Craney, J. L., & Bolhofner, K. (2004). Four-year prospective outcome and natural history of mania in children with a prepubertal and early adolescent bipolar disorder phenotype. *Archives of General Psychiatry, 61,* 459–467.

Geller, B., Warner, K., Williams, M., & Zimerman, B. (1998b). Prepubertal and young adolescent bipolarity versus ADHD: Assessment and validity using the WASH-U-KSADS, CBCL and TRF. *Journal of Affective Disorders, 51,* 93–100.

Geller, B., Williams, M., Zimerman, B., Frazier, J., Beringer, L., & Warner, K. (1998c). Prepubertal and early adolescent bipolarity differentiate from ADHD by manic symptoms, grandiose delusion, ultra-rapid or ultradian cycling. *Journal of Affective Disorders, 51,* 81–91.

Geller, D., Biederman, J., Jones, J., Park, K., Schwartz, S., Shapiro, S., et al. (1998). Is juvenile obsessive-compulsive disorder a developmental subtype of the disorder? A review of the pediatric literature. *Journal of the American Academy of Child and Adolescent Psychiatry, 37,* 420–427.

Geller, D., Donnelly, C., Lopez, F., Rubin, R., Newcorn, J., Sutton, V., et al. (2007a). Atomoxetine treatment for pediatric patients with attention-deficit/hyperactivity disorder with comorbid anxiety disorder. *Journal of the American Academy of Child and Adolescent Psychiatry, 46,* 1119–1127.

Geller, D., Petty, C., Vivas, F., Johnson, J., Pauls, D., & Biederman, J. (2007b). Examining the relationship between obsessive-compulsive disorder and attention-deficit/hyperactivity disorder in children and adolescents: A familial risk analysis. *Biological Psychiatry, 61,* 316–321.

Geller, D., Petty, C., Vivas, F., Johnson, J., Pauls, D., & Biederman, J. (2007c). Further evidence for co-segregation between pediatric obsessive compulsive disorder and attention deficit hyperactivity disorder: A familial risk analysis. *Biological Psychiatry, 61,* 1388–1394.

Geller, D. A. (2006). Obsessive-compulsive and spectrum disorders in children and adolescents. *Psychiatric Clinics of North America, 29,* 353–370.

Geller, D. A., Biederman, J., Faraone, S. V., Cradock, K., Hagermoser, L., Zaman, N., et al. (2002). Attention-deficit/hyperactivity disorder in children and adolescents with obsessive-compulsive disorder: Fact or artifact? *Journal of the American Academy of Child and Adolescent Psychiatry, 41,* 52–58.

Geller, D. A., Biederman, J., Stewart, S. E., Mullin, B., Farrell, C., Wagner, K. D., et al. (2003a). Impact of comorbidity on treatment response to paroxetine in pediatric obsessive-compulsive disorder: Is the use of exclusion criteria empirically supported in randomized clinical trials? *Journal of Child and Adolescent Psychopharmacology, 13* (Suppl. 1), S19–S29.

Geller, D. A., Biederman, J., Stewart, S. E., Mullin, B., Martin, A., Spencer, T., et al. (2003b). Which SSRI? A meta-analysis of pharmacotherapy trials in pediatric obsessive-compulsive disorder. *American Journal of Psychiatry, 160,* 1919–1928.

Geller, D. A., Coffey, B., Faraone, S., Hagermoser, L., Zaman, N. K., Farrell, C. L., et al. (2003c). Does comorbid attention-deficit/hyperactivity disorder impact the clinical expression of pediatric obsessive-compulsive disorder? *CNS Spectrums, 8,* 259–264.

Gilbert, D. L., Batterson, J. R., Sethuraman, G., & Sallee, F. R. (2004). Tic reduction with risperidone versus pimozide in a randomized, double-blind, crossover trial. *Journal of the American Academy of Child and Adolescent Psychiatry, 43,* 206-214.

Gilliam, J. E. (2001). *Gilliam Asperger's Disorder Scale.* Austin, TX: PRO-ED.

Glovinsky, I. (2002). A brief history of childhood-onset bipolar disorder through 1980. *Child and Adolescent Psychiatric Clinics of North America, 11,* 443–460, vii.

Goldstein, L. H., Harvey, E. A., & Friedman-Weieneth, J. L. (2007b). Examining subtypes of behavior problems among 3-year-old children: III. Investigating differences in parenting practices and parenting stress. *Journal of Abnormal Child Psychology, 35,* 125–136.

Goldstein, L. H., Harvey, E. A., Friedman-Weieneth, J. L., Pierce, C., Tellert, A., & Sippel, J. C. (2007a). Examining subtypes of behavior problems among 3-year-old children: II. Investigating differences in parent psychopathology, couple conflict, and other family stressors. *Journal of Abnormal Child Psychology, 35,* 111–123.

Greene, R. W., & Ablon, J. S. (2006). *Treating explosive kids: The collaborative problem-solving approach.* New York: Guilford Press.

Greenhill, L. L., Newcorn, J. H., Gao, H., & Feldman, P. D. (2007). Effect of two different methods of initiating atomoxetine on the adverse event profile of atomoxetine. *Journal of the American Academy of Child and Adolescent Psychiatry, 46,* 566–572.

Greenspan, S. I., & Wieder, S. (1997). Developmental patterns and outcomes in infants and children with disorders in relating and communicating: A chart review of 200 cases of children with autistic spectrum diagnoses. *Journal of Developmental and Learning Disorders, 1,* 87–141.

Greimel, E., Herpertz-Dahlmann, B., Günther, T., Vitt, C., & Konrad, K. (2008). Attentional functions in children and adolescents with attention-deficit/hyperactivity disorder with and without comorbid tic disorder. *Journal of Neural Transmission, 115,* 191–200.

Greves, E. H. (1884). Acute mania in a child of five years; recovery; remarks. *Lancet, ii,* 824–826.

Grigoroiu-Serbanescu, M., Christodorescu, D., Magureanu, S., Jipescu, I., Totoescu, A., Marinescu, E., et al. (1991). Adolescent offspring of endogenous unipolar depressive parents and of normal parents. *Journal of Affective Disorders, 21,* 185–198.

Gutstein, S. E., & Sheely, R. K. (2002). *Relationship development intervention with children, adolescents, and adults.* New York: Jessica Kingsley.

Hagerman, R. J., Smith, A. C. M., & Mariner, R. (1983). Clinical features of the fragile X syndrome. In R. J. Hagerman & P. M. McBogg (Eds.), *The fragile X syndrome: Biochemistry, diagnosis, treatment* (pp. 17–54). Dillon, CO: Spectra Publishing.

Hagino, O. R., Weller, E. B., Weller, R. A., Washing, D., Fristad, M. A., & Kontras, S. B. (1995). Untoward effects of lithium treatment in children aged four through six years. *Journal of the American Academy of Child and Adolescent Psychiatry, 34,* 1584–1590.

Halperin, J. M., McKay, K. E., Grayson, R. H., & Newcorn, J. H. (2003). Reliability, validity, and preliminary normative data for the Children's Aggression Scale—Teacher Version. *Journal of the the American Academy of Child and Adolescent Psychiatry, 42,* 965–971.

Halperin, J. M., McKay, K. E., & Newcorn, J. H. (2002). Development, reliability, and validity of the Children's Aggression Scale—Parent Version. *Journal of the American Academy of Child and Adolescent Psychiatry, 41,* 245–252.

Hamilton, B. E., Minino, A. M., Martin, J. A., Kochanek, K. D., Strobino, D. M., & Guyer, B. (2007). Annual summary of vital statistics: 2005. *Pediatrics, 119,* 345–360.

Hammad, T. A., Laughren, T., & Racoosin, J. (2006a). Suicidality in pediatric patients treated with antidepressant drugs. *Archives of General Psychiatry, 63,* 332–339.

Hammad, T. A., Laughren, T., & Racoosin, J. (2006b). Suicidality in pediatric patients treated with antidepressant drugs. *Archives of General Psychiatry, 63,* 332–339.

Hammen, C., Burge, D., Burney, E., & Adrian, C. (1990). Longitudinal study of diagnoses in children of women with unipolar and bipolar affective disorder. *Archives of General Psychiatry, 47,* 1112–1117.

Handen, B. L., Feldman, H., Gosling, A., Breaux, A. M., & McAuliffe, S. (1991). Adverse side effects of methylphenidate among mentally retarded children with ADHD. *Journal of the American Academy of Child and Adolescent Psychiatry, 30,* 241–245.

Handen, B. L., & Gilchrist, R. (2006). Practitioner review: Psychopharmacology in children and adolescents with mental retardation. *Journal of Child Psychology and Psychiatry, 47*, 871–882.

Handen, B. L., & Hardan, A. Y. (2006). Open-label, prospective trial of olanzapine in adolescents with subaverage intelligence and disruptive behavioral disorders. *Journal of the American Academy of Child and Adolescent Psychiatry, 45*, 928–935.

Handen, B. L., Johnson, C. R., & Lubetsky, M. (2000). Efficacy of methylphenidate among children with autism and symptoms of attention-deficit hyperactivity disorder. *Journal of Autism and Developmental Disorders, 30*, 245–255.

Hardan, A. Y., Jou, R. J., & Handen, B. L. (2005). Retrospective study of quetiapine in children and adolescents with pervasive developmental disorders. *Journal of Autism and Developmental Disorders, 35*, 387–391.

Hastings, R. P., Beck, A., Daley, D., & Hill, C. (2005). Symptoms of ADHD and their correlates in children with intellectual disabilities. *Research in Developmental Disabilities, 26*, 456–468.

Hazell, P. (2007). Drug therapy for attention-deficit/hyperactivity disorder-like symptoms in autistic disorder. *Journal of Paediatric and Child Health, 43*, 19–24.

Hazell, P. L., & Stuart, J. E. (2003). A randomized controlled trial of clonidine added to psychostimulant medication for hyperactive and aggressive children. *Journal of the American Academy of Child and Adolescent Psychiatry, 42*, 886–894.

Henin, A., Biederman, J., Mick, E., Sachs, G. S., Hirshfeld-Becker, D. R., Siegel, R. S., et al. (2005). Psychopathology in the offspring of parents with bipolar disorder: A controlled study. *Biological Psychiatry, 58*, 554–561.

Herman, B. H., Hammock, M. K., Arthur-Smith, A., Kuehl, K., & Appelgate, K. (1989). Effects of acute administration of naltrexone on cardiocavascular function, body temperature, body weight, and serum concentrations of liver enzymes in autistic children. *Developmental Pharmacology and Therapeutics, 12*, 118–127.

Himle, M. B., Woods, D. W., Piacentini, J. C., & Walkup, J. T. (2006). Brief review of habit reversal training for Tourette syndrome. *Journal of Child Neurology, 21*, 719–725.

Hinshaw, S. P. (2007). Moderators and mediators of treatment outcome for youth with ADHD: Understanding for whom and how interventions work. *Ambulatory Pediatrics, 7*, 91–100.

Hinshaw, S. P., Heller, T., & McHale, J. P. (1992). Covert antisocial behavior in boys with attention-deficit hyperactivity disorder: External validation and effects of methylphenidate. *Journal of Consulting and Clinical Psychology, 60*, 274–281.

Hollander, E., Baldini, R. N., Sood, E., & Pallanti, S. (2003). Risperidone augmentation in treatment-resistant obsessive-compulsive disorder: A double-blind, placebo-controlled study. *International Journal of Neuropsychopharmacology, 6*, 397–401.

Hollander, E., Phillips, A., Chaplin, W., Zagursky, K., Novotny, S., Wasserman, S., et al. (2005). A placebo controlled crossover trial of liquid fluoxetine on repetitive behaviors in childhood and adolescent autism. *Neuropsychopharmacology, 30*, 582–589.

Hollander, E., Wasserman, S., Swanson, E. N., Chaplin, W., Schapiro, M. L., Zagursky, K., et al. (2006). A double-blind placebo-controlled pilot study of olanzapine in childhood/adolescent pervasive developmental disorder. *Journal of Child and Adolescent Psychopharmacology, 16*, 541–548.

Howard, J. S., Sparkman, C. R., Cohen, H. G., Green, G., & Stanislaw, H. (2005). A comparison of intensive behavior analytic and eclectic treatments for young children with autism. *Research in Developmental Disabilities, 26*, 359–383.

Hoza, B., Gerdes, A. C., Hinshaw, S. P., Arnold, L. E., Pelham, W. E., Jr., Molina, B. S., et al. (2004). Self-perceptions of competence in children with ADHD and comparison children. *Journal of Consulting and Clinical Psychology, 72*, 382–391.

Hoza, B., Pelham, W. E., Jr., Dobbs, J., Owens, J. S., & Pillow, D. R. (2002). Do boys with attention-deficit/hyperactivity disorder have positive illusory self-concepts? *Journal of Abnormal Psychology, 111*, 268–278.

Hudziak, J. J., Althoff, R. R., Derks, E. M., Faraone, S. V., & Boomsma, D. I. (2005). Prevalence and genetic architecture of Child Behavior Checklist-juvenile bipolar disorder. *Biological Psychiatry, 58,* 562–568.

Hudziak, J. J., Derks, E. M., Althoff, R. R., Rettew, D. C., & Boomsma, D. I. (2005). The genetic and environmental contributions to attention deficit hyperactivity disorder as measured by the Conners' Rating Scales—Revised. *American Journal of Psychiatry, 162,* 1614–1620.

Hughes, C. W., Emslie, G. J., Crismon, M. L., Posner, K., Birmaher, B., Ryan, N., et al. (2007). Texas Children's Medication Algorithm Project: Update from Texas Consensus Conference Panel on Medication Treatment of Childhood Major Depressive Disorder. *Journal of the American Academy of Child and Adolescent Psychiatry, 46,* 667–686.

Hunt, R. D., Minderaa, R. B., & Cohen, D. J. (1986). The therapeutic effect of clonidine in attention deficit disorder with hyperactivity: A comparison with placebo and methylphenidate. *Psychopharmacology Bulletin, 22,* 229–236.

Institute of Medicine. (2004). *Immunization safety review: Vaccines and autism.* Washington, DC: National Academies Press.

Jain, M., Palacio, L. G., Castellanos, F. X., Palacio, J. D., Pineda, D., Restrepo, M. I., et al. (2007). Attention-deficit/hyperactivity disorder and comorbid disruptive behavior disorders: Evidence of pleiotropy and new susceptibility loci. *Biological Psychiatry, 61,* 1329–1339.

James, A., Lai, F. H., & Dahl, C. (2004). Attention deficit hyperactivity disorder and suicide: A review of possible associations. *Acta Psychiatrica Scandinavica, 110,* 408–415.

Jaselskis, C. A., Cook, E. H., Jr., Fletcher, K. E., & Leventhal, B. L. (1992). Clonidine treatment of hyperactive and impulsive children with autistic disorder. *Journal of Clinical Psychopharmacology, 12,* 322–327.

Jefferson, J. W., Greist, J. H., & Ackerman, D. L. (1987). *Lithium Encyclopedia for Clinical Practice.* Washington, DC: American Psychiatric Press.

Jensen, P. S., Arnold, L. E., Swanson, J. M., Vitiello, B., Abikoff, H. B., Greenhill, L. L., et al. (2007a). Three-Year follow-up of the NIMH MTA study. *Journal of the American Academy of Child and Adolescent Psychiatry, 46,* 989–1002.

Jensen, P. S., Hinshaw, S. P., Kraemer, H. C., Lenora, N., Newcorn, J. H., Abikoff, H. B., et al. (2001). ADHD comorbidity findings from the MTA study: Comparing comorbid subgroups. *Journal of the American Academy of Child and Adolescent Psychiatry, 40,* 147–158.

Jensen, P. S., Martin, D., & Cantwell, D. P. (1997). Comorbidity in ADHD: Implications for research, practice, and DSM-V. *Journal of the American Academy of Child and Adolescent Psychiatry, 36,* 1065–1079.

Jensen, P. S., Youngstrom, E. A., Steiner, H., Findling, R. L., Meyer, R. E., Malone, R. P., et al. (2007b). Consensus report on impulsive aggression as a symptom across diagnostic categories in child psychiatry: Implications for medication studies. *Journal of the American Academy of Child and Adolescent Psychiatry, 46,* 309–322.

Joffe, H., Cohen, L. S., Suppes, T., McLaughlin, W. L., Lavori, P., Adams, J. M., et al. (2006). Valproate is associated with new-onset oligoamenorrhea with hyperandrogenism in women with bipolar disorder. *Biological Psychiatry, 59,* 1078–1086.

Johnson, C. P., & Myers, S. M. (2007). Identification and evaluation of children with autism spectrum disorders. *Pediatrics, 120,* 1183–1215.

Kaufman, J., Birmaher, B., Brent, D., Rao, U., Flynn, C., Moreci, P., et al. (1997). Schedule for Affective Disorders and Schizophrenia for School Age Children—Present and Lifetime Version (K-SADS-PL): Initial reliability and validity data. *Journal of the American Academy of Child and Adolescent Psychiatry, 36,* 980–988.

Kemph, J. P., DeVane, C. L., Levin, G. M., Jarecke, R., & Miller, R. L. (1993). Treatment of aggressive children with clonidine: Results of an open pilot study. *Journal of the American Academy of Child and Adolescent Psychiatry, 32,* 577–581.

Kessler, R. C., Coccaro, E. F., Fava, M., Jaeger, S., Jin, R., & Walters, E. (2006). The prevalence and correlates of DSM-IV intermittent explosive disorder in the National Comorbidity Survey Replication. *Archives of General Psychiatry, 63,* 669–678.

Kessler, R. C., & Merikangas, K. R. (2004). The National Comorbidity Survey Replication (NCS-R): Background and aims. *International Journal of Methods in Psychiatric Research, 13,* 60–68.

Khalifa, N., & von Knorring, A. L. (2003). Prevalence of tic disorders and Tourette syndrome in a Swedish school population. *Developmental Medicine and Child Neurology, 45,* 315–319.

Khalifa, N., & von Knorring, A. L. (2005). Tourette syndrome and other tic disorders in a total population of children: Clinical assessment and background. *Acta Paediatrica, 94,* 1608–1614.

Klein, R. G., Abikoff, H., Klass, E., Ganeles, D., Seese, L. M., & Pollack, S. (1997). Clinical efficacy of methylphenidate in conduct disorder with and without attention deficit hyperactivity disorder. *Archives of General Psychiatry, 54,* 1073–1080.

Klein, R. G., Landa, B., Mattes, J. A., & Klein, D. F. (1988). Methylphenidate and growth in hyperactive children: A controlled withdrawal study. *Archives of General Psychiatry, 45,* 1127–1130.

Klein, R. G., Pine, D. S., & Klein, D. F. (1998). Resolved: Mania is mistaken for ADHD in prepubertal children, negative. *Journal of the American Academy of Child and Adolescent Psychiatry, 37,* 1093–1096.

Koller, H., Richardson, S. A., Katz, M., & McLaren, J. (1983). Behavior disturbance since childhood among a 5-year birth cohort of all mentally retarded young adults in a city. *American Journal of Mental Deficiency, 87,* 386–395.

Kolmen, B. K., Feldman, H. M., Handen, B. L., & Janosky, J. E. (1995). Naltrexone in young autistic children: A double blind, placebo controlled crossover study. *Journal of the American Academy of Child and Adolescent Psychiatry, 34,* 223–231.

Kovacs, M. (1992). *Children's Depression Inventory.* Los Angeles: Multi-Health Systems.

Kovacs, M., Akiskal, H. S., Gatsonis, C., & Parrone, P. L. (1994). Childhood onset dysthymic disorder: Clinical features and prospective naturalistic outcome. *Archives of General Psychiatry, 51,* 365–374.

Kovacs, M., Feinberg, T. L., Crouse-Novack, M., Paulauskas, S. L., & Finkelstein, R. (1984). Depressive disorders in childhood: I. A longitudinal prospective study of characteristics and recovery. *Archives of General Psychiatry, 41,* 229–237.

Kovacs, M., Goldston, D., & Gatsonis, C. (1993). Suicidal behaviors and childhood-onset depressive disorders: A longitudinal investigation. *Journal of the American Academy of Child and Adolescent Psychiatry, 32,* 8–20.

Kovacs, M., Paulauskas, S., Gatsonis, C., & Richards, C. (1988). Depressive disorders in childhood: III. A longitudinal study of comorbidity with and risk for conduct disorders. *Journal of Affective Disorders, 15,* 205–217.

Kovacs, M., & Pollock, M. (1995). Bipolar disorder and comorbid conduct disorder in childhood and adolescence. *Journal of the American Academy of Child and Adolescent Psychiatry, 34,* 715–723.

Kowatch, R. A., Findling, R., Scheffer, R., & Stanford, K. (2007, October 23–28). Placebo-contolled trial of divalproex versus lithium for bipolar disorder. Paper presented at the 54th Annual Meeting of the American Academy of Child and Adolescent Psychiatry, Boston, MA.

Kowatch, R. A., Fristad, M., Birmaher, B., Wagner, K. D., Findling, R. L., & Hellander, M. (2005a). Treatment guidelines for children and adolescents with bipolar disorder. *Journal of the American Academy of Child and Adolescent Psychiatry, 44,* 213–235.

Kowatch, R. A., Suppes, T., Carmody, T. J., Bucci, J. P., Kromelis, M., Emslie, G. J., et al. (2000). Effect size of lithium, divalproex sodium, and carbamazepine in children and adolescents with bipolar disorder. *Journal of the American Academy of Child and Adolescent Psychiatry, 39,* 713–720.

Kowatch, R. A., Youngstrom, E. A., Danielyan, A., & Findling, R. L. (2005b). Review and meta-analysis of the phenomenology and clinical characteristics of mania in children and adolescents. *Bipolar Disorders, 7,* 483–496.

Kratochvil, C. J., Michelson, D., Newcorn, J. H., Weiss, M. D., Busner, J., Moore, R. J., et al. (2007). High-dose atomoxetine treatment of ADHD in youths with limited response to standard doses. *Journal of the American Academy of Child and Adolescent Psychiatry, 46,* 1128–1137.

Kratochvil, C. J., Newcorn, J. H., Arnold, L. E., Duesenberg, D., Emslie, G. J., Quintana, H., et al. (2005). Atomoxetine alone or combined with fluoxetine for treating ADHD with comorbid depressive or anxiety symptoms. *Journal of the American Academy of Child and Adolescent Psychiatry, 44,* 915–924.

Kronenberger, W. G., Giauque, A. L., & Dunn, D. W. (2007). Development and validation of the outburst monitoring scale for children and adolescents. *Journal of Child and Adolescent Psychopharmacology, 17,* 511–526.

Kronenberger, W. G., Giauque, A. L., Lafata, D. E., Bohnstedt, B. N., Maxey, L. E., & Dunn, D. W. (2007). Quetiapine addition in methylphenidate treatment-resistant adolescents with comorbid ADHD, conduct/oppositional-defiant disorder, and aggression: A prospective, open-label study. *Journal of Child and Adolescent Psychopharmacology, 17,* 334–347.

Kutcher, S., Aman, M., Brooks, S. J., Buitelaar, J., van Daalen, E., Fegert, J., et al. (2004). International consensus statement on attention-deficit/hyperactivity disorder (ADHD) and disruptive behaviour disorders (DBDs): Clinical implications and treatment practice suggestions. *European Neuropsychopharmacology, 14,* 11–28.

Lacourse, E., Nagin, D. S., Vitaro, F., Cote, S., Arseneault, L., & Tremblay, R. E. (2006). Prediction of early-onset deviant peer group affiliation: A 12-year longitudinal study. *Archives of General Psychiatry, 63,* 562–568.

Lahey, B. B., Piacentini, J. C., McBurnett, K., Stone, P., Hartdagen, S., & Hynd, G. (1988). Psychopathology in the parents of children with conduct disorder and hyperactivity *Journal of the American Academy of Child and Adolescent Psychiatry, 27,* 163–170 [erratum, 516].

Lansford, J. E., Miller-Johnson, S., Berlin, L. J., Dodge, K. A., Bates, J. E., & Pettit, G. S. (2007). Early physical abuse and later violent delinquency: A prospective longitudinal study. *Child Maltreatment, 12,* 233–245.

Larson, J., & Lochman, J. E. (2002). *Helping schoolchildren cope with anger: A cognitive-behavioral intervention.* New York: Guilford Press.

Last, C. G., Hersen, M., Kazdin, A. E., Finkelstein, R., & Strauss, C. C. (1987). Comparison of DSM-III separation anxiety and overanxious disorders: Demographic characteristics and patterns of comorbidity. *Journal of the American Academy of Child and Adolescent Psychiatry, 26,* 527–531.

LeBlanc, J. C., Binder, C. E., Armenteros, J. L., Aman, M. G., Wang, J. S., Hew, H., et al. (2005). Risperidone reduces aggression in boys with a disruptive behaviour disorder and below average intelligence quotient: Analysis of two placebo-controlled randomized trials. *International Clinical Psychopharmacology, 20,* 275–283.

Leckman, J. F., Vaccarino, F. M., Kalanithi, P. S., & Rothenberger, A. (2006). Annotation: Tourette syndrome: A relentless drumbeat—driven by misguided brain oscillations. *Journal of Child Psychology and Psychiatry, 47,* 537–550.

Lee, D. O., Steingard, R. J., Cesena, M., Helmers, S. L., Riviello, J. J., & Mikati, M. A. (1996). Behavioral side effects of gabapentin in children. *Epilepsia, 37,* 87–90.

Leibenluft, E., Charney, D. S., Towbin, K. E., Bhangoo, R. K., & Pine, D. S. (2003). Defining clinical phenotypes of juvenile mania. *American Journal of Psychiatry, 160,* 430–437.

Leucht, S., Corves, C., Arbter, D., Engel, R. R., Li, C., & Davis, J. M. (2009). Second-generation versus first-generation antipsychotic drugs for schizophrenia: A meta-analysis. *Lancet, 373,* 31-41.

Lewinsohn, P. M., Klein, D. N., & Seeley, J. R. (1995). Bipolar disorders in a community sample of older adolescents: Prevalence, phenomenology, comorbidity, and course. *Journal of the American Academy of Child and Adolescent Psychiatry, 34,* 454–463.

Libby, A. M., Brent, D. A., Morrato, E. H., Orton, H. D., Allen, R., & Valuck, R. J. (2007). Decline in treatment of pediatric depression after FDA advisory on risk of suicidality with SSRIs. *American Journal of Psychiatry, 164,* 884–891.

Liberthson, R. R. (1996). Sudden death from cardiac causes in children and young adults. *New England Journal of Medicine, 334,* 1039–1044.

Lochman, J. E., & Wells, K. C. (1996). A social-cognitive intervention with aggressive children: Prevention effects and contextual implementation issues. In R. D. Peters & R. J. McMahon (Eds.), *Preventing childhood disorders, substance abuse, and delinquency* (pp. 111–143). Thousand Oaks, CA: Sage.

Lochman, J. E., & Wells, K. C. (2002). The Coping Power program at the middle school transition: Universal and indicated prevention effects. *Psychology of Addictive Behaviors, 16,* 40–54.

Lochman, J. E., & Wells, K. C. (2003). Effectiveness of the Coping Power program and of classroom intervention with aggressive children: Outcomes at a 1-year follow-up. *Behavior Therapy, 34,* 493–515.

Lochman, J. E., & Wells, K. C. (2004). The Coping Power program for preadolescent aggressive boys and their parents: Outcome effects at the 1-year follow-up. *Journal of Consulting and Clinical Psychology, 72*(4), 571–578.

Loeber, R., Brinthaupt, V. P., & Green, S. M. (1988). Attention deficits, impulsivity, and hyperactivity with or without conduct problems: Relationships to delinquency and unique contextual factors. In R. J. McMahon & R. D. Peters (Eds.), *Behavior disorders of adolescence: Research, intervention, and policy in clinical and school settings* (pp. xxx–xxx). New York: Plenum Press.

Loeber, R., Green, S. M., Lahey, B. B., & Stouthamer-Loeber, M. (1989). Optimal informants on childhood disruptive behaviors. *Development and Psychopathology, 1,* 317–337.

Lott, R. S., Kerrick, J. M., & Cohen, S. A. (1996). Clinical and economic aspects of risperidone treatment in adults with mental retardation and behavioral disturbance. *Psychopharmacology Bulletin, 32,* 721–729.

Lovaas, O. I. (1987). Behavioral treatment and normal education and intellectual functioning in young autistic children. *Journal of Consulting and Clinical Psychology, 55,* 3–9.

Luby, J., Mrakotsky, C., Stalets, M. M., Belden, A., Heffelfinger, A., Williams, M., et al. (2006). Risperidone in preschool children with autistic spectrum disorders: An investigation of safety and efficacy. *Journal of Child and Adolescent Psychopharmacology, 16,* 575–587.

Mackay, F. L., Wilton, G. V., Pearce, G. L., Freemantle, S. N., & Mann, R. D. (2008). Safety of long-term lamotrigine in epilepsy. *Epilepsia, 38,* 881–886.

Malone, R. P., Cater, J., Sheikh, R. M., Choudhury, M. S., & Delaney, M. A. (2001). Olanzapine versus haloperidol in children with autistic disorder: An open pilot study. *Journal of the American Academy of Child and Adolescent Psychiatry, 40,* 887–894.

Malone, R. P., Delaney, M. A., Luebbert, J. F., Cater, J., & Campbell, M. (2000). A double-blind placebo-controlled study of lithium in hospitalized aggressive children and adolescents with conduct disorder. *Archives of General Psychiatry, 57,* 649–654.

Manassis, K., Mendlowitz, S. L., Scapillato, D., Avery, D., Fiksenbaum, L., Freire, M., et al. (2002). Group and individual cognitive-behavioral therapy for childhood anxiety disorders: A randomized trial. *Journal of the American Academy of Child and Adolescent Psychiatry, 41,* 1423–1430.

Manassis, K., Tannock, R., & Barbosa, J. (2000). Dichotic listening and response inhibition in children with comorbid anxiety disorders and ADHD. *Journal of the American Academy of Child and Adolescent Psychiatry, 39,* 1152–1159.

Manassis, K., Tannock, R., Young, A., & Francis-John, S. (2007). Cognition in anxious children with attention deficit hyperactivity disorder: A comparison with clinical and normal children. *Behavior and Brain Functions, 3,* 4.

Mannuzza, S., Klein, R. G., Truong, N. L., Moulton, J. L., III, Roizen, E. R., Howell, K. H., et al. (2008). Age of methylphenidate treatment initiation in children with ADHD and later substance abuse: Prospective follow-up into adulthood. *American Journal of Psychiatry, 165,* 604–609.

March, J. S., Biederman, J., Wolkow, R., Safferman, A., Mardekian, J., Cook, E. H., et al. (1998). Sertraline in children and adolescents with obsessive compulsive disorder: A multicenter, randomized, controlled trial. *Journal of the American Medical Association, 280,* 1752–1756.

March, J. S., Franklin, M. E., Leonard, H., Garcia, A., Moore, P., Freeman, J., et al. (2007). Tics moderate treatment outcome with sertraline but not cognitive-behavior therapy in pediatric obsessive-compulsive disorder. *Biological Psychiatry, 61,* 344–347.

March, J., Silva, S., Petrycki, S., Curry, J., Wells, K., Fairbank, J., et al. (2004). Fluoxetine, cognitive-behavioral therapy, and their combination for adolescents with depression: Treatment for Adolescents with Depression Study (TADS) randomized controlled trial. *Journal of the American Medical Association, 292,* 807–820.

March, J. S., Swanson, J. M., Arnold, L. E., Hoza, B., Conners, C. K., Hinshaw, S. P., et al. (2000). Anxiety as a predictor and outcome variable in the multimodal treatment study of children with ADHD (MTA). *Journal of Abnormal Child Psychology, 28,* 527–541.

Martin, A., Koenig, K., Scahill, L., & Bregman, J. (1999). Open-label quetiapine in the treatment of children and adolescents with autistic disorder. *Journal of Child and Adolescent Psychopharmacology, 9,* 99–107.

Masi, G., Millepiedi, S., Mucci, M., Bertini, N., Pfanner, C., & Arcangeli, F. (2006a). Comorbidity of obsessive-compulsive disorder and attention-deficit/hyperactivity disorder in referred children and adolescents. *Comprehensive Psychiatry, 47,* 42–47.

Masi, G., Milone, A., Canepa, G., Millepiedi, S., Mucci, M., & Muratori, F. (2006b). Olanzapine treatment in adolescents with severe conduct disorder. *European Psychiatry, 21,* 51–57.

Matson, J. L., Benavidez, D. A., Compton, L. S., Paclawskyj, T., & Baglio, C. (1996). Behavioral treatment of autistic persons: A review of research from 1980 to the present. *Research in Developmental Disabilities, 17,* 433–465.

McClellan, J. M. (2007). Olanzapine and pediatric bipolar disorder: Evidence for efficacy and safety concerns. *American Journal of Psychiatry, 164,* 1462–1464.

McCracken, J. T., McGough, J., Shah, B., Cronin, P., Hong, D., Aman, M. G., et al. (2002). Risperidone in children with autism and serious behavioral problems. *New England Journal of Medicine, 347,* 314–321.

McDougle, C. J., Epperson, C. N., Pelton, G. H., Wasylink, S., & Price, L. H. (2000). A double-blind, placebo-controlled study of risperidone addition in serotonin reuptake inhibitor-refractory obsessive-compulsive disorder. *Archives of General Psychiatry, 57,* 794–801.

McDougle, C. J., Kem, D. L., & Posey, D. J. (2002). Case series: Use of ziprasidone for maladaptive symptoms in youths with autism. *Journal of the American Academy of Child and Adolescent Psychiatry, 41,* 921–927.

McDougle, C. J., Kresch, L. E., & Posey, D. J. (2000). Repetitive thoughts and behavior in pervasive developmental disorders: Treatment with serotonin reuptake inhibitors. *Journal of Autism and Developmental Disorders, 30,* 427–435.

McDougle, C. J., Naylor, S. T., Cohen, D. J., Volkmar, F. R., Heninger, G. R., & Price, L. H. (1996). A double-blind, placebo controlled trial of fluvoxamine in adults with autistic disorder. *Archives of General Psychiatry, 53,* 1001–1008.

McGee, R., Feehan, M., Williams, S., Partridge, F., Silva, P. A., & Kelly, J. (1990). DSM-III disorders in a large sample of adolescents. *Journal of the American Academy of Child and Adolescent Psychiatry, 29,* 611–619.

McGee, R., Williams, S., & Silva, P. A. (1984). Background characteristics of aggressive, hyperactive, and aggressive-hyperactive boys. *Journal of the American Academy of Child Psychiatry, 23*, 280–284.

McMahon, R. J., & Forehand, R. L. (2003). *Helping the noncompliant child: Family-based treatment for oppositional behavior* (2nd ed.). New York: Guilford Press.

McMahon, R. J., Wells, K. C., & Kotler, J. S. (2006). Conduct problems. In E. J. Mash & R. A. Barkley (Eds.), *Treatment of childhood disorders* (3rd ed., pp. 137–268). New York: Guilford Press.

Mesibov, G. B., Shea, V., & Schopler, E. (2005). *The TEACCH approach to autism spectrum disorders.* New York: Kluwer Academic/Plenum.

Messer, S. C., Angold, A., Costello, E. J., Loeber, R., Van Kammen, W. B., & Stouthamer-Loeber, M. (1995). Development of a short questionnaire for use in epidemiological studies of depression in children and adolescents: Factor composition and structure across development. *International Journal of Methods in Psychiatric Research, 5*, 262.

Michelson, D. (2004, Oct. 19–24). Active comparator studies in the atomoxetine clinical development program. Paper presented at the 51st Annual Meeting of the American Academy of Child and Adolescent Psychiatry, San Francisco, CA.

Michelson, D., Adler, L., Spencer, T., Reimherr, F. W., West, S. A., Allen, A. J., et al. (2003). Atomoxetine in adults with ADHD: Two randomized, placebo-controlled studies. *Biological Psychiatry, 53*, 112–120.

Michelson, D., Allen, A. J., Busner, J., Casat, C., Dunn, D., Kratochvil, C., et al. (2002). Once-daily atomoxetine treatment for children and adolescents with attention deficit hyperactivity disorder: A randomized, placebo-controlled study. *American Journal of Psychiatry, 159*, 1896–1901.

Michelson, D., Faries, D., Wernicke, J., Kelsey, D., Kendrick, K., Sallee, R., et al. (2001). Atomoxetine in the treatment of children and adolescents with attention-deficit/hyperactivity disorder: A randomized, placebo-controlled, dose-response study. *Pediatrics, 108*, 1–9.

Mick, E., Biederman, J., Pandina, G., & Faraone, S. V. (2003). A preliminary meta-analysis of the child behavior checklist in pediatric bipolar disorder. *Biological Psychiatry, 53*, 1021–1027.

Mick, E., Biederman, J., Santangelo, S., & Wypij, D. (2003). The influence of gender in the familial association between ADHD and major depression. *Journal of Nervous and Mental Disease, 191*, 699–705.

Mick, E., Spencer, T., Wozniak, J., & Biederman, J. (2005). Heterogeneity of irritability in attention-deficit/hyperactivity disorder subjects with and without mood disorders. *Biological Psychiatry, 58*, 576–582.

Miklowitz, D. J., George, E. L., Axelson, D. A., Kim, E. Y., Birmaher, B., Schneck, C., et al. (2004). Family-focused treatment for adolescents with bipolar disorder. *Journal of Affective Disorders, 82*, (Suppl. 1), S113–S128.

Miklowitz, D. J., Otto, M. W., Frank, E., Reilly-Harrington, N. A., Wisniewski, S. R., Kogan, J. N., et al. (2007). Psychosocial treatments for bipolar depression: A 1-year randomized trial from the systematic treatment enhancement program. *Archives of General Psychiatry, 64*, 419–426.

Milberger, S., Biederman, J., Faraone, S. V., Murphy, J., & Tsuang, M. T. (1995). Attention deficit hyperactivity disorder and comorbid disorders: Issues of overlapping symptoms. *American Journal of Psychiatry, 152*, 1793–1799.

Moffitt, T. E. (1990). Juvenile delinquency and attention deficit disorder: Boys' developmental trajectories from age 3 to age 15. *Child Development, 61*, 893–910.

Moffitt, T. E., & Silva, P. A. (1988). Self-reported delinquency, neuropsychological deficit, and history of attention deficit disorder. *Journal of Abnormal Child Psychology, 16*, 553–569.

Molina, B. S. G. (2007, October 23–28). Substance use and delinquency through 6–8 years:

Comparison to local normative comparison group (LNCG). Paper presented at the 54th Annual Meeting of the American Academy of Child and Adolescent Psychiatry, Boston, MA.

Molina, B. S., Flory, K., Hinshaw, S. P., Greiner, A. R., Arnold, L. E., Swanson, J. M., et al. (2007). Delinquent behavior and emerging substance use in the MTA at 36 months: Prevalence, course, and treatment effects. *Journal of the American Academy of Child and Adolescent Psychiatry, 46,* 1028–1040.

Moreno, C., Laje, G., Blanco, C., Jiang, H., Schmidt, A. B., & Olfson, M. (2007). National trends in the outpatient diagnosis and treatment of bipolar disorder in youth. *Archives of General Psychiatry, 64,* 1032–1039.

Morrison, J. (1980). Adult psychiatric disorders in parents of hyperactive children. *American Journal of Psychiatry, 137,* 825–827.

Morrison, J. R., & Stewart, M. A. (1971). A family study of the hyperactive child syndrome. *Biological Psychiatry, 3,* 189–195.

Mosholder, A. D., Gelperin, K., Hammad, T. A., Phelan, K., & Johann-Liang, R. (2009). Hallucinations and other psychotic symptoms associated with the use of attention-deficit/hyperactivity disorder drugs in children. *Pediatrics, 123,* 611–616.

MTA Cooperative Group. (1999a). Fourteen-month randomized clinical trial of treatment strategies for children with attention deficit hyperactivity disorder. *Archives of General Psychiatry, 56,* 1073–1086.

MTA Cooperative Group. (1999b). Moderators and mediators of treatment response for children with attention deficit hyperactivity disorder: The MTA study. *Archives of General Psychiatry, 56,* 1088–1096.

MTA Cooperative Group. (2004a). National Institute of Mental Health Multimodal Treatment Study of ADHD follow-up: 24-month outcomes of treatment strategies for attention-deficit/hyperactivity disorder. *Pediatrics, 113,* 754–761.

MTA Cooperative Group. (2004b). National Institute of Mental Health Multimodal Treatment Study of ADHD follow-up: Changes in effectiveness and growth after the end of treatment. *Pediatrics, 113,* 762–769.

Myers, S. M., & Johnson, C. P. (2007). Management of children with autism spectrum disorders. *Pediatrics, 120,* 1162–1182.

Nagaraj, R., Singhi, P., & Malhi, P. (2006). Risperidone in children with autism: Randomized, placebo-controlled, double-blind study. *Journal of Child Neurology, 21,* 450–455.

Newcorn, J. H., Halperin, J. M., Jensen, P. S., Abikoff, H. B., Arnold, L. E., Cantwell, D. P., et al. (2001). Symptom profiles in children with ADHD: Effects of comorbidity and gender. *Journal of the American Academy of Child and Adolescent Psychiatry, 40,* 137–146.

Newcorn, J. H., Kratochvil, C. J., Allen, A. J., Casat, C. D., Ruff, D. D., Moore, R. J., et al. (2008). Atomoxetine and osmotically released methylphenidate for the treatment of attention deficit hyperactivity disorder: Acute comparison and differential response. *American Journal of Psychiatry, 165,* 721–730.

Newcorn, J. H., Spencer, T. J., Biederman, J., Milton, D. R., & Michelson, D. (2005). Atomoxetine treatment in children and adolescents with attention-deficit/hyperactivity disorder and comorbid oppositional defiant disorder. *Journal of the American Academy of Child and Adolescent Psychiatry, 44,* 240–248.

Newschaffer, C. J., Croen, L. A., Daniels, J., Giarelli, E., Grether, J. K., Levy, S. E., et al. (2007). The epidemiology of autism spectrum disorders. *Annual Review of Public Health, 28,* 235–258.

Nolan, E. E., & Gadow, K. D. (1997). Children with ADHD and tic disorder and their classmates: Behavioral normalization with methylphenidate. *Journal of the American Academy of Child and Adolescent Psychiatry, 36,* 597–604.

Orvaschel, H., Walsh-Allis, G., & Ye, W. J. (1988). Psychopathology in children of parents with recurrent depression. *Journal of Abnormal Child Psychology, 16,* 17–28.

Ostrander, R., Crystal, D. S., & August, G. (2006). Attention deficit-hyperactivity disorder, depression, and self- and other-assessments of social competence: A developmental study. *Journal of Abnormal Child Psychology, 34,* 773–787.

Ozonoff, S., & Cathcart, K. (1998). Effectiveness of a home program intervention for young children with autism. *Journal of Autism and Developmental Disorders, 28,* 25–32.

Palumbo, D. R., Sallee, F. R., Pelham, W. E., Jr., Bukstein, O. G., Daviss, W. B., & McDermott, M. P. (2008). Clonidine for attention-deficit/hyperactivity disorder: I. Efficacy and tolerability outcomes. *Journal of the American Academy of Child and Adolescent Psychiatry, 47,* 180–188.

Pappadopulos, E., Macintyre, J. C. II, Crismon, M. L., Findling, R. L., Malone, R. P., Derivan, A., et al. (2003). Treatment recommendations for the use of antipsychotics for aggressive youth (TRAAY), Part II. *Journal of the American Academy of Child and Adolescent Psychiatry, 42,* 145–161.

Pappadopulos, E., Woolston, B. A., Chait, A., Perkins, M., Connor, D. F., & Jensen, P. S. (2006). Pharmacotherapy of aggression in children and adolescents: Efficacy and effect size. *Journal of the Canadian Academy of Child and Adolescent Psychiatry, 15,* 27–39.

Pauls, D. L., Alsobrook, J. P., Phil, M., Goodman, W., Rasmussen, S., & Leckman, J. F. (1995). A family study of obsessive-compulsive disorder. *American Journal of Psychiatry, 152,* 76–84.

Pauls, D. L., Leckman, J. F., & Cohen, D. J. (1993). Familial relationship between Gilles de la Tourette's syndrome, attention deficit disorder, learning disabilities, speech disorders, and stuttering. *Journal of the American Academy of Child and Adolescent Psychiatry, 32,* 1044–1050.

Pavuluri, M. N., Graczyk, P. A., Henry, D. B., Carbray, J. A., Heidenreich, J., & Miklowitz, D. J. (2004a). Child- and family-focused cognitive-behavioral therapy for pediatric bipolar disorder: Development and preliminary results. *Journal of the American Academy of Child and Adolescent Psychiatry, 43,* 528–537.

Pavuluri, M. N., Henry, D. B., Carbray, J. A., Sampson, G., Naylor, M. W., & Janicak, P. G. (2004b). Open-label prospective trial of risperidone in combination with lithium or divalproex sodium in pediatric mania. *Journal of Affective Disorders, 82* (Suppl. 1), S103–S111.

Pavuluri, M. N., Henry, D. B., Carbray, J. A., Sampson, G. A., Naylor, M. W., & Janicak, P. G. (2006a). A one-year open-label trial of risperidone augmentation in lithium nonresponder youth with preschool-onset bipolar disorder. *Journal of Child and Adolescent Psychopharmacology, 16,* 336–350.

Pavuluri, M. N., Henry, D. B., Devineni, B., Carbray, J. A., & Birmaher, B. (2006b). Child mania rating scale: Development, reliability, and validity. *Journal of the American Academy of Child and Adolescent Psychiatry, 45,* 550–560.

Pearson, D. A., & Aman, M. G. (1994). Ratings of hyperactivity and developmental indices: Should clinicians correct for developmental level? *Journal of Autism and Developmental Disorders, 24,* 395–411.

Pediatric OCD Treatment Study (POTS) Team. (2004). Cognitive-behavior therapy, sertraline, and their combination for children and adolescents with obsessive-compulsive disorder: The Pediatric OCD Treatment Study (POTS) randomized controlled trial. *Journal of the American Medical Association, 292,* 1969–1976.

Perlis, R. H., Miyahara, S., Marangell, L. B., Wisniewski, S. R., Ostacher, M., DelBello, M. P., et al. (2004). Long-term implications of early onset in bipolar disorder: Data from the first 1000 participants in the systematic treatment enhancement program for bipolar disorder (STEP-BD). *Biological Psychiatry, 55,* 875–881.

Perrin, S., & Last, C. G. (1996). Relationship between ADHD and anxiety in boys: Results from a family study. *Journal of the American Academy of Child and Adolescent Psychiatry, 35,* 988–996.

Pfiffner, L. J., McBurnett, K., Rathouz, P. J., & Judice, S. (2005). Family correlates of oppositional and conduct disorders in children with attention deficit/hyperactivity disorder. *Journal of Abnormal Child Psychology, 33,* 551–563.

Pliszka, S. R. (1989). Effect of anxiety on cognition, behavior, and stimulant response in ADHD. *Journal of the American Academy of Child and Adolescent Psychiatry, 28,* 882–887.

Pliszka, S. R. (1991). Anticonvulsants in the treatment of child and adolescent psychopathology. *Journal of Clinical Child Psychology, 20,* 277–281.

Pliszka, S. R. (1992). Comorbidity of attention deficit hyperactivity disorder and overanxious disorder. *Journal of the American Academy of Child and Adolescent Psychiatry, 31,* 197–203.

Pliszka, S. (2007a). Practice parameter for the assessment and treatment of children and adolescents with attention-deficit/hyperactivity disorder. *Journal of the American Academy of Child and Adolescent Psychiatry, 46,* 894–921.

Pliszka, S. R. (2007b). Pharmacologic treatment of attention-deficit/hyperactivity disorder: Efficacy, safety and mechanisms of action. *Neuropsychology Review, 17,* 61–72.

Pliszka, S. R., Borcherding, S. H., Spratley, K., Leon, S., & Irick, S. (1997). Measuring inhibitory control in children. *Journal of Developmental and Behavioral Pediatrics, 18,* 254–259.

Pliszka, S. R., Carlson, C. L., & Swanson, J. M. (1999). *ADHD with comorbid disorders: Clinical assessment and management.* New York: Guilford Press.

Pliszka, S. R., Crismon, M. L., Hughes, C. W., Corners, C. K., Emslie, G. J., Jensen, P. S., et al. (2006). The Texas Children's Medication Algorithm Project: Revision of the algorithm for pharmacotherapy of attention-deficit/hyperactivity disorder. *Journal of the American Academy of Child and Adolescent Psychiatry, 45,* 642–657.

Pliszka, S. R., Greenhill, L. L., Crismon, M. L., Sedillo, A., Carlson, C. L., Conners, C. K., et al. (2000). The Texas Children's Medication Algorithm Project: Report of the Texas consensus conference panel on medication treatment of childhood attention deficit/hyperactivity disorder, Part I. *Journal of the American Academy of Child and Adolescent Psychiatry, 39,* 908–919.

Pliszka, S. R., Maas, J. W., Javors, M. A., Rogeness, G. A., & Baker, J. (1994). Urinary catecholamines in attention deficit hyperactivity disorder with and without comorbid anxiety. *Journal of the American Academy of Child and Adolescent Psychiatry, 33,* 1165–1173.

Pliszka, S. R., Matthews, T. L., Braslow, K. J., & Watson, M. A. (2006). Comparative effects of methylphenidate and mixed salts amphetamine on height and weight in children with attention-deficit/hyperactivity disorder (ADHD). *Journal of the American Academy of Child and Adolescent Psychiatry, 45,* 520–526.

Pliszka, S. R., Sherman, J. O., Barrow, M. V., & Irick, S. (2000). Affective disorders in juvenile offenders: A preliminary study. *American Journal of Psychiatry, 157,* 130–132.

Polzer, J., Bangs, M. E., Zhang, S., Dellva, M. A., Tauscher-Wisniewski, S., Acharya, N., et al. (2007). Meta-analysis of aggression or hostility events in randomized, controlled clinical trials of atomoxetine for ADHD. *Biological Psychiatry, 61,* 713–719.

Posey, D. J., Erickson, C. A., Stigler, K. A., & McDougle, C. J. (2006a). The use of selective serotonin reuptake inhibitors in autism and related disorders. *Journal of Child and Adolescent Psychopharmacology, 16,* 181–186.

Posey, D. J., Wiegand, R. E., Wilkerson, J., Maynard, M., Stigler, K. A., & McDougle, C. J. (2006b). Open-label atomoxetine for attention-deficit/hyperactivity disorder symptoms associated with high-functioning pervasive developmental disorders. *Journal of Child and Adolescent Psychopharmacology, 16,* 599–610.

Power, T. J., Costigan, T. E., Eiraldi, R. B., & Leff, S. S. (2004). Variations in anxiety and depression as a function of ADHD subtypes defined by DSM-IV: Do subtype differences exist or not? *Journal of Abnormal Child Psychology, 32,* 27–37.

Prasad, S., Furr, A. J., Zhang, S., Ball, S., & Allen, A. J. (2007). Baseline values from the electrocardiograms of children and adolescents with ADHD. *Child and Adolescent Psychiatry and Mental Health, 1,* 11.

Quintana, H., Birmaher, B., Stedge, D., Lennon, S., Freed, J., Bridge, J., et al. (1995). Use of methylphenidate in the treatment of children with autistic disorder. *Journal of Autism and Developmental Disorders, 25,* 283–294.

Redl, F. (1966). *When we deal with children.* New York: Free Press.

Reeves, J. C., Werry, J. S., Elkind, G. S., & Zametkin, A. (1987). Attention deficit, conduct, oppositional, and anxiety disorders in children: II. Clinical charateristics. *Journal of the American Academy of Child and Adolescent Psychiatry, 26,* 144–155.

Reich, W., & Earls, F. (1987). Rules for making psychiatric diagnoses in children on the basis of multiple sources of information: Preliminary strategies. *Journal of Abnormal Child Psychology, 15,* 601–616.

Reichenberg, A., Gross, R., Weiser, M., Bresnahan, M., Silverman, J., Harlap, S., et al. (2006). Advancing paternal age and autism. *Archives of General Psychiatry, 63,* 1026–1032.

Reinblatt, S. P., & Riddle, M. A. (2007). The pharmacological management of childhood anxiety disorders: A review. *Psychopharmacology (Berl), 191,* 67–86.

Reinecke, M. A., Dattillio, F. M., & Freeman, A. (2006). *Cognitive therapy with children and adolescents: A casebook for clinical practice* (2nd ed.). New York: Guilford Press.

Research Units on Pediatric Psychopharmacology Autism Network. (2005a). Randomized, controlled, crossover trial of methylphenidate in pervasive developmental disorders with hyperactivity. *Archives of General Psychiatry, 62,* 1266–1274.

Research Units on Pediatric Psychopharmacology Autism Network. (2005b). Risperidone treatment of autistic disorder: Longer-term benefits and blinded discontinuation after 6 months. *American Journal of Psychiatry, 162,* 1361–1369.

Rich, B. A., Schmajuk, M., Perez-Edgar, K. E., Fox, N. A., Pine, D. S., & Leibenluft, E. (2007). Different psychophysiological and behavioral responses elicited by frustration in pediatric bipolar disorder and severe mood dysregulation. *American Journal of Psychiatry, 164,* 309–317.

Riddle, M. A., Geller, B., & Ryan, N. (1993). Another sudden death in a child treated with desipramine. *Journal of the American Academy of Child and Adolescent Psychiatry, 32,* 792–797.

Riddle, M. A., Nelson, J. C., Kleinman, C. S., Rasmusson, A., Leckman, J. F., King, R. A., et al. (1991). Sudden death in children receiving Norpramin: A review of three reported cases and commentary. *Journal of the American Academy of Child and Adolescent Psychiatry, 30,* 104–108.

Rifkin, A., Karajgi, B., Dicker, R., Perl, E., Boppana, V., Hasan, N., et al. (1997). Lithium treatment of conduct disorders in adolescents. *American Journal of Psychiatry, 154,* 554–555.

Rinsley, D. B. (1983). *Treatment of the severely disturbed adolescent.* New York: Jason Aronson.

Rizzo, R., Curatolo, P., Gulisano, M., Virzi, M., Arpino, C., & Robertson, M. M. (2007). Disentangling the effects of Tourette syndrome and attention deficit hyperactivity disorder on cognitive and behavioral phenotypes. *Brain and Development, 29,* 413–420.

Roessner, V., Robatzek, M., Knapp, G., Banaschewski, T., & Rothenberger, A. (2006). First-onset tics in patients with attention-deficit-hyperactivity disorder: Impact of stimulants. *Developmental Medicine and Child Neurology, 48,* 616–621.

Rohde, P., Lewinsohn, P. M., & Seeley, J. R. (1991). Comorbidity of unipolar depression: II. Comorbidity with other mental disorders in adolescents and adults. *Journal of Abnormal Psychology, 100,* 214–222.

Ruchkin, V., Henrich, C. C., Jones, S. M., Vermeiren, R., & Schwab-Stone, M. (2007). Violence exposure and psychopathology in urban youth: The mediating role of posttraumatic stress. *Journal of Abnormal Child Psychology, 35,* 578–593.

Rugino, T. A., & Janvier, Y. M. (2005). Aripiprazole in children and adolescents: Clinical experience. *Journal of Child Neurology, 20,* 603–610.

Rutter, M., Tizard, J., & Whitmore, K. (1970). *Education, health and behavior.* London: Longman.

Rynn, M. A., Siqueland, L., & Rickels, K. (2001). Placebo-controlled trial of sertraline in the treatment of children with generalized anxiety disorder. *American Journal of Psychiatry, 158,* 2008–2014.

Sachs, G. S., Baldassano, C. F., Truman, C. J., & Guille, C. (2000). Comorbidity of attention deficit hyperactivity disorder with early- and late-onset bipolar disorder. *American Journal of Psychiatry, 157,* 466–468.

Sadler, W. S. (1952). Juvenile manic activity. *Nervous Child, 9,* 363–368.

Safren, S. A., Lanka, G. D., Otto, M. W., & Pollack, M. H. (2001). Prevalence of childhood ADHD among patients with generalized anxiety disorder and a comparison condition, social phobia. *Depression and Anxiety, 13,* 190–191.

Sanchez, L. E., Campbell, M., Small, A. M., Cueva, J. E., Armenteros, J. L., & Adams, P. B. (1996). A pilot study of clomipramine in young autistic children. *Journal of the American Academy of Child and Adolescent Psychiatry, 35,* 537–544.

Satterfield, J. H., Faller, K. J., Crinella, F. M., Schell, A. M., Swanson, J. M., & Homer, L. D. (2007). A 30-year prospective follow-up study of hyperactive boys with conduct problems: Adult criminality. *Journal of the American Academy of Child and Adolescent Psychiatry, 46,* 601–610.

Satterfield, J. H., Satterfield, B. T., & Schell, A. M. (1987). Therapeutic interventions to prevent delinquency in hyperactive boys. *Journal of the American Academy of Child and Adolescent Psychiatry, 26,* 56–64.

Scahill, L., Aman, M. G., McDougle, C. J., McCracken, J. T., Tierney, E., Dziura, J., et al. (2006). A prospective open trial of guanfacine in children with pervasive developmental disorders. *Journal of Child and Adolescent Psychopharmacology, 16,* 589–598.

Scahill, L., Blair, J., Leckman, J. F., & Martin, A. (2005). Sudden death in a patient with Tourette syndrome during a clinical trial of ziprasidone. *Journal of Psychopharmacology, 19,* 205–206.

Scahill, L., Chappell, P. B., Kim, Y. S., Schultz, R. T., Katsovich, L., Shepherd, E., et al. (2001). A placebo-controlled study of guanfacine in the treatment of children with tic disorders and attention deficit hyperactivity disorder. *American Journal of Psychiatry, 158,* 1067–1074.

Scahill, L., Leckman, J. F., Schultz, R. T., Katsovich, L., & Peterson, B. S. (2003). A placebo-controlled trial of risperidone in Tourette syndrome. *Neurology, 60,* 1130–1135.

Schachar, R., & Tannock, R. (1995). Test of four hypotheses for the comorbidity of attention deficit hyperactivity disorder and conduct disorder. *Journal of the American Academy of Child and Adolescent Psychiatry, 34,* 639–648.

Scheffer, R. E., Kowatch, R. A., Carmody, T., & Rush, A. J. (2005). Randomized, placebo-controlled trial of mixed amphetamine salts for symptoms of comorbid ADHD in pediatric bipolar disorder after mood stabilization with divalproex sodium. *American Journal of Psychiatry, 162,* 58–64.

Schur, S. B., Sikich, L., Findling, R. L., Malone, R. P., Crismon, M. L., Derivan, A., et al. (2003). Treatment recommendations for the use of antipsychotics for aggressive youth (TRAAY): I. A review. *Journal of the American Academy of Child and Adolescent Psychiatry, 42,* 132–144.

Schvehla, T. J., Mandoki, M. W., & Sumner, G. S. (1994). Clonidine therapy for comorbid attention deficit hyperactivity disorder and conduct disorder: Preliminary findings in a children's inpatient unit. *Southern Medical Journal, 87,* 692–695.

Shaffer, D., Fisher, P., Lucas, C. P., Dulcan, M. K., & Schwab-Stone, M. E. (2000). NIMH Diagnostic Interview Schedule for Children Version IV (NIMH DISC-IV): Description, differences from previous versions, and reliability of some common diagnoses. *Journal of the American Academy of Child and Adolescent Psychiatry, 39,* 28–38.

Sharp, B. W. (2007). CMAP ADHD and aggression algorithm [letter]. *Journal of the American Academy of Child and Adolescent Psychiatry, 46,* 1.

Shaw, P., Eckstrand, K., Sharp, W., Blumenthal, J., Lerch, J. P., Greenstein, D., et al. (2007).

Attention-deficit/hyperactivity disorder is characterized by a delay in cortical maturation. *Proceedings of the National Academy of Sciences, 104,* 19649–19654.

Shea, S., Turgay, A., Carroll, A., Schulz, M., Orlik, H., Smith, I., et al. (2004). Risperidone in the treatment of disruptive behavioral symptoms in children with autistic and other pervasive developmental disorders. *Pediatrics, 114,* e634–e641.

Sikich, L., Frazier, J. A., McClellan, J., Findling, R. L., Vitiello, B., Ritz, L. et al. (2008). Double-blind comparison of first- and second-generation antipsychotics in early-onset schizophrenia and schizo-affective disorder: Findings from the treatment of early-onset schizophrenia spectrum disorders (TEOSS) study. *American Journal of Psychiatry, 165,* 1420-1431.

Sikich, L., Hamer, R. M., Bashford, R. A., Sheitman, B. B., & Lieberman, J. A. (2004). A pilot study of risperidone, olanzapine, and haloperidol in psychotic youth: A double-blind, randomized, 8-week trial. *Neuropsychopharmacology, 29,* 133–145.

Simonoff, E., Pickles, A., Wood, N., Gringras, P., & Chadwick, O. (2007). ADHD symptoms in children with mild intellectual disability. *Journal of the American Academy of Child and Adolescent Psychiatry, 46,* 591–600.

Singh, M. K., DelBello, M. P., Kowatch, R. A., & Strakowski, S. M. (2006). Co-occurrence of bipolar and attention-deficit hyperactivity disorders in children. *Bipolar Disorders, 8,* 710–720.

Smith, B. H., Barkley, R. A., & Shapiro, C. J. (2006). Attention-deficit hyperactivity disorder. In E. J. Mash & R. A. Barkley (Eds.), *Treatment of childhood disorders* (3rd ed., pp. 65–136). New York: Guilford Press.

Snider, L. A., & Swedo, S. E. (2004). PANDAS: Current status and directions for research. *Molecular Psychiatry, 9,* 900–907.

Snyder, R., Turgay, A., Aman, M., Binder, C., Fisman, S., & Carroll, A. (2002). Effects of risperidone on conduct and disruptive behavior disorders in children with subaverage IQs. *Journal of the American Academy of Child and Adolescent Psychiatry, 41,* 1026–1036.

Solanto, M. V., Abikoff, H., Sonuga-Barke, E., Schachar, R., Logan, G. D., Wigal, T., et al. (2001). The ecological validity of delay aversion and response inhibition as measures of impulsivity in AD/HD: A supplement to the NIMH multimodal treatment study of AD/HD. *Journal of Abnormal Child Psychology, 29,* 215–228.

Spencer, T., Biederman, J., Harding, M., O'Donnell, D., Wilens, T., Faraone, S., et al. (1998). Disentangling the overlap between Tourette's disorder and ADHD. *Journal of Child Psychology and Psychiatry, 39,* 1037–1044.

Spencer, T., Biederman, J., Steingard, R., & Wilens, T. (1993). Bupropion exacerbates tics in children with attention-deficit hyperactivity disorder and Tourette's syndrome. *Journal of the American Academy of Child and Adolescent Psychiatry, 32,* 211–214.

Spencer, T. J., Abikoff, H. B., Connor, D. F., Biederman, J., Pliszka, S. R., Boellner, S., et al. (2006). Efficacy and safety of mixed amphetamine salts extended release (Adderall XR) in the management of oppositional defiant disorder with or without comorbid attention-deficit/hyperactivity disorder in school-aged children and adolescents: A 4-week, multicenter, randomized, double-blind, parallel-group, placebo-controlled, forced-dose-escalation study. *Clinical Therapeutics, 28,* 402–418.

Spencer, T. J., Sallee, F. R., Gilbert, D. L., Dunn, D. W., McCracken, J. T., Coffey, B. J., et al. (2008). Atomoxetine treatment of ADHD in children with comorbid Tourette syndrome. *Journal of Attention Disorders, 11,* 470–481.

Sprich, S., Biederman, J., Crawford, M. H., Mundy, E., & Faraone, S. V. (2000). Adoptive and biological families of children and adolescents with ADHD. *Journal of the American Academy of Child and Adolescent Psychiatry, 39,* 1432–1437.

Stehr-Green, P., Tull, P., Stellfeld, M., Mortenson, P. B., & Simpson, D. (2003). Autism and thimerosal-containing vaccines: Lack of consistent evidence for an association. *American Journal of Preventive Medicine, 25,* 101–106.

Steiner, H., Petersen, M. L., Saxena, K., Ford, S., & Matthews, Z. (2003). Divalproex sodium for the treatment of conduct disorder: A randomized controlled clinical trial. *Journal of Clinical Psychiatry, 64,* 1183–1191.

Stephens, R. J., Bassel, C., & Sandor, P., et al. (2004). Olanzapine in the treatment of aggression and tics in children with Tourette's syndrome—a pilot study. *Journal of Child and Adolescent Psychopharmacology, 14,* 255–266.

Stewart, S. E., Illmann, C., Geller, D. A., Leckman, J. F., King, R., & Pauls, D. L. (2006). A controlled family study of attention-deficit/hyperactivity disorder and Tourette's disorder. *Journal of the American Academy of Child and Adolescent Psychiatry, 45,* 1354–1362.

Stigler, K. A., Dieno, J. T., Kohn, A. E., Erickson, C. A., Posey, D. A., & McDougle, C. J. (2006). A prospective, open-label study of aripiprazole in youth with Asperger's disorder and pervasive developmental disorder not otherwise specified. *Neuropsychopharmacology, 31,* S194.

Sukhodolsky, D. G., do Rosario-Campos, M. C., Scahill, L., Katsovich, L., Pauls, D. L., Peterson, B. S., et al. (2005). Adaptive, emotional, and family functioning of children with obsessive-compulsive disorder and comorbid attention deficit hyperactivity disorder. *American Journal of Psychiatry, 162,* 1125–1132.

Sverd, J., Gadow, K. D., Nolan, E. E., Sprafkin, J., & Ezor, S. N. (1992). Methylphenidate in hyperactive boys with comorbid tic disorder: I. Clinic evaluations. *Advances in Neurology, 58,* 271–281.

Swain, J. E., Scahill, L., Lombroso, P. J., King, R. A., & Leckman, J. F. (2007). Tourette syndrome and tic disorders: A decade of progress. *Journal of the American Academy of Child and Adolescent Psychiatry, 46,* 947–968.

Swanson, J. M. (1992). *School-based assessments and intervention for ADD students.* Irvine, CA: K.C. Publishing.

Swanson, J. M., Elliott, G. R., Greenhill, L. L., Wigal, T., Arnold, L. E., Vitiello, B., et al. (2007a). Effects of stimulant medication on growth rates across 3 years in the MTA follow-up. *Journal of the American Academy of Child and Adolescent Psychiatry, 46,* 1015–1027.

Swanson, J. M., Greenhill, L. L., Wigal, T., Kollins, S., Stehli-Nguyen, A., Davies, M., et al. (2006). Stimulant-related reduction of growth rates in the preschool ADHD treatment study (PATS). *Journal of the American Academy of Child and Adolescent Psychiatry, 45,* 1304–1313.

Swanson, J. M., Hinshaw, S. P., Arnold, L. E., Gibbons, R. D., Marcus, S., Hur, K., et al. (2007b). Secondary evaluations of MTA 36-month outcomes: Propensity score and growth mixture model analyses. *Journal of the American Academy of Child and Adolescent Psychiatry, 46,* 1003–1014.

Swedo, S. E., Leonard, H. L., Garvey, M., Mittleman, B., Allen, A. J., Perlmutter, S., et al. (1998). Pediatric autoimmune neuropsychiatric disorders associated with streptococcal infections: Clinical description of the first 50 cases. *American Journal of Psychiatry, 155,* 264–271 [erratum, 578].

Swensen, A., Michelsen, D., Buesching, D., & Faries, D. E. (2001, October 23–28). Effects of atomoxetine on social and family functioning of ADHD children and adolescents. Paper presented at the 48th Annual Meeting of the American Academy of Child and Adolescent Psychiatry, Honolulu, HI.

Symons, F. J., Thompson, A., & Rodriguez, M. C. (2004). Self-injurious behavior and the efficacy of naltrexone treatment: A quantitative synthesis. *Mental Retardation and Developmental Disabilities Research Review, 10,* 193–200.

TADS Team. (2007). The Treatment for Adolescents with Depression Study (TADS): Long-term effectiveness and safety outcomes. *Archives of General Psychiatry, 64,* 1132–1143.

Tallian, K. B., Nahata, M. C., Lo, W., & Tsao, C. Y. (1996). Gabapentin associated with aggressive behavior in pediatric patients with seizures. *Epilepsia, 37,* 501–502.

Tannock, R. (2000). Attention deficit disorders with anxiety disorders. In T. E. Brown (Ed.), *Attention-deficit disorders and comorbidities in children, adolescents and adults* (pp. 125–175). Washington, DC: American Psychiatric Press.

Tannock, R., Ickowicz, A., & Schachar, R. (1995). Differential effects of methylphenidate on working memory in ADHD children with and without comorbid anxiety. *Journal of the American Academy of Child and Adolescent Psychiatry, 34,* 886–896.

Taylor, E., Schachar, R., Thorley, G., Wieselberg, H. M., Everitt, B., & Rutter, M. (1987). Which boys respond to stimulant medication? A controlled trial of methylphenidate in boys with disruptive behavior. *Psychological Medicine, 17,* 121–143.

Tohen, M., Kryzhanovskaya, L., Carlson, G., DelBello, M., Wozniak, J., Kowatch, R., et al. (2007). Olanzapine versus placebo in the treatment of adolescents with bipolar mania. *American Journal of Psychiatry, 164,* 1547–1556.

Tourette's Syndrome Study Group. (2002). Treatment of ADHD in children with tics: A randomized controlled trial. *Neurology, 58,* 527–536.

Troost, P. W., Steenhuis, M. P., Tuynman-Qua, H. G., Kalverdijk, L. J., Buitelaar, J. K., Minderaa, R. B., et al. (2006). Atomoxetine for attention-deficit/hyperactivity disorder symptoms in children with pervasive developmental disorders: a pilot study. *Journal of Child and Adolescent Psychopharmacology, 16,* 611–619.

Turgay, A., Binder, C., Snyder, R., & Fisman, S. (2002). Long-term safety and efficacy of risperidone for the treatment of disruptive behavior disorders in children with subaverage IQs. *Pediatrics, 110,* e34.

Tyrer, P., Oliver-Africano, P. C., Ahmed, Z., Bouras, N., Cooray, S., Deb, S., et al. (2008). Risperidone, haloperidol, and placebo in the treatment of aggressive challenging behaviour in patients with intellectual disability: A randomised controlled trial. *Lancet, 371,* 57–63.

Valicenti-McDermott, M. R., & Demb, H. (2006). Clinical effects and adverse reactions of off-label use of aripiprazole in children and adolescents with developmental disabilities. *Journal of Child & Adolescent Psychopharmacology, 16,* 549–560.

Vance, A., Costin, J., Barnett, R., Luk, E., Maruff, P., & Tonge, B. (2002a). Characteristics of parent- and child-reported anxiety in psychostimulant medication naive, clinically referred children with attention deficit hyperactivity disorder, combined type (ADHD-CT). *Australian and New Zealand Journal of Psychiatry, 36,* 234–239.

Vance, A. L., Costin, J., & Maruff, P. (2002b). Attention deficit hyperactivity disorder, combined type (ADHD-CT): differences in blood pressure (BP) due to posture and the child report of anxiety. *European Child and Adolescent Psychiatry, 11,* 24–30.

Vetter, V. L., Elia, J., Erickson, C., Berger, S., Blum, N., Uzark, K., et al. (2008). Cardiovascular monitoring of children and adolescents with heart disease receiving stimulant drugs: A scientific statement from the American Heart Association Council on Cardiovascular Disease in the Young Congenital Cardiac Defects Committee and the Council on Cardiovascular Nursing. *Circulation, 117,* 2407–2423.

Villalaba, L. (2006). Follow up review of AERS search identifying cases of sudden death occurring with drugs used for the treatment of attention deficit hyperactivity disorder (ADHD). Available at *www.fda.gov/ohrms/dockets/ac/06/briefing/2006–4210B-Index.htm.*

Vitiello, B. (2008). Understanding the risk of using medications for attention deficit hyperactivity disorder with respect to physical growth and cardiovascular function. *Child and Adolescent Psychiatric Clinics of North America, 17,* 459–74, xi.

Volkow, N. D., & Swanson, J. M. (2008). Does childhood treatment of ADHD with stimulant medication affect substance abuse in adulthood? *American Journal of Psychiatry, 165,* 553–555.

Volkow, N. D., Wang, G. J., Fowler, J. S., & Ding, Y. S. (2005). Imaging the effects of methylphenidate on brain dopamine: New model on its therapeutic actions for attention-deficit/hyperactivity disorder. *Biological Psychiatry, 57,* 1410–1415.

Wagner, K. D., Ambrosini, P., Rynn, M., Wohlberg, C., Yang, R., Greenbaum, M. S., et al. (2003). Efficacy of sertraline in the treatment of children and adolescents with major depressive disorder: Two randomized controlled trials. *Journal of the American Medical Association, 290,* 1033–1041.

Wagner, K. D., Jonas, J., Findling, R. L., Ventura, D., & Saikali, K. (2006a). A double-blind, randomized, placebo-controlled trial of escitalopram in the treatment of pediatric depression. *Journal of the American Academy of Child and Adolescent Psychiatry, 45,* 280–288.

Wagner, K. D., Kowatch, R. A., Emslie, G. J., Findling, R. L., Wilens, T. E., McCague, K., et al. (2006b). A double-blind, randomized, placebo-controlled trial of oxcarbazepine in the treatment of bipolar disorder in children and adolescents. *American Journal of Psychiatry, 163,* 1179–1186.

Wagner, K. D., Redden, L., Kowatch, R., Wilens, T., Segal, S., Chang, K., et al. (2007, October 23–28). Safety and efficacy of divalproex extended release (ER) in youth with mania. Paper presented at the 54th Annual Meeting of the American Academy of Child and Adolescent Psychiatry, Boston, MA.

Walitza, S., Zellmann, H., Irblich, B., Lange, K. W., Tucha, O., Hemminger, U., et al. (2008). Children and adolescents with obsessive-compulsive disorder and comorbid attention-deficit/hyperactivity disorder: Preliminary results of a prospective follow-up study. *Journal of Neural Transmission, 115,* 187–190.

Walkup, J. T., Labellarte, M. J., Riddle, M. A., Pine, D. S., Greenhill, L., Klein, R., et al. (2001). Fluvoxamine for the treatment of anxiety disorders in children and adolescents. *New England Journal of Medicine, 344,* 1279–1285.

Wals, M., Hillegers, M. H., Reichart, C. G., Ormel, J., Nolen, W. A., & Verhulst, F. C. (2001). Prevalence of psychopathology in children of a bipolar parent. *Journal of the American Academy of Child and Adolescent Psychiatry, 40,* 1094–1102.

Webster-Stratton, C. (2000). *The Incredible Years training series bulletin.* Washington, DC: U.S. Department of Justice, Office of Justice Programs, Office of Juvenile Justice and Delinquency Prevention.

Webster-Stratton, C., & Reid, M. J. (2003). The Incredible Years parents, teachers, and children training series: A multifaceted treatment approach for young children with conduct problems. In A. E. Kazdin & J. R. Weisz (Eds.), *Evidence-based psychotherapies for children and adolescents* (pp. 224–241). New York: Guilford Press.

Weissman, M. M., Gammon, G. D., John, K., Merikanggs, K. R., Prusoff, B. A., & Sholomskas, D. (1987). Children of depressed parents. Increased psychopathology and early onset of major depression. *Archives of General Psychiatry, 44,* 847–853.

Weissman, M. M., Prusoff, B. A., Gammon, G. D., Merikangas, K. R., Leckman, J. F., & Kidd, K. K. (1984). Psychopathology in the children (ages 6–18) of depressed and normal parents. *Journal of the American Academy of Child Psychiatry, 23,* 78–84.

Welner, Z., Reich, W., Herjanic, B., Jung, K. G., & Amado, H. (1987). Reliability, validity, and parent-child agreement studies of the diagnostic interview for children and adolescents (DICA). *Journal of the American Academy of Child and Adolescent Psychiatry, 26,* 649–653.

Welner, Z., & Rice, J. (1988). School-aged children of depressed parents: A blind and controlled study. *Journal of Affective Disorders, 15,* 291–302.

Wigal, S., McGough, J., McCracken, J. T., Clark, T., Mays, D., & Tulloch, S. (2004, October 19–24). Analog classroom study of amphetamine XR and atomoxetine for ADHD. Paper presented at the 51st Annual Meeting of the American Academy of Child and Adolescent Psychiatry, Washington, D.C.

Wilens, T. E., Biederman, J., Brown, S., Tanguay, S., Monuteaux, M. C., Blake, C., et al. (2002). Psychiatric comorbidity and functioning in clinically referred preschool children and school-age youths with ADHD. *Journal of the American Academy of Child and Adolescent Psychiatry, 41,* 262–268.

Wilens, T. E., Faraone, S. V., Biederman, J., & Gunawardene, S. (2003). Does stimulant therapy of attention-deficit/hyperactivity disorder beget later substance abuse? A meta-analytic review of the literature. *Pediatrics, 111,* 179–185.

Willemsen-Swinkels, S. H. N., Buitelaar, J. K., Nijhof, G. J., & van Engeland, H. (1995). Failure of naltrexone hydrochloride to reduce self-injurious and autistic behavior in mentally retarded adults. *Archives of General Psychiatry, 52,* 766–733.

Winterstein, A. G., Gerhard, T., Shuster, J., Johnson, M., Zito, J. M., & Saidi, A. (2007). Cardiac safety of central nervous system stimulants in children and adolescents with attention-deficit/hyperactivity disorder. *Pediatrics, 120,* e1494–e1501.

Wolraich, M. L., Lambert, E. W., Baumgaertel, A., Garcia-Tornel, S., Feurer, I. D., Bickman, L., et al. (2003a). Teachers' screening for attention deficit/hyperactivity disorder: Comparing multinational samples on teacher ratings of ADHD. *Journal of Abnormal Child Psychology, 31,* 445–455.

Wolraich, M. L., Lambert, W., Doffing, M. A., Bickman, L., Simmons, T., & Worley, K. (2003b). Psychometric properties of the Vanderbilt ADHD diagnostic parent rating scale in a referred population. *Journal of Pediatric Psychology, 28,* 559–567.

Wozniak, J., Biederman, J., Kiely, K., Ablon, S., Faraone, S. V., Mundy, E., et al. (1995). Mania-like symptoms suggestive of childhood onset bipolar disorder in clinically referred children. *Journal of the American Academy of Child and Adolescent Psychiatry, 34,* 867–876.

Wozniak, J., Crawford, M. H., Biederman, J., Faraone, S. V., Spencer, T. J., Taylor, A., et al. (1999). Antecedents and complications of trauma in boys with ADHD: Findings from a longitudinal study. *Journal of the American Academy of Child and Adolescent Psychiatry, 38,* 48–55.

Zanarini, M. C., Frankenburg, F. R., & Parachini, E. A. (2004). A preliminary, randomized trial of fluoxetine, olanzapine, and the olanzapine-fluoxetine combination in women with borderline personality disorder. *Journal of Clinical Psychiatry, 65,* 903–907.

Index